Hebrew Christianity:
The Thirteenth Tribe

Contemporary Religious Movements:
A Wiley-Interscience Series

Edited by IRVING I. ZARETSKY

Hebrew Christianity: The Thirteenth Tribe

B. Z. SOBEL

A WILEY-INTERSCIENCE PUBLICATION

JOHN WILEY & SONS,
New York • London • Sydney • Toronto

Library of Congress Cataloging in Publication Data:

Sobel, B Zvi, 1933-

    Hebrew Christianity; the thirteenth tribe.

    (Contemporary religious movements)
    "A Wiley-Interscience publication."
    Bibliography: p.
    1. Missions to Jews—History. 2. Religion and sociology. I. Title.

BV2620.S65   261.2   74-3351
ISBN 0-471-81025-8

Printed in the United States of America

10 9 8 7 6 5 4 3 2 1

Acknowledgments

For permission to reprint copyright material, acknowledgment is hereby gratefully made to the following publishers and individuals:

Archives, National Lutheran Council: for the selections from *The Lutheran Parish and the Jews, An Analytical Study* and *The Lutheran Parish and the Jews—A Survey*, prepared by Harold Floreen.

Cambridge University Press: for selections from *The Christian Attitude to Other Religions*, by E. D. Dewick.

Conference on Jewish Social Studies: for selections from *Essays on Anti-Semitism* (2nd rev. ed.), edited by K. Pinson 1946; and the journal *Jewish Social Studies* for permission to use selections from *Legitimation and Anti-semitism as Factors in the Functioning of a Hebrew-Christian Mission*, by B. Z. Sobel, Vol. 23, No. 3 (1961), pp. 170–186.

Daedalus, the Journal of the American Academy of Arts and Sciences: for selections from "Historical perspectives on the American Ethnic Group," by Oscar Handlin in *Ethnic Groups in American Life*, spring 1961.

Dallas Theological Seminary: for permission to quote from *Aids to Jewish Evangelism*, © 1959.

Friendship Press, New York: for the selections from *The Jew and The World Ferment*, by Basil Matthews, © 1935; and for selections from *What now for the Jews*, by Conrad Hoffmann, © 1948.

The Globe, Toronto: for the selections from October 29, 1930 issue of *The Globe*.

Harper and Row: for the selections from *Modern Nationalism and Religion*, by Salo W. Baron, © 1947.

Home Mission Board, Southern Baptist Convention: for *What of the Jews*, by J. Gartenhaus, © 1948.

The Hebrew Christian Alliance of America: for the selections from the *Hebrew Christian Alliance Quarterly*; copyright by the Hebrew Christian Alliance of America.

The Jewish Journal of Sociology: for permission to use selections from "The Tools of Legitimation—Zionism and the Hebrew Christian Movement," by B. Z. Sobel, first published in *The Jewish Journal of Sociology*, Vol. 10, No. 2, December 1968. It is reprinted by permission of the editor.

Alexander R. James: for the selections from *Varieties of Religious Experience*, by William James.

The Macmillan Co.: for the selections from *Jews in a Gentile World*, edited by I. Graeber and S. H. Britt, © 1942.

The Mennonite Publishing House, Scottdale, Pa. 15683: for the selections from *Judaism Meets Christ*, by Roy Kreider, © 1960.

Oxford University Press, Inc.: for the selections from *The Theory of Social and Economic Organization*, by Max Weber, © 1947.

Dr. Hugh J. Schonfield: for the selections from his volume, *The History of Jewish Christianity*.

Prentice-Hall, Inc., Englewood Cliffs, N.J.: for the selections from *The Human Perspective in Sociology: The Methodology of Participant Observation*, by Severyn T. Bruyn, © 1966, p. 281.

Random House, Inc.: for selections from *Social Movements in the United States*, by C. Wendell King, © 1956.

The Society for Promoting Christian Knowledge: for selections from *The Jews and Judaism During the Greek Period: The Background of Christianity*, by W. O. E. Oesterley; and for the selections from *A Theology of Election: Israel and the Church*, by Jakob Jocz.

Society for the Scientific Study of Religion, Inc.: for permission to use selections from "Protestant Evangelists and the

Formulation of Jewish Racial Mystique," by B. Z. Sobel, first published in the *Journal for the Scientific Study of Religion,* Vol. 5, No. 3 (fall 1966), pp. 343–356.

The Student Christian Movement Press, Ltd.: for selections from *The Jew in the Christian World,* by H. Kosmala and R. Smith.

The World Council of Churches: for selections from *Missions and the New Situation in Asia,* by E. Bervan in the *International Review of Missions,* No. 9, July 1920.

Contents

PART TWO   HISTORICAL BACKDROP

PART THREE   SOCIOLOGICAL EVALUATION

Hebrew Christianity:
The Thirteenth Tribe

Introduction and Methodological Note

This study was begun some years ago, when as a staff member with the Anti-Defamation League I became aware of the phenomenon known as Hebrew Christianity. It was brought to my attention by a group of Jewish women in Newark, New Jersey, who asked that a group called the Messengers of the New Covenant be investigated with regard to their methods of proselytizing among Jews. Their concern had been aroused when one of their number announced her conversion to Christianity but asked to continue her membership in the other group (a B'nai B'rith chapter) and thereupon proceeded to "infiltrate" the organization with proselytizing literature of various kinds. In the course of carrying out the requested investigation, I became thoroughly fascinated with what appeared to be one of the most unique of missionary enterprises. I had had some previous familiarity with missionary groups and had never ceased to wonder about the lack of thought and verve, the absence of even the slightest spark of creativity that marked (and marred) these efforts. Most of the "traditional" missionary organizations devoted to Jewish work satisfied themselves with tracts, articles, and verbal arguments calling the Jews, like Circe, to forsake their past, their loved ones, their "Jewishness," and become as a new babe in Christ. By inference, if not more plainly stated, being Jewish was depicted as an unfortunate, burdensome cross to have to bear, and the road to Damascus was made to seem a rather attractive way of relieving the "burden."

It was immediately evident to me, however, that although Christianity was the faith of those who involved themselves with the Messengers, there was a conscious attempt made to emphasize a certain difference. The difference was that the group proclaimed themselves not only to have remained Jewish after their conversion to Christianity but in fact to have enhanced and improved their "Jewishness" *as a result of their conversion*. The members of the group identified themselves not alone as Christians but as Hebrew Christians—a specific and distinct kind of Christian, bearing a special relationship to the new faith.

While seeking additional information about Hebrew Christianity, I was amazed to learn that almost no research had been carried out in this area, nor indeed had much been published other than in-house tracts and reams of apologia. The one scholarly work extant was primarily historical and provided little or no data of ethnographic or sociological value.[1]

The need for such a study seemed obvious, and equally obvious was the existence of a number of important procedural and methodological problems. Was the research to be empirical, based on an intensive study of one or two Hebrew Christian groups, or would it prove more fruitful to trace the phenomenon within the context of the general missionary approach to the Jews, analyzing it as a socioreligious movement in terms of social processes, ideological developments, and theological presuppositions. This dilemma was resolved when I chose to do both; that is, to carry out a field study with the Messengers of the New Covenant as well as a larger and more intensive analysis of the phenomenon itself against the backdrop of traditional Christian efforts to convert the Jews. With the development of the so-called Jesus movement at the beginning of the 1970s, an additional phase of field work was undertaken.

Another problem was determining where and how to limit the scope of the study. I early realized that Hebrew Christianity was an international movement; however, I could not undertake a study of each of its national units as discrete entities. There was the additional complication of language barriers—Hungarian, Polish, Dutch, Russian, German, and Norwegian sources existed, which were beyond my powers of translation. But once again an alternative presented itself: although the movement had spread to the continent and the United States, it had begun in England; almost all its theoreticians and leaders were English, American, and German; and all important documents and sources were in these two tongues and Yiddish—primarily, however, in English. I therefore confined myself largely to an analysis of the English and American branches, which in the last analysis *are* the movement.

An additional methodological difficulty existed, and this too was resolved, but not quite so satisfactorily as the others. How was I to go about the field study? Should I identify myself to the members of the organization, telling them my intentions and purposes in studying the group, or should I attempt to appear as an earnest but doubting seeker wishing to know and to understand? In view of the generally acrimonious climate that has ever marked the relationship between Jews and the various missionary enterprises and evangelistically inclined individuals who have sought their conversion, I felt that it would be impossible to establish a satisfactory rapport if the group knew that my interest was scientific rather than personal and that in fact I was a Jew with no marked inclination to convert. Thus I chose the latter course, which did indeed result in the establishment of rapport, but it presented problems as well.

I was troubled at every turn by two reactions—first a sense

of questioning discomfort brought about by knowingly entering relations in which I did not lie or deceive but certainly did
not tell the whole truth, and second by questions about the
methodological justification of my chosen approach.

I never indicated that I was close to conversion or that I was
becoming convinced of the truths being proferred. I chose
instead the role of the basically ignorant but questioning outsider, who for a variety of unstated reasons was seeking clarification of a phenomenon that interested him. I did not reveal
confidences; I did not upset or interject myself into relationships between believers. I carefully attempted to avoid involvement in intragroup dynamics as either catalyst or participant.
I did not "experiment" with people to test reactions to hypoth-
esized situations. I did not try to undermine faith or to
buttress faith. I attempted at every juncture to take seriously
the faith of the believer, to engage as Weber put it in "sympathetic understanding" of that which I was analyzing and
studying.

However, although I never considered the possibility of
feigning conversion, it is absolutely clear that when I posed
as an interested party the converts assumed that I was a
postulant and that I was preparing for conversion: simply my
continued presence convinced them of that, my verbal non-
commitment notwithstanding.

There is no doubt that a great deal of data (i.e., a world of
"in" experiences, given only to the twice-born) was closed
to me. I could not share fully nor observe fully the joy and
the meanings derived by converts. As workers in this field well
know, the respondents' changing views of the observer influence the data he can collect,[2] and to gain the widest acceptance
and the broadest knowledge the observer must succeed by a
community's standards.[3] Success in this instance could only
have meant full conversion.

In addition to the view that the community has of the
observer, the level of participation reciprocally affects the ob-

server. As Elliot Liebow understood, ". . . the degree to which one becomes a participant is as much a matter of perceiving oneself as a participant as it is of being accepted as a participant by others."[4]

Recognizing the limits thus imposed, in morally evaluating my position I firmly decided that I would act "as if" I had announced my purpose: as if I were a formally announced social scientist participating as an observer or observing as a participant. I would not feign any conviction or experience that I had not had.

Both Gold and Junker delineate four levels of participant observation:

1. The complete participant, in which case the observer's role is concealed.

2. The participant as observer, in which case the observer role is subordinated to his more obvious participant role.

3. The observer as participant, in which case the observer's role is fully revealed and emphasized.

4. The complete observer, in which case the observer is on the scene of the action but does not formally participate.[5]

It is clear that my role was that of "complete participant" (level 1) in the technical sense of not revealing my role to the observed; but it was incomplete in that I set moral limits on the role playing I would allow myself. Certainly much extraordinary work has been done by way of role playing. In Festinger's *When Prophecy Fails,* for example, observers were "complete participants" in every sense except that they did not believe in what they were doing or saying: they feigned conversion and even extrasensory experiences and certainly influenced the group, both by their number and by their prophecy-fulfilling experiences.[6]

There has been a great deal of criticism of such "dishonest" research in which the observer poses as a true participant: Barnes, Jarvie, Shils, and Williams, among others, all reject

this method and suggest that there is no justification for dis-
simulation on the basis of public or intellectual need.[7]

> An intrusion into privacy could be justified only as an emer-
> gency measure necessary for the maintenance of public order,
> or the protection of the society as a whole, if it might otherwise
> be severely threatened. The growth of sociological and psycho-
> logical knowledge scarcely falls into this class of emergencies. . . .[8]

> The ethic of science is ill-served by fraudulent methods of study.[9]

I tried to walk that fine line between roles: I was a participating observer but I did not violate my own convictions; and
in thus acting "honestly" I believe I was following a legitimate
path for the social scientist.

Most of the literature on participant observation deals with
levels 2 and 3 (above) in which the social science role of the
observer is more or less made public (or at least is not purpose-
fully hidden) and the moral issue just stated does not arise.
In some cases, however, the hidden type of research is also
discussed without concern for the moral issue.[10] In this literature the methodological pitfalls and values of participant
observation are of chief concern. Although anxiety, bias, sex,
and the role chosen by the observer are still recognized as
factors that may distort the perceptions of the participant,[11]
virtually all analyses share the (now) classic view of Kluckhohn
that participant observation expands the range, relevance, and
even reliability of the data available.[12] However, researchers
are still not entirely comfortable with such idiosyncratic
data,[13] and Bruyn has devoted a book to philosophically legitimating this method. He emerges with no doubts:

> It is a methodology which is producing a scientific design of
> knowledge that transcends history and the particular social sys-
> tems in which people live. At the same time, it is a methodology
> which retains the integrity of the values and beliefs of people
> living in these systems by means of expressive descriptions and

accurate formulations of their cultural lives. Such a method has strong implications for the formal field of ethics and the applied fields of social design and planning. It is a scientific method with a challenging new perspective—a human perspective.[14]

I believe that an ultimate test of the acceptability of this research method can be performed with two checks. One is the assurance that no spiritual or material harm has fallen on those who were the subjects of the analysis; second is the assurance that the phenomenon was grasped, unfolded, and revealed with accuracy and precision. I believe that both these considerations have been met, but subsequent researchers will confirm or upset this evaluation.

Although I made extensive use of the checklist for data collection in situations of unstructured observation,[15] much went unrecorded and unobserved. In some areas a structured interview technique would have yielded a bit more than the unstructured and open-ended device that I utilized, yet I feel that on the whole my choice of research plan was vindicated. This became evident to me when I chose to identify myself as an objective observer with only scholarly interest in the phenomenon of Hebrew Christianity at a National Convention of the Hebrew Christian Alliance of America. I was able to gain many new insights and some additional data on this occasion, but both leadership and rank and file exhibited a certain reticence, which made the experience less than fully rewarding.

There is scant doubt that the methodological approach utilized provided a "natural" setting in which the rhythms of the group could be grasped and its tones recorded in a manner and to a degree that would not have been possible using another format. Nonetheless, there are purely methodological pitfalls—foremost among them a two-pronged and seemingly paradoxical tendency for the investigator to identify with the subjects of the study on the one hand and to stand in judgment on the other. This difficulty tends to occur in all participant observer exercises, but it can be particularly poignant and painful when the investigator role is unclear to the subject population. I am still moved when I remember a day spent with a member of the group which culminated in his taking dinner with my wife and me. All during the day he had witnessed to me, telling me about the meaninglessness of his life prior to his conversion, about his travails since his conversion and about his burning faith and belief in salvation and the ultimate joys to be had when "king Messiah returns to earth." Dinner at my home continued the pattern of the day, with H. H. witnessing, quoting scriptural proof texts, and playing with my children; finally, as the hour grew late, he asked if he might speak with my wife alone. Later that evening my wife told me that H. H. had told her with tears in his eyes how much he valued me and cared for me and how pained he was that I was destined for hell rather than the bliss of heaven. He had begged her as a good wife to help him to save me because he could not stand the thought of my damnation.

Although not every subject's interest in my soul was selflessly motivated, sufficient affect was cast in my direction during the field research to shake me with a recurrent sense of guilt for not being able to reciprocate love proffered. Nor could I reciprocate it in the designated fashion, which in the context meant nothing more nor less than conversion. During the entire field work period not an opportunity nor a moment was missed to approach me with the message, and as time progressed the message became more and more insistent and increasingly impatient. At the outset the professional missionary staff was relatively nondirective in approaching me; but with time (after 3 or 4 months) impatience was manifest and a certain contentiousness insinuated itself into their witnessing to me. What was wrong with me? Why didn't I see the obvious? Was I a fool? A knave? Both? At the outset of the field

study Mrs. F. continually assured me of her love for the
Jewish people, Jewish food, Jewish habits, Jewish souls; but
as time elapsed and I continued unconverted, the virtues of
the race were remarkably transformed into defects as I was
assured that "it [the unconverted state] really wasn't all my
fault and could and must be attributed to evil indoctrination
on the part of rabbis and other Jewish leaders."

The nonprofessionals and the rank-and-file membership
were somewhat less impatient with me throughout, and I was
"worked on" at every opportunity—including bus rides, car
rides, meetings, casual coffee hours, prayer and testimony sessions, and on one occasion while buying a suit. In addition to
the guilt referred to previously, I had to guard against a growing sense of chagrin and hostility brought about by the web
of love being spun about me.

Once while returning in a car from a Bible conference with
five members of the group, I heard "love" repeated so often
that I found it difficult to continue. Not only "love" in the
abstract, or "love" in the sense of man for God or God for
man, but love for the Jews, of enemies, of the saved state, of
children, of nature.

I was told how unhappy I was so often and by so many
people that it seemed downright churlish of me to refuse the
cure. My reactions were admittedly complicated by the fact
that so many of the members of the group were by any objective standards the most victimized, the most downtrodden, the
least happy or most joyless group of people I have encountered. As will become evident, Hebrew Christians tend to be
essentially marginal people who suffer from a long list of
defeats and frustrations ranging from the psychological to the
economic to the social. This simple datum is of central importance both in understanding the phenomenon of Hebrew
Christianity and in determining its relationships to the broader
spectrum of marginal religious groupings.

Because the individual participant tended to be so marginal,

there was a great deal of marginal behavior, as well as numerous marginal and unattractive personalities, making for tension around the sympathy–judgmental paradox under which
the investigator worked. In the local group and in the national
samplings encountered at the Convention of the Hebrew
Christian Alliance, as well as in the more recent Jerusalem
sample, there were relatively few individual participants whom
I could have called healthy or normal. There were and are an
inordinate number of depressives associated with the phenomenon of Hebrew Christianity, including a number of people
with marked suicidal tendencies. In this sense Hebrew Christianity is more akin to cultic phenomena like theosophy, outer
space groups, and scientology, than to more sectarian phenomena such as Pentacostalism and Holiness groups, early
Methodism and Quakerism. The belief pattern of Hebrew
Christians (other than the twofold chosenness of the members
by virtue of race *and* faith) is decidedly within the context
of a Protestant fundamentalist denominational framework,
whereas the psychosocial makeup of the membership is closer
to the sect-cult pattern.[16] Members were constantly assuring
me that plots were being hatched against them by Jewish
organizations and leaders, who themselves knew how potent
the Hebrew Christian message was and were trying to block
it off. Stories of individual persecutions at the hands of these
"enemies" abound and are exchanged among believers on
frequent and diverse occasions.

A key sociological datum about Hebrew Christian believers
which they share with religious sects on the Protestant fringe
is their marginality—their neither-fish-nor-fowl status. They
are Christian but decidedly not quite Christian in the way a
gentile Baptist or Methodist is Christian. They are Jewish but
cerainly not in the manner in which an Orthodox or Reform
or Reconstructionist Jew is Jewish. They are suspect in the
eyes of the former and rejected as renegades or weird cultists
by the latter. Until the recent appearance of the Jesus revival,

involving some Jewish youth, the typical Hebrew Christian was a middle-aged or elderly first- or second-generation American Jew, of minimal education and minimal economic attainment. He was or tended to be either an isolate in terms of institutional affiliation or a wanderer from group to group in search of personal identity, affiliation, and social anchorage. The individual was a man or woman who seemed to be buffeted about by life somewhat more than usual; a loser more often than not for whom both the organized Jewish community and the established Christian churches appeared (and in fact were) too cold, too institutionalized, too distant to be able to afford comfort and direction.

He was a Jew with strongly ambivalent feelings about being Jewish, manifesting a wavering shift between feelings of self-hatred at one point along the scale to downright anti-Semitism at the extreme pole.

Thus with respect to the sociopsychological characteristics of membership, we are able to see in Hebrew Christianity a pattern found time and time again in the literature of sectarian movements within the Judeo-Christian context; its ideal typical foundations have been outlined by such scholars as Weber, Troeltsch, Niebuhr, Wilson, O'Dea, and Wach with, however, a difference that emphasizes that Hebrew Christianity is *sui generis*. Hebrew Christianity is essentially a missionary effort, a device rather than a sect, whose methodology and legitimation processes constantly pull it toward the sectarian abyss, although thus far it has not fallen in. Hebrew Christianity might best be described as a "reluctant sect" whose study holds importance and relevance on at least three levels.

First, it provides an opportunity to trace the growth and development of a socioreligious movement from its genesis within a centuries-old missionary endeavor, showing how it assumed certain sectarian overtones and pointing out its present bifurcated "pulls," both in the direction of sectarian status within Protestantism, and in the direction of anti-institutional fundamentalism. Furthermore, in dealing with a group of converts who in essence deny their apostasy, it affords an opportunity to test the relevance of Weber's assertion that ". . . it is very common for violations of an order to be confined to more or less numerous partial deviations from it, or for the attempt to be made, with varying degrees of good faith, to justify the deviation as legitimate."[17] And finally, this effort to legitimize a new status has led to the buttressing of a factor that it in large measure sought to obviate—anti-Semitism.

It is hoped, of course, that in addition to shedding some light on these three dominant themes, the study will add to the general body of knowledge in the fields of sect and sect formation, social movements, and social change.

NOTES

1. Hugh Schoenfield, *The History of Jewish Christianity; From the First to the Twentieth Century* (London: Duckworth, 1936).

2. Cf. Arthur J. Vidich, "Participant Observation and the Collection and Interpretation of Data," *American Journal of Sociology,* Vol. 60 (1955), 354–360.

3. Cf. Joseph D. Lohman, "The Participant Observer in Community Studies," *American Sociological Review,* Vol. 2 (1937), 890–897.

4. Elliot Liebow, *Tally's Corner: A Study of Negro Streetcorner Men* (Boston: Little, Brown and Co., 1967), p. 256.

5. Raymond L. Gold, "Roles in Sociological Field Observations," *Social Forces* Vol. 36 (1958), 217–223; Buford Junker, *Fieldwork* (Chicago: University of Chicago Press, 1960), pp. 35–38.

6. Leon Festinger, Henry W. Reicken, and Stanley Schachter, *When Prophecy Fails* (New York: Harper & Row, 1956).

7. J. A. Barnes, "Some Ethical Problems of Modern Fieldwork," *British Journal of Sociology,* Vol. 14 (1963), 118–134; I. C. Jarvie, "The Problem of Ethical Integrity in Participant Observation," *Current Anthropology,* Vol. 10, No. 5 (December 1969), 505–508; Edward A. Shils, "Social Inquiry and the Autonomy of the Individual," in *The Human Meaning of the Social Sciences,* Daniel Lerner, ed. (New York: The World Publishing Co., 1959), 114–157; T. R. Williams, *Field*

   Methods in the Study of Culture (New York: Holt, Rinehart & Winston, 1967).

8. *Shils, op. cit.*, p. 132.

9. Williams, *op. cit.*, p. 45.

10. See Howard S. Becker and Blanche Geer, "Participant Observation: The Analysis of Qualitative Field Data," in Richard N. Adams and Jack J. Preiss, eds., *Human Organization Research* (Homewood, Ill: The Dorsey Press, Inc., 1960), pp. 267–289.

11. See S. M. Miller, "The Participant Observer and 'Over-Rapport,'" *American Sociological Review*, Vol. 17 (1952), 97–99; C. G. Schwartz and M. S. Schwartz, "Problems in Participant Observation," *American Journal of Sociology*, Vol. 60 (1955), 343–353; Arthur J. Vidich, "Participant Observation and the Collection and Interpretation of Data," *American Journal of Sociology*, Vol. 60 (1955), 354–360.

12. Florence R. Kluckhohn, "The Participant Observer Technique in Small Communities," *American Journal of Sociology*, Vol. 46 (1940), 331–343. Kluckhohn also recognizes that the range, relevance, and reliability of the data are simultaneously limited by participant observation.

13. See Becker and Geer, *op. cit.*, who advise rendering participant observations into quantifiable material so that others may be "convinced" by the data.

14. Severyn T. Bruyn, *The Human Perspective in Sociology: The Methodology of Participant Observation* (Englewood Cliffs, N.J.: Prentice-Hall, Inc., 1966), p. 281.

15. See Claire Selltiz, Marie Jahoda, *et al.*, *Research Methods in Social Relations*, 2nd rev. ed. (New York: Henry Holt and Co., 1959), pp. 209–210.

16. This is discussed further in Chapter 6.

17. Max Weber, *The Theory of Social and Economic Organization*, Talcott Parsons and A. M. Henderson, transls. and eds. (New York: Oxford University Press, 1947), p. 125.

Part One

Jesus in Jerusalem
and the Messengers

1

Jesus in Jerusalem

Hebrew Christianity has not received a great deal of attention from scholars interested in religious phenomena or from institutional leadership in either the Christian or Jewish camps. Main line Protestantism in recent decades has embraced an ecumenical approach that negates a missionary outreach generally and one with respect to Jews specifically. Since the limited numbers and marginal character of the Jews reached by the movement precluded the possibility of much concern among organized Jewish bodies, the movement has remained buried in obscurity.

With the dawn of the 1970s, however, a new dimension has emerged which has transformed prior obscurity to heightened concern, at least for Jewish leadership. This shift was brought about by an important change in the demographic outreach of the movement from one that appealed to highly marginal "burnt-out cases" in the latter stages of life to one that had begun to make an impact on dozens if not hundreds of the young scions of the highly affluent American Jewish community. Where previously the movement could be ignored as a haven for the defeated and confused tailenders of the general upward social-economic move of American Jewry, a less cavalier attitude was indicated when the children of the middle classes began to show interest in the Hebrew Christian message.

American Jewry has demonstrated a remarkable proclivity for being in step with trends and shifts appearing in American middle-class society at large. In a not completely playful manner the American Jew might be described as economically mobile, highly educated, urbanly oriented, culturally hip, increasingly intermarried, politically stable and liberal, consumer focused, religiously congregational, philanthropically committed, bureaucratically organized, voluntarily associated, and personally alienated. I think it evident that Jews reflect certain dominant trends abroad in American society and seem in fact to be the standard bearers for—though not necessarily the originators of—these developments. Whether it be in economic structures, styles of life, or patterns of education, Jews seem to be less in the vanguard than to be exemplars of specific and general change.

Thus most observers of the American Jewish scene agree that a disproportionate share of actors in the counterculture of the 1960s were and are Jewish. Whether among the new left, the dope culture, the drop-outs, or the cultists, young Jews, while of course a minority in absolute terms, seemed to be disproportionately represented. When the zeitgeist indicated an emphasis on instant relevance, personal freedom from the bonds of tradition in all its forms, a negation of institutions, a commitment to doing one's own thing, and preoccupation with sex, drugs, and to a lesser extent violence, we were able to trace the hegira of hundreds, indeed thousands, of Jewish youth in the direction of these commitments.

As could have been predicted, the new anarchism did not fulfill its promise, and the sought-for salvation was at best illusive and chimerical. With the end of the 1960s and early 1970s countertrends have begun to set in: a new conservatism is replacing the inchoate and inarticulate freewheeling of the past decade. A search for roots and social anchorage is no longer considered to be a cop-out. It is now felt that the past might have relevance for the present and the future.

I do not mean to suggest that the *ancien regime* has been restored through the aegis of a Children's Crusade. It was, in fact, never destroyed. Nor am I suggesting that the shift of many young people in the direction of older verities is unidimensional. The growth of satanic cults, Buddhist spinoffs, diverse communitarian sects, food faddists, and so on, would seem to suggest that ferment persists and that answers, personal and communal, are being sought along all points of the experimental compass. Ferment associated with adolescence is not a development of the 1960s. As Erikson has noted, each successive stage in the life cycle brings with it a crisis, a turning point, a crucial period of increased vulnerability and heightened potential.[2] In adolescence the crisis faced is that of identity—the young person must define himself psychologically and find his niche in society.

Under the best of circumstances this is a difficult and trying period for the adolescent, but as Keniston and other observers of the youth scene have pointed out, it is being inordinately complicated by the increasing preparation required for adult functioning and the growing gap that results between biological and social maturity.[3] In the post gesellschaft 1960s, American society confronted a widening abyss between biologically mature young people who were being stymied at every turn in making life decisions and were being commensurately tested by life situations. Under the impact of this reality, we should not have been surprised that a kind of anarchic backlash emerged to be dubbed the counterculture.

For historical and cultural reasons, middle-class Jewish culture was if anything even more protective and inhibiting of its adolescent stratum than the general culture. Thus the seemingly greater impact of prevailing youth trends on Jewish youth during the 1960s. With the waning of many of the more salient features of the counterculture came a return to more familiar categories of stability and self-definition, not least among them the category of religion.

As James, Underwood, Starbuck, and others have noted, conversion is essentially an adolescent phenomenon. It is a response to internal crisis, and given the existential realities of growing up American in the 1960s, it was an alternative that lent itself to the needs of a generation.

But one is converted to or by something specific, embracing, and demanding. Conversion has nothing to do with the gentlemanly assumption of a new role. Whatever form it takes, it transforms life, it is wrenching and cataclysmic. An esoteric movement, a cult, a personality, an overarching idea can all be the objects of conversion. A Jesus of Nazareth, a Buddha, a Maharishi can become the fulcrum, the orientation point for the conversionary experience. But can a sanctified sociology fulfill the role? And this in fact is how contemporary Jewry has been defined by its critics, both insiders and outsiders. Erikson suggests that ideology is the key element in the resolution of identity crisis: "An ideological system is a coherent body of shared images, ideals, and ideas which . . . provides the participants with a coherent, if systematically simplified, over all orientation in space and time, in means and ends."[4] Religion can provide such a system, but if Neusner is correct in asserting that being a Jew in America in our time means primarily to join an organization,[5] and in fact provides little or nothing in the way of a demanding ideological commitment, then we must suppose that such a Jewish context will be unable to meet the new demands of at least a sizable segment of youth in the 1970s. Most young Jews will not convert to Christianity or any other transcendental cause; but given the nature of the Jewish community—its familial structure, its smallness, its continued sense of singularity—even a visible minority movement in this direction will be threatening.

Indeed, since 1971 some leaders and many within the Jewish public have become increasingly disturbed about inroads made by missionaries bearing the Hebrew Christian message to college and university campuses. Assertions to the effect that 1972 saw the conversion of between 6000 and 7000 Jewish youth to

Evangelical Christianity[6] cause much consternation among Jews; and although the real figure is probably closer to 600 or 700, the effect is still considerable. A B'nai B'rith Hillel report prepared by S. Z. Fishman indicates that the number of Jewish youth actually baptized is probably smaller yet, but the same report also notes that a residual spiritual effect on hundreds of youngsters subjected to evangelical efforts cannot be so easily ignored.[7] Fishman suggests that counterefforts in educational and spiritual rearmament are indicated if the exertions of the missionary are to be further minimalized.

One can easily understand how the Hebrew Christian approach would prove particularly viable at this time from an understanding of the American Jewish praxis. Being Jewish involves little theological or ideological commitment that is not widely shared on a surface level by most of American society. In the postwar decades of the 1940s and 1950s, Zionism and the birth of Israel could and did capture the loyalties and imagination of thousands of Jewish youth. In the 1960s radical politics, the antiwar movement, and the civil rights thrust provided the systems through which a type of Jewish commitment, a Jewish messianism, could be expressed. But with the "guarantees" and ordinariness of Israel after 1967, the casting out of whites from the black liberation movement, and the end of the Vietnam war all coming at about the same time, these external struts to Jewish communal identity disappeared. At the same time, the mild deism of contemporary Jewry was put to a test to which it was and is not yet ready to respond from within. Being Jewish and being educated Jewish means essentially staying within the ethnic camp, being loyal to the group, appreciating the tradition, and identifying in some fashion with Israel and with the "plight" of Jews wherever they might be. The greatest sin is defection—denying one's Jewishness, copping out—a certain amount of success is predictable for a movement which has as a singular linchpin the assertion that belief in Jesus' messiahship is an unquestionably Jewish position involving ultimate loyalty to the true ethnic

community. If it is true that American youth who turn with
such zeal to Jesus of Nazareth are in effect reclaiming the
father who has absented himself (or been totemized) from the
traditional role, the same needs must be fulfilled for Mrs.
Portnoy's offspring. But traditional Judaism is unable to supply the personalized father figure of a Jesus. Judaism is ill-
equipped to give an antinomian absolution to its prodigies,
and in fact the case histories of a number of Hebrew Christian
converts among contemporary youth indicate a need for just
these elements: (a) an uncomplicated faith not requiring sophisticated scholarship to be fathomed; (b) a visible, graphi-
cally apprehensible father figure who loves totally and forgives
totally; (c) a sense of communal continuity; (d) a set of symbols,
ideas, and orientations against which a personal identity can
evolve.

With respect to item (c), an interesting and conceivably significant recent development has been the appearance in Israel,
primarily in Jerusalem, of dozens of young American Jewish
converts to evangelical Christianity who can add the legitimating claim of not only not having left the Jewish fold but of
having come home to the Jewish country. Their stories reflect
the variables noted earlier, demonstrating both continuities and
discontinuities with past Hebrew Christian experience, which
are discussed following and interspersed with the presentation
of the cases. Also included for purposes of contrast and analysis
is the case history of one convert who returned to the fold of
traditional Judasim, commenting on his previous ties from
the reclaimed Jewish perspective.

CASE HISTORIES [8]

1. Stuart

We first heard about Stuart while talking with the director of
Habad House. The Lubavitch Hassidic movement established

the house in 1972 to educate young Jews, mostly American, in the ways of Hassidism. In the last few months the director has received at least 20 letters from concerned parents in the States whose children had accepted Jesus and left for Israel. The letters are often hysterical, full of pain and guilt, becrying the writers' "ruined lives." They beg the Habad people in Jerusalem to search for their children and try to convince them to return to Judaism. One of the letters was from Stuart's mother.

Stuart was always an ideal son, reports Mr. K (director of Habad House), quoting from the mother's letter. He was the valedictorian of his high school class and did excellent work his freshman year in college. The trouble began when he was a sophomore. If it appeared that he was going to receive an A in a course he would drop it in midsemester. He was looking forward to a trip with his choir, but just before the group left he gave up his coveted place to another student. That spring he left school to visit his sister in California. Soon after, he announced to his parents that he had accepted Jesus.

Shocked and worried, the mother wrote that Stuart had been taken to a psychiatrist who said that the boy was terribly off balance and would "buy the Brooklyn Bridge if I tried to sell it to him." Shortly following the visit, Stuart left home, presumably to do missionary work in Jerusalem. Although he still writes to his parents, he gives no return address and does not speak of plans to return.

Mr. K explained that after reading Stuart's mother's letter he had made a special effort to find the boy. He discovered that the youth is being watched by the Israeli government, which is looking for an excuse to ask him to leave the country. On several occasions he has broken into army camps and in other ways disturbed the peace in his zeal to make converts. The Habad director pointed out that the letter suggests a rather common cause for the conversion: "masochism and a lack of horse sense."

About a week after hearing the story, we visited the home on Mount of Olives where a group of Jewish believers live together. As we talked in their bedroom, we noticed a shy, thin boy sitting alone on the side. Unlike his more vocal friends, he was strumming absently on a guitar, not contributing to the theology lesson being conducted. In his too-large Bermuda shorts and socks with loafers, he resembled a little boy away at summer camp for the first time.

At one point in the conversation, an older member of the group suggested we might like to hear a song that "the Lord taught to Stuart." The boy then began to play a beautiful melody, singing in an excellent, clear voice:

> All we like sheep have gone astray
> We have turned everyone to his own way
> And the Lord hath laid upon Him
> The iniquity of us all.
>
> He was oppressed and He was afflicted
> Yet He opened not His mouth
> He was brought as a lamb to the slaughter
> But He opened not His mouth
>
> For He was wounded for our transgressions
> He was bruised for our iniquities
> The chastisement of our peace was upon Him
> And with His stripes we are healed.
>
> Of whom did Isaiah speak?
> It was Jesus, It was Jesus.

The group joined in, smiling warmly at one another. After the singing, Stuart seemed to relax a bit and began to talk. As he spoke, he rocked back and forth in his seat, clutching his knees. He told us:

> I came from a really religious family. We kept kosher and everything and my father helped found a conservative synagogue in my town. I didn't have anything to do with Hillel at my college but I did have a seder in my room with some Jewish friends. That was really neat. As for Christianity, I was a real intellectual. I had all the arguments why it couldn't be true.
>
> But then things started getting bad and I decided to leave

school and hitchhike across the country to see my sister. Things began to happen on that trip. Strange things. I kept saying it was just coincidence but finally I couldn't hold out any longer. I got the last piece of the puzzle and everything made perfect sense. I was a believer.

When I told my parents they took me to a psychiatrist. Now, I used to be a very nervous person, much more nervous than I am now. But at the psychiatrist God gave me strength. Everything went smoothly. It just kind of flowed. The psychiatrist said I was fine and my parents were much happier. Then I decided to come here and spread the Word.

At my ulpan [rapid Hebrew langugage] class I had to give a speech so I told about Jesus. I was really nervous before I had to do it, like I always have been when I'm forced to talk in class. I prepared lots of notes. But when I got up there I didn't need the notes at all. The Lord just put the words in my mouth and everything went beautifully.

You know, when we go out in the streets to missionize I'm sometimes scared about being attacked by the yeshiva students. But once they actually start beating us up I feel great. I'm suffering for Jesus, the way He suffered.

The wonderful thing about Christianity is you don't have to be smart and study Talmud for a hundred years before you can know God. The Lord knew we weren't all going to be brilliant geniuses so He made it so even someone stupid like myself can have a relationship with God. Now I can say to Him, "Hey, Dad! Help me!" And He does.

2. Commentary: Deeds and Faith

Beware of those who insist on mutilation—"circumcision" I will not call it; we are the circumcised, we whose worship is spiritual, whose pride is Christ Jesus, and who put no confidence in anything external. . . . If anyone thinks to base his claims on externals, I could make a stronger case for myself: circumcised on my eighth day, Israelite by race, of the tribe of Benjamin, a Hebrew born and bred; in my attitude to the law, a Pharisee; in pious zeal, a persecutor of the church; in legal rectitude, faultless. But all such assets I have written off because of Christ. I would say more: I count everything sheer loss, because all is far outweighed by the gain of knowing Christ Jesus my Lord, for whose sake I did in fact lose everything. I count it so much garbage, for the sake of gaining Christ and finding myself incorporate in him, with no righteousness of my own, no legal recitude, but the righteousness which comes from faith in Christ, given by God in response to faith. All I care for is to know Christ, to experience the power of his resurrection, and to share his sufferings, in growing conformity with his death, if only I may finally arrive at the resurrection from the dead.[9]

We are fortunate in this case since we have the testimonies of both Stuart and his mother to work with. Disparities appear between them, and an even fuller story emerges.

Stuart's mother stresses that her son was ideal, he was number one in his class. But Stuart refers to himself as "stupid" and claims that in Christianity he has found a place for those who, like himself, are not "brilliant geniuses." He reports that he was always nervous when forced to speak in class. Even now, in ulpan, he reverts to his old role as striving student, preparing copious notes for an oral presentation.

Clearly intelligence and academic achievement were highly valued in his home. He had identified these demands with the requirements of Judaism. But he does not see himself as living up to the standards. One might conjecture that the courses he dropped midterm were actually courses he was doing poorly in. Alan Mintz, criticizing American Jewish life asks: "Who doesn't know many smart people who, because they could not be *brilliant* in school, deliberately begin to fail, then to lie in order to avoid the anxiety of being discovered?"[10]

Even now, Stuart wants desperately to believe he is pleasing his parents. Perhaps he was never told what the psychiatrist had said about him. It could be, however, that Stuart has twisted the story in his own mind, not willing to admit he has failed his parents by receiving a "bad report."

Like Paul in Philippians, Stuart has finally despaired of fulfilling the Law. For as Richard Rubenstein has pointed out,

"Jewish law is the same in its secular and religious form: Perform well and you will be rewarded, perform badly and you will be damned."[11] This is the law of achievement imposed on middle-class youth. Among Jews it most frequently takes the form of academic excellence as proof of good performance. For Stuart, the law had become an unbearable yoke.

Paul took seriously the need to achieve a right relationship with God. But when he concluded that it was impossible for an ordinary man like himself to fully observe the commandments, he discovered another way. No longer would obedience to the Father be the criterion for salvation. Rather, he identified himself with Jesus, one who has a perfect relationship to God. Through this identification, through faith alone, Paul too could be saved.

We see that following Stuart's conversion, formerly difficult tasks, such as speaking to a psychiatrist or to a class, began to "flow." Since faith, not deeds, is what God requires, the youth is less nervous now for he knows that he has been accepted fully by God—whom he can call Dad. He might have strived unsuccessfully all his life for such acceptance from his own father.

Of course there was a time when Stuart's parents accepted him totally. It was the time before deeds and achievement could be expected of him. In infancy one is powerless and passive; but parents, all potent and all accepting, never fail to come through. Stuart has regained this sense of childhood trust and freedom from obligation to perform. He can return to the passivity of an infant, sure in his faith that God will help him.

As Erikson has said, "All religions have in common the periodical childlike surrender to a Provider or providers who dispense earthly as well as spiritual health . . . the insight that individual trust must become a common faith."[12] Of course the emphasis placed on this theme differs with the religious group involved. In the case of the Jesus people it takes on a dominant role in the worldview of the believers.

Queried about how they supported themselves. Stuart and

his fellow believers told us again and again that there was no need to worry about such matters. "Our Father takes care of His children." When discussing their activities in missionizing, their performance in ulpan, their needs for food and shelter, they repeatedly emphasized that they never doubted that the Lord would see them through.

A believer put the matter of regression in startlingly clear form:

> One night I was taking dope and began to experience this sense of all perfection. I remained in one position for hours, thinking: I could just sit here like this forever. It was like being wrapped in whipped cream. I felt like I had returned to a time when I was a kid, before my mother went back to work.

A song heard from one of the group is illustrative:

> You've got to be a baby
> You've got to be a baby
> You've got to be a baby
> To get to heaven.

Stuart's song suggests that Jesus, through his suffering, has saved man from his iniquity. The inquity, the inadequacy, the sin that is relieved can take many forms. In this case it seems to be the iniquity of nonperformance, of not living up to the secular law of modern Jewish life. Through Christianity, Stuart has been relieved of his guilt. For he has now reentered the time when deeds and achievement are not required of man. All that is asked of him is faith and trust.

3. Ann

The Reverend Wallace H. Heflin, pentecostal pioneer for 46 years, came to Israel from his camp in Asheland, Virginia, to

proclaim the "soon coming of the Lord." The Pentecostal Conference on Biblical Prophecy which he organized took place in
Jerusalem at the Binyanai Ha-Ooma Conference Hall. There,
flanked by Israeli flags, the minister and his family preached
to the company of believers he had brought with him and to a
small group of Israelis and tourists. His followers were from
Readers Digest America. Most of the rest of the audience were
interested onlookers. It was at one of the afternoon sessions,
intimate and emotional, that we first met Ann.

She was sitting in the huge, almost empty auditorium. (The
nonbelievers came in the evening.) This was only a warmup
session, yet it was charged with excitement, at least for the
petite, attractive girl at our side. She sang with great joy,
clapped her hands, and danced in her place. When the minister made a particularly telling point she nodded her head in
affirmation, "It's true, it's true." At a pause in the meeting, she
turned and asked why we were not taking part. "Aren't you
believers yet?" When we confessed that we were not, she smiled
happily. "Paise the Lord! He has sent you right to me so I can
witness."

Ann was an American, living now in Jaffa and attending
ulpan. We indicated that we could find her a place to stay the
night in Jerusalem. She admitted that she had no particular
place to stay and promised she would consult the Lord and see
if it was His will. At this point, the minister called everyone
to come to the front and be touched by the Holy Spirit. One
by one, the audience went forward and received a light touch
on the forehead, after which they stretched out on the floor.
Ann soon joined the row of prostrate bodies. When she came
to, we approached her and she informed us that she had
received the Lord's permission to accept our invitation.

That evening we discussed her story:

I always had a good relationship with my parents. I really love
them. My father is a good man and he believes in God, although

he doesn't know Jesus yet. I know I've put them through a lot of anxiety since I accepted Jesus but I don't worry about it. The Lord is making them suffer now for His own purposes. I have a feeling He is paving the way for their salvation.

In college I studied art and slept with lots of men. The things I admired most in my lovers—self-confidence, strength of will, pride . . . these are precisely the things I now realize are wrong. It is not what the Lord wants. I used to think premarital sex was right, but now I see how mistaken I was. The Lord takes care of His children and He has written in my heart what I must do and not do. I am incapable of sin now!

My last year in college I lived with a non-Jewish boy for eight months without telling my parents. Toward the end I began to feel very guilty about it: I couldn't sleep at night. I was a sinner and I knew it. I see now that I put my faith in people, mostly men, and this was my mistake. People are of the flesh. This is what I realized by dying to my own fleshly life. Now I love people but I don't trust them. I only trust God who is of the spirit.

After my affair ended and I graduated from college I went home and confessed everything to my parents. They forgave me and everything was great. I lived at home for six months and worked for my father. I still couldn't get rid of the idea that I was a sinner. Then my father got the idea to send me to Israel so I could be steeped in Jewish faith and maybe find some direction for the more moral life I wanted to lead. So about three months ago I came here and enrolled in an ulpan I found in Jaffa.

About a month and a half ago I met a married couple at the ulpan who were believers. I began to visit their home and sit in on prayer meetings they held in their living room. At one of those meetings I opened myself up and asked the Lord into my heart. Just like that He came to me and I was saved forever. Since then my life has been perfect. I am totally at peace with myself. I have no desire for sin.

I always had a kind of fascination with religion. When I was young I used to think a lot about death. In college, I went through a stage where I was interested in Judaism. I went alone every Saturday morning to a synagogue about an hour from my school. But it didn't change my life and I stopped going after a while. Judaism is just for this world anyway. In Christianity I have perfected my life and received everlasting life as well.

As we talked, it became obvious that Ann did not know the Bible very well and that her theology was rather unclear. When questioned or challenged on a point she had made, she grew confused, searching in her memory for the appropriate Christian response. For instance, we asked her why a merciful God would let her parents burn in hell for eternity if they fail to accept Jesus. She got upset and said she was unsure about this particular point but certainly the Lord was right and whatever happened would be good.

We asked her if she would join us at dinner, but she explained that the Lord had told her that morning not to eat today.

> It's really amazing the way the Lord can tell me what I should do and then I just do it, without any effort. I used to really like to eat but now if the Lord wants it, I can do without food and feel no hunger. I used to have the habit of smoking, but the Lord rids one immediately of all bad habits. It's so easy now to be pure. All one has to do is accept the Truth. The Lord takes care of the rest.

4. Commentary: A New Puritanism

> Nature sets its desires against the Spirit, while the Spirit fights against it. They are in conflict with one another so that what you will to do you cannot do.[13]

Like Stuart, Ann came to Christianity with a deep sense of iniquity and guilt. For Ann, the sense of being a sinner was bound up with her earthly desires—particularly sex. Unlike Stuart, who had transcended the burden of Law, Ann was actually seeking law. She had been free to indulge her needs and lusts, but unable to find outer or inner controls, she wished to rid herself of her desires entirely.

It is a fundamental theme of Christianity that the works of the flesh are at odds with those of the spirit and that through

faith in Jesus one may "crucify the lower nature with its passions and desires."[14] Stories of conversion to Christianity are
filled with testimonies like Ann's. The sinner loses all craving
for that which he had once so greatly needed and yet had
sensed was evil. But how does this happen?

James suggests that there exists a "hot place" in man's consciousness that is the "habitual center of his personal energy."
When one is converted, the "excitement shifts"; religious aims
and ideas take a central place in his consciousness.[15] When
this occurs, as it did with Ann, the once-vital needs and
desires lose all significance as the personal energy becomes
directed toward a new center. The "degree of spiritual excitement allows sovereignty of spirit over flesh."[16]

We have yet to explain Ann's desire to achieve this sovereignty. The Jewish tradition has always accepted the earthly
life and man's material needs. It has sought not to vanquish
them but rather to control them through law. We may assume
that Ann's parents, modern and liberal Jews, had provided a
permissive and accepting environment. In this, the most liberated and unrepressed (at least sexually) of societies, why
would one develop guilt concerning the demands of the id?

The psychiatrist, Jarl E. Dyrud, suggests a possible interpretation:

> Everybody talks about this new youth—so free and happy. Well,
> these permissively raised kids have had to develop their own
> internal constraints on their behavior—and these are a great deal
> more rigid and punishing than the average good parent would
> have given them, if he had taken the trouble to set limits.[17]

In other words, the freedom from the controls of law can be
a hellish blessing. In an effort to be liberated, parents and society allow youth to be their own moral authorities. Given only
vague outlines of how one should behave, and in exercising
their license, failing to see a satisfying life emerge, the young
seek authority. Ann is a dramatic case of one who has found in

God someone who will always tell her precisely what to do. This is what she never had. When she relied on her own instincts, she failed to find happiness.

Ann's puritanical approach to the life of the body is not unusual among the converts studied. One older woman we met told us she liked the young Jesus people because "They are my type. I never liked drinking, cigarette smoke upsets me, and I have always been repelled by sexual excess. These people lead good clean lives." While she was right in saying their lives are "clean" she was wrong in assuming they are "her type." She has always been like that, whereas most of the converts' stories parallel that of Ann: a past involvement with sex, drugs, or drinking leading to a radical reversal and acceptance of the "Christian life."

This purity of life style is perhaps the most striking feature of the group studied. When entering one of the apartments maintained by the group at Mount of Olives, in Jerusalem, one is immediately impressed by its extraordinary neatness. Anyone who is familiar with American college dormitories is accustomed to disarray—books and clothes strewn about, empty bottles and remnants of food, full ashtrays. The room where six believers lived had the air of an army barracks during inspection.

Chastity, it appears, is very important. The house just mentioned was only for males and one married couple. Girls were quartered in a church down the road. All those asked about it insisted that sex was no longer important in their lives. Perhaps when God sent them a wife it would be different.

Drug use, of course, is anathema. Perhaps the tritest theme in the conversion stories is that of the dramatically cured drug addict. In one extreme case, a boy had been using $160 of heroine a day. Immediately following his conversion, he lost all need for the drug and exhibited no withdrawal symptoms. A doctor told him that his recovery was the most complete and spectacular he had ever seen.

The new life is a satisfying one. As one boy put it, "You only have to invite Jesus into your heart once. You have to smoke, eat, ball chicks again and again. The thrill doesn't last. Only Jesus lasts." Another explained the fruits of his conversion this way: "I wanted to *be* but I didn't want this body that holds me to the ground and gets sick, dirty, painful. The physical life was holding me down. With Christ I am above all worldly needs."

Returning now to Ann, we see that besides conquering her once sinful nature, she has found a life style free of complications. Her problems in the past had been mostly related to men, and the lesson she learned—"you can't trust people"—suggests that she must have encountered some painful experiences. It may be that her turn from sensuality to a chaste life was motivated not only by a conviction that her sexual activity was morally wrong but also by the realization that it had brought her hurt and betrayal. By leaving that world behind, she has also escaped the traumas of relationships.

She loves all men now, but in a sense she has ceased to have deep involvements with them, the kind that may lead to disillusionment and hurt. The Lord, however, cannot betray her.

5. Joshua

Several of the believers encountered at the Mount of Olives home attend Ulpan Etzion on Rehov Gad. A boy named Ron invited us to come there one day and watch him give an oral presentation to his class on Jesus. When we arrived at the ulpan, we realized that we had forgotten to ask the classroom number and began to wander around the building, searching for the right room. A tall, good-looking boy stopped us in the hall and asked if he could help. His big green eyes had the same happy, glazed look noticed previously in other believers, and he was carrying a Bible in a carved leather case over his shoulder. He introduced himself as Joshua—a man of God.

When we explained our mission, he insisted on helping us try to locate Ron. After about a half hour we agreed that Ron had failed to come that day. Joshua suggested we go somewhere and talk. "It was no accident you came here and couldn't find your friend. We were meant to meet. I'm missing my class now, but don't worry. God wants me to talk to you."

We found an empty classroom and there we heard his story:

I was born in Israel, but I moved to America when I was eight. I went to a Christian college. I never really got into the school activities. I was always off on my own trip. Except for sports. I played on all sorts of teams. But the friends I made on the teams were cold. I was looking for real friends, and of course, the perfect lover. I've found that now.

It was strange how it happened. I was brought up to hate Jesus and Christianity. Everything I ever heard about it seemed false. One night when I was really lonely and down, I went walking in the streets. Around two in the morning someone came up to me out of nowhere and said "Jesus loves you." Just like that I knew it was the truth. I had heard it a hundred times, but suddenly it made sense. I decided that morning to come back to Israel and convert Jews. In a moment I was no longer a son, a student, and an athlete. I was simply a man of God. I pulled out of my old life completely. I don't think I was missed.

All I can remember about God from my religious training is this one line: "Thou shalt have no other Gods before me." That really impressed me, except that I saw that no one believed it. Even my parents, who are good people, kept making things into Gods—their apartment, food, *me*. They made me into a God! I guess they loved me and I loved them but it wasn't anything like the kind of love I can have now—now that I know I have a soul.

Look at Israel today. Does it believe in God or in its own might? The problem is that Judaism thinks your works will save you. But only faith can do that. They're trying to get back faith here. A guy like Shlomo Carlebach, [a Habad Hassid with a mission to the counterculture Jews whom he attempts to bring back to the fold of traditional Judaism] does his best to make people religious. He's really a sincere guy. He dresses up Judaism and tries to make it palatable. But you know what happens? Everyone starts worshipping him instead of God. They idolize Carlebach. These people are lacking a real relationship with the Lord, so they figure the best they can do is worship a man who seems to have that kind of contact.

Through Jesus, every man can have it himself. The God of Judaism just isn't someone you can relate to. Now I know that God is a comfortable, relaxed father who is really in love with me. I have a lot of respect for Jewish culture. But that isn't enough. It's just the icing. Now I've got the cake, too.

When I saw the Truth I knew I had to do something big about it. And that doesn't mean a nine-to-five job. It means going off and living communally with other believers the way Jesus wanted us to. In the commune I live in now I have such great friends. Real, loving people. I want you to come and meet them because I really love you.

Why don't you let me pray for you? We'll read John together. It's a really heavy book. Then I'll pray that the Lord enter your heart as He did mine. You've got to let me save you. I love you too much to let you go on without Jesus.

6. Commentary: Intimacy and Community

But if we walk in the light, as He Himself is in the light, then we share together a common life. . . .[18]

Joshua's conversion experience is not an unusual one. A single statement changed his life. James notes,

The simplest rudiment of mystical experience would seem to be that deepened sense of the significance of a maxim or formula which occasionally sweeps over one. "I've heard that said all my life" we exclaim. "But I never realized its full meaning until now."[19]

Joshua wanted a friend, a perfect lover, a God he could be comfortable with. He lacked a sense of community at his school. The sports world introduced him not to fraternity, but rather to people who were cold. His parents idolized him, hence dehumanized him. Nowhere could he find the bases on which to establish ties of love.

The difficulty can be viewed on two levels. First, it is symptomatic of our society in general. Urbanization, isolated nuclear families, institutionalized religions leave little place for the needs of men to have a small community in which they can locate themselves and from which they may deal with the broader society. In response to this, young people seek to create their own communities. These efforts are more or less successful, depending on their basis.

Religion is ideally suited to serve as the ground for a creation of community. People are able to share their belief. That which is most significant and compelling in their lives is a common ground for communication and commitment to each other. Judaism has traditionally served this need in an exemplary way. But as we have noted, Judaism's sense of community has grown unwieldy and the concept of shared faith no longer is applicable. For Joshua, Judaism had already been tasted and rejected. Christian love offered a new option.

On a more personal level, Joshua was seeking one-to-one relationships of intimacy and love. We return to Erikson's theory of life cycle. In adolescence each individual must establish who he is and what he stands for. "It is only when identity formation is well on the way that true intimacy . . . is possible."[20] A youth who is not yet intimate with himself avoids at all costs a deep intimacy with another. What follows is a sense of isolation and estrangement from others.

Joshua was hampered in his efforts to rid himself of loneliness by his lack of a clear idea of who he was. He sensed that he must be more than his societal roles—"student, son, athlete."

These titles located him in the system but gave him no sense of unique importance. Anybody could have put on his uniform and played with the team.

The crucial step for Joshua in the effort to establish an identity on which to base intimacy was the sense of being recognized, accepted, and loved beyond his roles. This he managed to achieve by realizing that Jesus loved him. Now he knew suddenly and surely who he was: "a man of God."

He had located himself in the world. Who am I? A child of God, accepting and proclaiming certain truths about reality through which I define myself. He had also established a place in relation to society. I am a believer—a member of that small group who truly know Jesus. We are distinguishable from them—the sinners—by our views which oppose theirs.

Has Joshua succeeded in resolving the identity crisis in a way that will make intimacy possible? We cannot tell here. It is clear, however, that his need for friends and community has been overwhelmingly satisfied. The groups of young believers that live communally, together missionize in the hostile world, and share the conditions of life and are thus able to establish the fraternity they seek. As they suffer at the hands of the nonbelievers they are welded together even more strongly.

Perhaps a return to Judaism would not have been enough. A gradual reclaiming of one's heritage does not provide the drama and pathos of joining a new and embattled faith community. And would it be sufficient to simply grow into yet another new role? Through conversion, Joshua became, mysteriously and irrevocably, a "new man." The "old" man, a vague figure at best, was left behind with few regrets.

7. Milt

The Diaspora Yeshiva on Mount Zion was established following the Six Day War in 1967 to meet the needs of young Jewish men who were eager to learn and practice orthodox Judaism but lacked the necessary training to enter an ordinary yeshiva. The American rabbi who founded the institution introduced us to one of his students who had formerly been involved in the Jesus movement. Milt was a tall, serious young man with brooding eyes. In contrast to the believers we met, he was quite reticent, and his story was gleaned one sentence at a time.

I first heard about Jesus when I was still in California flipping out. I thought it was nonsense. Not for me. But everyone has to search for their essence in some way. I knew our society was all wrong and I was looking for a better way. At first I thought I'd go to the Orient and enter a monastery. Finally I decided that for me the best thing would be to go to Israel and give the kibbutz a try. I knew I wasn't developing harmoniously. I wanted to get back in touch with nature and history. Get rid of the socialization of my parents and start living deeply. You couldn't do it in California.

On the kibbutz I met several believers. I thought they were crazy but I knew that whatever *I* had was of no value. I was ready to try anything new. My wife and I decided to leave the kibbutz and come to Jerusalem. [NOTE: This was the first time Milt mentioned that he was married. It later was learned that he married before leaving California and that his wife was a non-Jew.] Accepting Christianity wasn't a matter of rejecting Judaism. It was just that my Jewish knowledge was fragmentary and this offered a kind of *whole* understanding.

The most attractive part was the love. I became very close to my friends who were believers. We figured that through Christ we'd learn how to love—really love. Now I see that the love thing was superficial. We were trying to prove something to each other. I began to feel very let down after a while. I had a terrible inner feeling that it just wasn't true—all the stuff we were supposed to believe. I think a lot of believers have this feeling but they can't admit it to themselves.

Even though I had doubts, I was planning to be baptized in Solomon's Pools. I would have gone through with it, too, although it's a heavy thing to think about now. But something

happened. The day of my baptism I was wandering around
Mount Zion and came across this yeshiva. I knew immediately
that I couldn't go through with the baptism. I wanted to come
here and study. It was just awful when I had to tell my five
best friends that I no longer believed. But I saw another way.

Anyhow, I've been here for six months now and I know I've
found what I was looking for. Sure Christianity is easier—all
you have to do is feel and believe. But I'm learning here and
I'm getting the harmony I was looking for. We have a kind of
little society up here that is fundamental and good. My wife is
studying in the girls' school and she is really loving it too.

I see now that the Jews for Jesus is just another phase of the
2000-year effort of the church to destroy Judaism. The best
teacher is the oldest one. I don't need J.C. to mediate anymore.
He's just like a cloud now between me and God. He can't purify
me—I have to do it myself. J.C. made a lot of mistakes in his
life. He wanted to be pure so badly he never got married. But
this is wrong. Wedded life is very important. Why do I call him
J.C.? I guess to prove he was just a regular guy.

8. Commentary: Back to the Garden

Senator William Fullbright has said "The great society has
become a sick society." There is no doubt that something has
gone wrong in American life. This is not the place to rehearse
the faults of contemporary society. What concerns us here is
the response of young people unwilling to acquiesce to the
ways of a world they deem spoiled, inadequate, and unworthy
of the effort required to succeed on its terms.

The responses can be divided into two categories. The first
is that of radical or revolutionary endeavor. In the 1960s many
young people were fired by the belief that through struggle
one could change society for the better. The optimism inherent in this approach is dying. Far more common now is the
second response. It is reactionary, and it is becoming increasingly appealing.

There was a time, according to the ideology of the second

approach, when life was simpler, purer, better. Let us stop
fighting the establishment and attempt instead to recapture for
ourselves this superior world. The movement to establish communes, to return to the more basic and meaningful agrarian
life reflects this hope. The renewed interest in religion, at least
in Milt's case, may be indicative of the same trend. For the
religious life is now identified with the kind of society in
which one would find a personally meaningful style of life.

Milt had despaired of life in the world he knew. He saw
that "our culture . . . weakened the whole fabric of individual
experience."[21] He had considered going East to a monastery
but had decided, because of a basic identification as a Jew, to
try Israel first. He was, in effect, shopping around. Confronting the world and saying, "Show me a better way." The kibbutz was apparently not the answer. Religion, however, seems
to hold the key.

Now just as there are two responses to society, there are also
two religious forms. Leo Baeck refers to them as the classic
and the romantic.[22] The classic form, like the social activist
response, seeks to change the world through action. It looks
toward a future of perfection. The romantic, on the other
hand, sees its golden moment in the past. The former has an
ethical imperative, the second may dissolve into feeling.

Baeck states that no religion exhibits the pure form of either,
but each has a dominant note. Christianity is the romantic
religion *par excellence*. Milt turned to Christianity as a romantic. But what of his return to Judaism? Baeck identifies Judaism as a classic religion. In fact, however, Judaism has strains
of the romantic, and it is these strains that attract Milt. He is
not particularly concerned with prophetic injunctions nor
with fighting society. Rather, the orthodox life style of the
yeshiva, communal and secluded, serves as the kind of retreat
he was seeking.

The most intriguing aspect of Milt's story is his emphasis on
love and the need to learn how to love well. This makes even

more unusual the position of his wife in his narration. She is
not mentioned at all until midway in the conversation. He
reports that "I was dissatisfied. I decided to go to a kibbutz."
Suddenly, out of nowhere, a wife appears who also apparently
decided to go to a kibbutz. But then he decides to believe in
Christianity. Fortunately, his wife seems to be in accord. At
the crucial moment, he loses credulity and makes the radical
move of entering a yeshiva. Later we hear that the wife is also
in the yeshiva, now a confirmed orthodox Jewess.

Now it could be that Milt's wife experienced all the same
changes of heart simultaneously with her husband and as luck
would have it has followed a parallel spiritual course throughout. More likely, however, she has followed his lead, and the
give and take between them is at a minimum. His comment
that he is just now learning the importance of marital life suggests that his attraction to the love promised in Christianity
belies a previously undeveloped idea of love and an inability
to exchange it on a more prosaic level.

9. Daniel

We met Daniel at a concert given by a group of young Christians from the Midwest. It was a rather straight crowd that
turned out for the event in Christ's Church in the Old City of
Jerusalem. They were mostly in their mid-twenties or older.
The music was pleasant and the mood happy, but the emotional excitement of other meetings was lacking. It could have
been any respectable group of people attending a concert.

After the performance we began talking to people and asking
if any were Jewish. An elderly man, himself a Jew, introduced
us to Daniel, who seemed to be about 30 years old—clean
shaven, short hair, crew-neck sweater. He gave the appearance
of a Jewish mother's dream son. He explained that he was an
Israeli citizen, although he had originally come from California. This was his story:

I was a businessman in the States. But besides being interested in business I was also concerned about truth. I kept reading books about religion and trying to figure out the answers. I had been bar mitzvahed and had a good Reform education, but frankly, I found Judaism to be about the worst religion in the bunch.

On a trip to India I became convinced that Hinduism is right and when I returned I bored all my friends for the next few years preaching the doctrines. But then I began to read the New Testament. Slowly, very gradually, I started to see that this was the truth.

I wasn't a Christian yet, but I was on my way. Then four years ago I came to Israel with the Jewish Agency. The place just grew on me. I became a citizen and a good Zionist. I decided that rather than start a new business I would become a writer. I've been writing ever since and supporting myself on my money from the States. Of course, now I've become a believer and this influences what I write.

The book I'm working on is about the causes of anti-Semitism in Germany before World War II. It shows how the same forces are at work today—with Jews all being in the professions and things like that. The point is, the Jews will always suffer until they accept Christ. If they would only do so, the Lord would take care of them.

Maybe you'd rather talk to some younger people. My conversion isn't very interesting. I wasn't on drugs or anything, although I'm really amazed by the stories I hear of people who were saved from addiction. It defies medical science! But anyway, my story isn't very emotional. I simply searched and finally came to understand the essential truth. Now I have a better grasp on history and events. I see that the return to Zion was no accident. The Lord is preparing for Apocalypse. It's going to be really exciting. You can understand everything if you just read the New Testament. Really, it makes a lot of sense.

10. Commentary: Truth

Traveling in the circles of contemporary skeptics, one may go far without encountering a man who knows beyond a doubt that

he is right. There is much posturing, but underneath it lurks
the sense that all truths are relative, that our theories of today
will be replaced by better ones tomorrow, that the complexities of reality will simply not yield to the strictures of our
minds. Daniel, then, is an anomaly in our doubting world of
the educated. But he is not alone among believers in his grasp
on truth.

As we note later, Hebrew Christians, as is so often the case
with fundamentalists of every stripe and faith, tend to view all
phenomena in monistic terms. Everything is explained from
within the most limited and limiting frame of reference, and
always in terms of a somewhat static core structure, unmoving
and unmovable for all times. Certainly one of the most attractive aspects of faith for many believers is the key it provides,
which can unlock all mysteries and interpret all experience,
historical and personal. It is difficult to understand reality
without a theory or set of theories that will organize it.

No doubt the Freudian literary critic or the Marxist histo-
rian may have much the same need as the believer. But the
truth of Christianity for our subjects has an overwhelming
explanatory power. Indeed, it precludes the need to look elsewhere for enlightenment. The essential truths proclaimed in
the Bible are seen as sufficient tools for interpreting all events.

"I've only read one book since I became a believer and that's
the Bible" was an oft-repeated boast. Once we suggested to
someone that he might enjoy Kazantzakis' *The Last Temptation of Christ.* "I'm sure it's interesting," we were told, "but I
don't read other books any more. Why should I? The Bible
has everything a man needs to know." When asked why they
did not delve into Christian theology for new insights into
their faith, the converts responded that "theology is the interpretations of men. We want only the word of God."

Not only is Christian truth sufficient unto itself, it is also
relatively simple to learn. The believers often compare the ease
of learning Christianity and the involved study necessary to

grasp the fragments of Jewish faith. Dr. L. Streiker writes in *The Jesus Trip* that the fundamentalist Christianity of the Jesus people does not require arduous study. Its teachings about the Bible and the Christian life can be learned from one placard proclaiming "Four Easy Steps To God."[23] Anti-intellectualism and the rejection of the academic world are certainly elements in the believers' attraction to this approach to truth.

Of course Daniel presents rather an extreme example of what is a common drive in all those who come to accept funda-mentalism: "I wanted to know the truth." Most people do not state it quite so bluntly, nor do many ever verbalize it at all. Yet in his unsophisticated declaration, Daniel reflects the usu-ally more subtle need to understand life. "To be in possession of an absolute truth is to have a net of familiarity spread over the whole of eternity."[24]

Daniel's interest in applying his new-found truth to historical analysis is not unusual. The believers we encountered were fond of discussing history, particularly the history of the Jews, and discovering the ways in which the biblical prophecies match the facts. It is no accident, they maintain, that the Jews who rejected Jesus were soon after punished by the destruction of the temple. It is understood that before the Messiah can return there must occur a great holocaust in which nonbeliev-ers suffer. Following the holocaust, the people are to be regath-ered in the homeland to await the return. Even those from the North Country (Russian immigrants) are to be brought back to the Land. Since there were 2000-year intervals between Adam and Abraham, Abraham and Moses, Moses and Jesus, it seems likely that the second coming will occur around the year 2000.

The interest in interpreting Jewish history and the great sense of satisfaction with the pattern that emerges suggests a rather interesting attraction of Christian truth. Jewish theol-ogy has confronted the holocaust with much confusion. The

Jewish theology of history is wordless before the massive suffering of good people. Although Jewish responses are possible, the Christian theodicy seems to make more sense to the young converts.

The possession of Truth implies the responsibility to educate others, and this responsibility is not taken lightly by the believers. Daniel's book is one of the quieter routes that have been chosen. Most of the believers prefer to missionize in the streets, distributing literature on Hebrew Christianity and testifying to the nonenlightened. Many had decided to come to Israel to convert other Jews.

Missionary work is a crusade of great intensity and as such has a social value of its own for the missionaries. Besides uniting the believers in their shared effort, it provides them with a definite purpose and goal in life. Daniel did not continue devoting his life to business because it was not sufficiently exciting or meaningful. No doubt the careers the other converts were anticipating appeared equally unrewarding. Here they have found a task with a point, clearly a "life's mission."

Of course the driving need to proselytize can be seen in another light as well. As Jacob Burckhardt has noted in *Force and Freedom*, "religions of great intensity often confine themselves to condemning, destroying, or at best pitying what is not themselves."[25] Yet this is not the approach of the believers who insist on saving others as well. Perhaps, as Milt suggested, there remains a lingering doubt about the validity of the truth they have adopted. People wish to confirm that which they believe is indeed correct. One means of assurance is an ever-growing consensus among others. Each new person who accepts Jesus is additional confirmation that one has chosen the right path.

There is a tendency to view all people who are respected as incipient Christians, although secret ones. We were told by several believers that Shlomo Carlebach is really a Christian but is hiding it for the time being. There are, we were informed, hundreds of "closet believers" in yeshivot (schools of higher Jewish learning) in Jerusalem. Because of pressures from the outside, these people fear testifying to their faith openly; but the widespread existence of such believers is assurance of the truth.

Daniel's mode of conversion makes an interesting contrast to the conversion experience of the majority of the subjects. James quotes Starbuck as distinguishing two kinds of conversion, the volitional type and the type of self-surrender.[26] Most of the believers we studied fall into the latter category. In this type of conversion, worry, fear, and sin dissolve in a sudden and dramatic triumph of emotion and insight. In the former case, of which David is an example, a man makes a gradual and conscious decision to build a new life.

Daniel's conversion did not happen dramatically, nor did it follow a period of personal turmoil, guilt, and doubt. There is no indication that his interest in truth ever became so obsessive that it interfered with his functioning. His was not a crisis resolved but rather a growing acceptance of an alternative approach. For the others, however, a conversion was not the result of intellectual inquiry. On the contrary, it was only a relaxation of the intellect and a surrender to emotion which allowed for the resolution of the problems that had beset them.

THE BELIEVER

Many believers emphasize the human aspect of Christ and see him as "a person like themselves": a man who was tempted by the sin of the flesh, a man who was ridiculed by the mob, a man who was insulted and spat upon, and yet gave up his life for the sins of mankind. The believers are in essence engaging in hero worship, individually identifying with Christ and his mission, and most of all his suffering. They too were tempted (and fell) into the muck of unrestrained sexuality, drug abuse, or personal indulgence. They are in awe of Christ for overcom-

ing temptation to which they fell prey and they seek through
imitatio Dei their personal rehabilitation and salvation.

> I see Jesus as a friend who shares one's suffering. I have a per-
> sonal relationship with Jesus and with God.
> Jesus was tempted by all the sins of the flesh and other routes of
> sin. But He resisted them. I have suffered through the sins of the
> earth, but now I, too, am resisting them.

Others see Jesus as the spiritual force that brought meaning
into a world of banality. Despite suffering, abuse, and ridicule,
Christ is able to elevate man, and his acceptance brings one to
a higher plane of existence.

> People would laugh at me; I cried a lot but I had peace in my
> heart. I feel that the reason people laughed at me was because
> they wished *they* could be such strong believers. They had noth-
> ing—I had everything.

The notion of Jesus as an escape from the physical, materialistic world was another dominant theme. The physical world
was a world of pain and shock and, ultimately, defeat.

> Now with Christ I don't worry about the materialistic, physical
> world. Christ is my escape from the world's troubles.
> Christ suffered so we could escape the body and we must move
> beyond our physical world in order to get peace.

To validate their claim as *Jews* who accept Christ, the Jewish
Jesus believers demonstrate their authenticity by "observing"
and "practicing" Judaism. But their definitions of Judaism
and Jewish practices are highly selective and by most standards
capricious. Most of the believers in Jerusalem claim to be
"biblical Jews" rather than traditional Jews, the latter being
defined as those who eat kosher and observe the Day of Atonement and other "minutiae." Their Judaism, it is claimed,

comes straight from the Bible: "We take our Judaism from the Patriarchs, Moses and Jesus. We don't do all those things like eating chicken soup. They are not Jewish. They are changes introduced much later by European Jews."

Preaching the word of Jesus, however, *is* the way to true and uncontaminated Judaism. The message of Jesus is the replacement, continuation, and completion of the law and mitzvoth (commandments).

> We are like the Jews in the Bible. They were the chosen people and they had to turn the world away from sin, many Gods, and so on. We too must get the people away from sin. In both cases the path was and is hard.

The biblical Jew loves his fellow man and especially his fellow Jews; he is one who has *returned* to the faith given the Jews by God and is now completed as a Jew through following *both* testaments of the Bible to their logical conclusion in Christ.

Some though not all the believers observe a few selected Jewish holy days such as Chanukah, which they like normative Jews see as a festival of freedom, Passover, seen as The Last Supper, and even Saturday prayer to be closer attuned to "traditional" brethren. Some wear Jewish stars with a superimposed cross around their necks, and most study Hebrew because it is the language of Scripture and can serve as a witnessing tool.

Most demonstrate a touching naïveté concerning their path to faith. All assert that they became filled with the Holy Spirit at one point or another. After praying hard they accepted Christ with all their heart, and this in turn meant that the absurd and the unexpected and unpredictable became everyday occurrences.

> I took a trip to Los Angeles and there found Christ. It was at night; I completely left the past and come to the City of the Angels. One night my mind was unhappy and Christ came into

me . . . the feeling was of being in love with all, a night of bliss. I felt Jesus in the room—the only difference between me and Jesus was the physical body. It took me eight days to realize Jesus was real. I was weak for a long time.

I found Jesus one day while at my locker in school. I asked Christ to go into my body and He went in. I asked God for help and I was really sincere in my wish and He went in.

I came to Jerusalem because in the middle of the night God told me to go. I didn't have any money but I prayed for the $2000 and people I never knew just came up to me and gave me the money.

God told me to go to Jerusalem, but I was without money. One day a lady just drove up to me and she happened to be a fellow believer. She said, "Here, take my car." So I did so and traded it in for the money and came to Jerusalem.

The believer is rewarded by a sense of palpable identity and intense meaning in life. This meaning is expressed variously, but all seem to arrive at a polarized view of the world in which phenomena are labeled good or evil with no intervening points on the moral continuum. The believers' job is to save mankind and especially the Jews from evil. Thus they wander the streets of Jerusalem handing out tracts, talking to passersby, and doing whatever they can to spread the word. Identity is buttressed by the proud assertion, "I am a Jesus believer and a Jew. I have finally woken up and seen the *real* me, the spiritual me, not the intellectual and physical me."

ORGANIZATION, APPROACH, AND REACTIONS

As with most missionary endeavors, it is nearly impossible to establish with certainty the number of conversions that have been made in a given time, or in our case, even how many believers are concentrated in Jerusalem. Our best estimate, garnered from a variety of Israeli sources and from field observation, is that there are now between 100 and 150 young Jews for Jesus in Jerusalem. There may be an additional 100 or so spread through the rest of the country, but our contact with these individuals was minimal because of their wide dispersion. Jews for Jesus are not organized in any systematic fashion either in America or in Israel. Most are not formally affiliated with the Hebrew Christian movement, although in approach and ideology they are strikingly parallel to the organized movement and should in fact be identified as Hebrew Christians.

As in other Hebrew Christian groups, the major approach or communal context in Jerusalem is the prayer meeting. The meetings, which are seldom scheduled for more than two evenings a week, are comprised of Bible readings, hymn singing, personal testimony, and prayer, mostly informal and spontaneous. The prayer meetings furnish a sense of spiritual rebirth, communality, reaffirmation of beliefs, and psychological reinforcement of the believer's daily existence in Christ.

To reach the unbeliever they daily take to the streets and witness to whomever will listen—but primarily to American Jewish tourists and students living in Jerusalem. They make every effort to establish contacts at the Hebrew University student dormitories, the American College in Jerusalem, the various Hebrew language ulpanim, and in the cafes, alleys, and streets of the Old City.

The major theme is, We come not to remove the Jew from Judaism but to complete the Jew with faith in his *own* Messiah Jeshua of Nazareth. Are you alone and confused? We can through Him provide love and certainty. Are you on a drug trip? We can help you not only to free yourself but can give you a trip you never have had nor could imagine in your wildest fantasy. Are you more sexually free and enjoying it less? In Jesus there is neither bond nor free, male nor female. The body is ephemeral: the spirit is eternal.

Near panic has erupted among some Jewish community leaders in America because of the recent increase in those associated with the Jewish Jesus group, and a similar reaction in

some circles in Israel has been brought on by the believers'
activities and presence in Jerusalem. In February 1973 Dr. Z.
Warhaftig, the Israeli Minister for Religious Affairs, submitted
a memo to Prime Minister Meir saying that missionary activity in Israel, particularly in Jews for Jesus circles, had increased.[27] Dr. Warhaftig asked for stern measures to counteract
this trend, specifically suggesting that active Jews for Jesus be
deported wherever possible and consistent with the law and
that current laws limiting the rights of Jews for Jesus to enter
the country under the Law of Return (i.e., qua Jews) be beefed
up. Not only in government circles associated with the
religious-political bloc, but in the general press as well a hue
and cry has arisen around the presumed dangers presented by
the Jews for Jesus activities.

Between January and April 1973 63 items relating to the
phenomenon appeared in such leading Israeli newspapers as
*Haaretz, The Jerusalem Post, Davar, Hatzofe, Al Hamishmar,
Maariv,* and *Yediot Achronot.* The material included interviews with Israeli and American believers, upset parents, teachers and religious leaders, political figures, and so on. The general thrust of opinion can be summed up as follows: Jews for
Jesus are missionaries like other missionaries, albeit with a
peculiar twist—their presumed Jewishness. The Jewish people
have never tolerated missionary activities while in the diaspora
and have no intention of doing so when reconstituted within
their own political framework. Jews for Jesus are practicing
deception when they claim to be Jews and thus at best are
engaging in marginal acts that should be reviewed through the
proper democratic and legal channels. Here the secular and
religious press part ways, with the religious press in favor of
immediate legislation and the secular press counseling modera-
tion. As far as can be determined, the Israeli public is split
along similar lines. Overall, however, the attitude seems to be
that an emergency does not yet exist; for the moment. Jews for
Jesus appears to be just one more example of the type of ex-

cessive, and strange behavior to be expected from individuals who are essentially lost American teenagers. "This too," it is assumed "will pass."

Less pacific has been the reaction of a small group of young religious zealots who have assumed the role of testing the Christian faith of Jews for Jesus by selectively beating them up, asking for their wallets and shirts, and otherwise harassing them. After striking believers in the face, zealots ask if they are prepared to turn the other cheek. Thus far they *have* been so prepared. Taking money or clothing from believers has been accompanied by claims that Christ required that believers share the goods of this world. The places of residence of believers have attracted dozens of zealots and the curious, who on one occasion "bombed" an apartment with red paint.

These activities, combined with the expressed concern of Israeli officials, have led to the growth of a type of catacomb Christianity among believers who are reluctant to be interviewed, to be approached by the outsider, or indeed to reveal that they *are* believers. Needless to add, the role has historical and even biblical validity and as such is embraced by many believers who view it as a vehicle for identifying with the sufferings of Jesus.

Difficulties notwithstanding, the believers will remain in Jerusalem, where they will continue to try to develop their outreach to the longer-established Israeli population, and not primarily among American youngsters as is presently the case.[28] Jerusalem fulfills symbolic, historical, and practical desiderata that cannot be gainsaid. Jerusalem *is* Zion, the place of the crucifixion, the place of the Lord's suffering and ultimate sacrifice. Jerusalem is the center of world Jewry, and it is presumed that whatever happens here will have ramifications for the whole world. It was here that the Jews rejected Christ: what would be the effect if it was here that they as a people repented and accepted Him? Clearly this would presage the second coming and the salvation of all. On a more pragmatic level, the constant assertion that one betrays the peoplehood of Israel through acceptance of Jesus of Nazareth, is given the lie by the visible Zionism of the Jewish believer. *They* have come home, while the majority of so-called Jews remain in the fleshpots of the diaspora. They are asserting their Jewishness by living in the Jewish state, speaking the Jewish language, and identifying with *the* Jewish cause.

DISCUSSION AND COMPARISON WITH THE HEBREW CHRISTIAN MOVEMENT IN THE PAST

The problems that confront these new converts are essentially the same problems confronted by prior generations of Hebrew Christians. First of all, there is no Hebrew Christian Church, which leads to the initial breach of legitimacy—the believer must pray in one of the existing "gentile" Protestant churches. There is no specific Hebrew Christian theology that differs in any significant way from standard Protestant fundamentalism. There exists no leadership cadre that could build a bridge between the Hebrew Christian and normative Judaism. There is no core of "role model types" that might be able to reach out beyond a small body of disenchanted and disinherited Israelis. Larger bodies abroad furnish only sporadic and unsure support, suggesting that in the crunch the believers will have only themselves to rely on, and this reed might indeed be too frail.[29]

As subsequent chapters indicate, there is a strong skein of continuity and similarity between past generations of Hebrew Christians and the "new breed" familiarly known as Jews for Jesus. In both generations we see that the movement's outreach is primarily directed at the psychologically disinherited, the wounded, the dissatisfied—but with two major and significant differences: (*a*) the new generation is younger, being comprised mainly of youngsters in the late teens and early twenties and (*b*) the marginality of the new generation vis à vis normative Judaism is less clear and distinct.

The latter point suggests in effect that the Hebrew Christian approach of legitimating conversion to belief in Jesus—so that it can be considered an embrace of "Jewishness" rather than a rejection—might be more successful than was the case previously. Between 1930 and 1945, prior to the remarkable postwar strengthening of Jewish affirmation and consciousness, the Hebrew Christian movement was to some extent gilding the lily in emphasizing "Jewishness" to people who had rejected or were at best ambivalent with regard to their Jewish identity. The new generation seems to be at least somewhat more comfortable with being Jewish and thus more needful of not appearing traitorous; these young people are less intent on becoming gentile than on becoming whole. What more effective device than to present the sought-after wholeness in existential, historical terms and not alone in a spiritual vein?

In the youthfulness of the believers we recognize the possibility that they are identifying with a broader trend within contemporary society—an urge to arrive at self-definition and an acceptable working through of the challenges of freedom.

CONCLUSIONS

We began by noting that young people in America are left to discover their identity in freedom. The society indicates, We'll give you a period of time to work it out. Decide who you are, what you really believe. The complexities of your world provide a whole smorgasbord of choices. Judaism does little to limit that freedom for its youth. It simply reminds them to "feel Jewish," which still leaves open myriad possibilities.

And so begins the freedom that grows unbearably difficult. Freedom to achieve or not to achieve. Freedom to indulge the carnal desires. Freedom to find one's identity. Freedom to criticize society and seek a better way. Freedom to discover truth. Our conversion stories, then, may be seen as expressing the same truth that Dostoevsky revealed in *The Grand Inquisitor*:

Man fears his freedom. But religion offers to relieve him of the burden. If one must sacrific his sovereignty, he gains much in return—all acceptance, inner controls, identity, community, Truth.

As Hoffer has noted, "freedom aggravates at least as much as it alleviates frustration."[30] Freedom can be exhilarating, but it is a frightening gift. This is the message of our conversion stories. They tell us that having the freedom to choose, to direct and control one's life, to create a place in society can become an impossible mandate. For some, the difficulty of the condition may necessitate a renunciation of that freedom in return for a sure and prescribed path.

Of course the matter may be seen in another light. The freedoms our society provides are, in truth, deprivations. While Stuart was free to succeed or fail on the basis of his own efforts, he was denied the acceptance that some societies and individuals offer to a person as his birthright, regardless of performance. While Ann was free to behave as she liked, she was never given the controls and limits that are needed if one is to learn how to live well. Joshua was free to play any roles necessary to help him establish his identity, but each of these roles denied him the reinforcement of his humanity without which he could not establish personal bonds.

Milt's freedom was that of an individual able to learn enough to see that the given order of his society is wrong. But that society did not offer to Milt meaningful avenues through which he might work for change. Finally, Daniel was blessed with the freedom of inquiry and doubt, yet deprived of any truth that rendered reality understandable. In short, the world of these converts had failed to provide for crucial human needs. Their answer was no retreat but rather a constructive resolution of the problems.

Seen in this way, the conversions to Christianity are necessary acts of freedom. The individual willfully embraces a tradition and way of life that can offer the "precious gifts" one needs to live in dignity. It is a sincere attempt to rescue one's self from meaninglessness, to create a world of order that will hold chaos at bay.

D. H. Lawrence has written: "Human beings are all vines ... seeking something to clutch, something up which to grow toward the necessary sun. . . . Such is freedom!—a clutching of the right pole."

If the pole our converts has clutched is indeed the right one, freedom has not been sacrificed but rather acted on. If in effect this freedom and identity resolution can be achieved within a prescribed framework of legitimacy (i.e., Jewishness), it is felt to be all the better.

NOTES

1. I am indebted to my students, Nancy Fuchs and David Morrison, for their extensive aid and assistance in the preparation of this chapter.

2. Erik Erikson, *Identity, Youth, and Crisis* (Faber and Faber, London, 1971), p. 96.

3. Kenneth Keniston, *The Uncommitted, Alienated Youth in American Society* (New York: Harcourt Brace Jovanovich, 1965).

4. Erikson, *op. cit.*, p. 190.

5. Jacob Neusner, *American Judaism* (Englewood Cliffs, N.J.: Prentice Hall, 1972), p. 15.

6. *Time,* June 12, 1972.

7. "Jewish Students and the Jesus Movement," mimeographed paper, B'nai B'rith Hillel Foundations, Washington, D.C., n.d.

8. The case history material in this chapter was gathered by a team consisting of the author and two students, Miss Nancy Fuchs and Mr. David Morrison.

9. The Letter of Paul to the Philippians, 3:1-11. *The New English Bible* (Oxford University Press and Cambridge University Press, 1961).

10. James A. Sleeper and Alan Mintz, *The New Jews* (New York: Vintage Books, 1971), p. 28.

11. Richard Rubenstein, *My Brother Paul* (New York: Harper & Row, 1972), p. 7.

12. Erik Erikson, *Childhood and Society* (London: Penguin Books, 1970), p. 247.

13. The Letter of Paul to the Galatians 5:17. *The New English Bible,* *op. cit.*

14. *Ibid.,* 5:24.

15. William James, *Varieties of Religious Experience* (New York: Random House, 1929), p. 193.

16. *Ibid.,* p. 265.

17. William Braden, *The Age of Aquarius* (New York: Pocket Books, 1971), p. 28.

18. The First Letter of John, 1:7.

19. William James, *Varieties of Religious Experience* (New York: Random House, 1929), p. 373.

20. Erikson, *Identity, Youth, and Crisis, op. cit.,* p. 135.

21. Edgar Friedenberg, *Coming of Age in America* (New York: Vintage Books, 1967), p. 10.

22. Leo Baeck, "Romantic Religion," in *Judaism and Christianity,* Walter Kaufman, transl. (Philadelphia: Jewish Publication Society of America, 1958), pp. 215–216.

23. Lowell D. Streiker, *The Jesus Trip* (New York: Abingdon Press, 1971). p. 35.

24. Eric Hoffer, *The True Believer* (New York: Harper & Row, 1951), p. 80.

25. Jacob Burckhardt, *Force and Freedom* (New York: Pantheon Books, 1943), p. 129.

26. James, *op. cit.,* p. 202.

27. *Jerusalem Post,* February 18, 1973.

28. At present a minimal number of native-born or veteran Israelis have been attracted to the movement (a matter of a few dozen in most major population centers), but the scanty evidence at my disposal to date indicates that the number is rising.

29. There is no evidence to support the rumors that Billy Graham has expressed his approval of the movement. The allegation of certain sources in the Israeli government that Graham has alloted $2 million to the Jerusalem work is also unsupported.

30. Eric Hoffer, *The True Believer, op. cit.,* p. 30.

2

The Messengers of
the New Covenant

I have already noted that the new Jews for Jesus phenomenon is essentially Hebrew Christian, although it is not formally organized as such. In their attempts to legitimize their conversions, in their pattern of Protestant fundamentalist belief, in their search for a satisfying personal identity, in their individual psychological makeup, Jews for Jesus share a great deal with the organized Hebrew Christian movement and are in fact Hebrew Christians in everything but formal affiliation. One might describe the Jews for Jesus as the new adolescent or youth wing of Hebrew Christianity, whose members remain outside the movement for reasons of style rather than ideology —a stylistic inclination which I believe to be largely a carry-over from the anti-institutional zeitgeist of the 1960s.

Notwithstanding a different social class positioning and a generational spread of some magnitude, the attitudes and responses of young Jews for Jesus and formally affiliated Hebrew Christians are remarkably similar with respect to normative Judaism, individual Jews, the synagogue, the rabbinate, modes of spiritual reinforcement, and religious exercises. The main difference seems to be the "heat" with which these attitudes are maintained—the Jews for Jesus being somewhat more temperate in their expression than the official Hebrew Christians. An additional difference appears when we examine the sex ratio—the organized movement has a predominance of females, whereas Jews for Jesus seem to be rather evenly balanced.

To arrive at a fuller understanding of both phenomena, it would, I think, be useful to turn to an exposition and analysis of the only two field studies carried out with Hebrew Christian groups to date. One was performed by me with the "Messengers of the New Covenant" and the other by Ira O. Glick with the "First Hebrew Christian Church of Chicago."

A small missionary group known as the Messengers of the New Covenant has been functioning in the Newark, New Jersey, area for more than three decades. It was not until some twenty years ago when its present director, the Reverend Isaac Levy Finestone, received a "call" to come to Newark from Chicago, that it achieved the modest degree of success it now enjoys. Until the arrival of Rev. Finestone the organization was housed in a store with little equipment or leadership, apparently sustained solely by the good will of several of the area's Protestant churches; there seemed to be no significant financial support. Rev. Finestone, a talented and able executive, introduced a modicum of organization, and soon an old mansion in a formerly Jewish neighborhood was secured. Now primarily a Negro neighborhood, the area was in the first stages of transition when the house was acquired.

The new headquarters (called The House of the Lord our Righteousness) provided a physical focal point for the realization of the objectives of the group and not incidentally relieved the Messengers of most of the stigma attaching to "storefront religion," thus imparting an aura of stability and rootedness that the organization most certainly had lacked. This organizational growth was furthered with the formation of an executive board and a board of trustees drawn primarily from among the Protestant clergy and laymen in the area. Although the functions of these boards were rather obscure, they provided by their very presence a point of contact with the "established" churches in the community.

The organization is directed by Rev. Finestone who is aided by his wife and two assistants, both ordained Baptist ministers, like Rev. Finestone. However, there appear to be only the most tenuous ties to the Baptists as a denomination, thus to all intents and purposes the Messengers are an unaffiliated group.

The group functions in most respects like a traditional missionary establishment. Rev. Finestone and his assistants[1] spend most afternoons during the mild seasons walking through the park, standing on street corners, and in door-to-door visitation, distributing their literature and preaching the gospel to whomever will listen. Much time is spent trying to consummate the possible conversion of individuals on whom it is felt an impression has been made. Finestone devotes considerable time and effort to fund-raising activity and the writing of tracts and articles for the various Messenger publications, as well as to the preparation of a weekly 15-minute radio broadcast.[2] For the latter purpose, the organization owns an impressive taping setup and broadcasting booth located in the basement of the headquarters building. The two assistant missionaries—one is a bachelor, the other a divorcé—live in the building, which from time to time takes on the aspect of a *domus conversorium*; they apparently spend as much time as possible in missionary activity.

This appears to be an unprepossessing organizational schema. However, the Messengers[3] have developed a refined set of group objectives requiring the utilization of a somewhat more imaginative approach.

GROUP OBJECTIVES

The objectives or goals of the Messengers, as adduced from their constitution, indicate clarity and simplicity of purpose.

> The purpose of this society shall be primarily to promote the cause of Christ among the Jews, by preaching the Gospel and by the distribution of Christian literature; to disseminate in the Christian Churches knowledge concerning the purpose of God toward Israel; and to receive funds and to acquire property to this end.[4]

The foregoing suggests a missionary society not unlike myriad other such societies aiming at the conversion of this or that particular group. But to accept this limited statement of goals as a definitive interpretation of the nature of the group would involve oversimplification, thus distortion. Although it is without any doubt correct to state the purpose of the group as being the promotion of "the cause of Christ among the Jews," this can serve only as a basic guideline to an understanding of the group's objectives. It points to the ultimate goal, which is the conversion of Jews to Christianity (although this is not made explicit); but it says nothing about the context within which this goal is to be pursued, nor does it hint at any possible ancillary or secondary objectives underlying the stated approach.

To more fully understand the objectives of the group, and ultimately the group itself, we must go beyond the acknowledged goals and utilize the accumulated data as a springboard to a broader interpretation. Research results point to a double-pronged set of objectives that can be referred to as primary-overt (the stated goals) and primary-covert, or the goals that are less apt to be verbalized or placed in a formal context.

Under the heading primary-overt there are three mutually supporting objectives: (1) to reach the Jews with the Gospel—that is, to plant the seeds for future conversion; (2) to convert Jews who find in Jesus of Nazareth their Messiah and Savior; and (3) to seek and gain the support of gentile Christians to this end.

The Primary-covert[5] objectives of the Messengers can be stated as (1) the succoring and strengthening of the new convert and (2) the creation of a "group" of converts as a basis of appeal to the unconverted Jew. The latter objective is a methodological tool for achieving the former as well as constituting a goal in its own right.

It is as a direct result of the existence of primary-covert objectives that the Messengers must be viewed as other than a traditional missionary structure. The traditional missionary enterprise to the Jews has been marked by an inflexible commitment to what were thought of as inviolable goals and methods. The goal of these groups was simply the conversion of as many Jews as possible, with little or no thought of follow-up or retention. The convert once won was either left to sink or swim on his own or paraded as a curiosity before various missionary societies and church groups, in a effort to secure additional support for the evangelistic undertaking. In any event, most traditional missionary groups make little or no provision for dealing with the convert *after* conversion.

The Messengers, recognizing the needs for retaining the fruit of evangelistic success and for building a base of receptivity for future converts, have gone far beyond the very limited primary-overt objectives by working in the direction of a community of interests. Conrad Hoffman has made the point that many European mission centers served as cells or *gemeinschaften* of the converted Jews, and it is this creation of a *gemeinschaft* environment for which the Messengers strive. The mission hall system of the past is viewed as an anachronism in no way suited to supply the continuity and momentum deemed necessary for ultimate success; thus strategic objectives articulated within an overall evangelistic scheme have been made operative where tactical goals had once (mistakenly) been thought sufficient. This enlarged objective has led the Messengers away from a previous role as a missionary society and in the direction of a "mission-church" structure, bearing similarities to both a mission and a church while being neither one nor the other.

METHODS AND EMPHASIS

Only when the missionary methodology of the Messengers is examined does it become possible to determine why the organization remains, as it were, in limbo between church and mission.

As noted previously, Hebrew Christianity has sought a new approach to Jews because only the most meager results have been produced by proselytizing activity among Jews. It has been concluded that the Jew is not receptive because he has been required to commit ethnic suicide in becoming a Christian, with the result that many Jews who would otherwise respond positively do not do so. Hebrew Christianity has, therefore chartered a course for itself that would obviate this fear, allowing the prospective convert to be a Christian and yet not be cast adrift communally, nor suffer guilt over possible feelings of disloyalty.

The field research carried out with the Messengers of the New Covenant and with the First Hebrew Christian Church of Chicago,[6] as well as a comprehensive analysis of the literature of the movement, indicate the prevalence of two major methodological emphases for achieving the aims of the movement. These can be stated as (1) emphasis on conversion to Christianity as constituting not a rejection of Judaism but its fulfillment, and (2) the assertion that contrary to popular belief, the "racial" Jew who embraces Christianity is representative of the "real Israel," while the "Rabbinic" Jew is at best in error and at worst a usurper and a fraud. The approach can be characterized in the following manner.

The Jew is approached and sought after *qua* Jew, as a representative of a great but fallen people who are destined, as a people, to play a significant role in the final stages of redemption. It is maintained that encouraging the Jews to assimilate among the Gentiles, allowing the "race" to die out, is to tamper with God's immutable plan for the Jews. It is averred that

Christianity is infinitely "more Jewish than Judaism"; that Christ in his earthly role appeared as a Jew in Judea; that the early Church was Jewish and that the Gentiles represented at best a poor second choice as bearers of the faith, made only after the cupidic Pharisees and their stiff-necked followers had rejected Jesus. What is more natural (it is reasoned) or more satisfying in the eyes of God than for this people Israel, His first beloved, to repent their sin and accept the salvation proferred by Yeshua Hamashiach (whom the Greeks, i.e., Gentiles, called Jesus Christ). The Jews as a "racial" group must still be viewed as chosen, while as a religious entity—as the upholders of an incomplete, therefore, unintelligible and indeed meaningless faith that must sooner or later be eschewed—they continue to suffer both here and in the hereafter.

Thus the stage is set for the emergence of a "super-Christian," one who combines the elements of "chosenness" in race as well as in faith. The Jew, therefore, will not and should not be confronted with an either-or choice (either acceptance of Jesus Christ as the Messiah or retention of his ethnic identity) but should be bolstered in his faith as a "returnee"—as one who has come back to what was his own—rather than as a disadvantaged newcomer or a stranger in what must ultimately be seen as his own house.

Thus it is assumed that the prospective Jewish convert is trying *not* to escape his Jewishness but to enrich it. For this reason the attempt is made to show how Christianity constitutes the only channel to this end by, as it were, completing Judaism, leaving the believer a truer representative of the "real" Israel. How is this to be accomplished? By creating an atmosphere or climate of familiarity wherein the convert will recognize a "Jewish" milieu that yet functions satisfactorily within a Christian framework. For example, it has been noted that Friday evening worship has become popular and prevalent among American Jews, and the Messengers have undertaken a similar practice. These informal services held at the headquarters building reflect admirably the marriage of the traditional fundamentalist Protestant missionary method and the Hebrew Christian emphasis, injected with what is conceived of as Jewish flavor.

The meetings follow a consistent pattern of opening prayer, the singing of one or two hymns, Old Testament exegesis, personal testimony, a closing prayer, and finally refreshments and "fellowship." The method and its resultant pattern are, I believe, deserving of closer scrutiny.

Old Testament Exegesis

The leadership of the Messengers has determined that the Old Testament is the most promising methodological channel through which to reach the Jews. Accordingly, the Old Testament is heavily relied on as an exegetical text, but is utilized with unmistakable allusion to its fulfillment in the Gospel accounts. It is explained that "though most Jews are really Unitarian in doctrine . . . most will show some respect for 'their' Bible. Build on the Old, then go on to the New."[7] All Friday evening services at the Messengers begin with a brief prayer that is followed with the study of a portion of the Old Testament that lends itself well to support or buttress a New Testament fulfillment. Thus in the biblical account of Joseph and his brothers, it is felt possible to apprehend the Christ.

> Joseph and Jesus both suffered rejection; Joseph by his brothers, Jesus by his people: they both displayed a transcendent love for their own—Joseph for his full brother Benjamin, Jesus for his people Israel: and both forgave—Joseph his brothers, Jesus the Jews.[8]

The attempt is made to show the Old Testament as a seed from which the events underlying the new dispensation sprang. In line with the larger methodological goal of proving that

Judaism is an incomplete and fragmentary structure, the basis of Judaism—the Bible—must be shown to be incomplete and fragmentary. Rev. Finestone has asked, "Are we to assume that God had no greater purpose in the Joseph story than to show how one man—Joseph—suffered at the hands of his brothers?" The answer supplied is that "God wanted to show a yet greater rejection and an infinitely greater forgiveness in the future." There is a suggestion of continuity here, of the old leading inexorably to the new and the new explaining the old. In discussing Jacob's wrestling with a man who enigmatically refuses to identify himself (Genesis 32:24–29), Rev. Finestone asks who this could be but Jesus himself, for did not Jacob say, "I have seen God face to face, and my life is preserved"? "If the Old Testament account of this encounter were to be depended upon in isolation and in the absence of the 'completing' New, how could we understand the significance of this revelation?" In Isaiah 53 we are given a description of the Messiah that fits only one man—Jesus. "How could we know this unless God provided us with the rest of the text in the New Testament?"

> The Old Testament instructs us with regard to the necessity for a blood atonement. But the temple and with it the possibility for sacrifice has been destroyed. God has not freed us of the need for blood atonement so how can we understand this requirement if not for his supplying us with his son as a substitutionary offering? The Old Testament is meaningless if it stands alone, and so by the same token is rabbinic Judaism which has substituted the Talmud for the word of God.[9]

This type of exegesis predominates at the Friday evening service of the Messengers, and its purpose can readily be discerned. It is to demonstrate the need for completion that speaks to the believer directly from the Old Testament sources. It is to emphasize the unique and inherent wholeness of Scripture where promises must be fulfilled and mysteries accounted for. On repeated occasions I was rhetorically queried "Would God lie?" When the answer was a firm negative I was triumphantly assured that this proves the New Testament, because only here has God fulfilled what he promises in the Old.

God's plan is complete and whole, and it is the incomplete man and Jew who fails to recognize this. Israel's revelatory experience is only one small part of the larger picture that can be said to be manifested in six portions of time.

In the *First* portion of time, in the Garden of Eden, man by disobedience failed God, and this period ended in paradise lost.

For the *Second* portion of time, God tested man under conscience. The sacrifice was established, the knowledge of good and evil, obedience and disobedience. This period ended in the judgment of the flood; God finding Noah only with faith in Him.

The *Third* portion of time was under human government, but man, like Satan, wanted power that belonged to God only; again man failed and this period also ended in judgment at the tower of Babel; there the human race was divided and scattered.

The *Fourth* portion of time was that of promise. God was progressively revealing more and more of His love and plans for the redemption of the human race. This period ended in judgment at Mount Sinai.

The *Fifth* portion of time was under law. God specially chose and prepared the nation of Israel, that all the world might know the power, the holiness, the love of the one true and living God. This period ended in the rejection of the Son of God, the Saviour of the world, the Holy One of Israel, by Jew and gentile. Judgment fell upon Israel and they were scattered throughout the nations of the earth, and gentile nations had all power without God.

In the present *Sixth* portion of time God is dealing with all humanity under Grace (unmerited favor). The rejected Son of God, Israel's Messiah, took the sinner's place and bearing the sins of all mankind, He cried "My God, my God, why hast Thou forsaken me?" (Matthew 27:46). He went all alone through the spiritual death, which is the separation of the soul from God. He, the Lamb of God. . . . It was all planned before the foundation of the world (Isaiah 48:16).[10]

Thus, the foregoing outline indicates that it would be erroneous to conceive Israel's story as completed with the last book of the Old Testament; and it is far greater error to consider the Rabbinic Jew who rejects so sizable a portion of Scripture as the real Israel of God's choice and plan.

Which group, which individuals, then, can be said to be the "real Israel" of Scripture? Obviously not those who deny and reject a substantial portion of God's revelation. The real Israel is comprised of those who believe that the whole Bible (Old and New testaments) is relevant and binding. These include the Gentile who is a "born-again Christian" (who may be referred to as a naturalized Israelite),[11] but most fully the Jew by birth who has joined the separated fragments of his heritage and destiny via his acceptance of Jesus of Nazareth as Messiah and Savior. In this connection, Rev. Finestone often digresses from the biblical text to reassert that the Jewish "race" was specially chosen from among all peoples. "He did not," says Rev. Finestone, "choose the Ethiopians, or the French, or the English—but us, yes us, the people of Israel to be His own and to carry out His orders and to spread the word." He adds, "Even though we rejected His Son we remain the chosen people, and when that day comes soon, when we repent our great sin, and recognize Him who was sent as our very own then will the world be saved."

The Hebrew Christian embraces and unabashedly clings to the biblical texts underscoring the chosen people concept, which in most sectors of modern Jewish expression have become an embarrassment to be explained away in any number of "accepted" categories. This attitude serves to fulfill a twofold function. On the one hand, the convert need not feel that he is entering the Christian fold hat in hand but rather that he comes bearing a special gift—that of the first and *immutably* chosen of God. Second, the acceptance of the notion of chosenness serves to maintain the connective link to the past. The entire community of Israel, unbeliever as well as believer, are chosen. The believer, however, has claimed his birthright, but the unbeliever has sought to exchange it for a mess of pottage; the latter rather than the former must be conceded the traitor.

Scriptural interpretation and exegesis can then be utilized as a legitimating tool in leading the convert to think of himself not as part of a fringe but as belonging to the normative structure itself, which is emerging from the encrustations of false theology and false interpretation to its preordained destiny.

Personal Testimony

But an individual desire or need for feeling one's self a part of the legitimate structure cannot bring this state about. There must be some tangible evidence to indicate that the acceptance of Christianity was not wholly an isolated act of the individual but was instead a personal link in a chain extending through history (and the biblical exegesis of the Hebrew Christian furthers this) as well as existing in the present. The Friday evening gatherings provide evidence that a *community* of like believers exists, for in listening to the testimony of others, it is possible to experience a sense of community and rootedness in a form of normative existence transcending as well as sanctioning individual involvement.

Rev. Finestone follows an undeviating pattern of asking for personal testimony following the period of Bible exegesis. He asks specific individuals if they will participate on any given evening, and without a murmur of dissent—in most instances with great eagerness—the individual rises and speaks in some detail concerning his or her road to faith.

In most cases the story told involves deep personal loss and bereavement, alienation and *anomie*. It is amazing to note the bond that appears between the one testifying and those who are listening until one realizes that essentially the same story is told over and over again. Since only the details vary, each individual is having his own experience validated and affirmed. The testimony is marked by frequent interruptions of "Amen" and "It's true, it's true," or "Isn't that wonderful, isn't that grand" when the climax is reached. During the testimony the faces of people in the group are uniformly wreathed in smiles at the mention of the conviction, the inward sense of personal sinfulness, and twisted in pain as the early period of despair and discontent is expounded. A few weep openly, and most appear agitated, fully involved, and nearly overcome with emotion. Some testimony seems to move the group a bit more than others—generally when the individual recounting his story is one who had been deeper in despair than most, for his conversion had thus been a greater "miracle." The group as a whole feels a stake and a share insofar as their existence (as a group) has provided a framework for the rescue. Mrs. S.G., for instance, always moved the group a little more deeply than the others. She began her testimony by saying that she really ought not to because it was "just too emotional" and that she "would cry"; then she would proceed to tell her story.

> You know I tried to commit suicide twice. I lost the two people that meant most to me one right after the other—my husband and my mother. I didn't know where to turn or what to do. I had nothing and nobody.
>
> I was on the cemetery and I was crying—I just couldn't help it. A strange woman saw me—a woman I had never seen before —and she sat me down in her car and spoke to me of the Savior. Soon I was baptized in the Roman Catholic Church, and the priest who baptized me was transferred a week later. [At this most people glanced knowingly at their neighbors, and there were various oohs and ahs from the assembled to indicate their complete awareness of how idolatrous Romanism treats a priest who would convert a Jew. The Reverend Courtney Stanton, one of Rev. Finestone's assistants, interrupted to say "Thank the Lord that you are among us now."] Yes, thank the Lord—I have

so much to be thankful for. After I was baptized my family rejected me, but my sister-in-law who is a nun comforted me and said, "Now that your people have rejected you come to my people." But I wasn't satisfied until God led me to Rev. Finestone, who searched the Scriptures with me and showed me what God really wanted me to do. Now I'm so happy—God is with me always. The rabbis never cared for me—they told me to go away. But not Mr. Finestone—he cared. I can't say any more. [At this point Mrs. S.G. broke down in tears and sat down amid chorused Amens.]

Most testimony was not accompanied by so much visual emotional stress, but it was nevertheless present, albeit under more effective control with most others. Even with V.H., who perhaps can best be described as being in a constant state of agitation and something of an ecstatic personality, the individual's deep emotional involvement became translated to laughter rather than tears. Curiously, however, the effect on the observer was very much the same as with Mrs. S.G.—namely, of controlled hysteria that in the absence of a restraining and yet reinforcing framework would break out. V.H.'s testimony follows:

I was brought up in a Jewish home but my religious education was nothing to brag about. My people were orthodox Jews, but they had no assurance in their lives of God's forgiveness. There was something missing in my life—I never knew what it was, but I knew something was missing. I thought that all religion was bosh and I was only interested in my career. [V.H. was an aspiring singer.] I thought if only I could make it, that emptiness would be filled up. How wrong I was! I never could get that one break so I sorta gave up and became a salesman. But I couldn't hold on to a job. I was really down in the dumps and one day just after I had applied for a job I wanted I asked God for a sign that I would get it. I was standing by my car and I noticed another car coming from the opposite direction—he went a block past me, turned around and drove up to me, and the guy inside asked me if I was Jewish. I was surprised but I told him yes and then he threw something into my car and said I would be damned to hell unless I truly believed in the Lord, Jesus Christ. Here was the sign from God that I had just prayed for, so I jumped right into my car and caught up with this guy. I asked him who he was and what he wanted, and I was soon convinced this guy really had something. I accepted Christ and was born again and everything is wonderful now. My wife who is a gentile but no Christian has left me[12] but I know that God has a purpose in mind and that soon He will restore her to me. One thing I can say is that both my wonderful children know the Lord and are Christians. [Amens] I have a job at Larkey's clothing store which gives me a wonderful opportunity to witness to my brethren and I want to tell you I'm making progress. [Amens] It's wonderful to do the Lord's work.

The testimonies of Mrs. S.G. and V.H. are representative of a number of similar cases in which a great personal loss through death or some other form of separation from loved ones wrought great havoc in the life of the respondent. The individual is assured of achieving great rapport and of eliciting genuinely felt sympathy from his listeners, who have experienced similar grief. Once while sitting in with a group of women before the services began, I was particularly struck by a form of spontaneous group therapy that was in progress. Each woman expressed her present happiness and contrasted this with the miserable past. A few were crying as they told how God had been so wonderful to them in this or that way, while the others answered Amen or nodded assent. I think there can be little doubt that each understood fully the travail and pain of the others and that they all gained immeasurable comfort and assurance from being together.

The testimony came primarily from those who had sustained great personal loss, but there was in addition the testimony of the converts who, at least as far as I could determine, had not been motivated by loss as much as by a sense of spiritual and temporal emptiness in their former lives. But here, too, the recognition of the existence of a group of like individuals who had themselves undergone similar trials proved to be rein-

forcing. Even a nearly blind old man who had lived a life
of emptiness by his own assertion (and the evidence he ad-
duces bears this appraisal out) is assured of a warm and sympathetic response from his listeners. Only among the Messengers or a similar group would A.S. have been taken seriously.

> It was eleven years ago that I found the Lord, I was a sinner, O
> I was a terrible sinner.
>   I was coming home from the movies—I used to go every night
> —and I had a few too many so I lost my way. I used to go home
> the same way every night by following a steel fence but somehow
> I lost it. [A.S. had to follow the fence because of his failing eye-
> sight.] I found myself in some kind of a school yard and I was
> getting worried. Nobody around. Nobody to help me. Well some
> women saw me and offered to help me back to the fence. She
> asked me if I knew Jesus, and I said I heard of him but that's
> all. I was so dumb then that I didn't even ask her if she was
> married. [A.S. is a bachelor who lived with a married sister.]
> Well I thought that was the last I'd hear of this lady, but the
> very next Sunday a Baptist preacher came to my house and
> offered to drive me to church. I accepted the ride, I accepted
> Christ, and now I'm about to get my "eleven-year pin" in Sun-
> day School.

Rev. Finestone capped A.S.'s testimony by attributing to him
"a vision of soul which more than made up for his poor vision
of eye." The convert's dull mentality was overlooked or rather
not seen by the group who recognized in him a kindred soul,
adrift and alone, who was a part of a glorious future, a consecrated community. A.S. for his part had experienced for perhaps the first time in his life a measure of acceptance and personal worth. If his experiences *in toto* were not entirely relevant to the other individuals in the group, the members certainly were sympathetic to the broad outline presented. A.S.'s
testimony gave him a sense of identity and purpose and the
group another brick in the wall of community.

The giving of personal testimony is the very cornerstone of

the Messengers' methodological emphasis. It assumes an importance here that is paralleled only in the most fundamentalist Protestant denominations, where it tends to be relegated to Wednesday or Sunday evening prayer meetings. Among the Messengers it serves to buttress the assertion that something essential was absent in Judaism, thus preventing meaningful spiritual involvement. Yet the testimony also performs the all-important function of stamping the individual conversion as a logical culmination of total Jewish experience, not an isolated response to personal despair. This is not to say that the rank-and-file member seeks through testimony a theological justification for his conversion. First and foremost, he seeks comfort and reassurance in being in or becoming part of a community of like individuals, but the way in which this is accomplished leads the individual through the process of justification.

Prayer and Hymns

Prayer and the singing of hymns is on the whole indistinguishable among the Messengers from the same practice in any fundamentalist group. The hymns chosen are such old American Protestant favorites as "O Come, Come, Emmanuel," "Not All the Blood of Beasts," "Near to the Heart of God," "Look to the Lamb of God," and "Love Divine"—sung with great gusto but without concern for musical accomplishment. There exist to the best of my knowledge no special Hebrew Christian hymns, nor for that matter do there seem to be favorites with any particular emphasis or allusion that might have special meaning for a Hebrew Christian.

No very significant divergences from a general fundamentalist tone or pattern can be discerned in the matter of prayer, but some small differences serve to distinguish it as peculiarly Hebrew Christian.

For one thing, the Hebrew name Yeshua Hamashiach (Jesus the Messiah) is often substituted in spontaneous prayer for the more familiar Jesus Christ. Also, the prayer is often begun with an appeal to the "God of Abraham, Isaac, and Jacob" and generally contains within it an appeal for "the lifting of the veil of blindness which blinds Israel" and the ultimate conversion of the Jews.

Aside from these few differences (which nevertheless serve to identify the Messengers as a special group of Christians with special spiritual concerns), almost the only other striking factor is the extraordinary facility with which almost all the Messengers (and Hebrew Christians generally) can compose a prayer without preparation or any advance warning. I was amazed at the germaneness of these spontaneous prayers often based on the testimony or exegesis of a particular evening and the way in which believers could weave together an often complex series of impressions and thoughts into a coherent and moving whole.

After the giving of testimony, when Rev. Finestone called up a congregant to lead the group in prayer, it was possible to witness a unified group, which had a shared past and whose members were bound by this past as well as by a common hope for the future to a sense and a presence of community.

THE VIEW OF JUDAISM

Like all Hebrew Christians, the individual Messengers hold to an interpretation of Judaism that assumes its utter insufficiency and error. Comments on the Jewish faith made in 1907 by W. T. Gidney can still be said to reflect the general viewpoint of the Hebrew Christian movement.

It [Judaism] deals with shadows only, the substance being conspicuous by its absence. It is a husk, or shell without a kernel;

a body without a soul; an empty cistern that cannot hold the Living Water. Judaism is an incomplete, imperfect religion. It leads nowhere. It is a blind alley opening upon a blank wall. Its ordinances cannot "give the guilty conscience peace, or wash away its stain" any more than the animal sacrifices of old.[13]

Many of the Messengers would be hard put to phrase a condemnation of Judaism in quite so forceful or literate a manner, but the raw elements contained in the statement can be found in the utterances of any member of the group.

There is first of all the charge that Judaism is materialistic, thus incapable of performing any spiritual task. In answer to a question I posed concerning any possible "reversion" of individual Messengers to Judaism, E.T. was utterly shocked and asked

> How could anybody return to Judaism after knowing Christ? I mean it's so empty, it's nothing. All you have in Judaism is materialism—a bigger car, a better house—you know what the Jewish religion says the successful man·is. In Christ you have everything—how could anybody return to Judaism? I don't see it.

Most of the testimony spoken by members of the group includes an allusion to the emphasis on wealth and material achievement that drove them as Jews, which is then contrasted with their present preoccupation with matters of the spirit.

Another basic element in the overall view of Judaism is that it fails as a faith. It cannot provide the basic desideratum of meaningful religion, namely, assurance.

> We [my wife and I] attended Friday evening services at the Temple, but we got very little out of it—stories, current events, etc. Nothing was ever said about being saved or assurance of where we would go after death. These subjects were never mentioned.

Most Messengers seek to explain their feeling that Judaism

provides no assurance in pointing out that sacrifice is no
longer a part of Jewish practice. This leaves the Jew with no
atonement and therefore no assurances of being saved. "Were
it not for the provision of God's grace, there would be no hope
for anyone"[14] has become something of a slogan to the Messengers, who continually contrast the insecurity of Judaism
with the surety to be found in Christ. Members of the group
repeatedly asked me how I knew "where I stood with God."
They added that they could never find out in the synagogue
or from the rabbis because there was no longer "blood," and
without "blood" there is no approaching God.

The failure of Judaism to claim an established religious or
temporal hierarchy was curiously disturbing to what are essentially a group of fundamentalist Protestants. Mrs. Finestone
asked, "Having no prophet, priest or king—how can they know
the will of Him Who loves them with an everlasting love . . .?"
This question evokes a noticeable response in the group, suggesting the comfort that they derive from the belief that the
sacrifice of the Lord has more than filled the gap. Yom Kippur,
or the Day of Atonement, is particularly scorned by the Messengers as a half-hearted and totally insufficient attempt to
close this gap within Judaism. The importance accorded to
Yom Kippur is thought to be proof enough that the need for
assurance still beats within the Jewish breast; but again, in
the absence of "blood," Yom Kippur and all the other "fasts
and ordinances" of Judaism fall far short of the mark.

In addition to being materialistic and unable to provide the
believer with assurance, Judaism is seen as a "dead faith," with
the mechanics relatively intact but totally devoid of fire and
passion. One early Hebrew Christian (not a member of the
Messengers) wrote:

Traditional Judaism . . . has developed its concept of God into
a base, abstract transcendental unit. I knew God in Judaism and
I never loved him. I learned to know Him in Christ, and He

won and changed my heart. . . . Before God was to me an "It",
a power which at best I feared; now He is a Person manifested
in the loving and redeeming Christ—dwelling in my heart
through the Holy Spirit.[15]

There would be few Messengers indeed who could not fully
acquiesce in this characterization of their former faith. S.K.,
who claimed to be the daughter of a rabbi, saw Judaism as
an empty vessel, with "a rule for this and a law against that"
but otherwise lacking real religious content.

> My father was very strict in his observance. Especially with my
> brothers he would always insist that they fulfilled the smallest
> letter of the law. They had to pray three times daily, put on
> T'filin [phylacteries] each morning and he would check to see if
> they were wearing their Tzitzes [fringed undergarment worn by
> orthodox Jews]. If they failed in any of these requirements they
> were punished on the spot. But my brothers did not feel any
> closer to God because of these things, and I even doubt that my
> father was satisfied through the law. It was all done because it
> was always done that way, because it was the rabbinic tradition
> and not out of belief that God was satisfied by it. It was empty
> and meaningless.

Particular scorn is reserved for what are viewed as the mechani-
cal observances of Rabbinic Judaism that stem from "questionable" sources and lead nowhere. One Messenger recounted the
joy he had experienced in watching his mother kindle the
Sabbath candles each week, until he realized that God does
not require this of men and that in fact the practice had become his mother's idolatrous substitute for real faith.

The Jewish festivals and holy days, it is averred, are mere
shadows and charades set in the place of the lost religious impulse of Israel. They may be beautiful, it is admitted, but they
are hardly a substitute for true faith, and certainly insufficient
as spiritual vehicles for salvation.

What then is Rabbinic Judaism? Whatever else it may be,

say the Messengers, it is not a faith. "Judaism is empty ceremonialism" is a catch phrase that always elicits a response from
the Messengers, who by and large did indeed experience Judaism on this level.

> What is Judaism? Is it eating bagels and lox on Sunday morn-
> ing? Well, I know plenty of gentiles who eat bagels and lox, too.
> I used to go to the synagogue and watch the people beat their
> breasts and then climb into big cars to go and do the same things
> they had just asked forgiveness for. They could only go through
> the motions and this they thought was enough. But was there
> really any change? Did God enter their hearts?

Almost every Messenger with whom I had contact referred to
this or that practice or ritual of Judaism, saying how beautiful
or how wonderful it was, only to conclude that it was in the
end a sham and a fraud because it was empty ceremonialism
emanating from a moribund faith.

Even if it were possible to give to Rabbinic Judaism the
status of meaningful religion, this status becomes inevitably
that of a lower development in the hierarchy of faith that has
at its apex Protestant Christianity. The present condition of
Israel and indeed of the world is explained against this backdrop of this lower case religion, Judaism, which lingers though
its day has long passed.

> We no longer live under the Mosaic Law, but under Messianic
> Law (Deuteronomy 18:15–19) the law of love which is so much
> higher than the law of works. Israel today does not know that
> God has graduated them into a higher class, another portion of
> time . . . .[16]

Thus Judaism is viewed not only as dead but as a dead
weight as well, in that by its continuing demands for allegiance it prevents what would otherwise be a natural movement
in the direction of Christianity. This is the core attitude toward
Judaism—namely, recognition of its lower standing in the hier-

archy of faith. In the maintenance of this datum, the Messengers can rationalize their leaving Rabbinic Judaism and yet insist that the action is a move along a continuum rather than a complete break, a natural developmental process rather than a crass desertion.

But still the necessity for this move must be established and its legitimacy underscored. Thus Judaism is accused of being unscriptural, a distortion of God's word, or at best the accumulation of lost threads. To the various feast days and observances of Judaism are applied the test of "scripturalness," and it is not surprising that they invariably "fail the test." I was repeatedly queried about the origins of festivals such as Chanukah, Purim, Tisha B'av, and even the high holy days, Yom Kippur and Rosh Hashonah. "Where," I was asked, "did these holy days stem from? Did God tell Israel to light the Chanukah lamps, to play games and get drunk on Purim?" These observances can be "explained away" as "folk customs"[17] and I was inevitably asked to explain the "more important" question of the scriptural validity of the Day of Atonement in the absence of the temple, the priesthood, and the atoning blood of sacrifice. The Messengers explain these as Rabbinic or Talmudic perversions of Scripture, debris that should have been swept away with the advent of the Messiah but are instead foolishly utilized to honor a long-extinguished flame. Kosher food is scorned as an oriental development based on the most meager of scriptural warrants; in any event, Kosher practice was superseded when the Savior appeared, and the present dispensation demands "not a kosher stomach but a Kosher heart."

The Talmud is perhaps the most condemned of the unscriptural underpinnings of Rabbinic Judaism. It is considered to be the sometimes sublime but more often corrupt effusions of a coterie of Babylonian rabbis who sought to maintain and strengthen their grip on the Jewish masses, against the inroads of Christianity, by resorting to lies, distortions, and outright paganism. "Who," it is asked, "gave the rabbis leave to legislate in the name of God?" Furthermore, and even more important, "By what authority did they replace God's holy word as revealed in the Bible with that of mere men as we have it in the Talmud?" This has led, it is said, to the formulation of a new religion called Judaism, which is itself utterly unscriptural, an "ism" among other bleak "isms" that mislead and befuddle. The accusation that Judaism is an "ism" and therefore evil is a rather curious modern fundamentalist touch that is no doubt peculiar to the American movement. Judaism is equated with those other arch evils represented by socialism, communism, fascism, totalitarianism, and so on, and is by virtue of a suffix condemned and scorned. It is remarkable to note the effect of this accusation on the rank and file, who see in it the proverbial straw that broke the camel's back. That is to say, not only is Judaism materialistic, not only is it incapable of providing assurance, not only is it a lower form of religious truth and expression, a dead faith dependent on perversion and distortion of Scripture for a questionable survival, an empty ceremonialism—not only this, but it is a secular perversion as well—an "ism" not unlike those other "isms" which are so disturbing and so steeped in evil and sin.

Short Circuiting of Jewish Ethos

These attitudes and these interpretations of Judaism strike a familiar note when viewed against the backdrop supplied by Protestant fundamentalism. It is possible to hear the same terminology, the same phrases, the same level of a somewhat distorted view of Judaism and oversimplified "theology" in a southern Baptist Church or in a Methodist Home Mission and among the Messengers or Hebrew Christians generally. How is this remarkable confluence to be explained, given that the Messengers claim to be Jewish Christians? One must of course expect that this form as any form of Christianity will espouse a Christological interpretation of reality, but what distinguishes it as peculiarly Jewish? The answer, it would appear, is that *it is in no way Jewish except insofar as the refutation of Judaism assumes a heightened central role in the explication and structuring of the participants' Christian faith*. In effect, the Messengers' view of Judaism is not significantly different from that of most fundamentalist Protestants. But the members of the group were not born into Protestant families, nor in most cases was their early socialization even peripherally within a Protestant mold. Thus we still must ask, how did these attitudes develop? We cannot adequately maintain that their conversion alone led to a new outlook contravening the former belief or affiliatory structure. This does not explain the numerous distortions or the general inability to comprehend even the simplest of Jewish observances, ritual patterns, or religious positions. It must be assumed that the act of conversion has resulted in a complete short circuiting of the Jewish ethos, wherein the believer approaches Jews and Judaism as one who experienced only the most peripheral contact with the reality. I would suggest that this particular type of conversion—that is, one where the convert avers that the conversion was in effect a nonconversion in its limited sense of moving from one *faith structure* to another—is uniquely susceptible to this short-circuiting effect. Because the presuppositions of such a conversion are in themselves so utterly naïve, and because its notion of what is required of the believer and of what has taken place within the believer can be described as the height of naïveté, it makes possible the emergence of a dream world that leads to a total restructuring of the past in the image of the present. This in turn produces an anomalous situation: a group basing their existence on a claim to historicity and an effort to reassemble the lost threads of a historical progression in what they deem to be its proper mold, find themselves heir to a historyless compendium of commonplaces and distortions.

In an effort to establish the legitimacy of their own form of Christianity, the Judaism that challenges this claim to legitimacy is completely transformed—it becomes a straw man, experiencing the usual fate of straw men. In seeking to refute Judaism point by point, the believer must perceive the entire structure as a cruel burlesque of its reality, and this attitude results in a complete short-circuiting of any Jewish ethos and the growth of an almost unparalleled naïveté. A mythology of the Jew and of Judaism is substituted for the unassimilable objective data, and what emerges is a striking compendium bearing only the vaguest relationship to the facts. This short circuiting, or inability to view Jews or Judaism except as an outsider who has had only the most perfunctory contact with the subject, stands forth in bold relief when we examine the attitudes held by individual Messengers toward individual Jews, the collectivity of Jews or the Jewish community, and finally the synagogue and the rabbi.

Attitudes toward Individual Jews and the Collectivity of Jews

Individual Messengers tend to view their former coreligionists in much the same light as the authors of the synoptic Gospels viewed the rabble that condemned Jesus and spared the thief.[18] Most Messengers (and Hebrew Christians generally) view the present-day Jews as the direct descendents of the inhabitants of biblical Israel—as if 2000 years of history had never passed. Qualities and defects are attributed to the modern Jews that reflect on the one hand a divorce from Jewish life and on the other a consciousness of the Bible as a living reality and force that would be difficult to find or duplicate among other believers.

The Jew, it is averred, is host to an innate spirituality that is, however, at all times compromised and distorted by its antithesis—materialism. There was not one member of the group who could discourse on the subject of the Jews without making reference to this duality that marked and marred his (the Jew's) personality.

In addition to the gift of spirituality, the Jew manifests special intellectual powers, and like his spirituality, these are most often misdirected toward unworthy goals. But here too there exists an unmistakable note of ambivalence, when it is suggested that the Jew's unbelief can be partially attributed to a certain naïveté or simplicity. Rev. Finestone suggests that in trying to convert the Jew, the missionary should endeavor to see that the conversation revolves about ". . . some purely Old Testament theme . . . as if you were to teach a class of adolescents."[19] At the same time, however, it is believed that the Jews are quite ignorant concerning the Old Testament, and Rev. Finestone assures the willing worker that "one need not necessarily have a very profound knowledge of the Old Testament to do satisfactory work with the average Jew. . .".[20]

It is asserted that the Jew is a difficult subject of evangelization—a stiff-necked and rebellious individual. One Messenger said in a radio testimony that "it is indeed a miracle when a Hebrew accepts Christ as his Lord and Master."[21] Inevitably, testimony either implicitly or explicitly underscored the greater wonder (and the greater victory) to be seen in the conversion of a Jew, as contrasted with the salvation of other mortals. But even though it is difficult to convert the Jew, he is reputed to be thirsting for salvation, and both the leadership and the rank and file of the Messengers are quite prepared to accept the thinnest of reeds as representing a milestone in evangelistic effort. I heard countless conversations among the members of the group in which they expressed surety that silence, partial agreement, or even good manners on the part of an individual Jew who had been approached with the "message" constituted proof of a hungering soul and the better part of a conversion. The willingness of a family to "live with" the

conversion of one of its members is mistaken for an evangelistic victory. This is so, no doubt, for at least two reasons.
First, it is a very necessary psychological salve to the individual
who would prefer to feel himself in some sort of dynamic relationship with those of his immediate family rather than being
merely tolerated, and the thought that he has "won" acceptance answers this need. Second, it appears that the Hebrew
Christians' interpretation of the Jew as a starved and ema-
ciated spiritual organism is so pervasive that the very toleration
of the convert by a Jew is taken to indicate a Jewish soul in
bud. The Hebrew Christian sees the modern Jew as the biblical seeker who is hungry for the word of God; he sees himself as the bearer of this word. But just as the Jews produced
Jesus and then killed him, their spiritual hunger is all too
often channeled into a materialistic morass.

The Synagogue and Rabbi

If the attitude toward the individual Jew and the Jews as a
group reflects a large measure of ambivalence—the Jew on the
one hand being God-chosen and highly endowed, and on the
other damned by his many defects of character and general
weakness—this ambivalence gives way to outright condemnation of rabbis and the synagogue. The Messengers and all
Hebrew Christians with whom I had contact viewed both the
rabbinate and the synagogue as instruments of the devil and
against a "factual" matrix that was almost unrecognizable. If
a short-circuiting effect is operative in the interpretation of
Judaism or in the attitudes maintained toward Jews generally,
it attains its zenith in attitudes toward the synagogue as an
institution and the rabbi as its mephistophelian major domo.
It must be remembered that all the Messengers, while
stemming from Jewish backgrounds of varying degrees of intensity and commitment, were all nonetheless familiar with

the functioning of the synagogue as an instrument of Jewish community, as well as with the role of the rabbi within this structure. Their postconversion views therefore, are not due to the absence of contact but are based on an entire reorientation stemming from a short-circuiting of the past.

To most Messengers the synagogue conjures up images of the medieval cathedral—dark, mysterious, and all-powerful to mislead. One leading Messenger told me that Jews were thrown out of the synagogue if they did not contribute a prescribed amount for its various funds. He related the following tale.

> I was witnessing to this little Jewish business man—he owns a candy store—who broke down and wept as he told me about giving what he could afford to give but having it rejected as being too little. You know what they did? They threw him out and told him he couldn't come back until he gave what they asked. Isn't that terrible?

The once-prevalent practice of "auctioning" ritual honors is interpreted as a sort of sale of indulgences. The Hebrew Christian somehow assumes that the individual who is unable to "bid" is denied participatory privileges and thus his religious needs are denied him on the grounds of penury. The synagogue is viewed as a fulcrum of power, either bestowing or denying basic religious rights on the basis of wealth or willingness to "give." But to the average Hebrew Christian the synagogue is an institution that wields secular power as well as great religious power. The Jewish community is viewed as an undifferentiated mass, dependent for both positive and negative sanctions—religious and secular—on the synagogue and its authorities. The individual Jew's loyalty is less to the faith than to the synagogue; and it is suggested that this loyalty extends to the secular domain, with Jews acting in all matters according to the requirements laid down by the synagogue. It is asserted that the individual Jew who balks at this or that prescription or proscription of the synagogue will be excluded and ultimately isolated from the family group as well as the synagogue.

The synagogue is furthermore perceived as a temple dedicated to the distortion and warped reformulation of the Bible. Repeatedly I was asked to explain the reason behind the reputed exclusion of prophetic messianic passages such as Isaiah 53 and Daniel 9 from the synagogue ritual. The questions were invariably answered by the questioners themselves, who believed that the synagogue was trying to kep true knowledge of the Messiah from the people. Even the synagogue practice of formal prayer was questioned as an unbiblical attempt to prevent direct communion between the believer and his God. It is thus maintained that the synagogue is a repository of stale and rigid formulas or rituals designed with one end in mind— keeping the Jews in line, bound not to God but to the synagogue.

The rabbi fares particularly badly as the leader of the synagogue. If the synagogue is most often viewed as the "synagogue of Satan," the rabbi appears as Satan himself.

Since its very inception Hebrew Christianity has deemed the rabbinate the single most effective stumbling block to the conversion of the Jews; accordingly, believers harbor an almost pathological hatred of rabbis as a group. Parsons has suggested that ". . . any movement which undermines the legitimacy of an established order tends to become particularly structured about an overt or implied challenge to the legitimacy of privileged statuses within it."[22] Hebrew Christianity does indeed seek to challenge the "privileged status" of the rabbi, but the Hebrew Christian has misunderstood and misinterpreted this status by attributing to it powers rarely if ever encompassed within it and certainly not in the American experience. The rabbis are said to have a degree of power and influence over the lives and fortunes of their congregants that most would fear to contemplate and few if any have ever actually wielded.

Most Hebrew Christians firmly believe that great numbers of Jews would convert if not for the influence of the rabbis.[23] S.K., a leading lay member of the Messengers, thus flatly maintains that "The reason the Jews don't accept Christ is their materialism and the leadership of the rabbis. The Jews follow the rabbis and they—the rabbis, of course—are leading them to Hell." It is thought that the rabbis, like Roman Catholic priests, can apply harsh religious sanctions to deviates, thus controlling their destinies. S.K., and V.H., and Rev. Finestone himself, repeatedly visit the rabbis in their areas in the expectation that the conversion of a rabbi would result in the entire congregation automatically following suit. The probability that the rabbi would be unceremoniously fired does not appear as a likely alternative, for it is naïvely asked "Is he not the shepherd of the flock?" Again it must be remembered that the new Protestant order to which the Messengers as individuals adhere does not itself support this interpretation.

Not only is the sociological positioning of the rabbi within the community totally misunderstood, but the conception of his personality as well gives rise to a grotesque stereotype that in view of the backgrounds of those who maintain it can only be explained in terms of Parsons's seminal suggestion and the short-circuiting effect. Thus the rabbis are seen as frauds who reject Christ for the community while they themselves "know in their hearts" that His claims are justified by Scripture. S.K., after visiting with one of America's leading rabbis, Dr. Joachim Prinz, asserted to me that "the rabbi knows, he knows in his heart but Satan is so powerful in him that he won't allow himself to be convicted." Other Messengers and Hebrew Christians maintain as the basis of rabbinic fraudulence an inability to "own up" to a mistake (the rejection). They are thus viewed as powerful men who are yet so weak that the tragic error of 1900 years' duration results in their cringing helplessly to an abominable lie.[24]

In part, the lie that the rabbis live is attributed to their desire to hold their notoriously well-paid positions. Again they are viewed as both all powerful, yet woefully dependent for their livelihood on toeing this or that line or doctrine. When I asked a random group of Hebrew Christians (Messengers and others who attended the National Convention held in Cincinnati, in June 1961) how much they thought rabbis were paid, I was astounded at the number of estimates in the $30,000 to $50,000 range. No respondent suggested a figure as low as $5,000, and most were convinced that with various fringe benefits rabbis were in the "upper economic brackets" along with presidents of medium-sized corporations and the highest paid professionals.[25]

No Messenger whom I interviewed knew how a Jew became a rabbi, nor were they even remotely aware of the extent or source of rabbinical authority. After many long talks with members of the group, one suddenly realizes that the rabbi is viewed as a sort of sanctimonious gangster who, after showing some prowess in general community affairs, "graduates" into the rabbinate, usurping in the process various and sundry powers. On the cover of one pamphlet in general circulation within the group (but directed at unbelievers) there is the plaintive cry: "When our Rabbis tell us to do things contrary to the word of God, what are we to do?"[26] The answer provided first establishes that the authority of the rabbis is usurped and entirely specious (in terms of the Bible), then it shows how and in what ways this authority "went wrong." The Hebrew Christian claims that the real authority for the Jews is not this shadowy, recondite religious buccaneer, who titles himself "Rabbi," but should instead be the Bible.

The numerous organizations that mark the Jewish community are interpreted as being essentially palliatives with which the rabbis and other Jewish leaders "religiously anesthetize" the community. There is widespread agreement with the condemnation of the rabbinate voiced by Joel Levy, who exclaimed in 1920: "They [the rabbis] profess to love their nation, build them synagogues or Temples, organize societies of benevolence and educate and make their people believe that all is well with them."[27] At every opportunity members of the group point to such seeming "successes" enjoyed by the Jewish community as impressive temples and well-functioning community institutions, suggesting that these are mere filler supplied by the rabbis to hold the Jews within a thoroughly rotten structure.

As if the foregoing were not sufficient to inspire the believer with a complete revulsion for the rabbinate as an institution and rabbis as men, the latter are accused of stupidity, an in-born inclination for violence, and finally sympathy with communism.[28] The "privileged status" of rabbis is attacked on the one hand because of a reputed usurpation of authority having no legitimate source and on the other because the rabbis as men are unworthy to occupy this high status. There are few members of the Messengers who cannot readily supply an instance of rabbinical stupidity, usually revolving around an asserted lack of biblical knowledge and understanding,[29] but including a general dullness of mind and an inability to deal properly with questions and positions of a believing Christian.

No member of the Messengers ever suggested that the rabbis were willing to resort to force and physical brutality; how-ever, repeated references to the "old days," when missionaries were beaten and publicly reviled seem to elicit tacit agreement about the "forces" that lay behind these attacks. Stories sup-plied by Hebrew Christian rabble-rousers such as S. J. Kliger-man and Jacob Gartenhaus concerning the physical and mental tortures inflicted on them by Jewish leaders, are readily understood as still another example of rabbinic excess.[30] Rev. Finestone at least twice mentioned that his father (a Chris-tian convert) was nearly blinded by members of the Jewish community in Constantinople, Turkey, who forced him to look into the noonday sun. It is interesting to note that the assembled were visibly moved and angry but not surprised at still another example of what unbelieving Jews and their leaders (rabbis) are capable of.

THE MEMBERSHIP

The Messengers of the New Covenant attempt, through various devices (exegesis, testimony, the structuring of a sense of community, etc.), to convince both converts and unbelieving Jews that they did not convert, hence are *not* traitors to their past—that as "completors" of an incomplete and thoroughly defective faith structure, *they* are the "real Israel." These efforts have led to what I have referred to as a short-circuiting effect wherein attitudes held toward Judaism as a faith and Jews as people, as well as the interpretation of Jewish community institutions and their functionaries are in fact highly distorted out-group views of normative Judaism, rather than in any way Jewish. I believe that it would be useful here to discuss the people who hold these attitudes—their backgrounds, socio-economic positioning, and general orientations.

I estimate that approximately 75 people in the Newark area are affiliated with the Messengers. There are between 12 and 25 adults who can be considered "regulars" in that they attend most Friday evening meetings of the group. The remainder can be split into two categories—those who have "graduated" into the gentile church but who still maintain an emotional affiliation to what was for many the vehicle of their conversion, and those who attend sporadically and affiliate only in a most tenuous and peripheral sense. The latter represent a blank page in terms of the field research carried out with the group itself, and little can be said about them beyond noting their existence.[31]

In the case of the "regulars" and the first category of the second group, we can generalize a bit with regard to socioeconomic class, the generational structure in terms of immigration to the United States, the level of Jewish education prior to conversion, the sex ratio and age composition within the group, and so on. Finally, some observations on the relationships with the nuclear family unit before and since conversion are possible.

It would appear that most of the Messengers (and, I believe, Hebrew Christians generally) fall into the middle and lower-middle class ranges. In the "regular" group it has been possible to isolate the following occupations: printer (1), pharmacist (1), store clerk (1), salesman (4), insurance agent (1), small businessman (dry cleaning shop) (1), draftsman (1). There are also two male regulars who are retired (both had been manual workers), and the rest of the group is comprised of housewives and elderly widows living on small pensions and/or social security benefits. The "graduated" affiliates or those who attend meetings only sporadically and who have made satisfactory adjustment within one of Newark's Protestant churches seem to fare slightly better on the whole. The latter group includes two small businessmen, a part owner of one of New Jersey's leading clothing chains, an engineer who was described as being self-taught (this individual may really be an expert draftsman), an insurance salesman (reputed to be well to do, he is the only convert on the Board of Directors of the Messengers). The rest of the second group is comprised largely of elderly ladies (about two-thirds of them widows) as well as a few men and women about whom no information was available.

The Messengers are not an affluent group of people, and in the case of the numerous widows and old people there is a decided tinge of not-so-genteel poverty. Upward mobility, a factor that distinguished the Jewish community as a whole, is limited in the extreme among the Messengers and in at least two cases has been totally reversed. I was able to visit the homes of three members of the group, and they were all strikingly similar in terms of type of furnishings, art choice, magazines, and so an. Furnishings in two of the three homes visited were quite old, and there was general clutter in all. The pictures were cheap reproductions of still lifes, pastoral country scenes, and other "realistically" conceived subjects. Significantly in all three there was an Israeli *objet d'art* or two—either a candelabrum (two homes) or a fruit bowl done in the easily identifiable material (green copper) that has become ubiquitous in American Jewish homes. Magazines were *Life* (all three) and *Readers Digest* (two). The homes were conspicuous for the absence of books; however, one boasted an organ and a grand piano in a small three-room apartment that housed two adults and a child. In sum, the homes must be seen as akin to the types most readily found in a working-class environment, albeit with some distinguishing marks.

As far as I could determine, the overwhelming majority of the Messengers are second-generation Americans whose parents immigrated mainly from Eastern and Central Europe. There are in addition four or five members of the group who are third generation. Most Messengers claim that their parents' home was a "traditional" one, but it soon appeared that in this application the term seldom bore the usual meaning. By "traditional" they meant to indicate that they were not Christians (or in any significant way sympathetic to Christianity) and that they attended synagogue on the high holy days. Aside from this very minimal connection, the homes of many of the group members were by and large devoid of meaningful Jewish content, as I learned in the course of my research. Not one male member of the group had received what could be described as an elementary school level Jewish education. Approximately a fourth of the male members and only three of the women known to me were able to read elementary "prayer book" Hebrew with any facility. Of these three women, however, two enjoyed a more than adequate familiarity with Hebrew, Jewish history, and even in a rudimentary fashion some Talmud. But these two women were so far ahead of the rest of the group that they represent anomalies rather than points along a continuum. Most of the group had *no formal Jewish education at all;* the remainder (with the exceptions just noted) had received the barest minimum in terms of simple and abbreviated preparation for the confirmation ceremony, and at this point (13 years of age) their Jewish education had been terminated. For the most part, the members of the group have no reliable knowledge of the Jewish religion. This is a complex problem because although surface glibness does exist (a literal familiarity with the Old Testament is almost universal), most knowledge of "Judaism" comes *after* conversion and then serves (thus being limited and circumscribed by) the need for legitimation and support. There is constant affirmation of the belief that now they are *true* Jews. L.L., for example, assured me that "Before conversion I never knew what it was to be a Jew. Now I know my heritage and it's so beautiful." S.K. also told me of *really* understanding only since belief in the Messiah of Israel changed her life. Indeed, there was not one member of the group who did not claim an insight into and a knowledge of Judaism based solely on his conversion to belief in "the Savior of Israel."

General educational attainment probably averaged 10 years of schooling, although most members have completed high school and only one has completed the equivalent of college (the pharmacist).[32] Again, this does not compare favorably with general educational attainment in the American Jewish community. A study by J. Fishman of the Greenfield Center for Human Relations revealed that 61 percent of Jewish heads of households in this country are high school graduates and 22 percent are college graduates.[33]

I estimate the average age of the group to be in the area of 50 or 55 years, accounting for the presence of approximately 10 pre-teen children. In other words, the group is primarily comprised of elderly people who in most cases have converted to Christianity rather late in life. The Messengers have a youth program run by one of the missionaries and one young convert (a 24-year-old printer), but it depends for continuity and numbers not on the children of the group members but on neighborhood children, most of whom are Negroes. On a visit I made to a meeting of the youth group where eight children were in attendance only one was the child of a group member; the rest were Negroes.[34]

The sex ratio is another striking characteristic of the group. The majority of the group are late-middle-aged and elderly women (50 to 70 years of age); most of them are widowed, divorced, or estranged from their mates. Among Hebrew Christians generally, I have observed a predominance of older women and a relative scarcity of men, especially young men. The reasons for this bias in the sex ratios are no doubt varied, but I suspect that it is at least partially explainable by the failure of the American Jewish religious milieu to provide an acceptable synagogue outlet for the intense religious commitment and enrapturement displayed by these women. Normative Judiasm provides no real *personal* religious role for women and grants them a rather stunted and attenuated religious role status. Moreover, for those whose personality bent or experience indicates the need for a central rather than a peripheral involvement, there exists no legitimate outlet. Also, and to a marked extent, the group members manifest all sorts of emotional scars. The men would not likely fall within the operating purview of a missionary in the course of their everyday existence; however, these stay-at-home women, in a large urban environment, are bound sooner or later to be approached or reached by a missionary. In the approach to a troubled individual the missionary can (and does) supply the necessary concern and involvement with the person's difficulties, making a conversion though by no means inevitable at least more likely to occur.

Once conversion does occur, a gulf generally opens between

the convert and his immediate family that in its initial stages often involves a complete break—a break invariably initiated by the family. Among the Messengers, however, I found that after a year (or two or three) the family tends to accept the convert, usually establishing as conditions of acceptance that no attempt be made to convert unconverted members of the family and that religion be treated as a taboo area of discussion. Of course this bargain becomes difficult for the convert to keep, and relations finally stabilize on a level of cold but correct cordiality. Some of the group members have explained that their reluctance to join a Protestant church is due to a desire to retain bruised but still intact ties to family, the better to witness to them. The members of the group, it must be remembered, are intensely committed to the fiction that they are still Jews, and any ties that remain with the original family group serve to buttress this claim. E.K. explained her refusal to join a Baptist church she regularly attends as follows: "I won't join because then I can't witness effectively to my family. They'll say aha—she joined a goyishe (gentile) church—she sold out."

One gathers that family relationships prior to conversion were loose at best, conversion tending to crystallize rather than radically change these relationships. In fact the convert gains a measure of heightened family status (in his own eyes) because he is now a serious concern of the family, whereas formerly he may very likely have been ignored or taken for granted. In any event he believes that being a hyphenated Christian—a Hebrew Christian—protects him from the accusation of apostasy and assures him of at least peripheral contact with his family, whether these ties are desired for evangelical purposes or for personal reasons.

The foregoing discussion allows us to draw the following conclusions about the membership of the Messengers of the New Covenant. The most active segment of the group is comprised largely of second-generation Americans of quite modest occupational and socioeconomic class attainment. There is a predominance of elderly and single females, and the group as a whole is not well educated, especially with respect to Jewish studies. They are for the most part people who have undergone great emotional difficulty, and they had had little formal religious involvement prior to their conversion. Usually their families extended little of the much-needed emotional (and in some cases material) support that was required during times of stress and during the years (for many) of declining physical vigor, and the resulting vacuum was readily entered by zealous missionaries who were both willing and able to supply the necessary support. They are finally a group of people who remain in many important respects ambivalent concerning their Jewish origin and their present relationship to both Jews and Judaism.

Anti-Semitism and Self Hate

One factor seems to characterize both the Hebrew Christians directly observed and the writings of the movement generally —namely the ambivalence with which they view Jews and Judaism. It is perhaps indicative of an often quixotic history that the very Christian group that styles itself as being more than Christian in that it is a *Jewish* Christian entity is in fact revolted by this bifurcation of its Christian faith, and specifically by its self-chosen "Jewish" qualification. Solomon Liptzin, writing of the feelings of such postemancipation German Jewish intellectuals as Borne and Beck, states that it was not *Judenhass* that motivated the negative feelings of what he refers to as Jewish Christians, but rather *Liebeshass*.[35] The same designation would be close to the mark in characterizing the very different "Jewish Christians" of the present, who feel constrained to underscore their Jewish roots and Jewish attachment but at the same time find it very difficult to experi-

ence the affirmation that they consciously seek. The matter is
further complicated by the ambivalence with which most
Hebrew Christians view the Gentile as well, indicating a marginal positioning that can have an overwhelming impact on
the convert. On the one hand there exists an overbearing desire to be a part of them (Gentiles) and to stop being a small
people accused always of being the Christ killer. On the other
hand there is a warped messianic expectation that the Jews
will "show them" when judgment day comes and ". . . they
appear before our Jewish Brother in Heaven." One Messenger
told the following story to prove to me how a Christian is better than a Jew because he can love his enemy; but the tale
shows something else indeed.

> When my husband was recuperating from a heart attack we lived
> in a house full of Irish Catholic families. Well—you know how
> superstitious they are and how many festivals they have where
> they drink a lot and dance around. One day they were making
> such a racket down below me that I went down to ask the
> O'Conners if they would please quiet down because my husband
> was ill. Well—she just put her hands on her hips and began to
> abuse me terribly. She shouted, "You lousy, dirty Jew—why don't
> you leave us alone—who cares if your husband is sick—Hitler
> should have come to America and gotten rid of the rest of you."
> I just looked at her and said, "My dear woman. I am a follower
> of the Lamb of God. Yes I am Jewish and proud of it and I am
> also a Christian and when you stand before God he will be my
> great Jewish Brother—Jesus of Nazareth. And if you believe your
> Bible there will come a day when you will beg to be able to
> touch a Jew's shirt—to kiss the hem of his garment."

The story is indicative of a general pattern among Hebrew
Christians that emerges from a reading of the literature of the
movement as well as through personal contact—that is, of
individuals who suffer more deeply than most Jews from anti-
Semitism. Most Hebrew Christians readily admit to a resentment against Jews before conversion, but they were and are

convinced that being Jewish is ineradicable. After conversion they can feel Christian (i.e., "better"), and they also have an eschatological answer to the question, Why Jews? They then are able to think of themselves and their sufferings in terms of "mission," where previously there had been inexplicable pain. What, it must be asked, is the specific source of this greater experience of pain by Hebrew Christians? I suggest that the Hebrew Christian suffers more intensely from anti-Semitism because he has assumed for himself the major burden for its very existence in an unregenerate guilt for the crucifixion of Christ. The psychologist Jung is reputed to have said that many Jews who were undergoing treatment with him experienced a sense of personal guilt for the crucifixion. This at first struck me as being extraordinary, but subsequent research in the matter of Hebrew Christianity has led me to conclude that it is indeed a factor in the phenomenon labeled Jewish self-hate. The Hebrew Christian constantly seeks atonement—not as the Christian who sees in the crucifixion man's utter sinfulness, but as the Jew who experiences a sense of personal guilt for a crime that is interpreted as a peculiarly Jewish crime. In the suffering the Jew experiences at the hand of the Gentiles, there is opportunity for a least partial atonement, and anti-Semitic rage becomes translated in this context into communion, thus absolution.

> The age long rage of Gentile against Jew burst forth. He smote me with the rope, he beat me with the cross and pressed it to my bleeding lips to kiss; then, that first sacramental blood grew sweet upon my lips. . . .[36]

This the author calls his first communion, and with this the burdensome guilt of an entire people is lightened. George Benedict, a leading Hebrew Christian during the early decades of the century, tells how he cried as a little boy when his teacher told of the betrayal of Judas Iscariot and how he assured her that he would "make it up" when he was grown.[37]

Another Hebrew Christian relates the following: "I came to where I found that a plot was being formed against Him in the Gospel of Matthew and I said, 'I will hate my people if they do any injustice to this man.' "[38] One of the Messengers concluded a description of his conversion by saying,

> After this [prayer and confession of faith in Christ] I felt different. I kept thinking to myself that I was a Christian and how great a feeling it was. I was able to see everything in a different light. Boy, I can't tell you how good it felt.

Another Messenger said,

> The first memory I retain of childhood is that Christian children would not play with me—the Christ killer. I really started coming to the Lord when I knew that Jesus loved little Jewish children.

That is, conversion was possible only after the respondent could feel personal forgiveness for an injustice for which he, as a Jew, was especially guilty. Glick quotes one of the Hebrew Christians interviewed in his study: "I feel that I am making up for all my ancestors, in atoning for their rejection of Christ for all the two thousand years."[39]

This sense of personal guilt for the crucifixion—or, more correctly, personal guilt as a Jew—is extraordinarily widespread both among the Messengers and other Hebrew Christians, leadership as well as laity; but there is also a general revulsion at the "perfidy" of the Jews, the meanness of their lives, and the poverty of their destiny. The customs and ritual practices of the Jews are pitted against those of the Christians, with the Jews faring rather badly in comparison.

> In Sheffield, as well as elsewhere my father was Shochet (i.e., ritual slaughterer) as well as Rabbi. As a little boy I once asked him to let me see him at his work. He took me along to the slaughterhouse and I saw him with his long knife keen as a razor

blade, draw it twice across the throat of a cow. It was a bloody and pitiful sight, and made me sick at heart.

While waiting for him, and while he sharpened his knives, I had looked about me. In an adjoining room I had seen a Gentile butcher strike a bull down with one stroke of a pick-axe on his skull.[40]

Even in the slaughter of a beast, this thoroughly alienated Hebrew Christian saw a "better" and more humane way than that of the Jews. Even the ghetto is perceived less as the cause of undesirable Jewish traits than as a catalyst for factors already operative.

But segregation [the ghetto] did not make the Jew less Jewish but more so. It intensified his prejudices and isolated him. These ghettos created by the Church of the middle ages produced the narrow streets, the dingy houses, the crowded rooms, the sordid occupations and the general isolation, which in turn created the crippled bodies, the weakened eyes, the bended backs, hollowed chests, the stunted esthetic (sic) sense, the cramped (sic) heart and the perverted mind.[41]

One Messenger asserted that he pictured two types of Jews: (a) the pious Jew and (b) the crooked Jew "like my grandfather who used to cheat at pinochle." In subsequent conversations it became evident that the latter type was felt to predominate. Like nearly all the Messengers and other Hebrew Christians with whom I had contact during my research, this individual had assimilated most of the negative (and some of the positive) stereotypes of the Jew; the significant difference was that each believer sought through personal and individual striving to overcome any onus. Ackerman and Jahoda claim that the Jewish anti-Semite permits himself to feel that he stands outside the Jewish group, thus allowing him to project "bad" qualities onto Jews, and thereby he conforms to the stance of the dominant majority.[42] This is partially true as we saw in the discussion of the short-circuiting effect; but the explanation is too simple and takes no cognizance of the internal pressures, contradictions, and striving that beset the man trying, as it were, to leap out of his skin. The Jewish anti-Semite, and specifically the Hebrew Christian, is often a man attempting an objective defense of his subjectivity; going outside the group to secure the necessary stance from whence he can explain himself to others, garbed in the clothes of the other. It cannot be simply maintained that this individual is, or is even attempting, solely to wash his hands of the matter, to disappear into the dominant group, or to shift blame onto those of the in-group who unlike him had not the courage or moral fiber to overcome this formidable ingrown sin. But he is nevertheless an anti-Semite in that he attributes to Jews as a group patterns of behavior or response that are negative and ultimately undesirable, manifesting in the process hostility toward the Jews. The Hebrew Christian seeks not so much a total rejection of the Jew as an opportunity to live "un-Jewishly" in an attempt to live down and repent group sin and perversity. In seeking an alternative for the Jew, it is determined that:

> There is only one remedy possible, and that is that somewhere, in some corner of the Jewish world, there should arise a great, overwhelming Jewish shame, a shame for itself, shame for all that is ugly, and for the ugliness with which we are soaked, a shame for God, for exile. . . .[43]

It is paradoxically believed that in becoming a Christian, the "shame" is dissipated, allowing for a "true" Jewish existence. The shame of the Jew is twofold, but the two elements are indissolubly interlinked: first and most important the rejection and crucifixion, and second the resulting debasement of the group soul. As proof of the connection, Hebrew Christians constantly refer to the uplift (spiritual and temporal) experienced by the converted Jew. It is, for instance, maintained that greed no longer exists once a true conversion is undergone; on another level, it is said that a somehow unworthy concern for life, which marks the unconverted Jew, disappears in the Christian. Unlike the Jew, the Christian is not afraid to die:

> I have stood at many death-beds and noticed that my Jewish co-religionists, even the very pious ones, always dreaded death, whereas true Christians had no fear of death; they were calm, peaceful, hopeful, because Christ and heaven were to them realities.[44]

In the same vein Rev. Finestone talked scornfully of how Jews would weep and cry and beat their breasts on Yom Kippur, suggesting that this behavior, while characteristically Jewish, was unworthy and even somehow disgusting. But it is unfortunate only when found in the Jew. Not more than 15 minutes after Rev. Finestone had condemned this behavior in the Jews, he reported the story of a Christian (a Gentile) who, upon becoming "convicted" of his sins knelt and wept on the floor of a mission house. This behavior was considered to be correct and praiseworthy, while its parallel among the Jews was execrated.

A corollary of the self-hate manifested by the Messengers is to be seen in the servile gratitude displayed toward Gentiles for any appreciation or acceptance they might manifest for the Hebrew Christian. Curiously, the members of the group never cease to wonder and express amazement that even the true Christian can "love the Jew." Among a few there is an aggressive insistence that they be loved, but most simply express quiet satisfaction that they can be loved at all. To illustrate the former attitude, I recall the behavior of J.J. at a Bible conference. She asked a missionary recently returned from Africa: "Did you have any contact with Jews in your work?" The missionary said that he did not meet many Jews. J.J. persisted: "Well, when you did come across Jews did you witness to them?" When assured by the missionary that he did, she said "That's good. You are a good Christian who knows Scripture and prays for the peace of Jerusalem." J.J. then spent the better part of an hour assuring the missionary that we (those sitting at table with him) were Jews and that there were many like us—believers in the Lord—obviously trying to assure him that the Jews were salvageable and that he must love us to consummate his Christian duty in winning us. Most Messengers, however, were far less aggressive and were content to relate stories of how this or that Gentile Christian had shown them love and had in effect accepted them notwithstanding their obvious defects and inherited guilt.[45]

Finally, it should be noted that although anti-Semitic effusions are quite common, and the element of self-hate is real and ubiquitous, the Messengers can by no means be thought of as a group of violent "haters." There exists here, as Ackerman and Jahoda have suggested, "a tendency to retreat;" that is, on the one hand a vacillation between deepseated hostilities seeking outlet and expression, and on the other hand a very definite element of restraint and ultimately of ambivalence.[46]

Conversion

I have, I believe, partially explained why one group of people convert to Hebrew Christianity rather than to a normative Christian structure, analyzing their conversion within the context of legitimation (see Chapter 6). I have not, however, dealt schematically with the process of *conversion* itself, to more adequately convey an understanding of the basic appeal of Hebrew Christianity, I must now expand on the general remarks in Chapter 1.

Brigham Young, in explaining his missionary approach and the underlying basis for its success, has said:

We gather those who are poor, who wish to be redeemed, who feel the oppression the high and the proud have made them endure. . . . Take those who are in enjoyment of all the luxuries of this life and their ears are stopped up; they cannot hear.[47]

This analysis is, I believe, a cogent one, and it has bearing on the present phenomenon. Press has observed that "the degree of receptivity to conversionary efforts will of course depend upon the circumstances which have shaped the life of the individual Jew. Personal problems tend to make the heart more open to spiritual truth . . . ."[48] Indeed the data appear to give this observation rather firm support. But the area of "personal problems" is a large territory, and for the Messengers it seems essentially to involve a number of diverse elements.

First there is the factor of a person in need of individualized concern; he is rather taken for granted by his present reference group or perhaps is living a marginal existence where he feels that he is of little concern or interest to anyone. The missionary's task is to fill this gap, and the existence of a community of "like" individuals sharing a common origin serves to support a convert's involvement. The Messengers, for example, make the convert or the prospective convert feel that he is the center of attraction. He is fawned over, looked to, cherished, and pursued. This factor, given the psychological state of most of those in the group or attracted to the group, is of considerable consequence. It ties in with the comments quoted earlier about rabbis "not caring" or "not speaking to the individual heart."[49] The individual member of the group required somebody or something of transcendent authority, and no Jewish "functionary" could fill this bill. What is demanded is a pastoral approach (that of the missionary) that acts as a medium to lead the seeker to a personal relationship with a personal God who above all else "cares." Underwood, for example, asserts that "man is more than intellect and will" and that man has the power to love but that he cannot love the impersonal.[50] This is of course debatable, but the group under study did contain individuals seeking with all their being personal involvement, personal relationships and ties to men *and* to God. God had no reality in their previous lives, where he was seen as abstract, distant, cold, and utterly unable to supply the protective warmth so intensely desired. But Jesus of Nazareth lived as a man, suffered and died as a man; in other words, they find Jesus understandable and relevant to their existence as human beings suffering and adrift.

Besides the need for a personal God and a primary relationship to others, there are those who come out of what King has called "sheer bewilderment." King's remarks about the individual in his relation to a mass movement can readily apply to many of those who because of discontent move into a religious group.

> The various circumstances of discontent render the individual especially receptive to suggestion. . . . Less attention has been given however to the situation in which sheer bewilderment (rather than the "will to believe") is also conducive to suggestibility. In this circumstance, the interpretation a person seeks may come from a respected friend, a newspaper columnist, or the leader of a social movement, but the degree of the individual receptivity will depend on both the extent to which he lacks a frame of reference and the intensity of his desire for meaning.[51]

In the testimony of Hebrew Christians, as well as in personal conversation with Hebrew Christians, it becomes evident that a "frame of reference" is exactly what is lacking before conversion and what is sought *through* conversion. Most Messengers, for example, readily admit to this "bewilderment," which they identify as "listlessness," "dissatisfaction," and "spiritual hunger;" and in their efforts to remedy this extreme situation, conversion—a new birth—seems to be the only possibility.[52] Anything less complete than total surrender will not do. But why surrender to Christianity? Underwood asks, Why does voluntary effort defeat itself? and Why does the surrender of effort accomplish "what volition fails to do?" He answers the second question as follows:

> When the direct assault on the besetting sin is abandoned, the noxious suggestion of inability begins to languish. The field of consciousness is now taken up with thoughts of Him to whom the surrender may be made. Thus instead of the suggestion "I am doomed to failure," the dominant suggestion comes to be: "my success is assured, for the invincible power of God is on my side." This suggestion of power releases psychic energy that the will had been impotent to stir so long as the suggestion of inability operated. Before, however, the new suggestion can do its work, the mind must be freed from all tension by the abandonment of voluntary effort. In Evangelical circles the suggestion is rendered the more potent by its strongly marked emotional affect, *since the surrender is made to a Person and not to a mere force; and above all to a Person thought of as One not only able, but also eager to save and Who has shown His eagerness by an act of redemptive love.*[53]

The factors of personhood (Christ) and redemptive sacrifice are of the utmost importance in relation to the seekers' "bewilderment;" these factors are not apparent within Judaism, which emphasizes exactly what is abhorrent in view of the individual's existential state—namely, voluntary effort, with its accompanying risk of continued failure and lack of surety. Judaism emphasizes the volitional in terms of *T'Shuva* or as Abrahams puts it, "the renewal of man's nature by repentance." Contrasting this with conversion, Abrahams notes that "it is a regular process not a catastrophe," and where the anomic seeker is no longer or never has been related to this "regular process," the catastrophe of conversion, with its surrender of will, speaks to his peculiar condition.

An additional underlying factor in the type of religious conversion with which we are dealing is self-hate, both in its group context as Jewish self-hate and on an individual level as a revulsion with and rejection of self. I have alluded to the former, but the latter plays a significant role, as well. The revulsion to self seemingly experienced by so many of the Messengers is not to be confused with an apprehension of sin. Its roots lie elsewhere. As has been suggested in relation to converts to the Salvation Army, it ". . . was not their sense of sin, but their desire to escape the misery, mental and physical, to which their vices had brought them. Their sense of sin was a post-conversion development."[54] Individual group members speak of their preconversion existence as an unbroken chain of defeats—in business or career, in personal relationships, in the failure to experience any meaningful tie to a group, in the absence of relevant values, and so on. I suspect that the sheer weight of failure and defeat, experienced on many levels, makes the prospect of partial melioration appear ridiculous and inconsequential, leaving open only the extreme avenues of accepting an untenable status or revolutionizing one's existence by breaking completely with the past and achieving a total reorientation through conversion. Yet paradoxically, in carrying out a complete break with the past the Hebrew Christian establishes and cements a negative bond to the Jews and to the Judaism that he had been fleeing from or had been unable to comprehend. His past is relived through a largely imagined relationship to his Jewish background—a past viewed as unsatisfying and deficient—and his conversion becomes structured as a point-for-point rebuttal of past misery and spiritual vacuity.

THE MESSENGERS: A LIMITED COMPARISON WITH THE FIRST HEBREW CHRISTIAN CHURCH OF CHICAGO

One group of Hebrew Christians besides the Messengers of the New Covenant has been subjected to empirical analysis.

A complete and detailed comparison of the two groups is not feasible within the present context, but I believe that noting differences and similarities will place the phenomenon of the Messengers in a more meaningful perspective. The comparison may serve to suggest the existence of a Hebrew Christian pattern, as well as to clarify the aspects of the study that might be viewed as isolated phenomena, having meaning in a particular instance but of limited value in an overall structuring of the movement.

The striking similarity of the two groups extends even to their size. Both the Messengers and the First Hebrew Christian Church of Chicago (HCCC) have approximately the same total number of adherents, with about the same breakdown in terms of "actives" and "inactives." Most of the members of both groups are second- or third-generation Americans, although the HCCC appears to have drawn more heavily on Jews with a German rather than an East European background. The socioeconomic positioning of both groups places them roughly in the lower-middle-class ranges, although here again there exists some divergence. Glick says that the HCCC members show a somewhat greater degree of upward mobility than was found among the Messengers. This can be partially explained, however, by the large numbers of relatively young people in the HCCC and the relative scarcity of younger people among the Messengers.

Glick asserts that ". . . a mutual possession of a number of shared traits tends to create a rather strikingly homogeneous group,"[55] and this applies equally well to the Messengers and to the HCCC. The observer is often hard pressed to remember that the individual members of the group cannot be thought of as completely interchangeable, one with the other. One is led to this response *because* of the almost total sameness of at least the external attributes of the group members—an impression that is buttressed by the constant recourse to slogans and the pat answers given to almost any question posed by an outsider. There exists a universe of discourse making it possible for Hebrew Christians of any background or affiliation to immediately engage a new acquaintance (in the Hebrew Christian fold) in conversation that reaches a degree of intensity and familiarity that could not be achieved in any other context without months of intimate association to build on.[56] In part, of course, this is explainable in view of the community of interests among Hebrew Christians and the quasi-sectarian nature of the movement; but beyond this it seems that great importance attaches to the aspect of homogeneity of personality that has other derivations and roots.

One basic difference between the two groups is to be seen in the church structure of the Chicago group—the Messengers still lacking such structure. The Chicago group operates as a Presbyterian church (in terms of church government) and utilizes a Presbyterian ritual with, however, a syncretistic overlay of a peculiarly Hebrew Christian character. Thus the star of David, reference to Yeshua Hamashiach (interchangeably rather than in place of the name Jesus Christ), the use of occasional Hebrew terms in sermons, the use of Jewish festivals as reference points for Christian exegesis, and so on, play observable roles in the church pattern. The Messengers, in addition to having no church structure, have a more fundamentalist theology than the Chicago group, still retaining more of the mission than the church flavor. Most of the Messengers worship at Newark's Emanuel Baptist Church. However, they have purchased one acre of land near Atlantic City, New Jersey, where they hope to begin not only a church of their own but an entire self-sustaining community. If the present theological stance is maintained, this will probably prove to be a most fascinating socioreligious experiment. The "statement of faith" that appears on the title page of the leading Messenger publication, *Grace to Israel*, clearly represents an interpretation of fundamentalist doctrine, announcing belief

. . . in one God, eternally existent in three persons; Father, Son, and Holy Spirit. We believe in God the Father, creator of all things visible and invisible. We believe in Jesus Christ our prophet, priest and king; who was begotten of the Holy Spirit: born of the Virgin Mary; who died for our sins, rose again from the dead and ascended into heaven; who will come again according to the Scripture. We believe in the Holy Spirit, our instructor and comforter. We believe the Bible is the inspired, inerrant word of God. We believe in the efficacy of the atoning blood of our Lord Jesus Christ, shed on the cross of Calvary for Jew and Gentile alike.[57]

Superimposed on this basic core of fundamentalism, the Messengers adhere to a dispensationalist outlook (shared by the HCCC), which emphasizes an ultimately triumphant Israel with Christ as Lord and Ruler. Finally, coupled with this fundamentalist dispensational approach, both groups are characterized by a rather attenuated antinomianism, which proves to be an ineffective missionary weapon in the fight against Jewish "legalism." Thus in the area of theology and church polity there are basic differences, as well as similarities, between the two groups.

In both the HCCC and the Messengers (and I suspect the movement as a whole) there are a great many "mixed" Gentile-Jewish marriages. Statistics in this area are of course unavailable, but I do not think that an estimate of 50 to 60 percent of the membership would be too high; probably, in fact, this figure is too low.

The attitudes maintained vis à vis the Jews, as well as the definition of who is a Jew, are about the same in both groups: being Jewish is a matter of race; that is, anyone who is born of Jewish parents is a Jew, and no power on earth can change this status. By the same logic a Gentile is anyone who was not born a Jew. A Christian is anybody (Jew or Gentile) who has accepted Jesus Christ as Lord and Savior.

Members of both groups are predisposed to identify with

the first Christians of the Apostolic Church. While this identification bears only the slightest resemblance to a formal process, the frequency with which members of both groups refer
to the "first Jewish Christians" and their readiness to draw
parallels between their situation and that of the believers of
the first century A.D. indicates the existence of a strong affectual involvement. Glick merely mentions these feelings without
attributing too much importance to them (p. 152), but I believe that this identification plays an important role as a
legitimating factor for Hebrew Christians. Glick contends
that the phenomenon of Hebrew Christianity can be largely
expained as a sociological rather than a theological "half-way
house" wherein the "ultimate" in assimilation—the adoption
of the dominant faith—can proceed with less pain or social
and personal dislocation. I agree with this analysis as far as it
goes, but I maintain that in view of the uncomfortable and
largely unnecessary marginality with which this accommoda-
tion saddles the convert, the position begs more questions than
it is able to answer.

THE QUESTION OF MARGINALITY

In her essay on biculturality, Jessie Bernard suggests that

> The nonghetto Jew is like the child of quarreling parents. He
> loves both yet allegiance to one often means or appears to
> mean disloyalty if not actual treason to the other. Still he can
> never achieve complete oneness save he deliberately turn his
> back on one or the other.[58]

If this contention is accepted at face value, we can say that the
Messengers and members of the Chicago group, as well as
Hebrew Christians generally, have simply "made believe" that
no choice was required of them. The Hebrew Christian has
insisted that he have his cake and eat it too, not alone in the

general area of culture to which Bernard referred but in the specific detail of religion as a reference point or watermark in the larger culture. Still, Bernard was correct in insisting that "he can never achieve complete oneness," for the Hebrew Christian does not accept the Hebrew and the Christian elements of his being in a one-to-one relationship. The Hebrew Christian has accepted Christian faith and Christian culture —he is a Christian; but at the same time he seeks to affirm an intangible and illusive element from his past (his imagined as well as his real past) which he identifies as "Jewishness" or being a "Jew," and in the process he becomes a good example of the marginal man. The "Jewish" Christian is in the anomalous position of having to prove his Jewishness to doubting Jews and his Christianity to questioning Gentiles. This has resulted in the sacrifice of the "oneness" of which Bernard speaks, since the internal gymnastics exacted by this situation place almost intolerable demands on the individual's spiritual and intellectual resources. No better indication of what is required of the individual in this position can be found than the following words of Sir Leon Levison (former President of the International Hebrew Christian Alliance):

> Our relationship to each other must be maintained in unity, because . . . we are a twice despised and twice exiled people— exiled along with the Jewish race, and exiled *from* the Jewish race because of our belief; despised like the Jewish race, but despised *by* the Jewish race because of our belief.[59]

Almost all Hebrew Christians (except the few who are completely removed from reality) are cognizant of their peculiar positioning and of their "neither fish nor fowl" status. Many evidence a certain embarrassment over their very anomalous situation, which often results in crude and adolescent attempts at proving themselves in this or that way to be "regular fellows." The L.T. family (man and wife) never ceased to assure me of their happiness and the perfectly "normal" life led by their son, who at the age of 11 and upon his parents' conversion shifted from a synagogue afternoon school to the Sunday school of a fundamentalist Baptist church. The lad himself seemed to take pains to tell me how much he loved baseball and all sports and how well adjusted he was to his new Sunday school.

But these attempts at "normalization" are as yet sporadic, at best affecting only surface phenomena. When pressed even in the slightest, the individual Messenger or Hebrew Christian will readily accept the burden of his anomalous position, bearing it proudly as the enigmatic will of an inscrutable but loving God, who has chosen him to shoulder this particular cross. The factor of marginality becomes intolerable only when seen in terms of the isolated individual or group that can provide no explanation or *raison d'être* for the difficult status. But when a group can form and an ideology can emerge to buttress and explain this marginality, it becomes transformed into a source of strength and the basis for an evolving order.

Stonequist's definition of the marginal man speaks very directly to the situation of the Hebrew Christian in a number of important respects. He states:

> The marginal man is the individual who lives in, or has ties of kinship with, two or more interacting societies between which there exists sufficient incompatibilities to render his own adjustment to them difficult or impossible. He does not quite "belong" or feel at home in either group. This feeling of homelessness or of estrangement does not arise in the same way or for the same reasons in all individuals, nor is it identical in all situations. For many it is a matter of incomplete cultural assimilation in one or both societies, for others it arises less because of lack of cultural assimilation than from failure to gain social acceptance, and in some cases it originates less because of obvious external barriers than because of persistent inhibitions and loyalties.[60]

The marginality of the Hebrew Christian can be explained

by all three of the factors Stonequist suggests, and often all three are operative in one individual. The Hebrew Christian, coming as often as not from a "sketchy" Jewish environment, finds himself imperfectly assimilated in the Jewish milieu and culture and alien to that of the Gentile—a stranger in both worlds. Often those who would feel it possible to bridge the cutural gap, moving away from Judaism to Christianity, are stymied less by "failure to gain social acceptance" than by the *fear* that they will fail and, as a result, they withdraw from the effort. Finally, there is the reluctance to move firmly into the Christian fold because of "persistent inhibitions and loyalties"—probably the most significant underlying cause of marginality in the Hebrew Christian, thus of his very exist- ence. Glick has asserted that the HCCC arose for two reasons: namely, the inability of the group members to break away (completely) from the Jewish group, and the antagonism dis- played toward the Jewish convert in the gentile church.[61]

I maintain that he is in error regarding the latter point but entirely correct about the former. Few among the Messengers or other Hebrew Christians intensively questioned could allude to any specific instance of "rejection" in the gentile church, although most claimed that "it was there." But almost all Hebrew Christians were intensely concerned with the problem of "disloyalty," and this produced overwhelming inhibitions about "joining" a gentile church. Here lies the basic cause as well as the basic dilemma of Hebrew Christianity.

What is a person to do who is a Jew only in name and who in fact is a Christian but cannot fully accept the sociological implications of this truth? How is this evident dilemma to be resolved and the marginality dissipated, or at least made mean- ingfully necessary for the individual believer? The choices that present themselves are relatively simple and straightfor- ward. Either the individual will resolve this marginality by making the necessary movement forward (or backward) or he will stabilize and institutionalize his marginal standing.

Hebrew Christianity is in large measure an affirmation of the latter choice. Although the reasons for the emergence of the movement and its individual units such as the Messengers and the HCCC are manifold and not easily reducible to separate components, there can be little doubt that the buttressing of a common marginality is an outstandingly important factor.

Glick, in an otherwise splendid study, makes the error of seeking the elegance of simplicity where simplicity does not exist. Satisfied to view Hebrew Christianity as a vehicle for the complete assimilation of the Jew who is desirous of it, he does not grapple with the problem of why Hebrew Christianity is the channel. Is this really a defensible choice for people desiring a stepping stone to complete assimilation and amalgamation? What of the thousands of American Jews who have moved into the dominant cultural mainstream without passing through the "intermediate" stage of Hebrew Christianity? There is little doubting the relevancy of E. C. Hughes's contention that one way of reducing marginality

> . . . is the elaboration of the social system to include a marginal group as an additional category of persons with their own identity and defined position. A number of people of similar marginal position may seek one another's company and collectively strive to get a place for themselves. . . . These marginal groups . . . consist each [sic] of people who are marginal in the same way, and who consciously seek to fortify a common marginal position.[62]

But this position takes no cognizance of a veritable ideology of marginality, in that it views marginality as part of a cyclic phenomenon pointed irrevocably in the direction of a normative structure. Although the Hebrew Christian is indeed a marginal man for all the reasons elucidated by Stonequist, and the formation of a group does provide a measure of acceptability and a buttress for this rather anomalous position, ideological factors exist that act not to absorb or alleviate this marginality but rather to consciously fortify it. If the group were to complete the "cycle" from marginality to integration (and this integration could occur only within Christendom), a prime methodological goal of the movement—that of providing a specifically *Jewish* witness—would be canceled out. This is not to deny that a strong ambivalence is present, wherein the group members seek this integration and yet hold back; such ambivalence does exist and is of the utmost importance in terms of the future of Hebrew Christianity. Nor do I suggest that there is equal acceptance or understanding of this ideological matrix among the rank and file on the one hand or the leadership on the other. But its very existence as a question is of central importance.

Hebrew Christianity has attempted to institutionalize and perpetuate a status of marginality for purposes of satisfying larger goals, while resolving its endemic *individual* trials through a community of interests. Still, however, the ultimate measure of a movement lies in the people who comprise it, and their needs and aspirations will in the long run determine any course to be followed. There can be little doubt that needs of the individual group members may be colored and influenced by ideology, but, their source is elsewhere.

NOTES

1. One of the two assistants is employed full time as a clothing salesman.

2. The program, "Israel's Heritage," is heard on Monday evening on station WAWZ (1380). It is advertised as "a program dedicated to better understanding" featuring "inspiring messages from the Hebrew scriptures, important interviews with Messianic Jewish believers, and interesting discussions on vital Jewish issues." (From a promotional card published and distributed by the Messengers of the New Covenant Incorporated.)

3. Hereafter I will occasionally refer to an individual as a Messenger to indicate formal affiliation with the group known as the Messengers of the New Covenant.

4. From the Constitution of The Messengers of the New Covenant Incorporated.

5. The use of the term "covert" should not be construed in a pejorative sense. It simply indicates primary goals that remain relatively unenunciated, thus linger below the surface.

6. Ira O. Glick, "The Study of a Marginal Religious Group" (Master's thesis, University of Chicago, 1951.).

7. *Grace to Israel*, published by The Messengers of the New Covenant Incorporated, Newark, N.J. (Autumn 1958), p. 7.

8. Field notes.

9. Field notes, Rev. Finestone.

10. Outlined in a letter to me from Mrs. Finestone (October 26, 1959). The material was a summation of Rev. Finestone's oft-repeated approach to the Bible as a revelation that did not begin nor cease with the story of empirical Israel.

11. This was how one Hebrew Christian supporter who is a Gentile described himself to me (a Gentile by birth, but a Jew by adoption and naturalization).

12. In conversation with V.H. it was determined that his wife had planned to leave him *before* his conversion.

13. W. T. Gidney, *Missions to Jews: A Handbook* (London: London Society for Promoting Christianity Amongst the Jews, 1899), p.80.

14. Isaac Levy Finestone, *The Abrahamic Hope*, tract (Newark, N.J.: The Messengers of the New Covenant, n.d.), p. 28.

15. T. B. Kilpatrick, quoted in "Can St. Paul be Understood?" *Hebrew Alliance Quarterly*, Vol. 1, No. 1 (January 1917), 32.

16. Ivy Finestone's letter (see note 10).

17. The Messengers are in favor of utilizing these as long as it is recognized that they are customs but not binding. At the Messenger headquarters there was a Chanukah menorah (seven-branched candelabrum) prominently displayed in the sitting room. On one occasion I asked one of the assistant missionaries why it was there. He said that it was there because it was a Jewish folk element that could have meaning for the Jewish believer, that there was nothing in his Christian faith which precluded its use. The same attitude is maintained among the young Jesus believers in Jerusalem.

18. "And the modern Israelite is not unlike his brethren whom we meet in the pages of Scripture." Jacob Peltz, "The Christian Approach to the Jew," *Hebrew Christian Alliance Quarterly*, Vol. 15, No. 4 (October and December 1930).

19. Isaac Levy Finestone, *Reaching the Jewish Nation for Christ*, tract, (Newark, N.J.: The Messengers of the New Convenant, n.d.), p. 7.

20. *Ibid.*, p. 6.

21. Testimony of George Rich, radio station WHBI, August 26, 1951.

22. Talcott Parsons, "Some Sociological Aspects of the Fascist Movements," in *Essays in Sociological Theory* (New York: Free Press, 1954), p. 139.

23. "I believe that many distressed and thoughtful Jews would reach out to embrace the blessed comfort of Christianity if it were not that they are directed in opposite paths by leading Jewish writers to whom they give a respectful and trusting ear." A. J. Kligerman and Morris Marsh, "When Jewish Leaders Face Christ," *Hebrew Christian Alliance Quarterly*, Vol. 29, No. 1 (Spring 1944), 9.
   Or referring to Jewish leaders' attitudes to Jesus as being negative, it is noted: "It's as disgraceful as it was in the days of the Lord's Ministry in Jerusalem. Now, as then, the ordinary searching and thinking Jew might come to the banner of Christ if the intellectually unscrupulous leadership did not seek to stamp Him out." *Ibid.*, p. 10.

24. "The Jews are victims of this two thousand year old fraud; they believed, as I also believed every basic falsehood fabricated by the merciless enemies of Jesus [the Rabbis] merely to conceal their own terrible mistake." Ladislaw A. Gross, "The Fatal Error of Israel," *Hebrew Christian Alliance Quarterly*, Vol. 21, No. 4 (Winter 1937).

25. In trying rhetorically to figure out the reason for the conversion to Catholicism of the Chief Rabbi of Rome in 1945, the editor asks what was behind it. "Was it honor that this rabbi looked for? As Chief Rabbi of Rome, he had all the honor that usually goes to one in so exalted a position. Nonsense! Was it money that beckoned him? No. It is well known among all that Jewish Rabbis of the type of Rabbi Zolli are well paid." "Across the Desk," by the editor, *ibid.*, Vol. 31, No. 2 (Summer 1945), 17. It should be noted that the question was posed at a time when the $30,000 to $50,000 range was totally unrealistic.

26. *The Rabbi Told Me So,* tract (New York: American Board of Missions to the Jews, Inc.).

27. Joel Levy, "Modern Jewish Leadership and Hebrew Christianity," *Hebrew Christian Alliance Quarterly*, Vol. 4, Nos. 3 and 4 (October 1920), 108.

28. "Their [the Rabbis'] organized attack on the Aedus Community Center was made through special articles in the Jewish Press, extensive correspondence and mass meetings in the synagogues. The local communist organization sent a group of ruffians to one of the open Forum meetings of Aedus Community Center with the express purpose of terrorizing the missionaries out of the place." *Ibid.*, p. 105.

29. "It is . . . rumored that even among Reform Rabbis there are not a few who enjoy a fair knowledge of Hebrew. . . ." *Ibid.*, p. 108.

30. A conversation on Jewish leaders between Hebrew Christians Marsh and Kligerman yields the following exchange. After noting that there were always Jews who accepted Christ, Marsh asks: "But hold now, Mr. Kligerman—it is intriguingly interesting to know what happened to these do-and-dare Jews, who accepted Christ in those days. Did they get the reception from their bigoted and prejudiced fellow Jews that Paul got in olden times?" Kligerman: "Yes, listen to this for an idea of the reception they got. They were beaten, they were scorned, abused, ostracized, offended, impoverished and even railroaded into insane asylums—all because they dared to accept God's promises concerning the Messiah. . . ." Kligerman and Marsh, *op. cit.*, p. 12. Going farther along this line than any of his colleagues, Gartenhaus, writing of a rabbi who tried to institute an adult education class for the study of the Gospel, claims: "Had such words been written half a century ago, the writer would have been ostracized by Jewish leaders, he might even have suffered physical torture at the hand of a mob." Jacob Gartenhaus, *What of the Jews* (Atlanta, Ga.: Home Mission Board, Southern Baptist Convention, 1948), p. 105.

31. It is impossible to determine the impact of the group because of the general scattering effect that gobbles up the majority of converts. Rev. Finestone claims that he is responsible for an average of three conversions a year but that many more are consummated elsewhere although begun through his efforts.

32. The 10-year figure is an estimate based on knowledge that some of the group have not attended school beyond the first eight grades.

33. *Changing Pattern of Jewish Life on the Campus* (Washington, D.C.: B'nai B'rith Hillel Foundation, 1961), p. 12. However, the universe provided by the Messengers is heavily biased in terms of the prevalence of older people in the group, whereas the Fishman study utilized a balanced sample.

34. At that time the children were engaged in a project of wall plaque making, constructing signs reading "God is Love" and/or "Jesus Loves Me."

35. Solomon Liptzin, *Germany's Stepchildren* (New York: Meridian Books, 1961), p. 45.

36. H. Steiner, "My First Communion," *When Jews Face Christ*, Henry Einspruch, ed. (Baltimore, Md.: The Mediator, 1932), p. 20.

37. See George Benedict, *Christ Finds A Rabbi: An Autobiography* (Philadelphia: privately printed, 1932).

38. Elinor Stafford Millar, "The Love that did not Fail," in Einspruch, *op. cit.*, p. 28.

39. Glick, *op. cit.*, p. 149.

40. Benedict, *op. cit.*, p. 39.

41. Elias Newman, "The Curse of Anti-Semitism or What Shall We Do with the Jews," *Hebrew Christian Alliance Quarterly*, Vol. 33, No. 1 (Spring 1947). It is true that Zionists reacted to the ghetto in much the same terms as did the Hebrew Christians, yet there exists a vast qualitative difference. The former sought to effectuate organic change, whereas the latter sought a reconciliation with the reputed cause of that which it thoroughly abhorred.

42. See Nathan W. Ackerman and Marie Jahoda, *Anti-Semitism and Emotional Disorder: A Psychoanalytic Interpretation* (New York: Harper & Row, 1950), p. 78.

43. Nathan Birnbaum, "Land and Faith," *Hebrew Christian Alliance Quarterly*, Vol. 2, No. 3 (July 1918), 123.

44. Arnold Frank, *What About The Jews?* (Belfast: Graham and Heslip Ltd., 1944), p. 87.

45. George Benedict in his relationship with his schoolteacher and Selig Cassel and others show a similar pattern of seeking Gentile approval and being overcome with gratitude when it appears. "The headmaster asked the boys to learn the Christmas story. Selig knew it best, and recited so faultlessly and with such feeling, that the teacher was so delighted that he kissed him. Dr. Cassel—when an elderly man—said that he still felt that kiss. It made a deep impression on him that a Christian should kiss a Jewish boy." Frank, *ibid.*, p. 30. Another example of gratitude and amazement (this time, however, to God) is to be seen in the final segment of a fantastic poem by Benedict, called "God's Salesmen," in which he shouts

    He picked me out, He picked me out
       And made me join "His crew,"
    I'm salesman for the living God
       And here, friend, to sell you.

    George Benedict, quoted by David M. Eichhorn, "A History of Christian Attempts to Convert the Jews of the United States and Canada" (Ph.D. dissertation, Hebrew Union College, 1938), p. 427.

46. See Ackerman and Johoda, *op. cit.;* p. 64.

47. Ray B. West Jr., *Kingdom of the Saints* (New York: Viking Press, 1957), p. 108.

48. Dolores Press, "The Contemporary American Jew and the Christian Faith" (unpublished Master of Religious Education thesis, Princeton Theological Seminary, 1961), p. 83.

49. A convert on her death bed was visited by relatives and a rabbi trying to convince her to "come back." The rabbi asked her what made her give up her Jewish faith and she said: "When I needed a friend, the Gittells [missionaries] were my friends. They did more for me than my own people and they taught me about my Jewish

Messiah and my Saviour. . . ." Immanuel Gittell, "Happenings Among the Branches," *Hebrew Christian Alliance Quarterly,* Vol. 32, No. 2 (Summer 1946), 32. Or again, "I have been greatly impressed with the fact that Jews almost universally testify that the main factor which led them to acceptance of the Christian faith was the friendly interest of some sincere and warm-hearted Christian." Stuart Conning, "What We May Learn from Christian Jews," *ibid.,* Vol. 32, No. 3 (Fall 1946), 7.

50. Alfred Clair Underwood, *Conversion: Christian and Non-Christian* (New York: The Macmillan Co., 1925), p. 263.

51. C. Wendell King, *Social Movements in the United States* (New York: Random House, 1956), p. 21.

52. I accept here James's definition of the phenomenon: conversion is the process, ". . . gradual or sudden, by which a self hitherto divided and consciously wrong, inferior and unhappy, becomes unified and consciously right, superior and happy in consequence of its firmer hold upon religious realities." William James, *The Varieties of Religious Experience* (New York: The Modern Library, 1929), p. 186.

53. Underwood, *op. cit.,* p. 185, my emphasis.

54. Underwood, *op. cit.,* p. 133.

55. Glick, *op. cit.,* p. 44.

56. I observed this phenomenon first hand at the national convention of the Hebrew Christian Alliance of America, in Cincinnati, Ohio, in June 1961.

57. From the Constitution of the Messengers of the New Covenant, Inc.

58. Jessie Bernard, "Biculturality: A Study in Social Schizophrenia," *Jews in a Gentile World,* Isacque Graeber and Steuart Britt, eds. (New York: Macmillan Co., 1942), p. 265.

59. Quoted in Hugh J. Schonfield, *The History of Jewish Christianity: From the First to the Twentieth Century* (London: Duckworth, 1936), p. 247.

60. Everett V. Stonequist, "The Marginal Character of the Jews," in Graeber and Britt, *op. cit.,* p. 297. He defines marginal Jews as follows: "They . . . are divided in their social allegiance, drawn forward by the Gentile world but uncertain of its hospitality, restrained by sentiments of loyalty to the Jewish world but repelled by its restrictions. They are self-conscious and feel inferior because their social status is in question. They are the partly assimilated, the partly accepted, the real Wandering Jews, at home neither in the Ghetto nor in the world outside the Ghetto." *Ibid.,* p. 307.

61. See Glick, *op. cit.,* p. 205.

62. E. C. Hughes, "Social Change and Status Protest: An Essay on the Marginal Man," *Phylon,* Vol. 10, 62, quoted in Glick, *op. cit.,* p. 109.

Part Two

Historical Backdrop

3

Jews and Christian Evangelization

Hebrew Christianity, as expressed through such groups as the Messengers or the more current Jews for Jesus, can be fully understood only when viewed against the backdrop of the history of Christian efforts to evangelize the Jews. These efforts are not recent. Indeed, they parallel the advent of Christianity, when there began a process that was to prove of inestimable significance for the world at large and particularly for the groups within the pale of its message.

That is, the attempt to encompass all mankind under the wings of one true faith, subject to one empirical entity—the Church—and centered in a once-for-all *(einmalig)* revelation of God to men. Christianity was neither the first nor the last faith to claim to possess absolute truth or to seek to spread its weltanschauung as extensively as possible; but in its insistence on the centrality in history of the incarnation and on salvation through Jesus Christ alone, a new dimension of unparalleled significance was brought to bear on world events.

We know that the ancient world was benign in its theomachies, that a certain liberality or spirit of tolerance set the tone of religious differentiation, until first Judaism and then Christianity appeared to remove any semblance of levity, as it were, and to place religion on a level of the utmost "seriousness." Judaism, notwithstanding its stern visage, continuously temporized, accommodating itself to the various compromises and antitheses of the cultures and religions that surrounded it. If the Bible is accepted as an authoritative guide to the spiritual meanderings, the theological vulnerability of early Judaism, we have a picture of a Judaism exhibiting a good deal more of flexibility, syncretism, and confusion than various apologists have been willing to attribute to it. That Judaism was in its very nature intolerant of other Gods and other theologoumenons cannot be denied; but it remained for its daughter faith, Christianity, to place the capstone on this trend, claiming a religious absolutism and exhaustiveness previously unparalleled in the religious and cultural unfolding of history.

From the earliest days of the Church the new faith excoriated, condemned, and anathematized pagan idolatry and polytheism, heeding John, who cried "Guard yourselves from idols."[1] The Church pressed the fight against paganism unceasingly,[2] attacking it first in Europe,[3] and pressing on into the "pagan East," bearing the message with zeal and a commitment sunk in the very sinews of the faith by the missionary charge of Christ—"Go ye therefore and teach all nations, baptizing them in the name of the Father, and of the Son, and of the Holy Ghost" (Matthew 28:19). On this single passage with its key imperatives—go; teach; baptize—it is possible to trace the unique character of the Christian message and its radical severance from its Jewish roots. The word for conversion in the Old Testament is *T'shuva*, which means "return." The emphasis here is on an inner dynamic, a highly personalized reaction to an internal seed, which does not lend itself to external mining. Kaufman Kohler has noted that although Judaism is a missionary faith, seeking the conversion of the heathen, it is yet ". . . based upon the conception of an original revelation of God common to all men, wherefore heathen sinners are also expected to repent and turn to God."[4] The Jewish conception of mission was essentially an attempt to permeate existing heathen structures with the ethical and spiritual values embodied in the Jewish weltanschauung, rather than an attempt to incorporate the heathen within a formal Jewish framework. The Christian conception of mission early assumed a different approach, embodying an assimilative drive ensconced within an activist shell reaching out to encompass and to amalgamate those who were without the camp, making of them part of the one body, the one Church. Conversion in this context came to mean something quite different from the Judaic *T'shuva*, for "it was no longer a return to God in repentance, but the adoption of a new faith . . . ."[5] Goldman has dichotomized the differing approaches to mission in Christianity and Judaism, noting that Judaism "knows of and preaches a 'mission' only in an ideal sense, through the force of a convincing example of moral and ethical conduct,"[6] whereas Christianity "claims to have a mission and to be obligated to the carrying out of the mission by reason of its assertion that the Christian faith alone can bring salvation."[7]

Christianity is the archetypal missionary faith[8] claiming not only superiority (a claim maintained by almost all religions) but completeness, exhaustiveness, finality, and absoluteness.[9] Insofar as it functions on this basis, it cannot but seek to disseminate its truths among all men, in as militant a fashion as is deemed necessary.[10] And the Jews from the very outset of the relationship between the two faiths have been pursued with a sometimes fluctuating but always persistent zeal. Not only have Jews been included in the evangelical spectrum (as all others were), but because of the peculiar relationship between the mother and daughter faiths, the feeling early arose that Christianity was *particularly* superior to Judaism—a faith it succeeded in the scheme of things. Because Judaism was viewed as the seedling from which the Church sprang, it seemed logical to conclude that the tree superseded the seed in every respect. A theological framework was supplied further to enhance this view, in which Judaism was a mere way station on the route to Christianity. As sophisticated a thinker as Sabatier could state with equanimity and in perfect orthodoxy:

> Between the religion of the prophets and the religion of Jesus . . . there is one more barrier to be broken down. In the "kingdom of God" the idea of the nation must give place to the idea of humanity. The universal God must be represented as the immanent God, as present in every human soul. His seat and temple could not be in Jerusalem or Palestine; it could only be in pure and humble hearts. The Hebrew nation must perish in order to free the human conscience from its Jewish yoke.[11]

The developments leading from Judaism to Christianity are viewed as a natural phenomenon within a progression of history from lower stages to higher stages, with the dynamic finally being disposed of in the ultimate revelation of God to man in Christ. The task set before Judaism was that of precursor to Christianity and it was believed that "After giving birth to the Gospel, Judaism dries up and withers like a tree that has borne its fruit, and whose season is past."[12]

But by some curious fillip of history, the Jews have persisted, not only as the remnant foretold in scripture but as a competitive entity, displaying varying degrees of vigor and assertiveness. Christianity has in every epoch needed to reaffirm its evangelical commitment generally and to the Jews specifically, noting that Judaism was only a first step but by no means a sufficient vehicle for individual salvation. It has been proposed that Judaism represents an inferior ethical development, lacking universal dimensions and universal applicability.[13]

But although various claims to the superiority of Christian ethics are made, the Christian approach to the Jew rests on two pillars—one theological, the other sociological.

On a theological level, the Christian approach to the Jews is developed in pellucid form, leaving little room for confusion. I believe it has been best stated by Hendrik Kraemer: "The core of the Christian revelation is that Jesus Christ is the sole legitimate Lord of all human lives and that the failure to recognize this is the deepest religious error of mankind."[14] Given this as a starting point, it becomes possible, indeed necessary, to include the Jews as objects of the missionary imperative. If anything, Paul's charge "To the Jews first" indicates a particular emphasis on the evangelization of the Jews. But even if this plea had not appeared in the New Testament, there would be no doubt left by Kraemer's stricture (and I believe his is consistent with the normative view)[15] that "all men" as individuals, rather than as representatives of this or that persuasion or people, are guilty of Sin and need the salvation attainable only in and through Jesus Christ. Thus the duty of the Christian toward the Jew is inescapable: the Jew is a sinner, as all men are sinners, and the Christian must understand with Jocz that

> The Church of Christ has been entrusted with a very definite task, to preach the Gospel. This task is not something supplementary or additional to the life of the Church, but the essence of its very existence, the *raison d'être* of the Church itself.[16]

Christianity, as noted previously, is essentially both a proselytizing faith and an imperialistic faith.[17] The possibility of the existence of other paths to and other truths concerning God cannot be recognized.[18] Leo Baeck has characterized Christianity as a Romantic religion, ever eager to incorporate all things within itself. He notes:

> . . . syncretism, the desire to fuse everything is characteristic of romanticism. Romanticism wants to mean all things and hence seeks to blend all the areas of human and super-human existence, to pull them together into a universal circle, a universal state, a universal art, a universal faith. . . .[19]

Seen in this light Judaism is a narrow, parochial, and highly particularistic phenomenon that cannot claim an extensive world view, let alone applicability in the face of the Christian revelation, which has incalculably broadened and thus superseded it. It has been said that Judaism has no serious claim on the souls of men, that it is a rivulet proceeding alongside the mainstream of events,[20] and as such, a disturbing anomaly. Not only has this view predominated in formulating the Christian approach to the evangelization of the Jew—the approach being essentially an attempt to fulfill Scripture vis à vis the Jew and to incorporate a lifeless entity into a universal mold—but it has (as one might suspect) communicated itself in every age as a singular alternative to the marginal existence of members of a despised minority. Conversion to Christianity has always afforded the individual Jew the possibility of affiliation with the dominant culture, and this factor has probably been a more effective instrument of missionary policy and appeal than any other. Once Christianity had assumed its central political dominance in Western civilization, and as a normative pattern began to evolve, it clearly became impossible to participate from the periphery of Christian culture. Thus the syncretistic romanticism alluded to by Baeck appeared at every turn, demanding either total absorption or an alternative in pariah status. Through the centuries there has been a continuous stream of conversions from Judaism to Christianity—some no doubt based on undiluted religious conviction; but great numbers were in large part attributable to a desire to assimilate with a majority culture that demanded assimilation as the price of full participation.[21] In a truly pluralistic society, it would have been possible to maintain full contact with the dominant culture and yet be part of a religious periphery. But Western civilization has been inextricably interwoven with Christianity, and in view of the nature of the Christian reality and the unique relationship between Judaism and Christianity, full participation against a matrix of religious marginality was impossible. The road to Damascus—conversion— was the one open road to assimilation with and participation in the dominant culture. In the fifteen centuries of Christian hegemony in the Western world, this path has been traveled by large numbers of the children of Israel. Western culture has been diffused and out-groups have been acculturated by way of the rite of baptism, and the Jews have displayed a lively enthusiasm for the ends if not always the means.[22] Most scholars have accepted the importance of the superior weltanschauung of Christianity (at least in terms of scope and breadth) as an underlying cause for conversion. Whatever its theological or spiritual satisfactions, Christianity always promised, in addition, assimilation to a broader cultural stream. As Kohler rather forlornly notes:

> To Jews ambitious to obtain worldly success, the temptation came in many forms to remove the barrier of creed by a few drops from the baptismal font, willingly bestowed by the ruling Church; and many a descendant of Abraham, eager to eat of the fruit from the tree of modern knowledge forbidden to him in the ghetto, was perplexed by the question whether he might not don the garb of Christianity in order to participate in its culture.[23]

BRIEF HISTORY OF CHRISTIAN EFFORTS TO EVANGELIZE THE JEWS

We have noted that the Christian approach to the Jew has been interwoven with two aspects of reality: the theological, wherein Christ is a gift and a necessity for *all* men (not least of whom are the Jews, who also play a peculiar eschatological role within Christianity); and the sociological, wherein as the condition of full participation in the dominant Christian culture, the Jew underwent a process of acculturation that presupposed his conversion. From the Church's victory with the conversion of Constantine in the fourth century, the history of Christian efforts to convert the Jews has been marked and

shaped by the tension between these two elements, with appropriate shifts in emphasis from one to the other in different
epochs and within diverse sociopolitical contexts. With few
extraordinary periods excepted,[24] the one factor that has remained constant is the belief in the necessity for including the
Jew as an object of the evangelical commitment of the Church.
At times the approach has involved proselytizing individual
Jews, sometimes evangelization of the whole group, and at still
other times a combination of the two approaches has prevailed.
Success or failure, too, has characteristically varied in diverse
circumstances. Statistics in this area are unreliable,[25] but it
cannot be doubted that conversions to Christianity have occurred in every age and in every environment within Christendom. Thus it appears that there has never been a time during
which the Jew has not been approached by missionaries or a
time when the movement away from Judaism and toward
Christianity was totally dormant. Indeed, Gidney divides the
evangelization of the Jews into six epochs or periods as follows: (1) from the advent to Pentecost, (2) the Apostolic Age,
A.D. 30–70, (3) the sub-Apostolic Age, A.D. 70–500, (4) sixth
century to the Reformation, (5) the era of the Reformation,
the sixteenth century (6) the seventeenth and eighteenth centuries.[26] One must of course add to this scheme the nineteenth
and twentieth centuries, which can be viewed together in terms
of methodological considerations, but not in terms of a socio-
historical matrix.[27] The first period is perhaps mere theological elegance, for Christ's coming did not in a sociological sense
immediately resolve itself into an active mission to the Jews in
any way comparable to later events of the genre. I believe, however, that the second period did mark the beginning of this
work, where at Pentecost 3120 Jewish souls were added to the
Church (according to the New Testament account). It has been
fairly widely assumed that until the efforts of St. Paul began
to bear fruit, the "Church" was about as "purely" Jewish as
the synagogue. Parkes, for instance, puts the breach between
Christianity and the synagogue between A.D. 80 and 90, when

the first Gospel is reputed to have been written, including the words "His blood be upon us and on our children!"[28]

The sub-Apostolic age (A.D. 70–500) was primarily marked by individual attempts to win the Jew, such as those of Justin Martyr, Origen, and Tertullian, as well as Hippolytus, Cyprian of Carthage, Eusebius, Gregory of Nyssa, Chrysostom, and others. These efforts were weak, essentially dialogical and disputive, and apparently resulted in little fruitage for the Church. During this period (or at least a substantial portion of it) the Jews could and did offer a spirited counteroffensive, winning in the process not a few converts from the dominant faith, and there is strong evidence to suggest that the Jews did not hesitate to take advantage of the relative weakness of the infant Church.

From the sixth century to the Reformation, Gidney, Thompson, Schonfield, and most Protestant sources for the period, see only black—the Roman Church and "her hate for Israel." Thompson notes:

> This decline in efforts to reach the Jews began soon after Apostolic times, when the Gentile branches, which had been grafted into Israel, "God's" olive tree, and made partakers of its root and fatness began to boast themselves against the natural branches. It culminated in the unholy wedlock of Church and State under the Roman emperor, Constantine. Henceforth, the apostate Church entirely ignored the Master's programme of missions and the luckless Jew became the special object of Christian hate and persecution.[29]

Thompson categorically disposes of the next fourteen centuries as a time of bitter persecution and neglect of the Jews. This despairing picture notwithstanding, both Thompson and Gidney recognize the efforts of individual Christians, who apparently transcended the fetters of "apostasy," such that "here and there the true light of love burned in a Christian breast."[30] Both men acknowledge Jewish converts who did not "forget their brethren, such as Nicholas of Paris, Paulus Christianus,

and Pedro Alfonsi,[31] as well as Gentiles, such as Paul of Burgos
and Raymond of Pennaforte (thirteenth century), who
founded a college in Murcia staffed by Dominican monks who
were trained for mission work among the Jews.[32] In the four-
teenth century a convert, Nicholas de Lyra, wrote "The Messiah and His Advent," a tract that sought to establish Christianity as the logical outgrowth of Judaism, beseeching his
former coreligionists to accept the logic and inexorability of
Scripture and to embrace Christianity.[33] Many converts followed this lead, and tracts on the truth of Christianity and
the falsehood of Judaism came to be expected from the pens
of numerous learned and semilearned converts. As noted
previously, these individual efforts were generally unsuccessful;
certainly they failed in terms of mass conversions where coercion played no role. However, Gidney has characterized these
efforts as essentially negative in that they were often accompanied by repressive and coercive measures through which entire communities were forced to the baptismal font.

The era of the Reformation is viewed by all Protestant
apologists as a period of phenomenal promise tempered and
obstructed by "carryover" from the era of "Romanist Apostasy." The Reformation witnessed a constant see-saw struggle
wherein seemingly each positive step toward the evangelization
of the Jews was countered and nullified by a negative factor.
In a positive vein there was John Reuchlin, who sought the
conversion of the Jews through love and understanding, yet at
all turns he had to contend with a Johann Pfefferkorn who was
consumed with a hatred for Jews, for which there is scant
parallel. More significantly, this period was that of the two
Luthers—the one who wanted to convert the Jews in a manner as enlightened as that which has since been propounded,
and the other who after failing to convert them became
extraordinarily venomous in his hatred of Jews.[34] As Thompson has put it, "The Reformation was the dawning of a brighter
day for the dispersed among the Gentiles, but a dawning dark-

ened with the lingering clouds of night."[35] Thompson says that the Reformation, with its renewed emphasis on the Bible and prophecy, led to a renewed interest in the "Elect Race." It appears that Holland and Germany were areas of particular interest in this direction, and in 1676 the synods of Delft, Leyden, and Dordrecht considered various methods for evangelizing the Jews of the Netherlands.[36] In Germany there was the work of the enigmatic Esdras Edzard, who founded a one-man mission to the Jews. Although Edzard worked in the seventeenth century, his methods and approach were curiously out of step with his period. He attempted to build a viable organizational structure with which to convert the Jews, and he wanted this organization to have relevance transcending his person. He sought to succor converts who were cut off from their roots in the Jewish community and not yet part of the Christian community, and to this end he willed a fund to be used by Jewish converts. A more comprehensive project following that of Edzard was the undertaking of the pietists, such as Philip Jakob Spener (1635–1705), August Hermann Franke (1663–1727), and their colleagues at the University of Halle.[37] In 1728 the "Callenberg Institutum Judaicum" for the training of Jewish missionaries was established in connection with the university, where tracts specifically aimed at the Jews were printed and from whence "many of them [students] went out on itinerant missions in Europe, Asia, and North Africa."[38]

But even with the modest beginnings of an institutional framework for approaching the Jew, the seventeenth and eighteenth centuries were primarily characterized by *individual* labors; there was very little of a sustained nature. I am inclined to agree with Schonfield that the most significant features of the Reformation and of the seventeenth and eighteenth centuries were not any notable *actual* successes among the Jews; rather, we should emphasize the rise of biblically centered Puritanism, with its apocalyptic expectations and the resulting resurgence of interest in the possibility of reaching the Jews via a "national" conversion.[39] It is here that we are able to distinguish a movement away from sporadic, unorganized attempts at reaching the Jews, as well as the disposal of the ambivalence that characterized the Catholic Churches' doctrinal and empirical approach to the Jewish problem. In its place we find a definite trend toward a self-sustaining structural means for including the Jews within the purview of Christianity.

Although modern missions to the Jews are generally agreed to be a development of the ninetenth century, they received their impetus from the Reformation. It was during the 1800s that the phrase "Jewish missions" came to be identified almost exclusively with evangelical (Protestant) Christianity, while Catholicism directed its organizational energies to the pagan world and only peripherally concerned itself with the conversion of the Jews. Gidney is quite right when he observes "Evangelical Christianity has in Jewish missions displayed far greater activity than the Roman and Greek Churches, and has, therefore made much greater impressions on the Jews. . . ."[40] The pattern for this overwhelming confluence of evangelical Christianity and the Jewish missionary enterprise is clear in the work of Martin Luther. The form of Luther's tract "That Jesus Christ was Born A Jew" has influenced both the scope and emphasis of these missions to the present day. Of particular importance was Luther's suggestion to use Jewish converts to help win over unconverted Jews. This stratagem, no doubt as old as organized human existence, has been very extensively and consistently utilized by the various Protestant groups working among the Jews.[41] Thus Schonfield wrote, "It had to wait for Jewish Christians to plead the cause of their brethren, before any real active work was started."[42] Men like Joseph Samuel C. F. Frey (1771–1837) and Ridly Herschell (1807–1864) spearheaded this effort in the early nineteenth century, and these men and others like them established the patterns that have with modifications dominated the scene to this day. (Both represented and extensively shaped an Anglo-American approach to the Jews, which is dealt with in greater detail below.) After 1800 the search for a viable institutional approach to the Jews shifted from continental Europe, especially Germany and Holland, to England and the United States, with associations like the London Society for Promoting Christianity Among the Jews, the American Society for Ameliorating the Conditions of the Jews, the Baptist Society for the Evangelization of the Jews, the American Society for Promoting Christianity Among the Jews,[43] and many others, assuming the center of the stage.

The modern period in the evangelization of the Jews was marked not only by changes in the geographical or even doctrinal base of the enterprise but by a complex interweaving of numerous other factors as well. The enlightenment, the rise of industrial capitalism, the emergence of modern nationalism—all ineluctably influenced the changing destinies of the Jews, and Western society in general. Here, more perhaps than in any previous era, did the siren call of assimilation beckon with the promise of success would that the religious barrier disappear:

> The tidal wave of cosmopolitan enlightenment achieved for the Church more than all her conversionists could. Captivated by the liberal thought of the age which beheld in creeds the work of priestcraft and superstition, the upper classes of Jew gradually broke away from their ancestral religion, which appeared to them as a shackle and a misfortune, and felt no scruple in taking a step which was the only means of freeing the Jew in the eyes of the Christian world from the yoke and the shame of centuries.[44]

Although the path to full assimilation had always been a factor in Judeo-Christian relationships in the Western World, never was its appeal so pervasive or its promises more bountiful than during the early decades of the modern era. In an age when religion as a creative matrix was in eclipse, it is ironic to note its increased efficacy as a vehicle of identification with a developing secular culture. The Jew was required to divest himself of his "Jewishness" via conversion, before being allowed access to the wider horizons attainable at the other end of the spectrum.

But again, conversion was always an individual rather than a group response. Jews availing themselves of the opportunities of Western culture by means of religious conversion did so in response to a call stemming not from the missionaries or the priests but from the votaries of secular culture. The missionaries, however, were not long in realizing the possibilities inherent in this tack, and during the latter part of the nineteenth century myriad Protestant missions to the Jews were launched—most under the auspices of American and English denominations. All the missions attempted to show the Jew not only otherworldly salvation but also a "this world" way— which led inexorably through a dominant Christian society.

THE ANGLO–AMERICAN EMPHASIS AND APPROACH TO THE JEWS

The Anglo-American approach to evangelization generally and to proselytizing the Jew in particular is marked by pervasiveness, tenacity, and zeal. In many other Protestant churches the evangelical demand was met by scriptural exegesis, metaphysical hair-splitting, temporizing, and relatively little actual accomplishment. The English and the Americans, however, most actively took up the standard of Christianity and bore it to all the corners of the earth. From China to India, Arabia to Afghanistan, North Africa to South America, devout men and women undertook the apostolic task of bringing the Gospel to all men; and notwithstanding rumblings to the contrary,[45] the Jews were by no means forgotten.

A cursory glance at Thompson's work, *A Century of Jewish Missions*, yields a stimulating insight into the completeness and extensiveness of the Jewish dispersion, as well as the desire and ability of Christian missionaries to pursue the Jew everywhere. No community seemed too small, none too somnolent or insignificant to escape the evangelical zeal of the modern missionary movement. Thompson comments on missions (or missionary journeys) to the Barbary States, Tunis, Kai Fung Foo (China), Turkey, Greece, Palestine, Scandinavia, East and West Europe, the Americas, Yemen, Mesopotamia, and elsewhere. Not only in distance but in terms of money, time, and effort, the responsibility to go to the Jew first seems to have been neither denigrated nor forgotten.

At the close of the nineteenth century efforts at converting the Jews were so extensive that the world appeared to be cluttered with a variety of missionary undertakings among the Jews. There were, for instance, no less than 32 American missions, supporting 80 missionaries on 47 different stations[46] enjoying an income of $55,000; some 28 British missionary bodies supported as many as 481 missionaries on 120 stations, with an annual budget reaching the half million dollar mark. There were also 40 or so missionaries representing some 20 European societies. All in all it is estimated that the Jews were being pursued by no fewer than 90 societies—648 missionaries working out of 213 stations and spending $673,000 annually. In the same period more than a million New Testaments in the languages spoken by Jews were distributed,[47] as well as countless tracts, printed exhortations, news sheets, and so on. The Jews were by no means being neglected as objects of missionary concern or endeavor.

Not only were the Jews being approached at all times and in all places, but with the shift in political and—more important—economic power from the continent to England and then to the United States,[48] there occurred a corresponding shift in missionary responsibility to these two centers. A peculiarly

Anglo-American approach to the Jew emerged, which early
was distinguished by the same vigor, assertiveness, and icono-
clasm that marked both the British and the Americans as outstanding mercantile pathfinders and creators.

As early as the sixteenth century the foundations were laid
for a unique pattern that permitted the rise to preeminence of
the following rather comforting thinking: that God could be
served well and effectively via the cash box and the ledger
books. Thus countless merchant "missionaries" were stimulated
to express in commerce a zeal and dedication that heretofore
had been appropriate only within the Church. It was early
possible to see that in the pursuance of commercial ends,

> . . . most ministers and businessmen were sincerely convinced
> that they were carrying out a noble plan for the benefit of
> mankind. Nothing but good could come they believed from ef-
> forts to provide a means of self-help for the poor. Trading com-
> panies and colonial projects promised to relieve distress and
> bring honor to the nation, glory to the crown and the extension
> of God's kingdom. Incidental profits to shareholders . . . were
> proof of the divine blessing upon beneficent enterprises.[49]

In studying the history of the missionary enterprise of the
West, it is amazing to observe how early the similarities between commercial and religious evangelism were recognized
and commented on.

Barton, in defense of the religious missionary, notes that
zealous merchants proselytized the East during the nineteenth
century for kerosene, bicycles, wheat flour, clocks, and other
"necessary" commodities, and he rhetorically asks how much
more defensible are the efforts of those who came in a purely
altruistic vein to present the claims of Christ. He uses a "soft
sell" approach and terminology that would have been readily
comprehensible to any commercial "realist" of the time. After
listing (in a not unsympathetic manner) the methods and

products of the merchant missionaries, he avers that the Christian missionary has *only* the good of the people in mind.

> He [the missionary] may not always be wise in his methods, but he cannot be charged with having any selfish purpose in his efforts. His teaching are never forced upon the people. They are perfectly free to refuse to attend his hospitals and schools, or to accept or reject his religion. He repudiates the use of force to accomplish the ends sought. It is his purpose to create a discontent for the old order of things only in so far as that old order is detrimental to the intellectual and moral advancement of the people. He presents to them that which he knows will elevate and enlarge the individual as well as to make society better. It is his universal rule not to force himself or his teachings upon an unwilling people, but to leave in every instance the acceptance of his teachings to the good judgment of the people who hear, while they are always free to decline to listen to him at all. He never attempts to destroy ancient customs or beliefs, but he simply offers to the Oriental all that he regards as best in the religion of Christ, which has created the best, and safest, and most benevolent society on earth, and has power to adapt itself to the requirements of every race and people. If we condemn the Christian foreign missionary, we must also condemn a thousand fold more the merchant missionary.[50]

No great effort is required to delineate the startling similarities in thought and expression between the ideal conceptualization of the missionary sketched by Barton, and the salesman of a less sublime inventory.

The psychological bent of the businessman was appended to the zealous devotion of the religionist, and the combination brought rather interesting results in both camps. As might be expected in this climate, the Jews and their evangelization appeared as an unshirkable challenge to men geared to challenge and committed to the belief in the ratiocination of all phenomena. It was merely a question of time and above all of methods chosen before the Jews and indeed all men could recognize in the certitude of Christianity the logic and truth of an outstanding product.

This development is perhaps more understandable in the case of America, where there was no established church. In such an environment, marked by the proliferation and growth of multitudinous sectarian groups, it became necessary for each body to find its own financial support. Thus a rather overt commercialism emerged[51] that was ostensibly and primarily geared to survival but became, like all such endeavors, part and parcel of the total ethos of the groups involved.[52]

One of the emerging characteristics of this ethos was abhorrence of failure of any kind, whether on the level of sheer commercialism or in the realm of religious faith. It is striking to observe the constant reference to numbers—whether numbers saved or numbers yet unsaved—in most of the missionary literature in the Anglo-American context. The statistic provided by J. F. A. de le Roi that 204,500 Jews were converted in the nineteenth century is quoted again and again to indicate the possibilities inherent in Jewish work. A proportional breakdown of the world's religious population is repeatedly quoted to prove that at least proportionally the Jews represent one of the most profitable missionary fields.[53] And so on.

It would be false and far from the mark to conclude, however, that the Anglo-American missionary emphasis is interchangeable with, let us say, the selling of bicycles, in its intent as in its methodological superstructure. The effort to convert the Jew is first and foremost a response to a religious impetus, and this is why the missionary response to failure assumes significant proportions.

There are two aspects to this view of failure. On the one hand there is the failure of the Jew, who is perceived as having suffered through the ages from his myopic inability to see the right and the true, contenting himself with second best; moreover, even his second best—Judaism—is collapsing under the strain of emancipation and modern life. On the other hand, there is the failure that attaches to Christianity, which has yet to fulfill its promise of a world in Christ.

The notion of the supposed failure of the Jew has led to an interpretation and a view of Judaism that in a rather fanciful manner disposes of nearly 2000 years of religious creativity in the dispersion as being a stygian artifact bereft of expression and devoid of real meaning. There is constant reiteration of this failure (which is overwhelmingly an Anglo-American interpretation), leading to the missionary appeal to abandon not so much a vehicle devoid of truth but one incapable of functioning reliably.

> For the Jew to accept Jesus Christ means exchanging a religion of obedience to law, of balanced reward and punishment for life in the radiant sunshine of a Father's love. . . . The center of Jewish worship was destroyed with the Temple at Jerusalem; and lacking that visible center the Jew has never found fullest expression for his God-given capacity for worship.[54]

The Jew, it is said, has failed to satisfy his human need in Judaism because Judaism being a theological dead letter, could not possibly perform a living role.

But as if the failure of Judaism to "function" successfully were not a sufficient indictment, there is the widespread growth of secularism among the Jews. Countless missionaries have commented on the "unbelief" of the modern Jew. In the view of most missionaries, although the orthodox Jew errs in his continued rejection of the Son, he at least makes obeisance to the Father; the secularist, however, denies even this. In the Anglo-American missionary tradition this state of affairs has provoked mixed feelings, though in sum it has probably been interpreted more as a blessing than anything else. On the one hand secularism indicates a depth of depravity unsurpassed even by those who have rejected Christ but still maintain belief in God, but on the other hand it is assumed that the depths have been plumbed and the only way now open points upward. Thus the various missionary groups exult over what they conceive of as the death rattle of Judaism—secularization. In this ultimate of all failures—the failure of a religious faith to elicit even pro forma loyalty from its adherents—the missionary sees the promise of putting over a new "product" to fill a black void. Judaism, he is assured, has failed, and like all failures it must leave the stage to those with the will and the vigor to compete. The classical approach to the Jew sought to save him from sin; the modern way, epitomized in the Anglo-American business approach, seeks to rescue him from secularism. Thus it is possible to view the present situation of the Jew in a rather sanguine light, hoping that success can be built on the ruins of a failure that was inevitable. Hedenquist goes so far as to state that "the largest group of Jews . . . that the Church confronts today are just secularized Jews."[55] There is implicit here both a plea and a call: a plea for the salvation of myriads who are lost and without hope, and a call to tend the garden of the Lord under the most propitious of conditions.

Still another aspect to the abhorrence and rejection of failure is the failure of the Church to achieve wholeness. This is primarily a Protestant concern, certainly one that goes beyond the Anglo-American experience alone. Unsurprisingly the impelling though somewhat ambivalent drive toward ecumenicity that is evident in Protestantism has extended to the Jews, and although various continental thinkers (notably Karl Barth) have provided the theological scaffolding, the assimilation and activation of this perspective are quite widespread in the Anglo-American missionary movement. Taking heart from the contention of Barth that an ecumenical Church implies the presence of the Jews, Hedenquist claims "One would be denying Jesus Christ Himself if one tried to deny this unity of His Church."[56] Thus for Judaism there is the additional challenge in the demand for ecumenicity—a demand not only to right its own peculiar failure but to fulfill itself *and* Christianity by recognizing its true mission, which is to be rejoined to the whole tree. Not only Judaism, but Christianity too, can be said to have failed barring this reconciliation.

During the greater part of the seventeenth century, the failure of the Jew appeared in much the same light as the failures of individual Christians and groups of Christians. Those who were saved were saved because it was part of the divine plan, and those who failed did so in fulfilling the negative side of this supernatural desideratum. But by the eighteenth century, as Oscar Handlin has observed in the case of America:

> . . . a missionary spirit had dissolved the earlier exclusive sense of election that had formerly separated one element from another. The desire to bar outsiders gave way to an urge to assimilate them; and a variety of groups came to consider themselves in competition for new adherents.[57]

Handlin further noted that "the rivalry for the loyalty of new members was stimulated thereafter by the constant appearance of new religious sects, which conducted unremitting raids upon the unaffiliated or the loosely affiliated."[58] Thus the dominant stamp of the American religious experience was no longer one of exclusivity but of amalgamation and the assimilation of those who remained without. It early became evident that the Jews represented the "outsider" *par excellence*. The Anglo-American approach to the Jew was in large measure shaped by this interpretation of the "condition of the Jews" as the hated and despised outsiders who must be brought under the sheltering wing of the Church. This must be done (so goes the reasoning) for two reasons: (1) the Christian is not a Christian unless he is willing to share his rich faith with all men, and (2) anti-Semitism is hateful and a total distortion of Christianity. It was but a short hop and a skip from this position to the conclusion that neglecting to approach the Jew was an anti-Semitic act in itself. Numerous articles and tracts pouring from the Anglo-American missionary presses hammered at this theorem, and it has become one of the best known missionary dogmas, which has retained and even expanded its currency. Basil Mathews, for instance, wrote:

> If I am sure from my own experience (as I am) that Christ makes sense of a universe otherwise tragically meaningless, if He is the root from which springs the growth of the fullest and freest life of fellowship; if in Him I find God revealed more fully than in any other way; if in Him both the individual and the community can find fulfillment and peace as nowhere else, then it is a definite act of anti-Semitism to fail to present Him to the Jew in convincing word and life.[59]

The absence of a program to approach the Jew is seen by some theoreticians as the *root* of Christian antipathy to the Jews, as well as a manifestation of anti-Semitism. Kosmala and Smith have even proposed that "anti-Semitism *begins* (my emphasis) when we refuse to share the gospel of Jesus Christ with our Jewish neighbor."[60] The reasoning behind this assertion constitutes an amazing affirmation of the essential "salvageability" of the Jews. It has been noted that:

> The lowest valuation a professing Christian could place upon any people would be to declare them too far gone for even the grace of Christ to save. The Christian believes that the Gospel can save a hardened criminal, a confirmed drunkard or a diseased pervert. If a Christian then says that the Jews are beyond the reach of the Gospel and leaves them strictly alone the implications are sickening.[61]

This interpretation of the Jew in Christendom, which saw in him a victim of Christian hate or, even worse, of Christian lethargy, provided a prime methodological context for his evangelization. If it is a manifestation of un-Christian hate to neglect the Jew, then it is an affirmation of Christian love to approach him. If the Jew has remained outside the Church because of hate, it is obvious that love will bring him nigh.

Thus Thompson could assure his readers that "if we would bring him [the Jew] within the influence of the pulpit evangel we must let flow through the open door of the Church a stream of love [and] . . . Jews by the thousand would enlist under the banner of the Cross."[62]

There is a countervailing thrust, however, in this Anglo-American pattern that is not so susceptible to documentation but appears nevertheless as a rather significant factor. That is, although the assimilation drive is strong and the demand for total victory potent, an element of guilt remains attached to the entire missionary enterprise. No other group within Christendom that was committed to the missionary undertaking produced so much in the way of apologetics not only for the methods utilized but for the very task itself. In both England and the United States (primarily since the turn of the century) such apologia appeared in response not only to outside critics but to the missionaries themselves, who obviously have experienced much doubt about the validity and "rightness" of the missionary endeavor. There exists, it would appear, a considerable degree of reticence about pressing forward with missionizing the Jew, founded no doubt on the conflict between the liberal secular ethic of tolerance on the one hand and an unadorned interpretation of the gospel imperative on the other. The Anglo-American approach to evangelization must, after all, be viewed not as a reflex to a pristine and ethereal Christianity but as something "rooted" in the total sociocultural experience. The Anglo-American commitment to toleration of the "other" at all turns calls into question the evangelization, followed by the absorption and destruction of the "other." This conflict has led to a rather interesting development—a syncretistic liberalism that allows for the delusory belief that evangelization involves not a superimposition, an amalgamative device, but a parallel growth in which Christianity does not displace but fulfills and completes an otherwise unfulfilled, incomplete structure. The main feature of this syncretistic liberalism is the assumption that Christianity will add to a religious structure its most meaningful and essential element— Jesus Christ—while accepting value and worth in the basic structure itself. Is there, then, an approach to the non-Christian that does not stop at interreligious cooperation, yet does not involve an offensive religious imperialism? Dewick answers this question as follows:

> One such answer maintains that Christianity "comprehends" and "fulfills" all the partial truths that are to be found in other religions, while at the same time purging them from their errors and supplementing them with truths and values that they do not in themselves possess. In them we see "broken lights"; in Christianity the full radiance of God's glory.[63]

This is a far cry from the old pattern, founded on the contention that Christianity must sweep away the debris of lesser faiths. And I further maintain that this development was not simply a methodological device but rather a response to contradictions and beliefs deeply rooted in the secular, liberal culture of the nineteenth century. When Kraemer quotes Gandhi, saying that missions involve "invading the sacredness of personality,"[64] he alludes not only to the individual personality but to the group integrity as well, and this has struck a responsive chord within the Anglo-American missionary enterprise. If ambivalence based on this secular-religious dichotomy influences the general missionary scene (as I believe it does), the picture vis à vis the Jews is even more pronounced. For at every juncture the person who desires to respect difference and to tolerate the other is confronted by a group that is "without" in terms of Christ but seemingly "within" in every other regard —ethically, religiously, and culturally. Although it can be said that other proselytized peoples live at a lower stage of civilization and culture, the situation of the Jews invalidates this reason for "interference."[65] Thus we see constant reappraisal and ubiquitous doubt about the real meaning of the evangeli-

cal demand when applied to the "nonotherness" of the Jews.
H. Richard Niebuhr has given voice to this basic ambivalence,
noting

> . . . when we try to convert men, we are to a large extent simply
> asking them to leave certain neighbors and social practices in
> favor of others, for Christianity and Judaism are both highly
> syncretistic things and neither the Christian nor the Jewish
> community is evidently founded on religion.[66]

All the attempts made within the Anglo-American context to
bridge the chasm between an ethic of toleration and absolutist
religious faith have followed one of two courses. In the first
instance, we find the growth of religious relativism (or more
correctly, Christian relativism), which holds as central the confession of sin and the relative character of all human endeavor.[67]
This ultimately leads to a "nonapproach" in the missionary
context generally and especially to the Jews, who after all
share a vast religious tradition with Christianity. The second
alternative has been marked by a willingness (at least theoretically) to draw distinctions between the chaff and the wheat,
the essential and the nonessential, permitting an acceptable
religious structure to be maintained if only Christ can be
absorbed as Savior and Lord. This has been the trend in the
Anglo-American tradition—namely, the view that Christianity
comes to bring Christ, not to destroy or to shunt aside any
religious structure that will fulfill and complete itself via the
acceptance and centralization of Christ. The missionary tradition denies the relativist attitude, as it must, but in doing
so does not shake off the peculiarly Anglo-American accretions and emphasis. In sum, these can be delineated as a
business pragmatism that recognizes the exigencies of time-
boundedness, a corollary abhorrence of all kinds of failure,
and an almost naïve assumption that wholesale love is possible
and will in the end prove victorious. In addition, an overriding accommodative political principle characteristic of the

Anglo-American missionary effort, becomes translated on the level of religion into a syncretistic emphasis, cementing the whole effort into a unique departure from the classical missionary approach. The traditional approach was an inflexible demand for the capitulation and removal of the "other" from the stage of history. This new approach too, of course, demands ultimate capitulation (for what else does the concept of missionizing imply?), but I think that the difference is real and not without significance. The one understands—if it does not relish—diversity, and as a result maintains some form of commitment to pluralistic society, whereas the traditional view is based on a sullen disavowal and rejection of all that lies outside its scope.

METHODS

Thus far I have alluded to a few of the theoretical underpinnings of what I conceive to be a unique approach to missionizing within the Anglo-American context. Now the actual mechanics or translation of these emphases into concrete efforts requires some comment. The Anglo-American approach is above all an "activist" undertaking, not limited to theorizing, and seeking hard results rather than illumination. Formerly, unworkable approaches had led missionaries to bewail the inscrutability and spiritual poverty of the Jews themselves. Now, however, the mistakes of the past were to be recognized as such and were expected to lead to reappraisal and directive change in the missionary approach.

At the beginning of the nineteenth century various Protestant groups in England recognized the existence of a fatal error in what had been the Catholic and later the continental Protestant approach to the Jews. The latter made repeated crude attempts to hack away at the Jewish corporate superstructure, seeking the conversion of the "genus Jew" rather than the Jews as individual men and women. These efforts were never very successful and generally led to a predictable survivalistic counterreaction. Not until the nineteenth century, however, was it acknowledged that all the Jews in one solid phalanx were not prepared to recognize the truth of Christianity. This realization led to the emergence or reemergence of the Pauline tenet of the "remnant" who are ever in existence among the Jews, which in turn paved the way for an approach to the "individual" that happened to be most suitable to the spirit of the times and the peculiar ethos of those who were placed in the forefront of the evangelistic scheme. At no previous time and in no other sociocultural matrix would the following conception of the missionary role as an adjunct of Christian eschatology have been expressed:

> The hindrances to conversion that exist in the Jew himself though somewhat varied in the different sections of the race are the result of religious pride, deep seated prejudice and false ideas of Christianity engendered by the teachings of the Rabbis and the unChristian treatment to which he has been subjected. The resistive force of these may have been made apparent in some measure, in the preceding narrative. The one hindrance that needs special consideration here is "that the blindness *in part* has happened to Israel until the fulness of the Gentiles become in." The veil is drawn so closely over many faces that the light of the glory of God in the face of Jesus Christ cannot illuminate their way to salvation. This blindness is judicial, that is to say permitted by divine purpose on account of their rejection of Jesus. Yet there is "at this present time also a remnant according to the election of grace" who shall be saved if the Gospel is preached unto them. Until there shall come out of Zion the Deliverer, who shall turn away ungodliness from Jacob we need look for no greater results than the calling unto His name of this remnant. After His appearing "all Israel shall be saved."[68]

Here we see a unique departure from the classical mold. There is first of all recognition of differences among Jews, as well as the assumption of some responsibility by Christians for the "un-saved" condition of the former. Rather than making a blanket demand that the Jews declare for Christ or dissolve, the author chooses to cite the scriptural tenet of "blindness in part." Only the Gentiles, in fulfilling their role in history, can correct this blindness. Not only is the "blindness" *in part only*, but there is and has always been a "remnant according to the election of grace"; that is, there have always been individual Jews receptive to the Christian message, and these persons *can* be saved. As Eckardt has noted, "if throughout the whole of the present dispensation the process of God's hardening of Israel is only partial, 'so that there is ever a remnant . . . what an incentive this is to the work of evangelism among the Jews.' "[69] Indeed, this datum proved to be just that—a remark-able incentive to work among the Jews. Thus, armed and for-tified with the scriptural promise of at least modest success, the Anglo-American organizational genius could begin to function with the minimal assurance of "fair return."

The transition from the old to the new approach was grad-ual and unprecipitous. At the end of the eighteenth century the most favored approach was still the tried and true method of using a convert to flatter the Christian community for their good sense in being Christian and flay former coreligionists for their cupidity and stupidity in remaining within Judaism. The man who is credited with being "the first convert in America" seems to have been satisfied to make only one foray into the missionary morass before retiring, seldom to voice in public his thoughts concerning the Jews as a group. The individual was one Judah Morris[70] of Boston, who on the occasion of his baptism (circa 1730) delivered an address grandiosely entitled "The Truth, the Whole Truth, and Nothing But the Truth." When the speech was published as a tract, a fiery preface by Increase Mather was added.[71] One is struck by the thought that Mather, if not Morris, had hoped for manifold results from this rather modest effort.

A more significant occurrence in the Jewish mission field in America was the arrival in 1816 of one Joseph Samuel C. F. Frey, who in 1819 formed a Society for the Evangelization of the Jews.[72] Frey wanted to build an ongoing organizational structure that would not see the Jews as an undifferentiated mass to be either saved *in toto* or similarly damned. Here was the beginning in the United States of a method and an approach that despite repeated and sometimes extensive change and reformulation, established the basic pattern that is still utilized in the Christian evangel to the Jews.[73]

Thompson, who appears to be the most reliable source for the period, outlines the methods and agencies in Jewish mission work, and these seem to be consonant with the theoretical structure sketched earlier. Most of the methods originated in England and were widely applied in the United States. I believe that a general overview would serve best to impart a sense of the project.

The primary method in all extensive missionary work is *itineration*. This was Christ's own plan and the one on which He sent forth the Twelve and the Seventy.[74]

The logical outcome of itinerant missions is the establishment of *mission stations*. Interest is awakened, souls are saved and the necessity of a local mission is immediate. . . . When the station is firmly established it becomes a base of operations from which itinerant journeys can be undertaken and around which outposts can be planted.[75]

The equipment of a large station is quite elaborate. The staff usually consists of one or more missionaries either Gentiles or Jews, who must understand Hebrew and the languages spoken by the Jewish community; assistants who spend much time in house to house visitation; colporteurs; Bible women who work among the Jewesses; teachers for the schools; and physicians, dispensers and nurses. The departments of work embrace preaching in the chapel or Mission Halls; street preaching; house to house visitation; distribution of literature by colporteurs and in the Book Depot; itineration to surrounding places; educational work including Day, Boarding and Sunday Schools,

Sewing classes and Mothers' meetings; and medical work by
means of hospitals, dispensaries and other professional practice.[76]

Among the various agencies employed, the preaching of the
Gospel holds the foremost place. In some communities . . . the
street corner is most successful. The gifts of consecrated women-
hood are in requisition for the more private forms of testimony
as they alone can cross the barriers that so closely confine the
Jewish women.[77]

Hand in hand with preaching should go the distribution of
the written word. . . . Not less than a million copies of the
Word of Life have passed into Jewish hands in the past century.[78]

An American adaptation of the Bible Depot is the Bible
Shop Window Mission, in which the open Bible and other
literature is placed in the window in such a way as to attract
the attention of passersby . . . .[79]

Postal Missions are finding a field for seed sowing among the
better class Jews and have already yielded some very precious
fruitage. The plan is to mail to Jews who are not readily ac-
cessible in other ways, such letters, tracts or books as might lead
them to consider the claims of Christ.[80]

In sending forth missionaries the modern tendency is toward
the formation of a central Board or Society, who appoint, commission, direct and become the channel of support of the
laborers.[81]

Discernible here is a clear-cut departure from the hit-and-run
tactics of the past, which are to be supplanted by an extensive
organizational structure emphasizing the probability of *individual* successes via an individual approach. The whole Jewish
people are to be approached, but with these differences: there
is to be recognition of sociological realities (e.g., different
social, economic, and even cultural outlooks and standards
among distinct groups of Jews); the enterprise is to be run in a
businesslike fashion in the expectation of a "fair return"
though not necessarily a groundswell; and finally, missionaries
are to assume at least partial Christian guilt for the failure of
many Jews to recognize the claims of Christ.

But new strategies notwithstanding, the ways of thinking

and patterns of reactions of centuries were not to be transcended so quickly or so easily. It was certainly possible to
adhere to an organizational outline, but not so easy to "rethink" the Jew himself. Thompson, I think, recognized this
difficulty when he appended the following to the listed methods
in Jewish missions.

> If there be a need in the twentieth Century, it is not for new
> methods, but for missionaries filled with the Spirit and with
> power, who can meet innumerable and almost insurmountable
> difficulties with unwavering faith, undaunted courage, undi-
> minished zeal and unfailing love.[82]

This was understood not only by Thompson but also by others
involved in the Christian evangel; however, the result *was* the
evolution of "new methods" that proved to be highly significant and thoroughly unique. Although the distinction between proselytism and evangelism had been posited earlier, it
was only within the Anglo-American context that it came to
play a central theoretical role.[83] To the credit of the missionary movement, its leaders were sufficiently objective and flexible to recognize the difficulty in maintaining love for that
which you feel it necessary to destroy and supplant. It was seen
and understood that a choice had to be made; either the Jew
must be wrested from himself and entirely recast in the Christian communal-religious mold (in which case he is to be proselytized and by definition unloved so long as he refuses the
proferred solution to his manifold ills), or he is to be evangelized, adding or removing only the essentials and leaving the
basic structure intact. In short, evangelization is viewed as a
positive rapprochement, and proselytism is seen as a total rejection: the one leaving ample room for love, the other throwing
insurmountable obstacles in its path. In evangelization the Jew
is implored not to cease being what he is—a Jew—but to stay
and be transformed.

> In proselytism the aim is to detach a convert from the tradi-
> tions, associations, and concepts of the religion in which he was
> brought up in order that he may be numbered among the ad-
> herents of the new faith. The proselyter seeks to build up his
> own organization at the expense of the organization from which
> the proselyte comes. In evangelism the concern is not the gain
> of prestige that may come to any organization through the con-
> verts who may be secured, but the sharing with them of a divine
> life, a quickening and transforming experience of God's redemp-
> tive love in Jesus Christ.[84]

Thus the basic decision arrived at in the Anglo-American
approach was to evangelize rather than to proselytize the Jew.
However, it is questionable whether the decision ever became
fully operative as a working principle. It was and is a goal of
the more "liberal" elements within the missionary enterprise,
but notwithstanding appeals for understanding, love, and
respect for the integrity of Judaism, it has been somewhat dis-
appointing as a methodological premise.[85] Although still maintained, it is not functional. This is not to say, however, that it
is a meaningless ploy. It has influenced the efforts of the entire
missionary movement and has resulted in the substitution of
something *approximating* a dialogue between the two faiths
for what had previously been an undifferentiated attack. It has
led to awareness that the Jew, if he is to be won for Christ,
must be approached with a message couched in love or at least
respect, in place of the former negativism. It has stressed indi-
viduality rather than the previous myth of a "Jewish collectivity" responding always as an unbroken mass. It has paved the
way for use of persuasion, as opposed to the former reliance on
various methods of coercion.

The results of the new approach were manifested in an
organizational context in two basic developments. The first I
will identify as operative missions, or separate organizations,
with professional staffs who in lesser or greater degree follow
the plan outlined by Thompson. These in turn can be broken
down into four primary types.[86]

The first and oldest type is that of the independent nonde-nominational mission. These were characterized by the absence of controls or direction from established Church bodies; they were staffed by the equivalent of the commercial buccaneer, that is, by an independent and usually less than responsible religious entrepreneur who more often than not vanished when his shoe-string financial operation collapsed (generally a matter of two or three years). Financial support for these efforts was shaky at best, and funds were usually raised by making appeals to missionary societies and individuals attached to the various free churches. The theological or doctrinal basis for these missions was generally eclectic and overwhelmingly fundamentalist. If the leadership—missionaries, colporteurs, and so on—had formal theological training at all, more likely than not they had received it at a marginal institution and in an attenuated course of study.

The second type can be described as a strictly denominational effort; that is, the organization was tied doctrinally, organizationally, and financially to one Christian denomination. The staff was expected to meet minimal educational standards established by the larger body, to follow its general theological orientation, and in turn to expect the full financial support by the denomination of the missionary undertakings. Such missions were not separate bodies but intrinsic parts of the general missionary outreach of the church.

The third type is an interdenominational effort—two, three, or more denominations working together. Here again control is exercised from outside the missionary enterprise, but usually less extensively and less effectively because of the existence of "many masters." Here there is more independence than in the second type because of the haziness of lines of authority. Also, such missions display the usual organizational antipathies and "border patrolling" peculiar to joint efforts in which larger group autonomy is maintained. There is also a tendency for minor points of theological or doctrinal nuances to cause dissension and disorganization.

The fourth type of operational mission is the strictly denominational "society," free from direct church control but confined to the members of a single denomination and governed by a special and separate board of directors elected by the members not of the denomination but of the *society*. Here we find complete professionalization, an assured income from the parent body, and fairly great autonomy within a defined doctrinal area. Interestingly this type of mission tends to exhibit a fundamentalistic tenor, notwithstanding the wide theological spectrum that may exist in the parent body.[87]

In the last 20 years there has been a relatively unsuccessful effort to give these separate undertakings a uniform mien or at least some degree of united guidance. Bodies such as the International Missionary Council's Christian Approach to the Jews, although recognized by most independent denominations and even some independent missions, have found that their own groups "prefer to work according to their own methods and to have no international organization advising or supervising their work."[88] The Anglo-American missionary scene is a microcosm of the broad societal picture, marked as it is by a startling degree of overorganization: there are few large organizations but myriad splinter groups, each demanding its place in the sun, each insisting that *it* has found *the* way. Partly because of this missionary morass, success according to the pattern of the operational mission has been limited in the extreme, leading in recent years to a reappraisal and finally to a new emphasis—the parish approach.

The parish approach, the second of the two major organizational patterns, has been defined by Bergstrom as "a normal congregation going about its normal business of witnessing to the saving power of Jesus Christ and including the Jew as a normal part of its outreach with the Gospel to the community."[89] This, as the definition indicates, is an attempt at "normalizing" the approach to the Jew by considering him a sinner like any other, in the same need as others for a "saving knowl-

edge of Christ." According to the thinking of the plan's proponents, the operational type of mission has committed the
error of separating and thereby stigmatizing the Jew, causing
the Jews to fear that they were to be proselytized and then separated from their normal reference matrix. The result, amply
evident to those involved in the missionary enterprise, was
the stiffening of "Jewish resistance" and the "ultimate defeat
of the Christian evangel." Not only has the operational mission
failed to gain converts, but it stands accused of being basically
"un-American" in act and outlook. Here again we have the
confusion and interaction of the secular ethic with the religious
imperative. Bergstrom firmly suggests that

> . . . a Jew living in any community is a normal member of that
> community—in regular standing—and not set apart simply be-
> cause he is a Jew. He is to be treated as a *person* in his own
> right, not lumped together with others in a nondescript group
> as "Jews." This at any rate is the "American ideal."[90]

In addition to the idealistic reasons, there is a pragmatic element, the desire to act in what is conceived to be the finest
interpretation of the Christian way. This motivation is a potent
factor in the evolution of the broader outlook just described,
since it is accompanied by the belief that the Jew will *have to*
react positively to such treatment. Almost all elements involved
in the evangelization of the Jew dwell on the effectiveness of
kindness and Christian love in winning him. Before completing the empirical research for this study I was inclined to
downgrade this factor, assuming that it played little or no role
in missionary efforts. However, in recognizing that so many of
the people who respond to the Christian evangel are marginal
members of the Jewish group in need of assurance and of kindness, I have been led to take serious note of the effectiveness
of this approach. In addition to individual marginality, most
of the Jews reached are second-generation Americans, the offspring of immigrant stock unsure of their place in the domi-

nant culture, and at all times responsive to an assimilative drive in the "American manner" (i.e., based on kindness, respect for diverse origins, and the assurance that all differences can be smoothed over in a new American culture).[91]

Another intent is to prove the "practicality" and "pragmatism" of Christianity in showing that love *can* work.

One of the favorite criticisms of the Jews is that Christianity, as a religion based on love, does not work; it is too idealistic and unrealistic. Hence in the field of Jewish evangelism, kindness can hardly be stressed enough.[92]

The parish approach makes it possible to reach the Jew in the "American way" as it were, emphasizing the workability of Christianity and the desire not to destroy but to assimilate— not in the narrow sense of fusion in which original identity is lost but in a broader sense that allows the basic reference group to remain intact. It is American pragmatism (though it has been used in England as well) at its fullest, promising methodological elegance leading to a formidable return. Gartenhaus attributes no fewer than six primary advantages to this method:

1. It is inexpensive. It saves the expense of scores of mission halls, equipment, and large staffs, salaries, and upkeep.
2. It covers a large territory, for it touches the Jew in the smallest community.
3. It arouses the conscience of the Church and makes it a unit of approach to the evangelized Jew in the midst of its own community.
4. It tends to soften the objection on the part of many Jews to the reproach of the so-called "mission."
5. It brings them into direct touch with the evangelical church, scriptural Christianity, true Christian worship and heartwarming fellowship.
6. It promotes a better understanding of true friendship between Jew and Christian.[93]

The methods used in the parish plan once again reflect the great stress on organization in the Anglo-American context. The churches are asked to follow a particular outline in pursuing the plan, the assumption being that a well-conceived program cannot fail. For Conrad Hoffmann, it is most important to be able to show the sincerity of the minister in charge and the interest of his lay people in including the Jews in their usual evangelistic outreach. Once this can be done he proposes the formation of a small group "or cell of church members who will qualify themselves to make the approach to Jewish neighbors their primary church activity,"[94] suggesting that the group be known as the St. Stephen's Society.

Once the group has been organized, Hoffmann advises special training for the work, and above all competent leadership. Emphasis should be on "personal work," which includes "friendly, neighborly visits . . . aimed at establishing such understanding and confidence that discussion of modern man's faith and his relationship to God may become quite natural."[95] A basic rule in utilizing the parish approach is: never rush things or act in any way precipitously. After awhile, however, and once the foundations have been laid "the neighbor may be invited to church or the suggestion may be made that he visit the minister for personal consultation."

When the preliminaries have been completed it is suggested that a more rigorous course be followed. One useful device is the forum or lecture, which should be open to the public. Hoffmann says that topics such as the following: "The Church and Anti-Semitism," "Palestine and Zionism," "Jewish and Christian Ideas about God," "God's Design for Israel," and "The Refugees and Displaced Persons," are "sure to interest Jewish neighbors."[96]

Hoffmann realistically notes that "in certain neighborhoods a special center . . . will be needed as some persons may be hesitant to come to a church,"[97] whereas it would be difficult to object to a community center.

A rather interesting proposal by Hoffmann is that an approach *through* the children will often be the most successful because "whereas parents frequently have little or no interest in religion or the church, they nonetheless are eager that their children should have religious instruction and attend Sunday School."[98]

The difference between the parish approach and the methods advocated by Thompson for the operational mission is far-reaching and highly significant. Whereas in the latter we see a separate device for mounting a persistent attack with the intention of separating as many Jews as possible from their coreligionists and if necessary from the Jewish people as well, the former represents the refined approach as between gentlemen of differing persuasions, with the one opening the doors of unity to the other. One has the advantage of "above-boardness" while the other is somewhat insidious and has led, notwithstanding a sincere effort to the contrary, to the denigration of the Jew and perceptions of him as something of a child or as a curious type of simpleton.[99] I suggest that this becomes so because in straining to do the "right thing," to avoid errors and offense, and yet to experience a modicum of success, the Jew must be typed and stereotyped, and techniques are thus of necessity oversimplified. This difficulty is apparent in the tone and substance of an article by Nels Bergstrom officiously titled, "How the Pastors and Their People Carry On a Witness to their Jewish Neighbors On the Parish Level," which I believe warrants extensive quotation here.

1. Be your Christian self and you will not offend or close the door for yourself.

2. Don't make a head-on approach to the Jewish community as such. Witness to the *whole* community, *including* the Jews. We know of a case where a group of earnest Christians of various denominations including Lutheran have made such a head-on approach to the whole Jewish community of their city. In no time at all they were marked by the Synagogue and every door

was closed. In five years of strenuous work they do not know of a single convert. This, we maintain is not Jewish evangelism at its best.

3. Don't advertise "Christian witness to the Jews" in any form.

. . .

6. Include the Jews in Church surveys and all visitation programs. Don't be dismayed by a mazuzah [sic] on the door-frame. A pastor or layman is visiting in a Jewish home or over the back fence with his neighbor. When religion is mentioned he is quite likely to say, "O, I'm a Jew!" And that is supposed to end the conversation on that subject for good and all! Too often it does. But the less timid will say, not the feminine, "O, we love the Jews!" but a more masculine "So what?" and the conversation continues. Approach any man as a *person*, not as an Englishman, a Swede, a Jew, or a Chinese. We make it almost a rule less he makes an issue of it."

7. Be friendly. Christian friendship is probably the greatest weapon for breaking down prejudice among the Jews or any of thumb. "Never let a Jew know that you know he is a Jew unother people. "Win them for yourself first, then win them for Christ."

8. Be neighborly. Be civic minded. Show interest in the neighborhood. An application of Christian principles to community affairs catches the interest of the Jew. Religion that is restricted to personal salvation without any concern for the community is beyond his ken.

(a) Watch your vocabulary. Our "Christian" words do not always carry the same connotation to a Jewish listener.

. . .

10. . . . Dr. Dan B. Bravin of Pittsburgh is a past master in the art of preparing sermon titles for Jews. From the beautifully lighted bulletin board you will see advertised subjects like these:

"Man's Quest for Security"

"When God Speaks—You Listen"

"The Conversion of Isaiah the Prophet"

"Three Charges Against the Church"

"Monotheism or Money-theism."[100]

12. Maintain a warm and active church family life. This appeals to the Jew. He has it in the Jewish community. He is afraid he will not find it in the Christian congregation.

13. Avoid negative reference to other churches.[101]

Thus although a new method and a new approach are posited, the old pitfalls are only too evident, leaving a residue of a seemingly permanent inability to launch a successful Christian approach to the Jews. Despite repeated attempts to evolve a viable structure for this effort, peculiar obstacles to a significant program of evangelization remain.

NOTES

1. John, 5:21.

2. This is not to say that the Church remained pure of pagan and other syncretistic influences, but rather that it consciously strove to eliminate these forces at all junctures as threats to the one faith and the one revealed incarnate God.

3. See E. D. Dewick, *The Christian Attitude to Other Religions* (Cambridge University Press, 1953), p. 113, ff.

4. Kaufmann Kohler, "Conversion to Christianity," *Jewish Encyclopedia* (New York: Funk and Wagnalls, 1903), Vol. 4, p. 249.

5. *Ibid.,* p. 250.

6. Felix Goldman, "Converts," *Universal Jewish Encyclopedia* (New York: The Universal Jewish Ency. Inc., 1941), Vol. 3, p. 341.

7. *Ibid.,* p. 342. It should not be assumed, however, that this dichotomy was always present in such pristine clarity. There were specific instances of Jewish proselytizing drives manifesting much the same absolutist trends discernible in Christianity, but these were generally of a deviant variety and never occupied the stage in the same or similar degree as has been the case in normative Christianity.

8. Again, I should like to emphasize that Judaism did experience a missionary urge of the same genre, that later became identified almost exclusively with Christianity. At a time approximately coterminous with the appearance of Jesus there was a disagreement between the sages Hillel and Shammai, with Hillel insisting on widespread religious propaganda among the heathen and Shammai holding to the belief that converts weakened rather than strengthened the faith, thus should be carefully screened before admittance to the community of Israel. Shammai's view prevailed and the process of conversion became so trying and difficult an experience that the possibility of large numbers of proselytes was precluded.

9. See Dewick, *op. cit.,* p. 143, ff.

10. A sense of military urgency underlies much of the missionary ethic

and methodology. "The missionary may be openly hostile or outwardly courteous; he may deprecate the study of other religions
as a waste of time, or he may encourage it as useful. But if he is
polite it is with the politeness of a diplomat dealing with a hostile
foreign power. If he studies other religions (and some missionaries
of this type have made notable contributions to scientific knowledge
in their field) it is with a motive similar to that which prompts the
commander of an invading army to study carefully the nature of
the country before him—in order that he may conquer it the more
quickly and effectively." Dewick, *op. cit.*, pp. 40–41.

11. Auguste Sabatier, *Outlines of A Philosophy of Religion Based on
     Psychology and History* (New York: Harper Torch books, 1957), p.
     129.

12. *Ibid.*, p. 130.

13. Here again, this claim was not made vis à vis Judaism alone but
     in relation to all other faith structures. It is assumed (as in the
     following quotation) that spirituality is a peculiar contribution of
     Christianity. Speaking of Christian nurses working in a leper
     colony, Arnold Frank rather gratuitously suggests that "only their
     devotion to Christ and Christ dwelling in their hearts by faith
     enabled those nurses to do that superhuman work, to attend to the
     boils and unsightly, distorted bodies of the lepers, who were
     Mohammedans and utterly indifferent to everything spiritual."
     Arnold Frank, *What About The Jews* (Belfast: Graham and Heslip
     Ltd., 1944), p. 68.

14. Hendrik Kraemer, *The Christian Message in a Non-Christian
     World* (New York: Harper & Row, 1938), p. 433.

15. Cf. Robert E. Speer, *Missionary Principles and Practice* (London:
     Fleming H. Revell Co., 1902); William Newton Clarke, *A Study of
     Christian Missions* (New York: Charles Scribner's Sons, 1910); Ed-
     mund Davison Soper, *The Philosophy of the Christian World Mis-
     sion* (New York: Abingdon-Cokesbury Press, 1943); James L. Barton,
     The Missionary and his Critics (London: Fleming H. Revell Co.,
     1906); Archibald G. Baker, *Christian Missions and a New World
     Culture* (Chicago: Willett, Clark & Co., 1934); Kenneth Scott
     Latourette, *The Christian World Mission in Our Day* (New York:
     Harper & Row, 1954).

16. Jacob Jocz, *Is It Nothing To You?* 2nd ed., rev. (London: Church
     Message to Jews, 1941), p. 66.

17. Soper charges that missionary Judaism was a religious imperialism
     because it demanded the total inclusion of the full convert. This
     seems to me a misapplication of the term based on a faulty under-
     standing of the normative Judaism of the age. Cf. Soper, *op. cit.*,
     p. 34.

18. Cf. Speer, *op. cit.*, for a good cross section of opinions regarding the utter superiority and total uniqueness of Christianity. These feelings are expressed by missionaries, but there is little evidence to suggest that they run counter to a general viewpoint within the Church as a whole.

19. Leo Baeck, "Romantic Religion," in *Judaism and Christianity*, transl. Walter Kaufman (Philadelphia: Jewish Publication Society of America, 1958), pp. 215–216.

20. The view of the Jew is discussed in greater detail in Chapter 6.

21. This of course does not take note of the Jews who were forced to convert merely to save their lives and not in any effort at "spiritual" emancipation.

22. This is not to say that voluntary conversions were so numerous that the facilities of the Church were tried. Quite the contrary; but over the centuries Jewish zeal for the wider horizons of Western civilization has provided a constant stream of conversions to the dominant faith.

23. Kohler, *op. cit.*, p. 250.

24. Here I take cognizance of the classical Church theory prevalent at various times in the middle ages, which envisioned the perpetual existence of the Jews as a lesson in apostasy for Christendom, as well as punishment for their (the Jews') crime.

25. The figure of 204,500 worldwide Jewish conversions in the nineteenth century is repeatedly quoted in missionary literature.

26. W. T. Gidney, *Jews and their Evangelization* (London: Student Volunteer Missionary Union, 1899), p. 86.

27. Glick views Christian efforts to convert the Jews as falling within three rather than six periods, as follows: first period—Christ to A.D. 400; second period—A.D. 400 to eighteenth century; third period—eighteenth century to present day. I believe Gidney's efforts to be more finely conceived and thus of greater use in determining trends and shifts in the missionary endeavor among the Jews. Cf. Ira O. Glick, "The Study of a Marginal Religious Group" (Master's thesis, University of Chicago, 1951).

28. See James William Parkes, *The Conflict of the Church and the Synagogue* (London: Soncino Press, 1934), p. 79. According to Parkes, these words could only signify a final separation.

29. A. Thompson, *A Century of Jewish Missions* (Chicago: F. H. Revell Company, 1902), pp. 87, 88.

30. *Ibid.*, p. 89.

31. Most of these individuals displayed the characteristic zeal and fanaticism of the convert, causing great fear and consternation among their former coreligionists.

32. Thompson, *op. cit.*, p. 89, ff.

33. *Ibid.,* p. 90.

34. An article in the *Hebrew Christian Alliance Quarterly* entitled
    "Jewish Evangelism in the Reformation Period" by Frank J. Neu-
    bery, [Vol. 32, No. 2 (Summer 1946), 12], lists the reasons for
    Luther's turning against the Jews, and all the reasons are white-
    washes. About the only "bad" thing the author permits himself
    to say was that Luther was not the right kind of individual for
    Jewish work, and notwithstanding Lutheran Church views on the
    Jews, this church is to be commended because it "has been one
    of the most active denominations in Jewish mission work."
      In 1523, before Luther underwent a change in his attitude, he
    wrote what appears to be an extremely enlightened tract called
    Das Jesus ein Geborener Jude Gewesen ["That Jesus Was Born a
    Jew"], containing the following oft-quoted passage: "Those fools
    the papists, bishops, sophists, monks have formerly so dealt with
    the Jews, that every good Christian would rather have been a
    Jew. And if I had been a Jew, and seen such stupidity and such
    blockheads reign in the Christian Church, I would rather be a pig
    than a Christian. They have treated the Jews as if they were dogs,
    not men, and as if they were fit for nothing but to be reviled.
    They are blood relations of our Lord, therefore if we respect flesh
    and blood, the Jews belong to Christ more than we. I beg, there-
    fore, my dear Papists, if you become tired of abusing me as a
    heretic that you begin to revile me as a Jew. Therefore, it is my
    advice that we should treat them kindly; but now we drive them
    by force treating them deceitfully or ignominiously, saying they
    must have Christian blood to wash away the Jewish stain, and I
    know not what nonsense. Also we prohibit them from working
    amongst us, forcing them, if they would remain with us to be
    usurers." Quoted in Hugh J. Schonfield, *The History of Jewish
    Christianity: From the 1st to the 20th Century* (London: Duck-
    worth, 1936), pp. 184–185. But in a tract published in 1543 entitled
    "The Jews and Their Lies" we have a different Martin Luther.
    What he suggests here sounds almost like a program for genocide.

35. *Ibid.,* p. 90.

36. Thompson, *op. cit.,* p. 91.

37. *Ibid.,* p. 91–92.

38. *Ibid.,* p. 92.

39. Schonfield quotes Reineck as saying in 1713, "The general topic
    of conversation and discussion at the present day is about the con-
    version of the Jews." Schonfield, *op. cit.,* pp. 198–199.

40. W. T. Gidney, *Missions to the Jews: A Handbook* (London: Lon-
    don Society for Promoting Christianity Amongst the Jews, 1899),
    p. 111.

41. See Armas Kustaa Ensio Holmio, *The Lutheran Reformation and*

the Jews: The Birth of the Protestant Jewish Missions (Hancock, Mich.: Finnish Lutheran Book Concern, 1949). This rather pedestrian work does contain some worthwhile insights into some of the significant departures from old patterns which marked Luther's work.

42. Schonfield, *op. cit.,* p. 211.

43. See Thompson, *op. cit.*

44. Kohler, *op. cit.,* p. 251.

45. In missionary literature, particularly in the publications of Hebrew Christians, there is the plaint that the Jews have been left out or have been disregarded in the evangelical scheme.

46. The following figures are from Thompson, *op. cit.,* pp. 263–264.

47. Thompson, *op. cit.,* p. 265.

48. See R. H. Tawney, *Religion and the Rise of Capitalism* (New York: Mentor Books, 1947).

49. Louis B. Wright, *Religion and Empire* (Chapel Hill: University of North Carolina Press, 1943), p. 152.

50. Barton, *op. cit.,* pp. 17–18.

51. Robin M. Williams Jr., *American Society—A Sociological Interpretation,* 2nd ed., rev. (New York: Alfred A. Knopf, 1960).

52. In this context I was amazed to find books with titles such as, *How You Can Develop Your Business Ability, How to Turn Your Ability into Cash, How to Do Business Over the Telephone,* prominently displayed on the bookshelves of a fundamentalist Baptist mission to the Jews.

53. The repetitions of these figures are to be found in works by Jocz, Kraemer, Schonfield, Reich, the articles in the *Hebrew Christian Alliance Quarterly,* and numerous tracts issued by a variety of missionary bodies.

54. Basil Mathews, *The Jew and the World Ferment* (New York: Friendship Press, 1935), p. 149.

55. Gote Hedenquist, "The Christian Approach to the Jews," *The International Jew—and the Ecumenical Church: Addresses delivered at the Pre-Evanston Conference on the Christian Approach to the Jews at Lake Geneva, Wisconsin, August 8–11, 1954* (New York: The National Council of the Churches of Christ in the U.S.A.), p. 2.

56. Hedenquist, *ibid.,* p. 5. He goes on to quote Barth: "The existence of the Synagogue alongside the Church is a wound, indeed a void in the Body of Christ which is utterly intolerable."

57. Oscar Handlin, "Historical Perspectives on the American Ethnic Group," *Daedalus,* Vol. 90, No. 2 (Spring 1961), 226.

58. *Ibid.*, p. 226.
59. Mathews, *op. cit.*, p. 166.
60. Hans Kosmala and Robert Smith, *The Jew in the Christian World* (London: Student Christian Movement Press, 1942).
61. Harold Floreen, *The Lutheran Parish and the Jews: An Analytical Study* (Chicago: The National Lutheran Council, 1940), p. 57.
62. Thompson, *op. cit.*, p. 227.
63. Dewick, *op. cit.*, p. 47.
64. Kraemer, *op. cit.*, p. 45.
65. Numerous missionaries still solace themselves with the thought that the Jews in the absence of Christ are at a lower stage of civilization than their neighbor. Those who maintain this view are not unimportant or without influence, and more is said about this in succeeding chapters.
66. Quoted in Arthur Roy Eckardt, *Christianity and the Children of Israel* (New York: King's Crown Press, 1948), p. 151.
67. *Ibid.*, p. 153.
68. Thompson, *op. cit.*, pp. 260–261.
69. Eckardt, *op. cit.*, p. 77.
70. Thompson says he was a rabbi, but there is no proof for this contention.
71. Thompson, *op. cit.*, p. 227.
72. *Ibid.*, p. 228.
73. The New York legislature refused a charter to the Society for the Evangelization of the Jews because, as they put it, the proselytizing of citizens is forbidden by the Constitution. The name was changed then to the American Society for Ameliorating the Condition of the Jews (chartered April 14, 1820).
74. Thompson, *op. cit.*, p. 79.
75. *Ibid.*, pp. 80–81.
76. *Ibid.*, p. 81.
77. *Ibid.*, pp. 81–82.
78. *Ibid.*, p. 82.
79. *Ibid.*, p. 82.
80. *Ibid.*, p. 83.
81. *Ibid.*, p. 83.
82. *Ibid.*, p. 85.
83. I say theoretical because as we see later, it has not always been possible to maintain quite so pellucid a separation, and where the emphasis has shifted, it has inevitably leaned toward proselytism.

In Chapter 6, *Peculiar Difficulties in Evangelizing the Jews,* this is discussed in greater detail.

84. Christian and Jews, Atlantic City, May, 1931, p. 43, "Major Problems and Issues in a Christian Approach to the Jews," Rev. Stuart Conning, quoted in *The Church and the Jewish Question* (Geneva: World Council of Churches, 1944).

85. A comparison of the renunciations required of the Jewish convert in past eras and social environments (see section on the *Ethnic and National Character of the Jews*) and the following program indicates that something new indeed exists. The quoted program, adopted in 1931, underscores an approach to the Jew that reflects the Anglo-American emphasis at its fullest expression. However, it should be noted that these tenets have been observed more fully in the breach than in the observance.

"The Aim and Basis of the Christian Approach to the Jew:

1. We are profoundly convinced that Jesus Christ is God's answer to the whole world's need. Having found Him to be the Way, the Truth, and the Life for ourselves, we are persuaded that what He is and does for us He can be and do for all men.

2. We confess with shame that so often the attitudes and conduct of Christians have not been in accord with the spirit of Christ and His teachings of love and brotherhood.

3. We urge Christians to repentance for the prejudice and unjust discriminations against the Jews, sometimes leading even to ostracism which, we have regretfully to admit, are not yet things of the past. We call on all our fellow-Christians to examine their own hearts and relationships and to cultivate Christ-like friendliness and good will toward their Jewish neighbors.

4. We gratefully recognize the rich religious heritage of Israel, a heritage which, through Jesus Christ, we have ourselves received and which gives us many great interests in common with the Jewish people. Alike worshippers of the one righteous, and holy God, share [sic] together in the ethical and spiritual values of the Old Testament, we desire to stand alongside the best Jewish leaders today against the rising tide of secularism and materialism that threaten the ideals which we both hold.

5. We believe that, having found in Jesus Christ our Redeemer, the supreme revelation of God and having discovered our fellowship with Him to be our most priceless treasure and the only adequate way to spiritual life, we should have an overmastering desire to share Him with others and very specially with those who are His own people according to the flesh. We therefore have a clear and compelling evangelistic purpose so to present Jesus Christ, by word and deed, to the Jews, that they may be attracted to His personality and recognize Him as their Christ, as in truth He was and is."

"Christians and Jews," a report of the Conference on the Christian Approach to the Jews, Atlantic City, N.J., May 12–15, 1931, quoted by James M. Black in "The Validity of the Christian Approach to the Jews," *International Missionary Council*, No. 2 (October 1931), 10.

86. I base the following typology on a pattern suggested by Elias Newman. See "Missionary Events," *Hebrew Christian Alliance Quarterly*, Vol. 16, No. 4 (October–December 1931).

87. The Zion Society, for instance, is a development of the Norwegian Lutheran Church, which does in fact manifest diversity in doctrine, although the Society does not.

88. Gote Hedenquist, (ed.), *Twenty-five Years of the International Missionary Council's Committee on the Christian Approach to the Jews, 1932–1957* (Uppsala: Almquist & Wiksells, 1951), p. 11.

89. Nels E. Bergstrom, "The Parish Approach," in Hedenquist, *op. cit.*, p. 63.

90. *Ibid.*, p. 65.

91. See "The Question of Marginality" in Chapter 2.

92. Harold Floreen, *The Lutheran Parish and the Jews: An Analytical Study* (Chicago: The National Lutheran Council—Division of American Missions, 1940), p. 38.

93. Jacob Gartenhaus, *What of the Jews?* (Atlanta, Ga: Home Mission Board, Southern Baptist Convention, 1948), p. 79.

94. Conrad Hoffman, *What Now for the Jews?* (New York: Friendship Press, 1948), p. 64.

95. *Ibid.*, p. 64.

96. *Ibid.*, p. 65.

97. *Ibid.*

98. The approach has historically been less *through* the children than *to* the children. For example, consider the following bland comment: "During the year November, 1939 to October 31, 1940 the number of professed conversions was fifty-four. The majority of those who professed to accept Christ were among the children. It is realized that it is difficult to tell whether this has been a genuine religious experience so that too much emphasis should not be put upon numbers." Eunice Nichols, "A Study of the Christian Approach to Jewish People in the City of Chicago" (Master's thesis, Presbyterian College of Christian Education, Chicago, 1941), p. 27.

99. For instance, in a manual for mission work among the Jews, we have a series of procedural suggestions that are horrifying and humorous at the same time. It is hard to take seriously, but it should be recognized that various individuals and groups of Christian activists do

just that. In an otherwise admirable attempt to view the Jews as individuals, we see a trend to do just the opposite, attributing a whole
host of stereotyped "traits" to Jews.

"6. Appeal to the heart. No one responds more quickly to loving
interest than does the Jew. (Statement by American Messianic Fellowship).

7. Be careful to define certain theological terms carefully to the
Jew. Don't overestimate him.

a. He has a different concept of sin. He feels that if he is fair and
honest in business, does not steal, murder or commit adultery, that
he is not sinning. Some of our pet sins such as gossip, unforgiveness
and evil thoughts are unknown to him.

b. He does not know what it is to be saved or lost.

c. His idea of repentance is like a mild feeling of being sorry for
wrong doing, rather than a turning away from sin.

d. His concept of Grace is that it is a girl's name.

e. The cross may be merely a sign on top of a steeple to show
that the building is a church.

f. He never heard of such terms as "Christ" and "saved by the
blood." (The above terms, misleading to Jewish people, were suggested by Mrs. Irene Fox—Southern Baptist material.)

g. The trinity might need to be explained to him. Intelligent
rabbis know better what we believe, but some unlearned Jews have
the idea that Christians believe in three Gods.

We must have loving patience in explaining some of these terms
to him." *Aids to Jewish Evangelism* (Dallas: Dallas Theological
Seminary, 1959), p. 16.

100. Thompson, too, thought that a commercial mien and a business
"front" were a perfect setting for reaching the Jew. Whether on the
parish level or in the operational mission vein, the Jewish image is
much the same, especially with respect to his reputed susceptibility
to some form of commercial seduction. "An entirely new method in
Jewish Missions was adopted in 1898. The promoters were F. F.
Wurts and Wistar Brown of Philadelphia. A store was rented, open
Bibles and tracts in various languages displayed in the window, and
a stock for sale and free distribution placed on shelves and tables.
At certain hours those in charge 'did business with the head of the
firm.' In other words, they prayed. Jews were welcomed at these
times as well as at any hour. There was no preaching. *The mercantile aspect seems to appeal to the Jews, and the work has been quite
successful.*" (My emphasis.) Thompson, *op. cit.*, pp. 249.

101. Bergstrom, *op. cit.*, pp. 70, 71, 72.

4

Hebrew Christianity

The attempt to evangelize and convert the Jews using an approach and methods similar to those employed in the evangelization of other non-Christian groups has met with repeated failure, or at best minimal fruits. Notwithstanding the relatively fresh elements brought to the evangelistic melange by British and American missionary societies and church groups, the difficulties seemingly inherent in *any* Christian approach to the Jews have continued to adumbrate all possibilities of success. The response to failure, however, has not been a rejection of the missionary imperative, nor a capitulation to those who suggest either the unsalvageability of the Jews or their essential "otherness" with respect to the Gospel of Christ. Rather, the response has been a continuously renewed effort to find a way to obey the scriptural admonition to bring the Gospel to all men and "to the Jew first."

The formation of the Hebrew Christian movement is one of the most significant attempts to overcome the long-standing refusal of the Jews to willingly convert in large numbers. This development had its roots in the missionary failures of the nineteenth century and emerged as a continuous force during the early 1900s.

To those within the missionary enterprise who had been able to retain an objective outlook[1] vis à vis Jewish steadfastness and the seeming immunity of Jews to conversionary appeals and efforts, it was clear that the approach was flawed. The appeal based on "collective love" for the Jew was a thoroughgoing failure, for this love, even when sincere, had become a condescending and clawing thing, divorced from its theoretical underpinnings and understandably rejected by those on whom it was lavished. The prolific distribution among the Jews of New Testaments and exhortative tracts in the variegated languages of the diaspora had similarly meager results because it too represented the imposition of a despised and rejected faith and, more important, a despised and *feared* community—Christendom. It was evident that the basic dilemma lay in the inseparability of Christianity from its empirical grounding and expression among the Gentiles. It was recognized that Judaism and Christianity were indeed indissolubly linked, but the linkage acted as a deterrent rather than as a spur to the eventual inclusion of the historical Israel under the wings of the Church. In this dilemma two possible courses of action presented themselves: either the Christ of the Gospels is to be totally recast in a Christological mold, free of nineteen centuries of religious creativity and development, and a beginning "begun" once again, or an attempt is to be made to recapture those elements—ensconced and often buried within the Christian tradition—that can be viewed as peculiarly the property and the inheritance of the Jews, utilizing these elements as a starting point for the inclusion of "those who have strayed." The first alternative, although retaining a few romantic adherents who forlornly protest what could have been "if," has been rejected by all responsible missionary agencies and theologians as being practically unsound and theologically absurd. The second, with all sorts of caveats, accretions, and addenda, has become the basis for a unique sociological and possibly theological development—the creation of a movement and the sowing of seeds for a church with its roots in a long-dead tradition (the

Apostolic Church), advocating not the assimilation but the banding together of converts to bear witness to their unconverted brethren and to *purify* their faith by returning it to its roots, which the converts alone can fully fathom as the recipients of a divine election. In other words, what is posited is something akin to a return to dormant truths by way of an empirical frame for these truths—Christianity—but climbing above the framework into an already prepared niche.

Before turning to a fuller analysis of the goals and philosophy of Hebrew Christianity, I think it would be useful to set the historical stage of its origin and early development.

THE MODERN MOVEMENT

Origin

Hebrew Christianity was born in England at the beginning of the nineteenth century through the efforts of a group of converts calling themselves the *Beni Abraham,* or sons of Abraham. It was on September 9, 1813, that 41 Jewish converts to Christianity met in London, setting forth as their purposes "to attend divine worship at the chapel and to visit daily two by two in rotation any sick member, to pray with him and read the Bible to him; and on Sunday all who could were to visit the sick one."[2] The goals of the organization were quite modest, and its intent was no doubt to function as something of a benevolent aid society among individuals with a similar background and in all likelihood similar difficulties. In 1835 the society changed its name to The Episcopal Jews' Chapel Abrahamic Society, whose stated purpose was "for visiting and relieving Jewish converts and enquirers."[3] It is probable that the society now expanded somewhat and undertook some proselytizing activity, but there is little evidence to indicate anything exceeding a very limited charitable character.

In 1882, however, a Hebrew Christian Prayer Union was founded (again in London) by one Dr. H. A. Stern, and its aims were considerably more ambitious than those of the earlier groups.[4] The Prayer Union sought to create or buttress a sense of unity among Jewish converts by bringing them together regularly for prayer and "religious intercourse."

All these efforts, however, represented something of a groping in the dark. Although little is known of their makeup, or even of their goals beyond a few highly generalized desiderata, it seems clear that the members of these organizations sought much the same kind of solace or support that one seeks in any quasi-religious body. Most of the members were no doubt "young in the faith," looking for anchor within a like group; moreover, they were very likely recent immigrants to England, made to feel uncomfortable in the churches and perhaps excluded entirely from social intercourse with their gentile coreligionists. I think it highly doubtful that more than a few envisioned larger goals and rewards in their banding together. Certainly at this point there was no thought of a separate denomination for Jewish converts, and little if any interest in becoming an organized missionary witness to their unconverted Jewish brethren.

Before the Prayer Union came into existence, however, a more significant development was in process. It attracted little attention and a miniscule membership, but its aims were considerably more ambitious, and the group was destined for a much longer span of life. This was the Hebrew Christian Union, organized in London in 1865 by Dr. C. Schwartz. The stated objects of this society included a definite missionary call in addition to the usual benevolent and sustaining functions for which its forerunners were organized. The objects were:

1. To promote a social and frequent personal intercourse among Christian Israelites by meeting together at stated periods.

2. To stir up and stimulate one another in the endeavor of uniting with and caring for our brethren.

3. To search the Scriptures together relating to Israel and Israel's king.[5]

But here again there is an almost total absence of clarity with regard to aims, although there is a vague notion that something more lasting and significant could result from the organization of an alliance. There is little suggestion of what this could be. However, a naïve faith that such an end will become evident in time is attested in a circular letter sent by Schwartz to all known converts on April 25, 1866. In inviting Jewish Christians to an organizational meeting, Schwartz readily admits that he is not sure why they should meet (except for mutual support and to know one another) or what would result from their meeting, but he asks them to come anyway.

> Dear Brother,
> It has occurred to us that it would be desirable and profitable that as many Israelites who believe in Jesus as can be brought together should meet in London on the 23rd of May.
> Our object is to become acquainted with one another and to be built up in our holy faith. There are special ties which bind us together as descendents of Abraham, and we believe that this conference for prayer and consultation might issue in a permanent union of Jewish Christian brethren in this land.
> We do not come before you with any definite plan for action, but would simply say that, as there exists an Evangelical and a Jewish, an Hebrew Christian Alliance also might be formed. We trust that you feel with us the desirableness and importance of such a meeting, and that we may reckon on your presence and on your prayers.[6]

Some 80 Jewish converts did feel the "desirableness" of such a meeting and met on the day appointed; but we have no record of anything being decided, and apparently no follow-up was carried out. I suggest that the formation of the Hebrew Christian Alliance was a rather confused, somewhat disoriented response to a vaguely felt need, rather than a well-conceived effort to establish a "Church-Witness" to the Jews. It was, however, a step in that direction, and by 1893 the efforts of Baron and Schonberger begin to show awareness of the possibilities inherent in a Jewish–Christian approach to the Jews, previously nonexistent within incipient Hebrew Christianity.

In 1893, David Baron and C. A. Schonberger organized a mission to the Jews in the teeming Jewish East End of London, calling it the Hebrew Christian Testimony to Israel. Here were planted the actual seeds of the modern movement. Structuring their efforts on the earlier Beni Abraham, the Prayer Union, and the largely dormant but nonetheless seminal Hebrew Christian Alliance of 1866, Baron and Schonberger were the first missionaries to see the possibilities of "a work" from *within* the Jewish fold. As the name of the organization indicates, they attempted to impress on the Jews that they came not as outsiders to draw Jews to an alien faith or an alien community; on the contrary, they came as Jews who, having discovered the lost fork in the road of their ancient faith, wanted to redirect their confused brethren rather than to untrack them. They very wisely insisted that they represented no particular church, and no foreign sect, but were Jews, bearing a Jewish message to fellow Jews. They maintained that their goal was not to convert Jews "but to bring as many as possible into a living relationship with God, in Christ, and to testify to both Jews and Gentile Christians that Christ and Israel are inseparable. . . ."[7] Thus, Baron and Schonberger are the first and most important proponents of what has come to be known as the Hebrew Christian approach to the Jews. Their efforts sparked the first real departure from the archaic and unsuccessful approach from *without* and turned attention to the need for an indigenous approach that would recognize the integrity of Jewish peoplehood, emphasizing an autonomous religious growth from *within*.

Thus far I have mentioned developments leading up to the formulation of a Hebrew Christian approach in Great Britain. There were also parallel developments in the United States, Germany, and to a lesser degree in Russia.[8] In the United States, however, there existed little in the way of original effort. The impetus for the movement stemmed from England, as did its leading proponents such as J. S. C. Frey (1771–1837) and Ridly Herschell (1807–1864). Neither man was able to get the movement off the ground, but the pair did pave the way for a series of attempts—all short-lived, all minor and insignificant.[9] All the Hebrew Christian associations seemed to be in the mold of the early English benevolent and aid society, largely lacking in clearly stated goals or intellectual underpinnings. In the United States the period between 1878 and the turn of the century appears to have been a quiescent one—not in terms of missionary activity, which was burgeoning, but in regard to further attempts to launch a Hebrew Christian organization. In 1901, however, the first of a long series of conferences was held (1903, 1908, 1913, 1914) that culminated in the formation of the American Hebrew Christian Alliance in 1915.[10] From this point on the American Alliance has enjoyed an uninterrupted existence, playing a not unimportant role in the worldwide movement, though in a highly delimited area. In this connection there is a symbiotic relationship between the English and American Alliances, reflecting in microcosm and in a very specific vein a historical pattern underlying the relationship between the two larger societies. In the specific case of Hebrew Christianity, England provided the intellectual stimulus and America the activist response. Thus although the American movement never produced a Levertoff, a Schonfield, or a Baron, it played the most active role in launching the International Hebrew Christian Alliance and in sustaining it once established.[11] Beginning with the twentieth cen-

tury, the English and American movements provided in concert most of the intellectual and organizational drive for the
worldwide movement, which by the 1930s included branch
units in Germany, Holland, Scandinavia, Hungary, and
Poland.

Numerical Strength

It is impossible to determine the numerical strength of the
movement either in its national unit or as a whole, but I
think that until the 1970's there were probably between 1000
and 2000 actual members, notwithstanding claims in the
neighborhood of 5000 or more. Statistics among missionaries
(and Hebrew Christians are no exception) are devastatingly
chaotic. For instance, the American Hebrew Christian Alliance
arrived at the figure of 50,000 Hebrew Christians (i.e., Jews
who have converted—not enrolled members of the Alliance)
in America, and 120,000 in the rest of the world (excluding
Catholics) as follows. The American Jewish Year Book for
1954 states that of the 222,000 Jews in Canada, 2202 are Protestants who claim Jewish birth. This, the Alliance correctly
notes as 1 percent of the Canadian Jewish population. But
they continue: 1 percent of the American Jewish population
(5 million) is 50,000 and 1 percent of the world Jewish population (12 million) is 120,000; ergo, there are approximately
170,000 Jewish Christians in the world today. In 1935 the
Hebrew Christian Alliance Quarterly announced that there
were 20,000 Hebrew Christians in the United States, claiming
1 percent (i.e., 200) as members of the Alliance. At the convention of the Hebrew Christian Alliance which I attended as
an observer (June 1961, Cincinnati, Ohio) Arthur Glass, a
member of the executive board of the Alliance, claimed a
membership "below 1000." The American unit is reputed to
be the largest within the International, and this is why I

assume that the world membership is no higher than the figure suggested—1000 to 2000. One caveat should be added, however. Although, the organization was never at any one time larger than, let us say, 2000 (before Hitler), there were probably many more members who subsequently faded into the gentile church, removing themselves from the rolls of Hebrew Christianity. We have no accurate means of determining just how many changed their affiliation, but if the pleas to converts not to desert the fold for the gentile churches printed in almost every issue of the *Hebrew Christian Alliance Quarterly* since 1917 are an indication of a trend to do just that, the figure is apt to be considerable.

Goals and Outlook[12]

Thus far I have reviewed in a very general fashion the origin of the Hebrew Christian movement, noting that it was developed largely in response to repeated missionary failures of the past. But this is only a partial explanation for a highly complex phenomenon. Hebrew Christianity is a multidirectional entity aiming sometimes for mutually exclusive goals, often subscribing to a variety of self-defeating methods, thus presenting the observer with a situational Gordian knot. At times this is understandable when we examine these conflicts as between individual points of view within the movement. But more often than not confusion appears in the individual point of view, leaving the observer with a somewhat schizoid ideological and organizational canvas to interpret. What, for instance, is the normative Hebrew Christian view of Judaism? Is it an essentially sound faith lacking only a capstone, as it were, in Christ, or is it a religious artifact to be cast aside? What is the Hebrew Christian viewpoint on the law? Does it have continuing relevance for the believer in Christ or has it been abrogated? What is the Hebrew Christian position vis

à vis a Jewish Church? Should the Hebrew Christian believer
join an existing denomination? No denomination? Or should
he organize a separate one? How is the Hebrew Christian
to relate to his gentile brethren? Is he to consider himself a
"babe in the faith," to be instructed by the gentile believer; a
twice-chosen child of God; or an equal among other believers?
What is the significance of Jewish peoplehood? Is it to be
embraced as a methodological tool to win the unconverted
brethren, or does it have relevance beyond this? How is the
refusal of the Jew to believe to be interpreted? As a peculiar perversity of soul of the Jew or as a response to persecution by the Gentiles?

All these questions are implicit (and some are made explicit)
in the statements, positions, and emotions of Hebrew Christianity as a movement and among individual Hebrew Christians. Clear-cut answers are elusive at best and at worst nonexistent. Usually two or three mutually exclusive responses
to the same question are maintained in the same policy position and as part of the same individual response. There is,
however, a series of dominant themes that forms the ideological
superstructure of the movement, and to a lesser extent the
motivational basis for the individual member, although in
specific cases such themes are tempered, abbreviated or radically reinterpreted. Foremost among these positions, and the
two most widely and unreservedly subscribed to, are the importance of Hebrew Christianity as a missionary witness to the
unconverted Jew, and the provision of a familiar supporting
structure for the Jewish believer in Christ.

Article II of the first constitution adopted by the American
Alliance contains a straightforward affirmation of these two
goals of the organization. They are simply:

1. To encourage and strengthen Hebrew Christians and to
deepen their faith in the Lord Jesus Christ.
2. To propagate more widely the Gospel of our Lord and Sav-

iour Jesus Christ, by strengthening existing Jewish Missions,
and fostering all other agencies to that end.

3. To provide for the evangelical Christian Churches of America an authoritative and reliable channel how best to serve the
cause of Jewish evangelization.[13]

At this point in the development of the movement the
organization is viewed as a secondary vehicle for the conversion of the Jews, its purposes being to strengthen all existing
work and to assist in the religious growth of the recent converts. No grandiose role is assumed by the Hebrew Christian
Alliance, and certainly nothing indicates a very startling break
with the more traditional missionary enterprises. Ancillary to
the established denominations (to which its members subscribe according to individual conscience), the Alliance is seen
as an aid to rather than as a well-tuned, independent instrument of evangelization.

This core of the Hebrew Christian position has remained
intact over the years—to serve as a witness to the unconverted
Jew and to be utilized as a cushion or support for the recent
convert. But many involved in these early efforts believed that
this was too limited a goal. Some predicted failure because
they felt the Jews would perceive their efforts as a transparent
front for the "same old missionaries;" thus they sought to
enlarge the movement's scope. The goal seemed utterly inadequate to others because it did not reach far enough into the
Jewish ethos, the Jewish reality, to ensure a firmer hold on the
Jewish religious pulse, which they sensed as a prerequisite for
success. For such reasons, the Hebrew Christian Alliance of
America moved steadily away from the initially modest goals,
not because they were inappropriate or insufficient but because
it was felt that headier goals were needed before the original
aims could be realized. In other words, I believe the later
ideological encumbrances were tactical additions rather than
responses to deep-felt needs of the rank-and-file membership.

By 1931 the Hebrew Christian Alliance of America had revised the original constitution, setting forth a considerably expanded set of objectives. These were:

1. To unite in a cooperative fellowship Hebrew Christians throughout America.

2. To establish and maintain local branches.

3. To advance the spiritual development and general welfare of Hebrew Christians and to stimulate propagation of the Hebrew Christian ideal in every sphere of Jewish life.

4. To extend practical aid to Hebrew Christians in distress in such ways as may be determined by the officers of the organization.

5. To provide for the education of Hebrew Christians aiming for useful service in Church, mission field, or society.

6. To witness unitedly to Church and Synagogue of the fulfillment of Israel's Messianic hope in Jesus Christ.

7. To encourage the propagation of Christianity among the Jews by Christian agencies.

8. To prepare and to publish literature setting forth the message of Hebrew Christianity.

9. To bring about a better understanding of the Jewish problem by Christians and of the Christian message by Jews.

10. To participate through the International Hebrew Christian Alliance in a world wide witness to the Jewish people that Jesus Christ is the Messiah of Israel.[14]

Here we see an expansion of goals and a revamped self-perception going far beyond the group's early aims. With the constitution of 1931, the signs of a movement emerge from what had been an organization. The Hebrew Christian Alliance is no longer to act as a mere stimulus, it is to establish branch units responsible for "the propagation of the *Hebrew* Christian ideal . . ."—a distinct and separate viewpoint. The branches are to "educate," permitting the Hebrew Christian to go to both church and synagogue to witness to Israel's messianic hope.

The message is to be sent forth by the group's own organs and by separate publications emphasizing that Jesus Christ is the Messiah of Israel.

Even here, however, although we can glimpse the beginnings of something more than a missionary undertaking, there remains a basic fidelity to the earliest aims, which were supportive and evangelistic. There is a decided enlargement on these, perhaps a straining at the leash; but the original outline, now bearing a sectarian coloration, is still discernible. All sorts of additions in terms of "what we should believe" and questions such as, "Where are we going?" begin to appear at this stage in the development of Hebrew Christianity. Some pulled in the direction of a most unusual syncretistic trend and were known as "Judaizers" (discussed in Chapter 5 in greater detail); others concentrated on the evolution of a particular "way"—a peculiar code of the Hebrew Christian believer, not too different from the code of behavior that might be advocated by a fundamentalistic Christian but containing sufficient reference to a Jewish "heritage" to set the actor apart as a special Christian, a Hebrew Christian. The best example of this is found in a code titled *Queries for the Solemn Consideration of the Members of the Hebrew Christian Alliance,* by Max Reich, a long-time president and ideologue of the American Alliance.

1. Are you at all times concerned to live worthy of the Name which you confess, making Hebrew Christianity to be respected?
2. Do you daily pray for the officers and members of the Alliance? Do you uphold the workers in South America in loving intercession? Do you pray for the local branches of the Hebrew Christian Alliance?
3. Are you careful to live within the bounds of your income, avoiding debts and obligations beyond your means? Do you live in godly simplicity?
4. Do you shun tale bearing, detraction, and all evil speaking?

5. Do you endeavor to live down anti-Jewish prejudice by living a noble life, in purity, integrity, dignity, sincerity, rather than by argument?

6. Do you keep a watch over your temper, avoiding sharp and cutting words, meeting false accusations in a spirit of meekness?

7. In your speech do you avoid superfluity of words, letting your yea be yea, and your nay, nay? Do you exercise care to speak the truth at all times?

8. Do you cherish love and harmony with fellow-believers, and as much as lieth in you with all men? When differences arise are they ended speedily and in a peaceable spirit? Do you love the poor?

9. Do you minister out of your substance, as you are able, to the work of the Hebrew Christian Alliance?

10. Are you careful to perform your promises? Do you avoid making pledges which you afterwards fail to fulfill? Are you a man of your word?

11. Do you cherish a forgiving spirit towards those who have injured you, not being overcome with evil, but overcoming evil with good?

12. Do you honor the Scriptures by reading them regularly to your household? Do you keep up the family altar? Do you bring up your children in the nurture and admonition of the Lord?

13. Do you avoid the use of strong drink, except medicinally, tobacco and other habit-forming drugs?

14. Do you maintain a separated life, apart from worldly amusements and entertainments which lower the temperature of the spiritual life, finding your joy in Christ and His truth?[15]

The Hebrew Christian is no longer viewed only as a convert from a particular communion who "naturally" wants the fellowship of his own group; he has now become a particular type committed to a distinct and unique religious path. The root for this development was implicit in the earliest formulations of the movement. The dangers were immediately evident to both leadership and external supporters (i.e., gentile churchmen), resulting in internal tensions that have in the past threatened the very existence of the movement.[16] Although

Hebrew Christianity was begun *only* as a "methodolgical device," it very soon was confronted with demands for clarification of its *raison d'etre,* and in fulfilling this need it developed a typical organizational thirst for survival. It wanted to grow; thus it could not remain a tool for missions or a benevolent aid society. The movement needed a reason for being that would establish it as the only logical organism for the task of evangelizing the Jews. In responding to this challenge the Hebrew Christian movement achieved an autonomous existence at the price of forswearing a primary goal of its infancy —namely, that it would act as an aid to missionary bodies already in existence. This in turn led to a series of often bitter struggles with various mission bodies and church groups over the issue of who could best do the job. During the struggle I believe that Hebrew Christianity was pushed toward the denominational abyss, where it continues to hover to this day, reluctant to take the plunge but refusing to reject the possibility for all time.[17]

The minutes of the conventions of the Hebrew Christian Alliance and the contents of a prodigious number of articles in the *Quarterly* reflect this struggle for supremacy in the Jewish mission field and its attendant movement away from an ancillary role, where the only alternative to the opposition of the Gentiles appears to be a separate institution—a church. The burden of the Hebrew Christian movement was put upon it by the Gentiles, for "who is to call Israel to Christ, awakening them from their stupendous sleep of nineteen hundred years, if not the Hebrew Christian?"[18] This implies that the Hebrew Christian is the only one who will be able to prepare a "place" for the Jew once he comes to Christ. It is suggested that this burden has been forced on the Hebrew Christian by the Gentiles' lack of concern for Jewish souls. When the Hebrew Christian is able to feel indignancy and wrath for the injustice committed against the Jews, accusing Gentiles of "indifference . . . to our Lord's commission to go to every creature,"[19] the heady sense of being disinherited and wronged comes into play in cementing not an organization but a movement.[20]

Thus the goals of Hebrew Christianity have emerged from an early period of reticence in which the organization posited modest, essentially supportive functions. The present organizational self-view is that of a distinct element performing a unique task within Christendom, giving rise to a "new" Christian approach to the Jews.

THE HEBREW CHRISTIAN APPROACH TO THE JEWS

It is evident that a movement without reasonably clear goals, and lacking any plan that sets it apart as necessary, will wither before it has an opportunity to function. Hebrew Christianity was begun largely to appease a whetted appetite for institutional life, but it would not have survived if it did not also contain the promise of fulfilling a unique role, in a manner possessing the seed of an "inner logic." What after all could be the excuse for creating still another Christian missionary endeavor with so many already in the field, each demanding its share of a limited financial reserve and a finite store of commitment among Christian supporters? If it could not be demonstrated to both gentile supporters and Jewish converts that Hebrew Christianity had a unique claim both on the potential Jewish believer and within the divine scheme for man, no doubt it would have aborted early in its career. That it did not do so constituted assurance that it was at least theoretically viable and pertinent in the overall Christian approach to the Jews.

The several presuppositions underlying the claim of Hebrew Christianity for a place in the missionary sun and a niche in the Christian panorama are quite simple. These are adduced as follows: (1) the Hebrew Christian will be more successful because he alone really knows the Jew, and because the Jew is sick and the ministration of loving minds and hearts readily available only among the closest of relatives promises the only cure,[21] and (2) the Hebrew Christian *qua* Hebrew Christian is in any event vouchsafed a unique scriptural role in the divine economy.

The first ideological premise is scripturally buttressed in Corinthians I (9:19), where Paul asserts:

> For though I was free from all men, I brought myself under bondage to all, that I might gain the more. And to the Jews I became as a Jew, that I might gain Jews; to them that are under the law, as under the law, not being myself under the law, that I might gain them that are under the law.

The Pauline meaning is unmistakable. Christ, though he appeared first among the Jews and preached his message exclusively to the children of Israel, did not proclaim a narrow parochialism, applicable only to a small segment of mankind in an insignificant corner of the Mediterranean world. His purpose was not to provide a melioristic salve to a troubled national psyche. Nor was his purpose (as Paul saw it) to uplift the "fallen away," reestablishing their former spiritual suzerainty—in which case the significance of Jesus the Christ would descend to the poverty stricken reaches of a crucified reformer. Christ came not to reform but to obviate reform, not to reestablish the old lines of demarcation between nations and classes but to establish one yardstick of differentiation—that between the believers and the blind, the saved and the damned, grace and sin. In Christ there is neither Jew nor Greek, bond nor free, and if these appellations or loyalties persist among men, they are to be respected insofar as they provide a channel for salvation, even utilized to the fullest toward this end if necessity warrants but they are never to be taken as a serious obstacle to the universal dissemination of

Christian truth. Paul was the pragmatist, the instrumentalist
par excellence comprehending (as did Jesus) the powerful
grip of group loyalties on men, and although he claimed personal freedom from its demands he was ever willing to man-
ipulate these to his singular end—man's salvation in Christ.
Thus he exhorted his following to employ the instruments at
hand—"becoming as a Jew to the Jews," and though they
might be free, putting themselves under bondage the better
to "win" mankind.

Hebrew Christianity, in taking note of the continuing
relevance of Jewish peoplehood, has embraced Paul's course of
action as a mandate for its existence and as a methodological
locus in its revamped missionary approach. In answer to the
often posited question, Why should there be a specifically
"Hebrew" Christian approach?, the answer is something of
an avowal of the "weakness of the flesh," wherein it is recognized that men are prone to demand a share in this world as
well as in the world to come, and if the latter can be assured
by doubling the rewards of the former this is both scriptural
and effective as well.

Thus the Hebrew Christian can cite both scriptural and
pragmatic justification for his singular approach, but how
is this approach to acquire bone and sinew? To what specific
loci within the Jewish experience is the approach to be
directed? What theological garment (if any) is to be the most
efficacious? A further question was adduced: Would it be
possible to structure a movement on instrumental grounds
alone, seeking only a more efficient way to do a particular job,
or is it not necessary and desirable for it to have autonomous
standing and goals beyond mere efficacy?

Even though Hebrew Christianity interpreted itself as a
compromise recognizing the Jews' desire to remain Jews, at
the same time it paradoxically claimed that the Jews who
believe are free and yet not free; that is, they are still chosen,
since election does not disintegrate in Grace. Not only is
Hebrew Christianity a legitimate (in terms of Scripture) ploy

for the conversion of the Jew, but there is a continuing theological role for the Jewish believer, not simply as a believer like any other but as a Jew.

AFFIRMATION OF RACIAL SEPARATISM
THE TWOFOLD CHOSENNESS OF ISRAEL

As the very term Hebrew Christianity attests, the approach of the movement will presuppose the continuing viability of some form of Jewish autonomous existence.

The scriptural basis for this affirmation can be found primarily in Paul's epistles to the Romans, where it is said of the Jews, "As concerning the Gospel, they are enemies for your sakes; but as touching the election they are beloved for the fathers' sakes."[22] Why is this true, given the rejection? Very simply, "For the gifts and calling of God are without repentance."[23]

In other words, once having been called, having been chosen, there is no turning back. Once having been singled out to fulfill a unique role—even though a critical evil now beclouds this destiny—the election retains its currency. For better or worse, the Jews are, and since their inception as a unified entity have been, the chosen of God, and notwithstanding their infidelity, they remain chosen.

If this be so, the Jews must continue as a "people apart" if they are to fulfill God's purpose for them. The failures of past missionary efforts have been attributed to a wrathful God, displeased that His covenant was being tampered with by those attempting to lure the Jew into an ersatz gentilism. As the Hebrew Christian interprets the divine organizational table it appears in the following stages:

After the election of Abraham the picture was:
Jews
Gentiles

With the advent of Christ and the rejection it became:
Christians
Jewish unbelievers
Gentile unbelievers
But God's real desire is to be:
Jewish Christians
Gentile Christians
Jewish unbelievers
Gentile unbelievers

In sum, the separate existence of the Jews has continuing
pertinency for God, thus for all believers. The Jews are to
be approached as Jews and their autonomous existence assured
because they remain the first beloved of God, and the combination of racial chosenness and religious election (Jewish birth
and Christian belief) represents the apex of the divine
pyramid. But having affirmed the idea of the continued separatism of Israel, the Hebrew Christian is left with a host of
problems less easily solved by resorting to scriptural proof
texts. What, for instance, is to be the here-and-now organizational rationale for a specially set-apart group of believers in
Christ? Is this twofold chosenness of the Jewish believer in
Christ to remain a mystery akin to that surrounding the choice
of Abraham from among all men? Or is the Hebrew Christian
set a task by and through this "double" blessing for which he
is specially endowed?

Most Hebrew Christian leaders and thinkers have assigned
to Hebrew Christianity a specific role, growing out of this
twofold chosenness, which goes beyond the evangelistic needs
of the Jews and impinges on all Christendom. The Hebrew
Christian is thought of as a believer with a pedigree, and more
than that, a believer with a mission to those lacking this
genetic distinction. Schonfield phrases the question thus:

To what purpose is all this Hebrew Christianity? Is it that
Jewish Christianity with its accumulated experiences of human
passions and Divine love has a potent message to give to a world

crying aloud for light and truth? Is it that these patient followers of King Messiah have a leading part to play in the restoration of peace and international brotherhood to a world
sown with dissension and distrust? Is there after all something
in the Mosaic vision of a "Kingdom of priests and a holy
nation" playing a mediatorial part between the nations and
their God?[24]

But rather than answer outright, Schonfield cryptically suggests that "those who seek an answer . . . go to the fountainhead and to the word of His revelation,"[25] implying that
Scripture holds the key and that the key will unlock the door
behind which Israel continues its claim to the divine election.
Here Hebrew Christian thought is quite similar to that of
modern Reform Judaism in its insistence on the role of
Israel as mankind's conscience through the guardianship of
the prophetic message. Both Reform Judaism and Hebrew
Christianity maintain the continued existence of empirical
Israel because of the divine mandate and also because Israel
is destined to uphold the purity of the prophetic utterances.

To make possible the execution of this task, it is believed
that God has not only elected Israel but has endowed it with
a form of collective charisma, wherein the Jews as individuals
and the Jews as an entity manifest peculiar spiritual gifts.

The fact alone that the Jew is a Jew, with all the intangible
charm of his race and culture and heritage, makes him the
outstanding star in the modern religious drama. He sees farther
and knows more of the deeper intent of the Scriptures than
all the Augustines and Abelards of the centuries. He has taken
Babel to Pentecost and laid his polyglot linguistic genius on the
altar of his blood-relative, Jesus. He shoulders the cross like a
joy-crowned martyr or hero and walks calmly though undaunted
up the Golgothas of family ostracism, gentile suspicion and ra-
binical scorn. And best of all he is the ideal Christian pragmatist
because he works up all of his Christian idealism into the warp
and woof of daily life.[26]

So powerful is this affirmation of the inherent quality of the "race" that the argument that *Judaism* has obscured these natural endowments achieves some prominence. The thought is posited that "the Hebrew Christian has a wonderful heritage . . ."[27] but when one is prepared for a follow-up assertion that perhaps the heritage has become obscured or impaled on a theological axe, one is instead informed that this heritage ". . . has been covered up in the exile by 'Judaism,' Gentilism, materialism. . . ."[28] It is plainly implied that the qualities of the Jew do not have their source in Judaism but in the individual's genes, with the only logical fulfillment of this potential resting in his conversion, whereupon "he will more and more slough off the map of the 'Goluth' in his face, and the beautifulness of Jerusalem will reappear."[29] The Jew, in short, has "soiled" his racial superiority, but in the receiving of Christ this exclusive quality will reappear as a glowing manifestation of his twofold chosenness.

The stress on the "racial" distinctiveness of Israel and the implication of a "double election" has in a paradoxical manner found support and, at the same time, resentment among some gentile Christians. This has occurred primarily among the fundamentalist groups, who in great part made Hebrew Christianity possible by their affirmation of dispensationalism, emphasizing the eschatological relevance of empirical Israel. We have noted a recurrent feeling among many gentile supporters of Hebrew Christianity that a special charisma attaches to the Jew who preaches Christ, in that he is *truly* in the apostolic succession both in faith and in flesh. When it can be asserted that "whilst God is no respector of persons, yet the Jews as a nation have specially and above all others been set apart by Him as missionaries . . ."[30] the road to a "racial" mystique is in the process of development. The belief that the Jew is placed by birth in a surer relationship to God, whereby "Jesus must be something more to the Jew than he *could be* (my emphasis) to the Gentile, for he was the legal king of

Israel,"[31] has led to the assumption of some rather grandiose and far-reaching tasks for the Hebrew Christian. The dispensationalist tenet that "Christ is still to be Israel's king and Israel is still to be Christ's own,"[32] would no doubt be assimilable by the gentile churches. But there is basis for conflict when, in a sort of reverse reading of Romans 11:11 (wherein Paul asserts that the gentile Church was given life in order to make Israel jealous), the Hebrew Christian says that the *Church* needs *Israel* to point out the way. In following this reasoning, Moses Klerekoper proposes two functions for Hebrew Christianity that might stagger a more modest apologist; but for Israel, representing "the foundation of the apostles and prophets"[33] the task is thought to be performable. These are: (*a*) fight Rome and bring St. Peter's authority to Jerusalem, and (*b*) reemphasize Christ's primary emphasis on the Jewish people.[34] Hebrew Christianity is to act as a purifying agency for the Church, pointing the way back to the fundamentals, and the only channel through which these fundamentals can be retraced is their original vessels—the Jews.

> . . . the most promising conception of Hebrew Christianity is the theological one [for] . . . if the Jew today feels that Christianity is an alien religion, it is in large measure due to the fact that popular Christianity is not the religion of the New Testament. Increasingly it is being realized that the truth of the New Testament was during the second to fifth century poured into molds of thought that subtly changed it. The Reformation was another period of subtle change. As a result, while the Gospel is as much today as in the first century the power of God unto salvation unto every one that believeth, to the Jew first and also to the Gentile, there is much preached as Gospel truth that is only man's explanation of it. It may well be the principal task of Hebrew Christianity to feel its way back to the primitive apostolic simplicity of the Gospel, and then to express it in thought forms that will speak to Jew and Hebrew Christian alike.[35]

Thus the Jew who believes must affirm his racial identity;

he must maintain a separate existence if he is to fulfill his unique role within Christendom. The "mission" concept of Israel is retained in its ethnic ("racial") kernel which, however, is stripped of its religious shell, to be replaced by Christianity.

As suggested earlier, the emphasis on a peculiar grace devolving on the born Jew, though in large measure fostered by gentile dispensationalists and fundamentalists generally, has in many instances led to tension between the Hebrew Christion and gentile supporters. The attempt of Hebrew Christians to paint a portrait of the Jew as "indestructible," "God's chosen," "brilliant," "good," and so on, probably backfires more than it catches fire. I am convinced that the reluctance with which most Church bodies view Hebrew Christianity is at least in part a reaction to this "intemperate" appraisal. A line such as "they [the Jews] survived because they are indestructible, imperishable and vitally involved in God's plan"[36] is not designed to make the gentile Christian "feel good inside," no matter how weighty its scriptural warrant. Many Christians have questioned this emphasis on "racial" distinctiveness, suggesting like Geoffrey Allen that since the past dies with a rebirth in Christ, any claims to special grace must be denied.[37] Jakob Jocz, himself a leading proponent of Hebrew Christianity, has warned that this approach is self-defeating:

> In assessing the Hebrew Christian position we shall have to keep the Pauline concern constantly before us. The fact of origin can be understood in two ways. It can be taken as a special privilege, and become a source of pride, or else it can be accepted as a fact in humble acknowledgement of God's will and purpose.[38]

More often than not, the Hebrew Christian answer to such questions has exacerbated rather than lessened tensions. Why Hebrew Christianity? Why the reerection of the middle wall of partition? Statements in answer to these questions have either emphasized the failure of gentile Christendom or affirmed the special spiritual qualities of the Jews—qualities that are inborn, thus ineluctable. When a Hebrew Christian writes: ". . . the weak points in the Church's offensive will be strengthened by the entrance of Jewish nerve into Church fibers, that the loop holes in her discernment will be filled by the vision of eyes that have seen the glory of God in the Prophets,"[39] a point of view is propounded that may appeal to the ego of the Jew, but without question extracts a heavy price from that of the church as a whole.

Thus we must ask why a group of orthodox Christian believers emphasize "racial" distinctiveness as a central tenet of belief, when there is substantial ground to believe that this emphasis is divisive and perhaps unscriptural as well (given Paul's warning against building up the middle wall of partition) and unnecessary (given the "all in all" that is Christ). One might call this alleged orthodoxy into question, maintaining that this is merely the esoteric belief of a sectarian grouping; or, it might be explained as a deliberate ploy through which an essentially missionary enterprise could achieve greater and more lasting success. The answer, I believe, lies somewhere between these alternatives, involving aspects of both, with the former achieving substance and momentum with increasing recognition of the possibilities inherent in the latter.

Clearly the avowal of a twofold chosenness and the insistence on maintaining the separateness (purity) of the Jew would not win undeviating support from gentile Christians, or for that matter from most Jewish converts. The Gentiles were faced with a flesh-and-blood attestation to their status as the "wild branches" merely "grafted on," displacing the no doubt more palatable, because largely theoretical secondary positioning that heretofore remained buried and harmless in scripture. For many (perhaps most) Jewish converts these positions amounted

to still another barrier to full assimilation within the wider
Western civilization; and as we have noted, such a desire
almost invariably plays a role in this type of religious conversion. Why then has this potentially self-defeating pair of prop-
ositions arisen? Why are they maintained with such fervent
commitment by Hebrew Christian leadership, some gentile
churchmen, and the small but vocal Hebrew Christian rank
and file? One could of course ask the same question of the
Jehovah's Witnesses or the adherents of Father Divine, answer-
ing it by stating the obvious—because people believe what
they say to be right and true. Surely all such groups were
aware that their deviation was real and that its affirmation
involved a breach with the established order. I think, however,
that Hebrew Christianity contains one special element that is
either absent or not at all conspicuous in the other groups.
This is the conscious attempt made by and through Hebrew
Christianity to hook its fortunes to a rising star *within* the
normative structure—not to purify, reform, and restructure by
moving to the periphery (or to accept a *fait accompli*, which
places one there), thus institutionalizing a marginal status
through a sectarian development. In most deviant or sectarian developments we can trace a "holding action" in which
the sectarian group tries to maintain, rediscover, and protect
a lost, neglected, or misinterpreted element or a group of elements that the dominant group is unable or unwilling to
recognize. We see this in Hebrew Christianity with regard
to the "twice-chosenness," the very acceptance of Jesus as the
Messiah and the general theological framework of the movement. However, the approach assumed leads not to a defense
of the periphery or a shouting into the wind but to a direct
embrace of the existing polity. All religious sects lay claim to
the guardianship of a unique truth or a pure and original
structure, and Hebrew Christianity is no exception. But rather
than try to protect its discovery by removing itself from the
"rotten core," it chose to embrace the one factor that was *not*

lost or negated but occupied a central position in the Jewish scene—Jewish peoplehood. Sects protect and protest from the fringe, but Hebrew Christianity chose to leap headlong into the already avowed nineteenth-century core of Jewish nationalism. The theological posture that pushed to the fore the concepts of twice-chosenness and racial separateness *may* be able to stand on the terms implied—that is, insofar as they represent the beliefs of a particular group of people and could be accepted for what they purport to be (articles of faith). At the same time, however, such concepts serve as pivots for the contention that the Jews can be evangelized successfully only through the maintenance of their group autonomy; thus they must be analyzed in this light as well.

There can be little doubt that Hebrew Christianity's recognition of the relevance of the ethnic factor played a determining role in the move against the church's desire to overcome national barriers. Hebrew Christianity went in the opposite direction to appeal to what was conceived of as the widest possible base within Judaism—namely, those who insisted on retaining their ethnic identity. If the primary aim of the movement was the emotional and religious sustenance of those already converted, racial distinctiveness and separatism would have played no role (we are all one in Christ Jesus), and the emphasis on twice-chosenness would perhaps have provided some comfort, but not enough to justify risking the ire and suspicion of the Church. But insofar as these concepts bolster and vindicate the concept of Jewish peoplehood, which is assumed to be the most persistently held desideratum of the Jew, the risk can be considered to be well worth the price.

The leaders of Hebrew Christianity are not sectarians;[40] they do not represent the religiously or the socially disinherited. Rather, they are missionizing innovators who, in the search for a new method, have approached sectarian differentiation: tactical considerations have led to developments bordering on theological schism.

DISCOVERY OF THE SOCIOLOGY OF THE JEW

There can be little doubt that the most outstanding methodological innovation of Hebrew Christianity is the embrace of
Jewish peoplehood and the stress on a Jewish ethnic configuration through which it is hoped that the Jews will more
readily respond to the message of Christianity. The idea itself
is not new, but its institutionalization as the cornerstone of a
distinctive religiosocial movement did indeed herald the
emergence of a new dimension in the evangelistic program for
the Jews.[41] It was at last recognized (as it could scarcely fail
to be) that the Jews were not merely a curious religious relic
who somehow persisted in clinging to a single thin strand out
of their past. Instead, they represented an unusual blend of
elements, not the least of which was their anomalous but nonetheless real ethnic–national character.

Missionaries have explained the failure of past efforts to
convert large numbers of Jews without recourse to coercive
measures in many ways. Explanations have ranged from the
contentions that the Jews are inherently unable to assimilate
Christian truth and that the conversion of the Jews must await
the last days to the suggestion that the absence of Christian
love in these undertakings was at fault. Finally, as we noted
in discussing the parish approach, it was asserted that "normalcy" was the missing ingredient. Hebrew Christianity, in
admitting the last of these explanations has rejected the others
totally, insisting that the cause of past failures lies in the
inability of missionary bodies to recognize not only a Jewish
faith but a "sociology of the Jew" as well. The Jew, it is maintained, cannot be approached simply as one who lacks Christian faith, for "in dealing with a Jew we must not consider
the soul of the individual only, but the spirit of the nation as
a whole."[42] This would not be a startling novelty if it led
merely to an avowal of particular methods to fit the needs of
a distinct group. However, since it involved the notion that a

separate *Jewish* path to Christ is warranted and needed, it must be seen as a radical break with any traditional missionary pattern. Individuals and bodies other than Hebrew Christianity have recognized the dilemma posed in carrying Christianity to non-Christian, non-Western peoples and have taken into account the sociological dimensions and complexities of the problems involved. The missionary movement has, as it were, "discovered" sociology, finding much of heuristic value in Kraemer's plaint that

> In its evangelistic fervour the missionary movement did not realize in the least that it had to do not with the individual, who as human beings simply were placed before the alternative to answer positively or negatively to the message and the appeal of the Gospel and act accordingly, but with societies and highly integrated forms of life, having through their great antiquity an unquestioned authority and command over the life of these individuals.[43]

But in giving recognition to this truth, neither Kraemer nor the conventional missionary movement advocates recourse to syncretistic philandering, wherein Christianity is made to accommodate any and all social forms with which it is confronted.

> Every religion is a living, indivisible unity. Every part of it— a dogma, a rite, a myth, an institution, a cult—is so vitally related to the whole that it can never be understood in its real function, significance and tendency as these occur in the reality of life without keeping constantly in mind the vast and living unity of existential apprehension in which this part moves and has its being.[44]

Hebrew Christianity has affirmed the outline of this position without going to the heart of the matter by asserting that the Jew cannot eject himself from his social moorings because these are part of an indivisible whole, although a different faith can be *added* without adversely affecting the integrity of the whole. In affirming the indivisibility of Jewish peoplehood and Jewish religion, Hebrew Christianity nonetheless seeks to remove the one without seriously disturbing the other. It is assumed that the really important element in this scheme is not the religion (which has been displaced by a higher form) but the ethnic–national group which persists in the same way as an African Negro continues to be a Negro though he may have thrown off paganism and adopted Christianity. In other words, what is posited is that a Jew is a Jew (by race) and he cannot stop being a Jew any more than he can choose to be a rhinoceros. Furthermore, and perhaps more important, even if such disaffiliation were possible, the Jews have shown little enthusiasm (as the Hebrew Christian sees it) for negating their attachment to a Jewish community. Thus it appears that the outstanding fault of the Christian evangelistic enterprise among the Jews has been the failure to use this "racial loyalty" for Christ. How is it to be used? By having "Jews" convert other Jews and by providing assurance that the act of conversion in no way involves disloyalty to one's past.

In the first instance, Hebrew Christian supporters have been warned that "It's hard to catch Jews with Gentile bait,"[45] whereas in the second it is maintained that

> We must now make it unquestionably [sic] to our non-Christian Jewish brethren that in the proclamation of this blessed truth we do not seek to Gentilize them or make them members of the Protestant Episcopal or any other Gentile branch of Christ's Church; but that we do earnestly desire to prove to them that they are at liberty to remain in the cherished love of family and racial life when they accept Him as the Messiah; for Jews *though not compelled* are ever left free in Christ to exercise their Jewish national loyalty in Judah's spiritual favor.[46]

If the Jew's reluctance to disentangle himself from his ethnic–national roots and loyalties was a strong factor in vitiating past missionary efforts, it has become an even stronger factor in the present age of nationalism, when the Jew like others seeks a "renaissance along nationalistic lines." Just as others desire to fulfill their destinies as "whole men" (i.e., as creatures of flesh and blood and spirit), so do the Jews require this freedom. Jews, like other groups, display a national genius that produces peculiar modes of expression, underlying insights, and a distinct creative matrix that can be channeled to Christ if only the impulse itself is respected and the methods utilized conform to a preestablished and definable pattern. Christ cannot be imposed by gentiledom but must come as it were from within. If not by means of an apocalyptic awakening wherein the nation as a whole will lift the veil that blinds it, then at least by injecting into the normative stream *Jewish* converts who will "work among their own people, preaching Christ in the way that will appeal to Judaism [sic] and to the deepest longings of the Jewish mind."[47]

Hebrew Christian ideologues have observed again and again that the renewed interest beginning in the latter part of the nineteenth century in a national revival (i.e., Zionism) is a factor that the missionary movement dare not ignore. The Jews it is averred *are* a nation insofar as loyalty or ties to a sociological entity, a community, are operative. Thus Hebrew Christianity realistically appears on the scene, not because of any doctrinal dissonance within the Church but "to witness more effectively to the Jewish people which also in these days is being formed or reformed into a homogeneous people."[48]

What, it is asked, could have held the Jews in such primordial darkness as to continuously and repeatedly call forth a "nay" to the claims of Christ? How could they refuse to acknowledge the validity of His claims unless some powerful block made it almost impossible for them to choose to do so?[49] The Hebrew Christian answer is suggested by Max Reich, who states that it is

> . . . the accusation that in becoming a Christian a Jew commits a sin against his people. The Jewish leaders in their age long rejection of Israel's Corner Stone have done their best to foster

> this feeling, and this more than anything else, keeps some of the
> noblest sons of Israel in the synagogue and seals the lips which
> would otherwise openly confess Jesus as the Christ. The fear of
> becoming traitors to their beloved mother-nation holds them
> back. . . .[50]

This passage implies that even those (and there are presumed to be many) who believe in Christ deny their faith
because they would have to leap out of their skins, as it were,
to choose Christ, and except for the strongest, this is impossible.
Once the Jews can be assured "that members of their own race
believe . . . and are lovers of their people, they [the unconverted Jews] are influenced and encouraged to examine for
themselves the claims of Christ."[51] As long as Christianity was
presented as the province and the property of Christendom, it
was rejected by the Jew, who refuses to undergo a process of
self-alienation, for "to the average Jew, Christianity is not
only an alien religion but it makes an alien of the Jew that
accepts it."[52]

Thus Hebrew Christianity suggested that past missionary
failures among the Jews could be largely explained by the
proselytizer's refusal to recognize the powerful community
bond that held the Jew to an ethnic-national configuration.
That is, "it could not be expected of the Jewish people that
they would in any way countenance either the objects or
methods of Christian propaganda which . . . represented a
disruptive force aiming at the piecemeal destruction of their
racial integrity."[53] It has been assumed that this reputed
desire to maintain "racial integrity" is the most powerful
cohesive factor underlying the continued existence of the Jews,
and it is therefore held that the integration and recognition
of the continuing pertinence of a Jewish sociological entity can
provide increased evangelistic returns.[54]

The recognition of the existence of Jewish peoplehood in and
of itself would, however, lead to few changes, but in determining to make of this recognition a cardinal methodological propo-

sition, Hebrew Christianity assumed a new and rather unique direction, not alone within the missionary movement but as an expression of a special form of Christianity as well.

NOTES

1. Here I mean simply those who continued to seek answers to failure on a multicausal level, rather than attributing it totally to a peculiar Jewish deficiency of soul or mind.

2. Hugh J. Schonfield, *The History of Jewish Christianity* (London: Duckworth, 1936), p. 219. This volume, together with the historical material in the *Hebrew Christian Alliance Quarterly* (1917–1951), The *American Hebrew Christian* (1952–1960), and in David M. Eichhorn, "A History of Christian Attempts to Convert the Jews of the United States and Canada" (Ph.D. dissertation, Hebrew Union College, 1938), provide the basis for the historical material in this chapter.

3. Schonfield, *op. cit.*, p. 219.

4. *Ibid.*

5. *Ibid.*, p. 220.

6. *Ibid.*, p. 221.

7. *Ibid.*, p. 213.

8. The Russian experience is a particularly interesting one, though limited in influence and relatively short-lived. In 1882 Joseph Rabinowitz founded a Jewish-Christian synagogue, where he hoped Jews would remain in every respect Jews (retaining most of the synagogue ritual, etc.) but could become a community of believers in Christ. Rabinowitz was an avid Jewish nationalist, and Schonfield describes him as the "Herzl of Jewish Christianity." He appears to have been a saintly and pious soul who truly underwent a conversion that entailed a return to the roots of Christianity: to the Jewish people. He eschewed all denominational affiliation, insisting that his belief was a Jewish belief, thus isolating himself and condemning his work to an inevitable demise.

9. Between 1855 and 1878 no fewer than six Hebrew Christian brotherhoods were organized in the United States. They lasted for periods ranging from three months to two years. Most collapsed as a result of denominational difference and conflict, while some went under for lack of organization or leadership. They were as follows:

    1855   The American Hebrew Christian Association

> 1859   The American Hebrew Christian Brotherhood
> 1865   The American Hebrew Christian Brotherhood
> 1868   The American Hebrew Christian Brotherhood
> 1868   The Western Hebrew Christian Brotherhood
> 1876   The Hebrew Christian Association

See Eichhorn, *op. cit.*, pp. 317–336.

10. Eichhorn, *op. cit.*, p. 412. Elias Newman gives us the following description of the founding of the American movement. Both the American and English organizations are interdenominational, rather than non-denominational; the American organization (reflecting no doubt the American religious canvas) is considerably more so, however.

"In 1914 the real foundation was laid when a group of us met in Pittsburgh. It was not a large assembly. There were just six of us: Ruben, a German Jew, a business man, founder of the New Covenant Mission, with a passion for souls; at that time a Methodist, later he joined the U. P. [sic] Church; Rohold a Palestinian, a man with a long sighted vision, indefatigable and energetic, possessing a large heart always open to his brethren, Presbyterian; Kuldell, a Jew from the Baltic Provinces, a cultured gentleman and a Lutheran Pastor of Pittsburgh; Wertheimer, a veritable Zacheus in stature and zeal, a little German Jew, a former Reformed Rabbi and Christian Science practitioner and finally a Baptist minister who is still holding forth the message of Truth; Sternhertz, a quiet slow and deliberate thinker, originally from Russia but educated in Sweden, a Swedish Lutheran Pastor; then also the present speaker, at that time a Presbyterian minister but since eight years a Lutheran Pastor. The first conference met in New York City, in the Assembly Hall United Charities Building, April 6 to 9, 1915. Elias Newman. "Looking Back Twenty-Five Years," *Hebrew Christian Alliance Quarterly*, Vol. 25, No. 2 (Summer, 1940), 23–24.

Rev. Jacob Peltz, in resigning as General Secretary of the Hebrew Christian Alliance of America, brings out into the open the difficulties of the Alliance. In addition to taking note of such typical Jewish characteristics as bubbling over with ideas, wanting to be the leader, and lack of continuity in plans and execution, he also notes: "Add to these difficulties the fact that members of our Alliance belong to various Christian denominations, with their distinctive theological emphasis, and it will be realized what a tremendous task it has been to keep our Alliance together as a united testimony for Christ." Jacob Peltz, "Editorial Notes and Comments," *Hebrew Christian Alliance Quarterly*, Vol. 18, No. 3 (October–December 1933), 12.

11. Schonfield states that the American Hebrew Christian Alliance got the ball rolling for the International, and on March 25, 1925, a joint letter of the British and American Alliance was sent. Schonfield com-

pares the letter to the epistle to Gentile believers sent by the first
council of Jerusalem (Acts 15), but it would seem that the analogy
is somewhat threadbare. There is an unmistakable touch of modern-
ity about the entire undertaking.

> Dear Brethren in the Lord Jesus our Messiah,
>
> We members of the Hebrew Christian Alliances of Great
> Britain and America send you hearty greetings.
>
> Since the days of the Apostles Hebrew Christians have been
> scattered units in the diaspora, ostracized by our unbelieving
> brethren and lost among the nations. We believe, however, that
> the times of the Gentile are being fulfilled and that the God
> of our fathers according to His Gracious promise, is about to
> restore Israel to her ancient heritage. We also believe that as
> Hebrew Christians, though a remnant weak and shall we have
> a share in the building up of "the Tabernacle of David that
> is falled (sic) down."
>
> We have therefore decided to hold D.V. an international
> Hebrew Christian Conference in London, England this year
> from Saturday, September 5 to Saturday, September 12, and to
> this we heartily invite you.
>
> . . .
>
> The Hebrew Christian Alliance of London will, . . . during
> the period of the conference, September 5–12, give themselves
> the pleasure of providing hospitality to all delegates who
> will have registered beforehand and will have received cards
> and badges. To such delegates full particulars, together with the
> programme, will be sent in due course.
>
> With cordial greeting. . . .

Schonfield, *op. cit.*, pp. 238–239.

12. Here I deal primarily with the American Alliance and to a much
    lesser degree with the International.

13. "The Editor's Notes," *Hebrew Christian Alliance Quarterly*, Vol. 1,
    Nos. 3 and 4 (July–October 1917), 82.

14. Jacob Peltz, "Notes and Comments by the General Secretary,"
    Hebrew Christian Alliance Quarterly, Vol. 16, No. 3 (July and
    September 1931), 16.

15. Max I. Reich, "Queries for the Solemn Consideration of the Mem-
    bers of the Hebrew Christian Alliance," *Hebrew Christian Alliance
    Quarterly*, Vol. 31, No. 3 (Fall 1945), 4.

16. These continue, but in much abated form; they do not constitute a
    real threat.

17. The call for the second annual conference of the Hebrew Christian
    Alliance of America, May 2–5, 1916, contains the following point
    reflecting on the why of Hebrew Christianity:

"When we look at the evangelizing agencies now in operation among Israel, how inadequate in number, some in quality, some in equipment, some in support. Who, if not we, shall take up the difficult task of making this grave problem of Jewish evangelization in these days of our opportunity, the main issue in our existence?"

18. S. B. Rohold, "Needs of the Jewish Mission Field," *Hebrew Christian Alliance Quarterly*, Vol. 1, No. 1 (January 1917), 3.

19. Elias Newman, "The Average Jew and the Gospel," *Hebrew Christian Alliance Quarterly*, Vol. 1, Nos. 3 and 4 (July and October 1917), 130.

20. The sense of wrong having been perpetrated is poignantly illustrated in the following quotation from an article by Elias Newman entitled "Looking Back Twenty-Five Years." Here the plight of the disinherited, the alienated is revealed, with the implicit suggestion that a separate Hebrew Christian existence is warranted and necessary.

"Twenty-five years ago when we began to unite we were warned, we were threatened, we were cajoled, we were urged not to form such an alliance. It was supposed to be unscriptural. We were (so they said) about to re-build the middle wall of partition. We had to watch our steps. If we wanted to eat a Jewish corned beef sandwich we were considered as Judaisers. If we wanted to get married we were told we must marry a Gentile; there were a few Hebrew Christian girls and they had to marry Gentiles and if we were imprudent to cast an eye upon one of these maidens, flesh of our flesh, we were considered in danger of apostasy, etc."

Hebrew Christian Alliance Quarterly, Vol. 25, No. 2 (Summer 1940), p. 24.

"Others were afraid that an alliance would only lead to the formation of a Hebrew Christian Church. Hebrew Christians must not unite. Union was only for Gentile Christians. Some of us were interested in Palestine and that too was wrong, we were told: our citizenship was above. We had no interests on earth. The Gentile Christian could maintain a dual allegiance: below where he shouted loudly and vociferously, 'God save the King' or 'My Country Tis of Thee'; and above, singing just as earnestly, 'Heaven is My Home' or 'I am a Stranger Here.' We Hebrew Christians could only look to heaven. To think of any kind of earthly Jerusalem was considered a mistake on our part. . . ." *Ibid.*, 24.

21. That the Jew is sick and restless is a pervasive theme among Hebrew Christians. "Anyone who has had close dealings with the Jew finds that inside of him there is an aching heart, a restless and sick soul." Gartenhaus, *What of the Jews?*, (Atlanta, Ga.: Home Mission Board, Southern Baptist Convention, 1948) foreword.

Or again: "The Jew in his suffering has not become the object of missionary activity. His disturbed equilibrium is not considered a cause for Christian action. The missionaries have given up this field to proponents of Jewish nationalism and to communistic agitators who have an easy mark in the disturbed (sic) Hebrew." *Ibid*, p. 24.

22. Romans 11:28.

23. Romans 11:29. Romans 2:29 seems to contradict this: "But he is a Jew, which is one inwardly; and circumcision is that of the heart, in the spirit, and not in the letter; whose praise is not of men, but of God." However, Romans, 2:28 states, "For he is not a Jew, which is one outwardly; . . ." This difficulty is overlooked in the ideational structure of Hebrew Christianity. In 1958 and 1959 there was a piece in every issue of *The American Hebrew Christian* on the current Israeli dispute on "Who is a Jew?" The believers recognized the significance of the matter for their own interests and they were on the side of the liberals (i.e., Ben Gurion: any one who has at least one Jewish parent and considers himself a Jew, is a Jew). Because of the nature of modern Judaism and present Jewish peoplehood, there can be no definitive answer to the question, Who is a *Jew*? I think, however, that the positions of Buber and Baron most closely approximate a normative approach. Kosmala and Smith quote Buber as follows: "Whoever regards Jesus as an historical personality be he ever so high, may belong to us; but he who acknowledges Jesus to be the Messiah already come, cannot belong to us; he who tries to weaken or to divert our belief in a redemption still to come, there is no agreement with him." Hans Kosmala and Robert Smith, *The Jew in the Christian World* (London: Student Christian Movement Press, 1942). p. 58.

Baron states: "As a permanent minority outside of Israel we are insisting upon the right of Jews and other minorities freely to pursue their own religion and cultural aims in a pluralistic society. We shall similarly have to learn to get along with much cultural pluralism in our own midst. I for one am prepared, therefore, to recognize, even for practical purposes, everyone as a Jew who (1) is born of Jewish parents and has not been converted to another faith; (2) is born of mixed parentage but declares himself a Jew and is so considered by the majority of his neighbors; and (3) one who by conscious will has adopted Judaism and joined the membership of the Jewish community." Salo W. Baron, "Who is a Jew? Some Historical Reflections," *Midstream*, Vol. 6, No. 2 (Spring 1960), 158–159.

24. Schonfield, *op. cit.*, p. 245.

25. *Ibid.*,

26. Rev. A. Cairns, "The Imperative Appeal," *Hebrew Christian Alliance Quarterly*, Vol. 9, No. 4 (October and December 1926) 121–122.

27. Max Reich, "Our Objective," *Hebrew Christian Alliance Quarterly*, Vol. 21, No. 2 (Fall 1936), 2.

28. *Ibid.*

29. *Ibid.*

30. F. L. Denman, *Hebrew Christians as Missionaries to Gentiles*, tract (London Society for Promoting Christianity Amongst the Jews, 1914), p. 13.

31. Schonfield, *op. cit.*, p. 227.

32. Elias Newman, "The American Jew and the Gospel," *Hebrew Christian Alliance Quarterly*, Vol. 1, Nos. 3 and 4 (July and October 1917), 131.

33. Moses Klerekoper, "Hebrew Christianity," *Hebrew Christian Alliance Quarterly*, Vol. 18, No. 2 (July and September 1933) 13.

34. *Ibid.*

35. H. L. Ellison, "The Riddle of Hebrew Christianity," *Hebrew Christian Alliance Quarterly*, Vol. 31, No. 1 (Spring 1945), 10.

36. Gartenhaus, *What of the Jews? op. cit.*, p. 23.

37. See G. Allen, *Theology of Missions* (London: Student Christian Movement Press, Ltd., 1943), p. 45 ff.

38. Jakob Jocz, *A Theology of Election: Israel and the Church* (London: Society for the Promotion of Christian Knowledge, 1958). But even Jocz assumes a peculiar role for the Jew *qua* Jew from which there is no escape. He is the "witness" *par excellence.* "As is the case with the Jewish people, the Hebrew Christian is a witness, though he may personally not be engaged in missionary work. His witness is implied in his position as a Jewish believer in Jesus Christ. As long as he maintains this position he is a witness in a special sense to his own people and to the Gentile Church." *Ibid.*, p. 181.

39. Fred Kendal, "Preparing Jewish Converts for Baptism," *Hebrew Christian Alliance Quarterly*, Vol. 25, No. 3 (Fall 1940), 9.

"In the midst of present day materialism and the revival of God-less Humanism, wholesale apostasy and unbelief which overshadows the Protestant Church, like a vast swarm of locusts covering the earth, eating away the very vitals, energy and vitality of the Christian testimony, in the midst of all this we of the Hebrew Christian Alliance have a definite message to proclaim and a vital testimony to give."

Elias Newman, "Seventeenth Annual Conference of the Hebrew Christian Alliance of America," *Hebrew Christian Alliance Quarterly*, Vol. 16, No. 3 (July and September 1931), 4.

40. That is, the leaders are not sectarians except insofar as Peter Berger's extended definition holds water. Berger maintains that it is more fruitful to think of sectarianism as a religious process of sociation. See Peter L. Berger, "Sectarianism and Religious Sociation," *American Journal of Sociology*, Vol. 64 (July 1958), 41–44.

41. As early as 1819 a convert named John David Marc wrote to Joseph

Frey outlining his ideas for the creation of a Hebrew Christian
Union, in which the efficacy and need for a national–ethnic approach
assume prime importance. In a list of the difficulties that block the
road to Christ for the Jew, Marc put particular emphasis on:

"3. The dreadful idea to separate from a nation, whose distinct
and lasting existence, as a peculiar people, God had so clearly
promised. . . .

4. That brotherly love which he enjoys amongst his own people,
but which he nowhere else observes in such degree.

5. The mere idea of going amongst Christians excites in him a
timidity indescribable.

6. The greatest difficulty lies in the way of the poor. Where is
he to seek for help and assistance in time of need? He stands alone
in the world; he is forsaken by his Jewish brethren; and to apply to
the Christians—the very thought is painful to his feelings, and from
their past conduct to the Jews he is apprehensive to be looked upon,
nay, even treated, as a self-interested hypocrite."

Quoted in Eichorn, *op. cit.*, p. 82.

42. Morris Zeidman, "The Place of the Mission in the Scheme of Jewish Evangelization," *Hebrew Christian Alliance Quarterly*, Vol. 17,
No. 4 (July and September 1932), 18.

43. Kraemer, *op. cit.*, p. 52.

44. *Ibid.*, p. 135.

45. Rev. A. Cairns, "The Imperative Appeal," *Hebrew Christian Alliance Quarterly*, Vol. 9, No. 4 (October and December 1926), 122.

46. Mark John Levy, "Jewish Ordinances in the Light of Hebrew-
Christianity," *Hebrew Christian Alliance Quarterly*, Vol. 1, Nos. 3
and 4, (June and October 1917), 138. The author appears to have
been a saintly but much abused soul; he was thoroughly convinced
that with the promise of ethnic–national autonomy the Jews would
drop all opposition to the claims of Christ. He labored tirelessly to
have Hebrew Christianity go "all the way" in Judaizing the movement, but he evidently achieved much more success among Gentile
sympathizers than among Hebrew Christians, who have always feared
the manifold implications of such a move (this is alluded to in
greater detail in the discussion of Judaizing as a method of legitimation). He did, however, induce the Protestant Episcopal Church to
recognize his position, and at their convention in October 1916 they
affirmed the following: "Our Jewish brethren are free to observe
the national rites and ceremonies of Israel when they accept Christ
(as the Messiah) according to the clear teaching of the New Testament and the practice of Christ and the Apostles" *ibid.*, 138.

Another argument brought forth for the "traditional" validity of this approach is the exchange between Justyn Martyr and Trypho, wherein it is said that the Jew can have recourse to his national customs and loyalties and yet be a completely acceptable believer. Lowe quotes the following exchange between Justyn Martyr and Trypho: "Trypho again inquired, 'But if someone . . . after he recognizes that this man is Christ, and has believed in and obeys Him, wishes however, to observe these institutions, [the law] will he be saved?" I said, "In my opinion Trypho such an one will be saved—if he does not strive in every way to persuade other men [i.e., Gentiles] who have been saved by Christ to do the same things as himself, telling them that they will not be saved unless they do so. Also, if some wish to observe such institutions as were given by Moses, from which they expect some virtue . . . along with their hope in this Christ, and wish to perform the eternal and natural acts of righteousness and piety, yet choose to live with the Christians and faithful, as I have said before, not inducing them to be circumcised like themselves or to keep the Sabbath, or to observe any such ceremonies, then I hold that we ought to join ourselves to such, and associate with them in all things as kinsmen and brethren.' " "Justyn, Dialogue" (Scribner's Antinicean Christian Library), quoted by William George Lowe, in "Jewish Christianity and Jewish Christians," *Hebrew Christian Alliance Quarterly*, Vol. 28, No. 3 (Fall 1943), 10.

47. "Across the Desk—the Editor," *Hebrew Christian Alliance Quarterly*, Vol. 33, No. 1 (Spring 1947), 18.

48. Moses Klerekoper, "Hebrew Christianity," *Hebrew Christian Alliance Quarterly*, Vol. 18, No. 2 (July and September 1933), 112.

49. Morris Zutrau illustrates the genuiness of this dilemma when he asks, "Have you not had the experience of talking with a Jew embittered by persecution, only to find that after you had spent hours with him, and even brought him to the point where he could not answer your arguments, yet he was just as much opposed to Christ as ever?" "The Printed Page Pointing Jews to Christ," *Hebrew Christian Alliance Quarterly*, Vol. 26, No. 2 (Summer 1941) 20. Zutrau's bland answer is, "That sort of Jew needs something else than a tract or a talk on the Trinity. He needs to know that the badge of a Christion is love" *ibid.*, 20.

50. Max Reich, "Missionary Turns Legionaire," *Hebrew Christian Alliance Quarterly*, Vol. 2, No. 4 (October 1918), 133.

51. Jacob Peltz, "The Hebrew Christian Alliance of America—a Questionnaire," *Hebrew Christian Alliance Quarterly*, Vol. 9, No. 4 (October and December 1926), 128.

52. H. L. Ellison, "The Riddle of Hebrew Christianity," *Hebrew Christian Alliance Quarterly*, Vol. 31, No. 1 (Spring 1945), 7.

53. Schonfield, *op. cit.*, p. 210.

54. Some Hebrew Christians, notably Jocz, have feared that this emphasis on the sociological approach might lead to an overvaluation on a "group" conversion to the detriment of *individual* salvation. He is afraid that Jews may find too much comfort in being assured that their Jewishness is immutable and will await a national conversion rather than take the step alone. He states: "For the individual to submit to Israel's 'fate' is to neglect the day of opportunity and despise the grace of God. No Jew dare wait for the rest of his people so that he can make the journey in company. The road to God is a lonely path and can be undertaken only by a decision of faith." *Theology of Election, op. cit.*, p. 183. Jocz recognizes the scriptural difficulty in asserting a national destiny that is too radical. If the Jewish nation is destined to accept Christ as a nation, what will this preclude for the believer who might say, "I cannot slough off my skin or my heritage"? Supplementing the answer just cited, Jocz says that ". . . a Jewish decision for Christ means today what it meant in the first century and what it will always mean to the believer, a rift, a break" *ibid.*, pp. 185–186.

5

Legitimation

The genius of Hebrew Christianity lies in its recognition of the existence of a Jewish "order" going far beyond the expression of Jewish faith. Not only did Hebrew Christianity take note of this reality, it also displayed a lively willingness to mold itself in accordance with what it conceived to be the dominant themes underlying the total structure.

Earlier missionary efforts among the Jews attempted to legitimize Christianity purely through faith. Hebrew Christianity, in recognizing that Judaism was a complex phenomenon embracing a way of life, saw this as an almost insurmountable barrier to an avowal of faith in a different religion, bearing no appeal to legitimacy except perhaps an abstract claim to religious continuity with the Old Testament. Rather than continue to attempt to overshadow the totality of Jewish experience, it sought to use Judaism as a framework, placing an act of faith in Christ within rather than without the existing scaffolding. The Hebrew Christian seeks adherence to a *normative system* and not alone to a church, simply because the Hebrew Christian has recognized totality, a peoplehood, and not *just* a church.

According to Max Weber, to be considered binding or legitimate is the strongest support a normative order can have. Weber points to a hierarchy of "order stability" wherein an order that is adhered to because of expediency is less tenable, less stable than one sustained by tradition. But an order that can claim legitimacy is viewed as being the most stable of the three, since it has "the prestige of being considered binding."[1]

One may view Hebrew Christianity as an attempt to provide a system within which the Jew could and would view Christianity as a binding or legitimate religious expression of one's Jewishness.

But before this could be accomplished, the factors[2] on which the legitimacy of normative Judaism was based had to be recast to permit them to ascribe legitimacy not to Judaism but to Christianity. Everything that once had militated against the acceptance of Chrsit would now be utilized to legitimize the embrace of Christianity. As Weber notes, "in times of strict traditionalism a new order, that is one which was *regarded* as new, could, without being revealed in this way, only become legitimized by the claim that it had actually always been valid though not yet rightly known, or that it had been obscured for a time and was now being restored to its rightful place."[3]

In fact, Hebrew Christianity asserts that the true tradition has been destroyed or obscured by a fraudulent development and that modern Judaism is living a lie.

We have no objection to Jews "strengthening their allegiance to their own religion" provided they do so by the way of their prophetic writings. We distinguish between *the religion of ancient Israel* and *modern Judaism*. The first leads direct to Him whom God has made Lord and Christ at His right hand. The second is the invention of Pharisaic rabbis and lawyers intended to keep Israel in ignorance of Him. The New Testament and not the Talmud is the true continuation of Moses and the Prophets.[4]

So old, they insist, is this tradition of faith in Christ, that it

may have antedated the establishment of Jewish peoplehood,
for even

> . . . Old Testament saints might be called Hebrew Christians in
> the sense that by faith they looked forward to the great sacrifice
> in their daily sacrifices. "Abraham saw My day and was Glad."
> We look back to the sacrifice of Christ and receive assurance and
> comfort.[5]

In assuming that the most unyielding obstacle to the conversion of great numbers of Jews was a fear (among Jews) of
destroying the tradition, of becoming renegades to family,
faith, and culture, Hebrew Christianity tried to provide assurance of the contrary. If the prospective convert inquired what
effect his conversion would have on his previous loyalties, he
could be assured that "upon accepting Christ he does not give
up anything *vital* (my emphasis) in Judaism, but rather has
light and meaning and vitality shed upon his ancient faith."[6]
If he asks why a national conversion has not occurred, or why
there are not many more Jewish believers in Christ, he could
be told that the fault lies not in the unacceptability of Christianity but that the "reason the mass of Jews are not in harmony with Christianity is that *they* are not fully Jews"[7] How is
this possible? Simply because "Judaism is Christianity in bud.
Christianity is Judaism in fruitage."[8] Those who refuse to take
note of this fact are in essence rejecting the very viability of
what they purport to be their faith. It is those who insist on
retaining the hollow shell that is called Judaism who are least
justified in calling themselves Jews, because "it is in us Hebrew
Christians that the line of faith is continued during the period
of our nation's unbelief, that we are the link between the true
and faithful in Israel in the past, and the converted and saved
Israel in the future."[9]

The use of Scripture is extensive and points not only to the
continuity of the "tradition" but to the emotional buttressing
as well. No matter how strong the appeal to the continuity

with tradition, affectual attitudes must play a supportive role. The convert must be able to trace his spiritual hegira with an intellectually acceptable traditional pattern; but it must also be possible for him to believe that he has had meaningful personal contact with and involvement in the whole. Especially in matters of faith, there is probably something very basic within the individual that rejects being placed on the receiving end of religious truths, and particularly as in the case of the Jew, truths of which he considers himself the fountainhead. There must exist the feeling that this is one's very own, one's most precious personal (in the collective sense of peoplehood, as well as in the individual sense) discovery and possession. This is illustrated in the following comment, which carries with it a ring of authenticity and sincerity:

> The writer was by his acceptance of Christ Jesus not gone through a delusion of the mind and heart, but by the guidance of God into the inheritance of his fathers, his own Jewish fathers. What a glory to see this, not to be on foreign ground, but on his own, his fathers' ground. There is nothing more glorious for a Jew than to discover this harmony of being on his own Biblical fathers' ground. This gives joy and firmness. Indeed he can say "Jesus is mine."[10]

Once it becomes feasible to identify one's self existentially with a phenomenon as well as with a relatively impersonal and abstract tradition, the supports of the legitimating process become correspondingly stronger. The combination of an appeal based on scriptural "legality" and an unbroken tradition lead to a strengthening of the all-important affectual involvement. The assurance that the "legal" positioning of Jew and Gentile is that the Jews are the good olive tree and the Gentiles the "wild branches grafted on contrary to nature" provides a cushion against the possibility of guilty usurpation of a destiny not inherently the Israelites, making it possible to *reclaim* rather than *lay claim*. This is an extremely old approach, as Hort indicates in noting that when Paul prayed in the synagogues it meant for the early Jewish believer in Christ "virtually a claim on their behalf to be the truest Israelites."[11] Not only were they heir to the tradition in terms of their unbreakable involvement with it, they were its legal inheritors as well.

In dealing with the phenomenon of faith it is virtually impossible to clearly separate affectuality and rationality. That is, we cannot trace a logical sequence or untangle that which is felt or internally experienced from that which is "rationally believed." "Submission to an order," as Weber has noted, "is almost always determined by a variety of motives; by a wide variety of interests and by a mixture of adherence to tradition and belief in legality. . . ."[12] Weber further said that "in a very large proportion of cases the actors subject to the order are of course not even aware how far it is a matter of custom, of convention, or of law."[13] It is the sociologist in the final analysis who "must attempt to formulate the typical basis of validity."[14] In this context there is little doubt that the primary basis for ascribing legitimacy to Christianity is an appeal to its legal and traditional continuity and connectiveness to the true and original faith of Israel. Affectual attitudes and any emphasis on rationality are subthemes in the overall phenomenon, considerably more elusive and much less subject to documentation than is the traditional–legal typology. We can, however, document and objectively analyze what I call the tools of legitimation, or the devices utilized by Hebrew Christians to underscore the traditional acceptability and legal basis for the avowal of Christianity as the *bona fide* religious expression of the Jews. This is to be accomplished in a number of ways, including especially: (*a*) embracing political Zionism to indicate continuing and intensified commitment to a Jewish ethnic–national destiny; (*b*) Judaizing, or the attempt to consciously syncretize Christianity via the Judaization of

Christian dogma; and (*c*) the possible creation of a Hebrew Christian Church that would embody and give institutional expression to (*a*) and (*b*).

EMBRACING ZIONISM

Hebrew Christianity began to achieve stability and organizational sophistication at about the same period in history that witnessed the emergence and phenomenal growth of political Zionism as a force among the Jews of the Western world. The ghettos of Europe, which had begun to disintegrate with the enlightenment, breathed their last at the end of World War I, and with this collapse new forces were set rolling in Jewish life, presaging radical change in the religious, cultural, economic, and social patterns of the Jews. Perhaps the most significant of the new forces was Zionism, not in its simplest definition as a political expedient for the oppressed among the Jews but in its larger context as an all-embracing response to the question, whither the Jews? Baron is no doubt correct in asserting that

> Despite its outward secularization, therefore, its professed attempt at "normalizing" Jewish existence on the level of other nations and its endeavor to unite the whole people from the extreme orthodox to the extreme agnostics, the Zionist movement was but an offshoot of the traditional Jewish messianic idea.[15]

Zionism like Judaism did not lend itself to one-dimensional analysis in its early formulation: like Judaism itself, it was an anomalous and highly complex response to an elusive reality. It is no doubt partly for this reason that large segments of world Jewry reacted vigorously to make the movement an expression often willy-nilly of this or of that position or outlook, and it is thus that Zionism, in begging definitiveness and

allowing for variegated interpretations of its nature and purposes, could be readily assimilated by Hebrew Christianity as
a legitimating tool.

How was this so? Partly because Hebrew Christian ideologues saw in the polar appeal of Zionism a threefold opportunity for evangelistic gain. First, insofar as Zionism based its
appeal on the entire spectrum of Jewish life from orthodoxy
to rabid antireligionists, an avowal of Zionism afforded an
opportunity to separate Judaism the religion from Jews the
people in a perfectly consistent (in terms of Zionism) fashion.
In this manner it was hoped that the Hebrew Christian would
appear as just another Jew—with, however, a different faith—
much as the religionist and the antireligionist considered themselves Zionists and Jews. Second, the embrace of Zionism could
indicate that Christianity need not upset the Jews' pattern of
ethnic–national loyalty; quite the contrary, insofar as Christian eschatology left ample room for the prophetic doctrine of
national restoration, Christianity could enhance this loyalty.
Finally, Zionism was "courted" on a pragmatic organizational
level. Because it afforded entree to an area that had captured
the imagination of so many Jews, it was no longer necessary
to move against the tide in this area as well as in the realm of
religious faith. In other words, it was possible to go "all out"
on this one aspect of Jewish life, without necessitating a compromise with Christian belief.

The messianic nature of Zionism appears to have been a
tailor-made strut in the legitimation of Christianity among
the Jews. If the Hebrew Christian's claim to being part of the
Jewish reality could be denied in terms of his rejection or
unauthorized reconstruction of Judaism the faith, this claim
could not (he felt) be rejected in terms of his birthright as a
racial member of the *Klal Yisroel,* the people of Israel. Insofar
as Hebrew Christianity needed a "handle" for its claim to
being Jewish, it had to be along national rather than religious
lines. But because Zionism was a religiopolitical movement, it

provided an unparalleled opportunity for displaying solidarity with the "secular" aspiration of the Jewish people on the one hand, while on the other crediting the motivation for this expression of unity to religious desiderata best expressed within a *Christian* framework. Political Zionism was explained by Hebrew Christians in terms of prophetic fulfillment as follows: ". . . it is itself a beginning; and in the light of prophecy it is thus shown at its outset to be a movement likely to have an important outcome."[16] What is this outcome to be? Nothing less than

> . . . the crowning event, that which is outside of Jewish expectation, will be the coming of the Messiah in glory whom they will recognize as none other than Jesus, the crucified. After a representative portion of the nation will have been restored to the promised land, the Son of man shall come in the clouds of heaven and manifest Himself to Israel as the Son of David whose right is to reign in Zion. Filled with remorse and contrition as they "look upon Him whom they have pierced," they shall repent and exclaim "Blessed is he that cometh in the name of the Lord."[17]

Zionism is viewed in terms of Jewish eschatology but through Christian spectacles. Thus although Judaism is indeed "fast ripening for its last tribulation,"[18] the final result will be not the restoration of national sovereignty alone nor the reinstitution of the temple sacrifice, but the Christian dispensationalist fulfillment in the reign of Christ over Judah and the world. In accepting Zionism as essentially a religious movement, the Hebrew Christian does not close the door to his own participation; on the contrary, he finds greater rationale and motivation than nonbelieving Jews can claim.

> If any class of Jews are really prepared for zionism it is the Christian Jew, for he thoroughly believes in zionism for Israel and zion's sake according to the divine program and purposes

of God for them. We Hebrew Christians are by the grace of God
the advance guard in the movement. . . .[19]

The long-term objective of Hebrew Christianity in adopting
Zionism is the legitimation of Christianity as a valid mode
of Jewish existence, but its shorter-term or tactical goal
is the acceptance (by Jews) of Jewish believers in Christ as
bona fide Jews who differ from their fellows only in regard
to their interpretation of the faith of Israel. Before Christianity could be demonstrated as constituting a legitimate,
indeed *the* legitimate religious expression of "Jewishness," it
had to be shown that Jews who espoused this doctrine would
continue to identify with and operate within a "Jewish"
framework. Thus, since the first Zionist Congress in 1897
Hebrew Christians have sought to prove this "identity" by
zealously supporting the goals and aspirations of political
Zionism.

> Hebrew Christians in my judgement owe a duty to generations
> yet unborn to vindicate manfully and persistently their inalien-
> able right to be considered a part of their people. They must
> make it manifest by word and deed that they feel themselves one
> with them, both in their sufferings and in their present struggles
> for national reconstruction.[20]

According to Reich, "Jews must be taught to recognize that
faith in Jesus as the Messiah leaves the national bond, with
its accompanying citizen rights, unbroken."[21] To substantiate
this claim, numerous plans for colonies in Palestine were formulated "to get young Hebrew Christian pioneers who will go
out and work on the land . . . [and] be second to none among
Jews in zeal and devotion."[22]

But as indicated earlier, the affirmation of Zionism promised
additional rewards. First, to be sure, it was important to stake
a claim to being Jewish that could not be set aside by any
deviation—be it to Christianity, communism, or agnosticism.

If one who was born a Jew identified himself as a Jew (and what firmer affirmation of one's Jewishness than a desire to see the people reconstituted a whole nation in their own land?), then he *was* a Jew. Furthermore, if it could be demonstrated that in becoming a Christian one not only remained within the fold, but did so with zeal, dedication, and scriptural enrapturement—a part of the nation in all respects not only in terms of aspirations but sharer as well in the sufferings that mark the life of the Jew—then how could the Jews continue to stigmatize the believer as apostate, traitor, assimilationist or worse? Not only was the embrace of Zionism intended to give the lie to these assertions, thus legitimating the believer as a Jew and Christianity as an assimilable expression of Jewish belief, it was also seen as a potent tool of evangelization.

Hebrew Christians, like so many fundamentalists, tend to view all phenomena in monistic terms. Everything is explained within the most limited and limiting frame of reference, and always in terms of a somewhat static core structure—unmoving and unmovable for time and eternity. Thus the Hebrew Christian thinkers and leaders saw two possible courses emerge in the collapse of the ghetto and the movement of East European Jewry to the Western world, with its unbridled freedom to threaten the old orthodoxy. Either the Jews would turn to secular movements such as communism, socialism, and Zionism, or they would at last open their hearts to the Gospels and surrender to their own Jesus of Nazareth. Everything falling between on the continuum would prove to be transitory and ultimately unsatisfactory. Of the "isms" bedeviling the emancipated Jews, it was believed that only Zionism (which was scriptural) promised evangelistic success by finally broadening the limited intellectual and spiritual scope of the Jew. The almost simultaneous origins of Hebrew Christianity and Zionism pointed to a joint destiny of the two, and by ignoring all other developments, trends, disputes, and forces within Jewish life, it could with perfect faith and equanimity be

asserted that "the Jews are electing a congress for their political end; we are forming an alliance for their spiritual awakening"[23] as if the two events were inextricably bound in history.[24] It is naïvely thought that if Jewish life is in flux, if
through enthusiasm for Zionism "the Jews . . . have acquired
a new interest in their Jewishness,"[25] this interest will have to
flow toward Christianity so long as Hebrew Christianity is
"within," so as to better cultivate this trend.[26] Until the 1970s
and the appearance in Jerusalem of dozens of young Jews for
Jesus, Hebrew Christian Zionism had had very little practical
or operational effect. It will be interesting and possibly highly
significant to see what effect the new visible "practical" Zionism of the young believers will have in fulfilling a legitimating
role.

JUDAIZING

If Hebrew Christianity could with little significant internal
opposition affirm political Zionism, making its goals and aspirations fit snugly into the larger ones espoused by the movement, this was by no means the case with the phenomenon
known as Judaizing. Zionism possessed the glad faculty of
being upholdable both in its intent *and* in its methods. Nothing—be it restored Jewish sovereignty, agricultural colonies,
the revival of the Hebrew tongue, or the rise of Jewish politi-
cism—prevented the whole-hearted embrace of Zionism by
Hebrew Christians.[27] All this could be said to enjoy scriptural
warrant, and at the same time it furthered a prime methodological tenet of the movement—namely, it corroborated the
contention that being a Jew was a matter of birth and a continuing commitment to a Jewish ethnic–national entity. The
believers sought to demonstrate that this commitment could
be supported at least as well by Christian faith, as by Rabbinic
Judaism. However, the question of Judaizing (i.e., the conscious

attempt to syncretize normative Protestant Christianity with an overlay of Jewish ritual practice and a loose involvement with the law) engendered considerable conflict within the movement and widespread condemnation of those who propounded it.

Even before Hebrew Christianity achieved viable organizational form, missionaries saw evangelistic possibilities in "adapting" Christianity to Jewish forms and patterns.[28] As long ago as 1890 a missionary by the name of Niles was described by Thompson as "a staunch advocate of the theory that converts ought still to observe the ceremonial law, and remain distinctively Jewish. . . ."[29] But even before the turn of the century the dangers of this course were apparent, and Niles's proposal was rejected. In Russia at about the same time, Rabinowitz put the plan to the test, celebrating the Jewish holy days and festivals, wearing a skull cap, and affecting a flowing beard.[30] In Poland, a convert named Lucky continued to pray in the synagogue, used phylacteries and prayer shawl, and considered the ceremonial law, if not binding, at least desirable for a Hebrew Christian.[31]

But these individuals lacked a significant following; they were tolerated *in spite* of their aberration and were indulged by Jews and Christians alike in a spirit of mild wonderment.

Only when the Hebrew Christian *movement* appeared on the scene did the question of the relationship of the Jewish-Christian to the ceremonial law acquire substance. There were at least two reasons for this. First, people naturally wondered whether the Jew, being approached with Christianity and finding it all or partly acceptable, would be finally won by the assurance that his old way of life would remain intact save for the addition of Christ. Second, if the contention of the Hebrew Christian that he was a special Christian was to have any meaning beyond its "racial" implications, would not the most logical source for the drawing of this "meaning" be that of the Jewish religious heritage?

Some of the leaders of Hebrew Christianity realized that

the claim to completed or "full" Judaism would require more than verbal affirmation if it was to have any weight in the conversion of Jews. "Why," it was asked, "could not the Jew who accepted Christ continue in his specifically Jewish ways much as others within Christendom worshipped and lived according to their own peculiar and diverse lights?" Some, particularly Levertoff, Schonfield, and Levy, insisted that the Jewish believer may indeed continue to celebrate certain Jewish festivals and to utilize the ritual objects and patterns of Judaism in a refined and perfect Christian framework. Levy and Levertoff proposed what amounted to Reform Judaism plus Jesus of Nazareth. Levy suggested:

> The feasts of the Lord enumerated in the twenty-third chapter of Leviticus (i.e., the Sabbath, Passover, Unleavened Bread, Pentecost, Trumpets, Day of Atonement and Tabernacles) have a three-fold fulfillment; (1) a national application to Israel; (2) an individual application to every Christian; (3) a dispensational or corporate application to the Church Universal. Confusion arises in the Church because we do not note the fact carefully and thus measure our doctrines by the yardstick of Israel's *God-given* (my emphasis) customs.[32]

Levy asserts that these festivals are God-given, thus not subject to man's abrogation. In addition, they serve as pointers or reminders of the ultimate fulfillment in Christ, so that while the Passover celebrates the emergence of Israel as a people it had a "spiritual" result when "Christ our Passover was sacrificed for us and rose again for our justification."[33]

Levertoff compiled a communion service for the use of Hebrew Christians, using as variegated sources the prophets, the Gospels, the Song of Songs, the Siddur (Hebrew prayer book), the Passover Haggadah, as well as the Book of Common Prayer of the Church of England. This service called for the use of *"Haloth* [Jewish loaves] on the platter at all seasons except on Passover when Matzoth [unleavened bread] should be used,"[34] and the suggested vestments included a prayer shawl and a skull cap. The prayer book was printed with alternating Hebrew and English pages.

But Levy, Levertoff, Schonfield, and later Lowe (a gentile supporter of Hebrew Christianity)[35] seemed to be a minority in the ranks of Hebrew Christianity. No sooner had the Hebrew Christian Alliance of America been born than a storm of unparalleled force arose over the issue of Judaizing, with scorn and anathema heaped on its supporters—especially Mark John Levy.

I contend that the Alliance was host within its ranks to three somewhat diverse approaches to the question of Judaizing. There were a few—notably Mark John Levy (see note 46, Chapter 4)—who staunchly advocated the incorporation into Hebrew Christianity of as much ceremonial law as was consistent with belief in Christ and the doctrine of salvation through grace alone.

The second camp was comprised of those who felt that there was some merit to a plan of "limited" Judaizing (although they would not have called it that) insofar as this might serve as a temporary "half-way house" for those believers still young and weak in the faith. Reich, for example, though as vehement in his denunciations of Levy as most, cautiously accepted some Judaizing: ". . . I can quite believe that many of our Jewish brethren coming by slow stages out of Judaism, might again dwell in a half-way house [but] . . . it is not God's ultimate [sic], but only a temporary make-shift."[36] Reich accepted the modal imperative but continually warned of its dangers and of the need to destroy the half-way structure once "its occupants obtain clearer light."[37] Most of those who accepted Reich's position (and Reich was undoubtedly the most influential thinker produced by Hebrew Christianity in the United States) could hark back to the early Church for support, where Paul pleaded for tolerance for "the weak ones" who could not completely sever themselves from the ceremonial law.[38]

The third position on the question of Judaizing ostensibly won the day—namely, that of outright and unqualified condemnation of what was considered a heretical and potentially schismatic road to ultimate defeat. The reasons for this opposition must be sought on a number of levels, none of which in isolation provide a key to its unraveling, but which do as a whole, I believe, point to a single theme—Judaizing won't work! Those who condemned Judaizing did so on the grounds that rather than assisting in the legitimation of Christianity, as its proponents had hoped, Judaizing would do just the opposite. Judaism would not "be contented were we to observe its national religious customs and yet believe in Jesus: If we would have its recognition we must deny Christ."[39] Furthermore, for a Christian to accept the law as binding would be to deny his justification by faith alone, and where would this leave a professing Jewish believer in Christ?

Another basis for the outright rejection of overt Judaizing lay in the revulsion with which so many of the Hebrew Christians—leaders as well as laymen—viewed the Jewish religion. These people were and are as truly alienated from normative Judaism as one might think possible. They did not leave the synagogue only to return with hat in hand, and as a despised minority only to once again partake of the onerous practices of the Jews.

Praise God! I am glad I am free. Once I was in a cage and that cage has been opened by Christ. God has let us out of the cage of Judaistic legalism, we are free and have no desire whatsoever to return to our cage.[40]

Also, what practical good could come of this projected return? Would it attract great numbers of Jews? The majority felt that it would not. Rev. Joel Levy suggested that the vast majority of Jews would see in it a trap because they knew that the messianic era must be free of the old law.[41] Moreover, if Hebrew Christianity were to begin the observance "of days and ordinances"[42] it might very well lead to the formation of a new sect. Again, why not assume that great numbers of Jews want to escape the burdensome load that is the law, rather than return to it? What then was to be the stand of Hebrew Christianity on Judaizing?

Although it appeared to be decisively defeated in 1918, the question continued to arise, showing particular strength in 1931, 1932, and the 1940s, but in a different form. The question of whether the law was binding was decisively answered in the negative at the very outset. But even here, in accepting the possible role of a half-way house, Reich had set the stage for the inclusion of Jewish rites and Jewish modes of observance, not as a binding religious commitment but as a methodological ploy for the more ready inclusion of tradition-steeped converts and as the basis of an appeal to those who had not yet taken the final step. Although Judaizing that would have meant the mandatory observance of this or that Jewish rite or festival (as Levy would have had it) was rejected, it was readily accepted insofar as it was "a matter of brotherly courtesy."[43] To participate in the Jewish religion as if it were binding would involve nothing less than the strengthening of the Jew "in his deadly error and to deny the Christ who redeemed us."[44] But to use now this, now that item of Jewish ritual, or to see in the observances of the various holy days some meaning for the Jewish believer, or to rely on Hebrew as an important language for prayer and in some cases exegesis—all of this was then (1918) and is now an important and thoroughly acceptable aspect of Hebrew Christian practice.

While it is quite true that Judaizing in its schismatic predilection has been set aside (though by no means is it a dead letter), Judaizing in its lightly syncretistic nature used as a legitimizing device is still a dominant theme. The very existence of a Hebrew Christian Church is sufficient evidence with which to adduce this.

THE HEBREW CHRISTIAN CHURCH

Again, as in the matter of Judaizing, the proposal to form a
Hebrew Christian Church met with a mixed reception from
the ranks of Hebrew Christianity and from various gentile
sources as well.[45] The reasons for this opposition are for the
most part obvious and involve the fear of causing further
schism in the Church with the creation of still another denomination, as well as the possible imputation that Christ could
not serve as the "all in all" for the believer. To suggest a
specifically Jewish Church implied a direct challenge to the
datum of Paul that there can be no distinction between Jew
and Gentile, and the creation of this Church would appear
as an attempt to rebuild "the middle wall of partition" which
could serve only a negative function among believers.[46]

A few among the leadership of the movement felt that a
Hebrew Christian Church was perhaps warranted in Europe,
where anti-Semitism was so firmly entrenched or where the
Roman Catholic Church was predominant but that it could
have little relevance in England or the United States, where
these factors played a minimal role.[47]

Still others felt that the one place where a Hebrew Christian
Church seemed "natural" and necessary was in a reconstituted
Jewish state, where the "revival of the Primitive Hebrew Christian Church"[48] could presage the conversion of all Israel and
where it would not come into conflict with the established
churches of the West that could, should, and would absorb the
Jewish converts who presented themselves for inclusion.

But although these objections to the creation of a Hebrew
Christian Church continue to be expressed, the general
trend within the movement has tended toward the creation of
a Church for the inclusion of the Jewish convert *qua* Jew in
the corporate body of Christ—a Church that manifests a peculiar Jewish system of ritual and observance.

If Judaizing, or the use of a patina of Jewish practice was to serve as a legitimating tool, it would require an institutional framework. Conceivably, this could be accomplished within a Hebrew Christian mission structure,[49] but only in skeletal form and without continuity and sociological substance, since the mission structure itself is limited. A church can provide the appurtenances of a system that a mission cannot. A mission can subscribe to a belief in the viability of a Jewish ethnic–national reality; but a church can provide a dynamic involvement with its various parts, demonstrating the inclusive nature of these beliefs in active forms of ritual, dogma, practice, and observance.[50]

To demonstrate the possibility of incorporating familiar patterns of liturgy and ritual into a Christian framework, a vessel for these practices must exist, and this would be possible only in a church.

Hebrew Christianity did not move in the direction of a church because of any felt need for Christian religious expression from within a Jewish framework. With the exception of perhaps two or three individuals, no Hebrew Christian theoretician speaks of any special spiritual benefits to be gained from this move.[51] The tendency toward the formation of a church must be viewed in the same light and by using the same criteria as has been applied to the creation of the Hebrew Christian movement generally, but now as a refined tool of legitimation. Where the movement sought to prove that the Jewish convert need not be one who seeks to escape his Judaism, membership in a Hebrew Christian Church unmistakably proved that the convert was a man who was *adding to* his Judaism by emphasizing the Hebrew prefix to his Christianity through membership in a community (not just an organization) of like believers. As Jacob Peltz has commented, the stigmatization as renegades of Jews who convert "is no longer tenable when they [the opponents] note that Jewish converts deliberately and proudly bear their identity as Jews when they join Hebrew Christian congregations."[52]

As Hebrew Christianity (the organization) sought to demonstrate to gentiles that the conversion of Jews was possible, the
existence of a Hebrew Christian Church crowned their claim
of the possibilities inherent in conversionary efforts among the
Jews. In the past, gentile missionaries and churchmen had
failed to notice the bountiful results of "Jewish work" because
the converts had become lost in the crowd. In displaying a community of believers, a "binding system" of Hebrew Christianity with a church polity, this success could become visible (and
could provide greater promise of stability), leading to the en-
couragement of those who may have become disheartened or
who may lack zeal for the work of converting the Jews. As
Reich stated in 1936 concerning the "disappearing converts"
and the unfortunate effect this was having on gentile support,
"we need a Hebrew Christian Church into which to gather
them. . . ."[53]

Where Hebrew Christianity desired to succor the new Christian, the creation of the church was seen as the most efficient
means of accomplishment. It was believed that by forming congregations "where the young convert . . . may find intelligent
sympathy and helpful fellowship"[54] a perennial stumbling
block to the conversion of Jews would be overcome. They
would also serve to protect converts from the attacks of their
former coreligionists. "Our babes need to be insulated against
buffeting from their own brethren. They must be able to give
a reason for the hope that lives within them."[55] Then not only
will the church be furnishing the needed emotional support, it
will also act as an irreplaceable educational adjunct in the life
of the Jewish convert.

If Hebrew Christianity itself can effectively gain converts,
how much more effective could this work be when buttressed
by a church that the convert may call his very own? This is the
one hope that seems to have induced widespread support for
the church idea, and the one goal that brooked little argument
even from persons who would otherwise have opposed such a

development. A. J. Kligerman, for instance, suggested the necessity for a Hebrew Christian movement "with scattered Hebrew Christian congregations ministered by Hebrew Christians,"[56] while Victor Buksbazen saw in it "a corporate testimony to the Jews as well as to the Church of Christ,"[57] and all agreed with Aston that its ultimate use was "the advancement of mission work among the household of Israel."[58] This position, however, is best summarized in a statement attributed to the Reverend Daniel Finestone, minister of a Hebrew Christian Church in Philadelphia.

> What of the Future? We feel the growing need of a Hebrew Christian Church in Philadelphia. This new approach to the Jews would be a far more effective witness to them than the present mission setup, due to the strong community and national spirit prevalent among the Jews in America today. Many Jews who are tender to the message of Christ do not wish to surrender their Jewish identity and become Gentiles, as they imagine forming a regular Church would make them . . . such a unique witness would have a potent appeal to .vast numbers of Americanized Jews and could not fail to impress the Jewish Community.[59]

In comparing the proposed Hebrew Christian Church with "a regular Church," Rev. Finestone reflects the general position of every Hebrew Christian leader at the present time.[60] They need this hybrid institution only on the level of an evangelistic imperative having no intrinsic religious value or insights to offer the believer. If the church can serve as a legitimate instrument, and yet not be a doctrinal white elephant, it is to be affirmed; this has indeed become the predominant Hebrew Christian viewpoint.

In sum, the creation of a Hebrew Christian Church can perform five major functions in the evangelization of the Jews: (1) it can show Jews that people who have converted did not do so to escape being labeled as Jews; (2) it can show Gentiles that the conversion of the Jews is possible; (3) it can insulate the recent convert from harmful influences; (4) in fulfilling items 1 to 3 it can lead to the development of a highly successful evangelistic method, which is the only one holding promise for (5) the elimination of a previous stumbling block in Jewish work, anti-Semitism.

It has rightly been concluded that no system can appear legitimate to a Jew if it harbors any taint of anti-Semitism. To the leadership of Hebrew Christianity, it was somehow self-evident that a born Jew could not be an anti-Semite; thus arose the rather naïve datum that a Hebrew Christian Church would by definition be free of this germ. "The only solution of this vexed problem [anti-Semitism] in the Gentile Churches is a strong and virile Hebrew Christian Church that will be self-supporting, self-governing, and self-propagating. . . ."[61]

Nevertheless, the entire legitimating structure *is* being under mined by the persistent and unusual quality of the anti-Semitism with which Hebrew Christianity generally is interlarded.

ANTI–SEMITISM

Paradoxically, feelings of anti-Semitism continue to dominate an effort primarily suggested as a means of overcoming this bias.

Hebrew Christianity, as part of the legitimating attempt, claims to be a sure-fire antidote to and opponent of anti-Semitism in all its forms. In embracing political Zionism the Hebrew Christian has announced his support for a development that would finally establish the Jews in a "normal" context among the nations. Zionism, giving rise to an independent Jewish state, would provide a geographical place for the persecuted Jew as well as an arena in which he might refute prevailing canards concerning Jewish economic and social parasitism, showing his gentile tormentors that he is capable of the best that is within man.

In adopting at least the veneer of Judaizing, the Hebrew Christian movement sought to prove to all that Judaism could still lay claim if not to sufficiency as a means of Salvation, then at least to some relevance as a mode of religious expression. The various semireligious holy days, the Hebrew language as a partial vehicle of prayer, the relative absence of Christological symbolism, the heavy emphasis on Old Testament exegesis—all were meant to affirm the "good seed" that lay ensconced and heavily overlaid within Judaism. There was a serious attempt to demonstrate to Jews and Gentiles the worth and inherent value of the Jew—and even, in some limited fashion, his religion. The Hebrew Christian in this way would pose the question to hostile gentiles: could a people who produced the prophets, the psalms, the Savior himself, possibly be all bad, completely unsalvageable?

In the development of a Hebrew Christian Church, the believer sought to convince his Jewish brethren that his was the most complete of commitments, that he was embarked on an effort not to disassociate himself from his Jewish roots but to strengthen them. Did he join a gentile church seeking to bury his past or to cast his lot with the persecutor or did he not stand up to the gentile world, pointing proudly to his Jewishness, affirming his continuing identification with his people in a *Hebrew* Christian communion? In showing the gentile Christian (and the unconverted Jews) that a Jew could remain a Jew yet be a good Christian, seeking not social advantage through membership in a majority Church but electing to stay among his own brethren, according to the flesh, the Hebrew Christian sought, in addition to evangelistic gain, to strike a blow against anti-Semitism. This would have constituted the legitimating success *par excellence*.

But tragically any blow struck has been without noticeable

effect. Numerous statements, articles, and quotations indicate the concern of Hebrew Christians with the problem and their desire to remove anti-Semitism as a factor in Judeo-Christian relationships; the cumulative impression garnered is one of abject failure in opposing prejudice from without, plus an unfortunate tendency to sustain and buttress it from within. Successful opposition to anti-Semitism could no doubt have become one of the strongest elements in a legitimating structure; it is instead the weakest link in the chain.

One course of exploration of the relation of anti-Semitism to Hebrew Christianity involves the possibility that the seeds of antipathy grow out of *any* conversionary effort (e.g. Hebrew Christianity), with those seeking to convert others attributing various negative qualities to the proselytees. After all, one might safely assume that those seeking a change believe that the religion to be replaced is deficient, wrong, evil, or perhaps all three. I think the assumption is valid as far as it goes. But does the conversionary effort necessarily lead to negative attitudes toward the *holders* of the offending doctrine? At least one investigator has said that his evidence indicates no correlation between missionizing intent and such negative feeling. Olson asks, "Are lessons with conversionist interests directionally more unfavorable than favorable to outside groups than lessons which have no missionary interest?"[62] He concludes that *"stress upon missionary themes as such do not in themselves necessarily encourage negative statements about other groups* in greater proportion than stress upon non-mission themes."[63]

I would maintain as a possibly more fruitful avenue of exploration the suggestion that manifestations of anti-Semitism on the part of Hebrew Christians are bound up in the inner tensions and contradictions of a movement of this nature based as it is upon the assertion of legitimacy, which must and indeed has led to a parallel attempt to undermine the accepted legitimacy of normative Judaism. As a result there has been a widening gulf of acrimony between the antagonists. This has led to what I have referred to as the short-circuiting of the Jewish ethos, wherein the convert loses meaningful contact with or understanding of the reality of his past affiliation and loyalties (whether these were fragile or strong) and can henceforth look at the reality only through the spectacles of the (new) system. This is so not only as regards central issues and doctrines but in *all* areas large and small, central and peripheral. Thus we have the anomaly of an individual or group of individuals who may have lived a considerable portion of their lives either within or on the margin of a system; who, once conversion is undergone, lose all sense of the reality of the former matrix, assimilating *in toto* the new outlook. The willingness or need of a convert to immerse himself in the newly found belief is not particularly startling. Less comprehensible is *the inability of the convert to understand or interpret his former condition in any way but as a total outsider who had never shared a set of common experiences or outlooks with other Jews.* The ethos has been short-circuited to the degree that the convert approaches it as any outsider—not to prove his orthodox avowal of the new but simply because he is *incapable* of viewing the old in any other way.[64] The Hebrew Christian who converts to a form of fundamentalist Protestantism views the Jews and Jewish experience in this light, and insofar as the new system might involve anti-Semitism, this too is readily absorbed.[65] The plaint of the non-Jew that he (the Jew) is a paradoxical creature—now satanic, now angelic, now reaching the heights of sublimity, now descending to the terrors of hell—becomes the lament of the Hebrew Christian.

> He is poor, he is rich, desperately poor, fabulously rich; he is a religious enthusiast and an agnostic, having no king but God, and not believing in God; custodian of the highest spiritual religion and a gross materialist; an ascetic capable of the most rigid self denial and a worshipper of the flesh pots; a rebel and

a sycophant; a capitalist and a communist, conservative and iconoclast; a war maker and a pacifist; there is no limit to the anomalies and paradoxes of the Jewish nature.[66]

This reflects not the self-analysis of a Jew but the tortured confusion of a fundamentalist believer confronted by what he sees as the terrible contradiction of God's Chosen, the People of the Book. Various legitimating efforts notwithstanding, the Jew is perceived as wholly the other, and it becomes possible to suggest an evil so ingrown as to be naturally unresponsive to the higher ethic of Christianity.

> Christianity demands a high moral standard which acts as a deterrent to many Jews. Their own peculiar faults of character—selfishness, love of money and material prosperity, habits of lying, doubtful commercial dealings, lack of the sense of sin and in some areas drinking and impurity—are challenged by the stricter Christian morality and cause a revolution in their moral outlook, and in many cases the change seems to be too demanding and radical.[67]

Thus the Jews, in their unconverted state, constitute a danger to civilized life.[68] Not only is this believed by Hebrew Christians with much the same intensity as by some gentile missionaries, but in the same degree as well. A "mystique" of the Jew arises as a result of this particular type of conversion,[69] where all touch with reality seems to be lost, leading one to assume that any contact the convert may have had with Jews was purely in the realm of ideas. Even in trying to defend the Jew against anti-Semitic onslaughts, statements take on a distant hue and become highly generalized. In place of a strong denial of group guilt or perfidy, in place of a sense of personal outrage, we hear instead, "Now those who accuse the Jews of every imaginable crime are not wholly wrong. Like in all falsehoods there are some grains of truth in their accusations against the Jews."[70] In conversation with Hebrew Christians, as well as in countless articles and tracts, one is

struck by the sincere (but miserably unsuccessful) attempts
to fight these anti-Jewish effusions. In their continuing and
uncompromising opposition the Jews play the devil's game,
and in this context no deviousness, no evil is beyond their ken.
For example, repeated references are made to the possibility
of "Jewish violence" against Christians,[71] but specifically
Hebrew Christians; the impression that emerges vis à vis the
Jews is of a blind, violent lot who spare the missionaries only
because "the angel of the Lord encamped round about His
servants and no harm befell them."[72]

Thus anti-Semitism—the one factor that had invariably
compromised and limited evangelistic success—plays a not
dissimilar role in the efforts of Hebrew Christians to win Jews
for Christ. In attempting to legitimate Christianity, the obvious need has arisen to undermine the previously established
legitimate order (normative Judaism), leading to the growth
and development of deep-seated antipathies.

NOTES

1. Max Weber, *The Theory of Social and Economic Organization*, A.
M. Henderson and Talcott Parsons, eds. and transls. (New York: Oxford University Press, 1947) p. 125.

2. Weber says that "legitimacy may be ascribed to an order by those
acting subject to it in the following ways: (a) by tradition; a belief in
the legitimacy of what has always existed; (b) by virtue of affectual
attitudes, especially emotional, legitimizing the validity of what is
newly revealed or a model to imitate; (c) by virtue of a rational
belief in its absolute value, thus, lending it the validity of an absolute and final commitment; (d) because it has been established in a
manner which is recognized to be legal." *Ibid.*, p. 130.

3. *Ibid.*, p. 131. I would contend that not only is this so in times of
"strict traditionalism," but also during periods when the *actual*
strength of tradition is weak where, however, respect for the tradition
nostalgic or otherwise, is still operative.

4. "Jewish Opposition to the Message of Christ," Editor's Notes, *Hebrew
Christian Alliance Quarterly*, Vol. 5, No. 2 (April 1921), 44.

5. M. Malbert, "The Influence of Hebrew Christians on the Destinies of Mankind," *Hebrew Christian Alliance Quarterly*, Vol. 2, No. 4 (October 1918), 142.

6. Jacob Peltz, "Christian Approach to the Jews," *Hebrew Christian Alliance Quarterly*, Vol. 16, Nos. 1 and 2 (January and March 1931), 39.

7. Max Reich, "The Relations Between Church and Synagogue," *Hebrew Christian Alliance Quarterly*, Vol. 16, Nos. 1 and 2 (January and March 1931), 1.

8. *Ibid.*. p. 2.

9. D. Baron, "Message to the Sixth Conference," *Hebrew Christian Alliance Quarterly*, Vol. 4, No. 3 (October 1920), 99.

10. Moses Klerekoper, "Why a Christian and *That* a Constant Christian," *Hebrew Christian Alliance Quarterly*, Vol. 20, No. 2 (Summer 1935), 4.

11. Fenton John Anthony Hort, *Judaistic Christianity* (London: Macmillan & Co., 1898), p. 93.

12. Parsons and Henderson, *op. cit.*, p. 132.

13. *Ibid.*

14. *Ibid.*

15. Salo Wittmayer Baron, *Modern Nationalism and Religion* (New York: Meridian Books, 1960), p. 237.

16. William Bell Dawson, "The Present Fulfillment of Prophecy," *Hebrew Christian Alliance Quarterly*, Vol. 15, No. 4 (October and December 1930), 3–4. Zionism is seen as predicted in Scripture, even to the year in which it would appear as a political force, in the following manner. "In 623 B.C. the Babylonian Empire was founded; the first of the four great empires in Daniel's prophecy. When Ezekiel dates the beginning of his book (which opens in 593 B.C.) as the 'thirtieth year,' he is therefore counting in the years of the Babylonian Empire.
    "From 623 B.C.—1260 years run to the winter of 637–638 A.D., the Saracen capture of Jerusalem.
    "Again, from 637–638 A.D.—1260 years run to 1897, the first Zionist congress." *Ibid.*, 34.

17. Joel Levy, "Modern Jewish Leadership," *Hebrew Christian Alliance Quarterly*, Vol. 4, No. 3 (October 1920), 117.

18. *Ibid.*

19. M. Ruben, "The Zionist Convention at Pittsburgh," *Hebrew Christian Alliance Quarterly*, Vol. 2, No. 4 (October 1918), 136.

20. Max Reich, "The Jewish Congress," *Hebrew Christian Alliance Quarterly*, Vol. 3, No. 1 (January 1919), p. 12.

21. *Ibid.*, p. 12.

22. Jacob Peltz, "Annual Report of the General Secretary," *Hebrew Chris-

tian Alliance Quarterly, Vol. 18, No. 2 (July and September 1933), 22. It should be noted that no Hebrew Christian colony had ever been successfully launched in Palestine.

23. M. Malbert, "Hebrew Christian Unity," *Hebrew Christian Alliance Quarterly*, Vol. 1, Nos. 3 and 4 (July and October 1917), 135.

24. Thompson, too, though not a Hebrew Christian, saw only one possible meaning to Zionism—the emancipation of the Jewish body and soul and the inevitable movement toward Christianity. "The bearing of this movement upon the evangelization of the Jews is of paramount importance. . . . That it is enlarging the conception of many, and consequently making them more ready to consider the claims of Christianity is indisputable." A. Thompson, *A Century of Jewish Missions* (Chicago: F. H. Revell Co., 1902), p. 58. He adds: ". . . when the heart turns homeward, the question must arise, 'why have I been an outcast?' The Jew who knows anything of history and of the New Testament must feel that there may be a connection between the rejection of Christ and the scattering of his nation. In these and many other ways there is a direct effect of zionism upon the relation of the Jew to the Gospel." *Ibid.*, p. 58.

25. N. Levison, "Are Jews Becoming More Jewish?" *American Hebrew Christian*, Vol. 39, No. 2 (Fall 1953), 5.

26. But although this was and continues to be the dominant approach to Zionism within Hebrew Christianity, there was also a countertrend that was anything but *naive*. Its proponents surmised that revived Jewish interest on one level may lead to a revival on another (i.e., religion), or that Zionism will fill a void that might otherwise be filled by Christian faith, or finally that the alleviation of Jewish suffering would lead to the false but comforting notion that the nation had been forgiven its sin without true repentence. Some characteristic quotations representing these points of view follow.

"Persecuted Jewry *must remain scattered amongst the nations*, live and suffer amongst the persecutors until the power of the Gospel of Christ will manifest itself in their hearts and then strike a death blow to the enemies of God, both persecuted and persecutor can be saved." Abraham Gradowski, "The Spiritual World Revolution and the Jews," *Hebrew Christian Alliance Quarterly*, Vol. 28, No. 2 (Summer 1942), 5.

"We do not think it is part of the Christian Church's duty to assist in the restoration of the Jews to Palestine while in unbelief, we should rather seek to point them to Moses and the Prophets and urge them to flee from the wrath to come and turn to God. . . ." "Editor's Notes," *Hebrew Christian Alliance Quarterly*, Vol. 2, No. 2 (April 1918), 50.

The same writer continues: "We thoroughly believe in the rightful Jewish claims to Palestine. We also believe in Israel's restoration and reconciliation. We certainly look for an immediate *partial return* [note the emphasis] fully warranted in the Scriptures, the result of this partial return is also indicated in the Word of God, but what we are chiefly concerned with now is Israel's condition and attitude. It is all very well to run with the crowd and sing the popular tunes, but such is not the right attitude of the loyal and true heart. We must at all cost lay bare Israel's true condition before God's people, which will enable us to adjust our prayers and sympathies in the right direction. . . . The tone, enthusiasm and temper displayed by happy Jews and their editors would make one think . . . that Jewry had already been rejuvenated and the new epoch ushered in. . . . Ancient Judaism taught, that before Israel's restoration takes place, the true Prophet will appear, who will guide the people and prepare them for the ushering in of peace. . . . [Finally,] when the spirit of 'grace and supplication' will be poured out upon them, Israel in the true attitude of repentance will recognize Him as the joy of their salvation and He will lead them! Yes, no other person will ever lead them successfully." *Ibid.*, pp. 51–54.

27. The one factor that *did* prevent full involvement of Hebrew Christianity was the violent hostility to this group of the Zionist movement itself. Up until the 1930s the Hebrew Christian Alliance repeatedly sought membership in the World Zionist movement; it was rebuffed, however, in all these attempts at formal affiliation. The conflict deteriorated into wild threats and counterthreats, and it was even suggested that if Hebrew Christians were not to be considered loyal to a Jewish state, then perhaps the Crown, for instance, ought not to trust those who claim Jewish faith to be loyal to England. (See J. H. Adeney, "An Illogical Attitude," *Hebrew Christian Allliance Quarterly*, Vol. 3, Nos. 3 and 4 (July and October 1919). It was also threatened to send a delegation of Hebrew Christians to Washington to see the British Ambassador "with the object of ascertaining information touching the Balfour Declaration and its bearing on Hebrew Christians." (See Minutes of the 8th Annual Conference of Hebrew Christian Alliance of America" [Toronto, Canada, May 29–June 2], *Hebrew Christian Alliance Quarterly*, Vol. 6, No. 3 (July 1922), 92. However, the Zionists helped to worsen the situation by refusing to listen to the Hebrew Christian viewpoint, while making almost no requirements for membership except sympathy with Zionist aims but rejecting a group who without doubt were most sympathetic. One is moved by the plaint of Henry Hellyer that, "A host of Jews who are so only in name, and who have no vestige of Judaism left in them are received with open arms, whereas a humble follower of the meek and lowly Nazarene must turn aside spurned, laughed at and hated." Henry L. Hellyer, "The Evangelization of Three Million Jews of America," *Hebrew Christian Alliance Quarterly*, Vol. 1, Nos. 3 and 4 (July and October 1917), 120. Thus, although formal affiliation was denied them, the Hebrew Christian movement is even more vehement in

their Zionist sentiments today, than in the past. In a regularly appearing department of the journal titled "Happenings in Israel," unvarnished chauvinism and pro-Israel sympathies are voiced by the editor on all occasions. One can only wonder about the nature of this involvement with the Jewish state were the Hebrew Christians to have been accorded a warmer reception within the ranks of Zionism.

28. Kraemer, who was an extremely perceptive observer of the missionary enterprise, has said in this connection: "To *decide* for Christ and the world He stands for implies a break with one's religious past, whether this past is Christian in the qualified sense of the word or non-Christian. This break is something radically different from taking a sympathetic attitude towards His personality and teaching." Hendrik Kraemer, *The Christian Message in a Non-Christian World* (New York: Harper & Row, 1938), p. 291. And this, it seems to me, is a thoroughgoing and quite correct (from the Christian *and* the sociological viewpoint) statement of the case regarding "adaptation."

29. Thompson, *op. cit.*, p. 241.

30. See Hugh J. Schonfield, *The History of Jewish Christianity: From the First to the Twentieth Centuries* (London: Duckworth, 1936), p. 227, ff.

31. See David M. Eichhorn, "A History of Christian Attempts to Convert the Jews of the United States and Canada," Ph.D. dissertation, Hebrew Union College, 1938.

32. M. J. Levy, "Jewish Ordinances in the Light of Scripture," *Hebrew Christian Alliance Quarterly*, Vol. 1, Nos. 3 and 4 (June and October 1917), 141.

33. *Ibid.*

34. Paul Levertoff, *The Order of Service of the Meal of the Holy King* (Milwaukee: Morehouse, 1928), p. 3.

35. Lowe suggested that the Feast of Tabernacles, even the rudimentary dietary laws could be observed by Hebrew Christians without compromising their Christianity. He even suggested that the gentiles should observe more of the law and said that the Jews should be: "encouraged to be Jews according to the standards of God as given to them as a 'peculiar people,' to whom pertain the covenants, and the promises, and the giving of the law, and all the 'things' that are theirs, if they will but keep them." George William Lowe, "Jewish Christianity and Jewish Christians," *Hebrew Christian Alliance Quarterly*, Vol. 28, No. 3 (Fall 1943), 12.

36. M. Reich, "Jewish Ordinances," *Hebrew Christian Alliance Quarterly*, Vol. 2, No. 1 (January 1918), 24.

37. *Ibid.*

38. See Hort, *op. cit.*, p. 127. Hort, however, also recognized the dangers inherent in a too ready indulgence for these tendencies. He described

the Epistle to the Galatians as an attack on Judaizers who were undermining the structure of the Church. "As we all know, the Epistle was
written in consequence of a retrogression among the Galatians due to
the seductions of Judaizing missionaries who not only attacked the
apostolic authority of St. Paul as invalid beside that of the Jerusalem
apostles . . . but were preaching, and apparently successfully preaching, to the Galatians the necessity of circumcision." *Ibid.*, p. 99.

39. "Editors Notes," *Hebrew Christian Alliance Quarterly*, Vol. 1, Nos.
3 and 4 (July and October 1917), 87.

40. Elias Newman, "Jewish Ordinances," *Hebrew Christian Alliance Quarterly*, Vol. 2, No. 1 (January 1918), 25–26. Some other comments in
this genre follow.

"Our brother is an English gentleman—of the *Jewish persuasion*—
does not even know the Jewish language; never studied in the Yeshi-
bah; never studied the Talmud, or the Jewish code of laws, with its
complicated one hundred and fifty caustic (sic) commentaries, in its
vernacular. He may have studied it but only in theory, as an outsider.
He cannot fully appreciate the true meaning of its heavy burden and
its complicated character. I contend with all due respect and Christian Charity that our brother does not know what he expects us to
adopt. He had not tasted as some of us have, 'the bread of affliction';
wasted his youth in the Yeshibath (sic) (Jewish college); raked (sic)
his brains on the argumentative discussion of the sages; spent sleep-
less nights on the bare benches of the Beth-Hamidrash (House of
Meditation); fasting Mondays and Thursdays . . ." *Hebrew Christan
Alliance Quarterly*, Vol. 2, No. 1 (January 1918), 27.

Rohold continues: "Can a Hebrew Christian conscientiously worship in a Synagogue? We have no hesitation in saying, *Certainly not!*
The synagogue is *Anti-Jesus!* The Synagogue teaches by her code of
laws, the Talmud, that Jesus was an imposter, a wicked man, a
sorcerer, an idolator, . . . teaches that He is in hell; and that his name
should not be mentioned without saying: Yimack-Shemoh-Wezickroe
(May his name be blotted out and his memory). The New Testament
is called *Avon Gilgon* (Margin of evil, or a blank page of sin). My
Lord is openly insulted there, reviled, slandered and blasphemed.
How can an honest believer have fellowship there? I shudder at the
very thought of it!" Rohold, *Hebrew Christian Alliance Quarterly*,
Vol. 2, No. 1 (January 1918), 27.

"A few years of real orthodox Jewish life would be more than
enough to cure the dear brother of his love of an infatuation with
Jewish observances. He would then be able to appreciate our position, and with us thank God for the liberty we have in Christ Jesus,
our dear Lord and Saviour.

"There is one point the brother must consider. He claims that the
brethren misunderstood him; that he firmly believes that the blood

of Jesus and the blood alone saves us from our sins, only the enforcement of Jewish observances upon Hebrew Christianity is to serve as a bait wherewith to catch our Jewish brethren." This may have been acceptable in past, but "at the present time these very ordinances which brother Levy thinks would make a splendid bait to win our brethren for Christ are neglected by thousands, yea hundreds of thousands of Jews." *Hebrew Christian Alliance Quarterly*, Vol. 2, No. 1 (January 1918), 26.

41. *Hebrew Christian Alliance Quarterly*, Vol. 2, No. 1 (January 1918), 31.

42. Ibid., 34.

43. A. J. Kligerman, "Hebrew Christianity and Gentile Christianity—Is There a Difference?" *Hebrew Christian Alliance Quarterly*, Vol. 17, No. 1 (January and March 1932), 19.

44. Reich, "Jewish Ordinances," *Hebrew Christian Alliance Quarterly*, Vol. 2, No. 1 (January 1918), 24.

45. Nobody seems to know just when or by whom the idea for a Hebrew Christian Church was first broached. Eichhorn notes at least three separate claims to being the first Hebrew Christian Church on these shores: on October 11, 1885, a mission in New York was dedicated as the "First Hebrew Christian Church in America"; on June 7, 1913, Benjamin Rohold established what he claimed to be the first Hebrew Christian Synagogue on the American continent, in Toronto, Canada; and in February 1922 a church in Philadelphia was dedicated as "the First Hebrew Christian Synagogue in the United States." As far back as 1825, a Jewish convert in the employ of the American Society for Meliorating the Condition of the Jews called for the creation of a Hebrew Christian Church, but there is no record of its having been established. Eichhorn, *op. cit.*, pp. 466, 439, 379, 121. Schonfield notes that the International Hebrew Christian Alliance established a commission "to inquire into the desirability and practicability of forming a Hebrew Christian Church," in 1931 with a favorable resolution being passed in 1933; but again there is no record of any Church actually being established. Schonfield, *op. cit.*, p. 243.

46. See Max Reich, "Our Objective," *Hebrew Christian Alliance Quarterly*, Vol. 21, No. 2 (Fall 1936), 1.

47. See Elias Newman, "Report of the 18th Annual Conference of the Hebrew Christian Alliance of America," *Hebrew Christian Alliance Quarterly*, Vol. 17, No. 3 (July and September 1932), 13.

48. J. H. Adeney, "Palestine of the Future and the Hebrew Christian," *Hebrew Christian Alliance Quarterly*, Vol. 3, Nos. 3 and 4 (July and October 1919).

49. This is in fact the case with the Messengers of the New Covenant, discussed in Chapter 2.

50. For example, the following proposed articles of faith for a Hebrew Christian Church, which outline the belief structure of the Hebrew Christian, would be inappropriate and thoroughly undesirable in a mission framework. These articles indicate to the believer as well as to the outsider that those who subscribe to it are in a position to activate (all or part of it) as a living element of personal existence.

"Hear O Israel, the Lord thy God is one Lord and thou shalt love the Lord thy God with all thy heart, with all thy soul and with all thy strength and thy neighbor as thyself.

"Article 1. I believe in God the source of all being, the Covenant God, the Holy One of Israel, our Heavenly Father.

"Article 2. I believe that God who spake at sundry times and in diverse manners in time past to the fathers through the prophets promised to redeem the world from sin and death in and through His annointed, Who would be a light to lighten the Gentiles and the glory of His people Israel.

"Article 3. I believe that in the fulness of time God fulfilled His promise and sent forth His Son, His eternal word Jesus the Messiah Who was born by the power of the Holy Spirit of the Virgin Mary, who was of the family of David, so that in Him the word was made flesh and dwelt among us full of grace and truth.

"Article 4. I believe that Jesus the Messiah is in very truth the Shekinah [the Spirit of God] the brightness of the Father's glory, the very impress of his person, that He was made unto us wisdom from God, and righteousness, and sanctification and that by His life, Death on the Cross and glorious Resurrection, He has accomplished our Reconciliation with the Father.

"Article 5. I believe that the Father sealed all that the Son was, did and taught by raising Him through the Holy Spirit from the dead, and that the Risen and Glorified Lord appeared to many and communed with them, and then ascended to be our Mediator with the Father and to reign with Him One God.

"Article 6. I believe that the Holy Spirit, the Paraclete Who proceeds from the Father and the Son, was sent to be with us, to give us assurance of the forgiveness of sin and to lead us into the fulness of truth and the more abundant life.

"Article 7. I believe that the Holy Spirit, Who beareth witness with our spirits that we are the sons of God, will quicken us in the resurrection when we shall be clothed in the body which it shall please the Father to give us.

"Article 8. I believe that the Church of the Messiah is the family of God in heaven and on earth, the sanctuary of the redeemed in which God dwells and of which the Messiah Jesus is the only Head.

"Article 9. I believe that the Old and New Testaments are the divinely inspired records of God's revelation to Israel and the World and are the only rule of life and faith.

"Article 10. I believe that it is the will of God, Who has graciously brought us into the new Covenant that we should strive to be witnesses, making the teaching and life of the Messiah our standard and example until He comes again to reign in power and glory.

"Article 11. I believe that the Church visible maintains unbroken continuity with the Church in heaven by partaking of the same blessed Sacraments of Baptism, and of Holy Communion and by confessing the same Father, Son and Holy Spirit, One Godhead."

"Proposed Articles of Faith for the Hebrew Christian Church," *Hebrew Christian Alliance Quarterly*, Vol. 18, No. 1 (June 1933), 30–31.

51. Klerekoper is one who does suggest that the Jewish Church can bring reward to the Church in general in at least two ways: "(2) To purge the Church of the leaven of paganism and worldliness by presenting afresh a Prophetic Christianity, by the exposition of the inseparable, interrelated books of the Bible, the Old and New Testaments. (3) To advocate the purification of the Church from idolatry, nationalism, and racial distinction . . . ." "Hebrew Christianity," *Hebrew Christian Alliance Quarterly*, Vol. 18, No. 2 (July and September 1933), 13.

Also, a few Gentile supporters saw some eschatological significance in the formation of a Hebrew Christian Church. William George Lowe observed that "if the remnant according to the Election of Grace is a Jewish Remnant, the re-establishment of Jewish Christianity will, according to Malachi 4:4–6, hasten the coming of the Messiah, even our Lord Jesus Christ, whom the Heavens must receive until the times of restitution of all things, Acts 3:21." W. G. Lowe, "Jewish Christianity and Jewish Christians," *Hebrew Christian Alliance Quarterly*, Vol. 28, No. 3 (Fall 1943), 12–13.

52. Jacob Peltz, "The Christian Witness to the Jews in North America—The Mission Approach," *Twenty-five Years of the International Missionary Council's Committee on the Christian Approach to the Jews, 1932–1957*, Gote Hedenquist, ed. (Uppsala: Almqvist & Wiksells, 1957) p. 58.

53. Max Reich, "Our Objective," *Hebrew Christian Alliance Quarterly*, Vol. 21, No. 2 (Fall 1936), 1–2.

54. Reich, "Appreciations," *Hebrew Christian Alliance Quarterly*, Vol. 1, No. 1 (January 1917), 39.

55. Fred Kendal, "Conserving Our Jewish Converts," *Hebrew Christian Alliance Quarterly*, Vol. 34, No. 3 (Fall 1948), 17.

56. A. J. Kligerman, "An Open Letter," *American Hebrew Christian*, Vol. 44, No. 2 (Fall 1958), 21.

57. Quoted in Peltz, "The Christian Witness to the Jews of North America," *The Christian Approach to the Jews, op. cit.*, p. 56.

58. F. A. Aston, "Consolidation of Hebrew Christian Forces," *Hebrew Christian Alliance Quarterly*, Vol. 20, No. 3 (Fall 1935), 7.

59. Quoted in Peltz, "The Christian Witness to the Jews of North America," *The Christian Approach to the Jews, op. cit.*, p. 56.

60. This became even more evident in personal conversation with Finestone, who is the brother of Rev. Isaac Levy Finestone, the missionary in charge of the Messengers of the New Covenant.

61. Morris Zeidman, "Relationship of the Jewish Convert to the Christian Church," *The Church and the Jewish Question, op. cit.*, p. 71.

62. Bernhard Emanuel Olson, "The Victims and the Oppressors; A Depth Analysis of the Protestant Images of their Own and Other Groups in Situations of Conflict, Deprivation and Persecution, as They Appear in Religious Educational Materials," (Ph.D. dissertation, Yale University, 1959), p. 430.

63. *Ibid.*, pp. 435–436. This of course is by no means a complete answer to the problem here, if only because Olson's material applies to the reactions of Sunday school and church school *children,* who are not *actively* involved as missionaries. There is scant doubt that an active involvement with *any* issue calls forth stronger reaction to success or failure than does peripheral exposure to the idea underlying an approach. However, Olson's work does·keep us from accepting any overly facile theory that missionizing or the idea of missionizing automatically leads to negative attitudes being adopted toward the subjects of the missionary enterprise. That the two so often go hand in hand is evident, but a part of the etiology must be sought elsewhere.

64. This positing of the absorption of the anti-Semitism of the other—the outsider—does not deny the importance and relevance of a *self*-hate that may have existed prior to conversion, but this new antipathy is essentially different. Cf. "Anti-Semitism and Self-Hate," p. 98 ff.

65. There was, however, some reaction to the heavy involvement of various fundamentalists in blatant and violent forms of anti-Semitism. Between 1930 and 1936 hardly an issue of the *Hebrew Christian Alliance Quarterly* does not speak out against anti-Semitism. The problem was acute for the Hebrew Christian Alliance, since because of its fundamentalistic color it was deeply involved if not in fact then by association with these anti-Jewish attacks. The *Quarterly* notes at one point that "any attempt to use the Scriptures as an excuse for an anti-Semitic attitude is a perversion of God's word and irreconcilable with the Spirit and teaching of the Lord Jesus Christ." ["To Christians and Jews of America—A Manifesto and A Call," *Hebrew Christian Alliance Quarterly*, Vol. 21, No. 2 (Fall 1936), 3.]
Or again, "We appeal to the true leaders of Fundamentalism, not

the noisy, spectacular vaudeville opportunists, but our pious, scholarly, godly, Christian gentlemen who have the evangelization of the Jew and of the world at heart, the fundamentalist teachers who are rightly dividing the word of God, who are truly the guardians of the faith, the heirs of the 'Fair Deposit,' the Faith once delivered to the saints, which we must preach, proclaim and protect at the cost of our lives, and until the end of our lives. To you Christian, men and women we appeal. Jesus said 'Lead My Sheep.' Protect the sheep from the wolves that have stolen into the sheepfold—the household of faith." ["Notes by the Honorary General Secretary," *Hebrew Christian Alliance Quarterly*, Vol. 20, No. 1 (April 1935), 15.]

Curiously, however, there exists no evidence that the Hebrew Christian Alliance has taken cognizance of anti-Semitism within its own ranks. It was (and is) thought impossible for a "racial" Jew to harbor these feelings. The foregoing comments—impassioned as they are—reflect the reactions of Christians appalled at un-Christian behavior rather than victims demanding justice.

66. Meyer Pearlman, "Whither Israel," *Hebrew Christian Alliance Quarterly*, Vol. 23, No. 2 (Summer 1938), 7.

67. Roy Kreider, *Judaism Meets Christ: Guiding Principles for the Christian-Jewish Encounter* (Scottsdale, Pa.: Herald Press, 1960), p. 44. When queried about the passage quoted, Kreider, a convert, maintained that he was speaking of prophetic and redemptive love and that the words were not therefore anti-Semitic.

68. This charge is leveled in a significantly large proportion of Hebrew Christian writings on the general subject of the Jews—their nature and destiny. A small representative sampling taken from issues of the *Hebrew Christian Alliance Quarterly* appearing between 1925 and 1944 can serve to highlight the tenor of these remarks.

"Whatever destruction our civilization proposes for itself, it would be well if the Jews were snatched from it like brands from the burning, since unsaved they are liable to play Nero's part, fiddling while Rome burns. They are undoubtedly singularly capable of reflecting whatever ideas are current, so that they are peculiarly fitted to become instruments of destruction. Dare we let them be so used?" (Paul P. Levertoff)

"Jewish immorality, almost unheard of in Eastern Europe, is a growing evil in our Jewish centers. If not counteracted by the Gospel, Jewish irreligion and vice will mightily aid the forces of ungodliness in corrupting our national life . . . the safety of society demands the instant evangelization of the Jew." (Rev. Thomas M. Chalmers) "The fear of God is departing from the nations; hence the irreligious Jew, and as such, we cannot but admit it, he is a menace and not a blessing." ("Editor's Notes") "The Jewish race is here. Not only is their number large but they have penetrated every sphere of our lives.

They are in our Universities, in all our professions; they are bankers
and merchants; the discontented are our labor leaders; they have
monopolized our amusements; they own our newspapers, they specu-
late in our real estate; they complicate our home conditions." (Frank
A. Smith) "It is this Jewish unbelief that is responsible for the post-
ponement of the Messianic Kingdom, and it will remain postponed
as long as this unbelief continues." (Anton Darms.)

69. Here I refer only to a convert who identifies himself as a Hebrew
    Christian.

70. The Managing Editor, "I Am Called Down by a Presbyterian Elder,"
    Hebrew Christian Alliance Quarterly, Vol. 21, No. 4 (Winter 1937)
    7.

71. An example of alleged violence against Christians is contained in a
    lengthy article by M. Mabbert, titled "Persecution is not the monop-
    oly of Christianity and Contrary to Its Principles." The author says
    that "the Jews were not at all backward in hurting the Christians'
    feelings with coarse jests about their religion . . . it is even recorded
    that in 415 A.D. the celebration of the feast of Purim led to horrible
    consequences. At Imnester, a small Syrian town between Antioch and
    Chabcia, they suspended a Christian lad on one of those gallows and
    flogged him to death." *Hebrew Christian Alliance Quarterly*, Vol. 5,
    No. 2 (April 1921), 67.

72. E. Greenbaum, "The Evangelist's Report," *Hebrew Christian Alliance
    Quarterly*, Vol. 2, No. 2 (January 1918), 21.

Part Three

Sociological Evaluation

6

Peculiar Difficulties in Evangelizing the Jews

In Chapter 3, I discussed the patterns assumed at different times and in diverse environments by the Christian evangel to the Jews. In providing an overview of these patterns, I have noted some of the more recurrent difficulties confronting individual Christians and missionary bodies in their efforts to convert the Jews. I now turn to a fuller discussion of three primary and seemingly insurmountable difficulties that have in the past bedevilled and which continue to stymie efforts to evangelize the Jews.

Even though the emerging Anglo-American approach took cognizance of past serious errors, showing an amazing degree of self-criticism and even perspicuity, the transition from recognition of these errors to their correction or removal has not proceeded apace. Intrinsic conservatism is not responsible for this inability to cause significant change—the Anglo-American pattern was in many respects revolutionary. Rather we must examine the difficulties themselves, which are inextricably tied to the relationship of Judaism and Christianity, the unique sociotheological characteristics of the Jews, and finally the persistence of a ubiquitous multicausal antipathy borne toward this people.

Some regard any difficulties encountered in evangelizing the Jews as essentially pragmatic. These observers believe that the obduracy of the Jew is the primary cause of failure, and they solace themselves with the thought that all hindrances exist in the Jew himself and "are the result of religious pride, deepseated prejudice and false ideas of Christianity. . . ."[1] This of course leads to simplistic attempts to educate the Jews, wherein the Jew is conceived of as in reality a Christian who has been unable to recognize this truth about himself because of prejudice and roguish leadership. Thompson, and to a lesser degree Gidney and Schonfield, are satisfied to attribute this myopia on the part of the Jews largely to "contact with the idolatrous practices of the Greek and Roman churches . . . ."[2] Only rarely do they venture a suggestion that goes beyond noting the very obvious—namely, that the Jew has not yet capitulated and that there must exist good reasons for this. Occasionally it becomes possible to glimpse greater insight in the writing and utterances of those involved in the missionary endeavor. By and large, however, the task of a more searching analysis has been left to the outside observer and to the historians, sociologists, and theologians who have concerned themselves with seeking a definition of the Jews and an analysis of their role(s) in the movement of events. With the possible exception of Jakob Jocz, for instance, nobody seriously involved in the traditional missionary enterprise has recognized the truth in Mayer's assertion:

> The Jews . . . are neither a nation nor a religious community in the usual sense of these words, rather they are both at the same time in such a way as to make any distinction between these two concepts impossible. The nation is at its foundation a religious community, and the religious community is a nation. The Jews are a "covenant."[3]

Instead, the tendency has been to continue to experiment with new methodological "gimmicks," taking little or no cognizance of the possibility that the peculiar nature of the Jewish reality, or the unique relationship between Judaism and Christianity, bears on any conceivable encounter between the two.

Mayer goes on to note that the Jews fail the basic test of being a nation, because they are not a "natural political unity"; and they do not belong under the heading "church" because a church is a "religious category without any direct and immediate relation to a people."[4] What characterizes the Jews, says Mayer, "is the unique relationships between religion on the one hand and society on the other."[5] They are peculiar. "They live among and with others but they are not the other, and notwithstanding their curious nature they display the most remarkable survival powers of any people."

Aside from this very basic difficulty, lesser problems have been recognized—some characteristic of work among the Jews and others endemic to the broader missionary undertakings. The most important of these broader difficulties is the lack of consensus among the myriad groups and denominations on everything from goal to method. In addition, some denominations (but primarily individuals) don't want to evangelize any one at all because they feel that Christianity is the religion of the Christians. Some value the independent existence of the Jews (for various and differing reasons) and do not want them to disappear. And so on, up and down the scale of possibilities.

But our interest at this point is not with those who are ambivalent about conversion of the Jews, or with those who manifestly do not seek this goal, but rather with those who do and have not been able to satisfactorally pursue this end. The question arises as to why if not total success, at least a greater degree of success, has not been forthcoming given the dominant position of Christianity and the great interest in the conversion of Jews manifested at all times by significant elements in the Christian community. What factor or combination of factors has continuously vitiated and hamstrung their efforts?

It would appear that although the matter is much too complex and variegated ever to arrive at simple conclusions, it is nonetheless possible to discern some recurrent factors in the history of the Christian approach to the Jews (and the relationship generally between Christians and Jews) that seem to play a very significant role in this failure.

THE DIALECTICAL RELATIONSHIP BETWEEN JUDAISM AND CHRISTIANITY

Christianity is a child of Judaism. It is put forth as the culmination, the fulfillment of God's plan for mankind as contained in the Old Testament. Whereas the Old Testament foretells the coming of a messiah who will set things aright and usher in the kingdom, the New Testament insists that this leader appeared in the person of Jesus of Nazareth. The Old Testament is a history of the relationship or encounter between man and God in microcosm as it were, the New Testament expands the promise to all men. The Old Testament outlines a complicated, sometimes contradictory "way" through sacrifice, the commandments, and law; the New puts forth the "ultimate sacrifice," faith, and grace as the only ways to salvation. The New in short, seems ever a response to the challenges of the Old, and even if one agrees that the Old can be understood with no reference to the New, the reverse is somewhat problematic. The relationship and dependency of the New Testament on the Old Testament is ineluctable and essentially unchallengable.

Christianity is not a mere offshoot of Judaism, with little but certain doctrinal debts owed to the one by the other. The relationships between Christianity and Judaism did not cease when the Church and the Synagogue diverged, but rather continued to intersect and converge.[6] Christian theology foresees an eschatological fulfillment wherein the wild branches and the olive tree itself will be one—that is, when the Jews will reassert their *rightful* role as the first and immutably chosen of God. The Messiah and Lord of Christianity is not viewed as relevant for the Gentiles alone but for all men, not least the Jews. The intimate relationship between God and the chosen people may have been interrupted by this people's rejection of the Son, but it has certainly not been set aside. "Hath God cast away His people? God forbid."[7]

But Judaism denies these assertions of a new covenant and rejects the messiahship of Jesus. Judaism voices a nay to the Christians yea. According to Judaism the Messiah and the Messianic age are yet to come to an unredeemed world, while for the Church the Messiah has come and is awaited again.

Rather than leading to a silence between Christianity and Judaism, the Jews' rejection of Jesus as the Messiah is part of the overall dynamic of the ongoing relationship and occupies a central position within Christianity: "For if the first fruit be holy, the lump is also holy; and if the root be holy, so are the branches."[8] The Jewish roots of Christianity are constantly referred to, to indicate and buttress the legitimacy of the new faith and to underscore the continuity of revelation. The Jews have not been forever shunted aside; indeed, their continued existence and their ultimate conversion contains an eschatological promise for those of the New Covenant. "For if the casting away of them be the reconciling of the world, what shall the receiving of them be, but life from the dead?"[9]

Although a continuing, intimate relationship clearly exists between Christianity and Judaism, its nature is not always evident, and there is always confusion about the active role Christianity must assume to the Jews. As suggested earlier, the Jews play an eschatological role, but they also act as testing arena for the Christians' fidelity to the demands of the Christian faith, and Christians have ever before them the admonition of Paul—". . . if God spared not the natural branches, take heed lest he also spare not thee."[10] The Christian can measure himself against the high and low water marks of Israel, with Israel always in full view both as a threat and as a gauge. Thus the Christian is confronted with a problem brought about by the very intimacy of this relationship. Should he leave the Jew alone (i.e., not evangelize him), thereby retaining in the Jew a witness to the folly of his rejection and also a positive witness to God's revelation in Christ? Or should the Jew be brought nigh, to hasten the final redemptive victory? Barth in commenting on the witness of the Jew notes that:

> The existence of the Jew probably is the symbol of the objective metaphysical fact, independent of all intellectual countermovements, that the Christian root of Western culture is still alive. Without credit to him and even against his will the Jew is witness to the continuing vitality of the Old and New Testament revelation. . . .[11]

A more active function for the Jews is envisaged by Eckardt:

> We are confronted by the paradoxical fact that, while Christianity originally broke away from Judaism partly for the purpose of universalizing the Judeo-Christian message, today Judaism has the function of protesting on behalf of universalism against the particularization of that message by Christianity.[12]

As a rule, those who emphasize only the continuing witness of Israel (*qua* Israel) are not the strongest advocates of an active mission, and so are not particularly troubled by conflicts or confusion generated by this intimate relationship and the Jews' enigmatic place in it. But to those who seek to hasten the millennium, and who base their hopes on the scriptural positioning of the Jews in the plan, the dialectical placement of the olive tree and the wild branches appears as a boon rather than a defect. Unlike other religious and ethnic groupings the relationship between Israel and the Church can be likened to that between the branch and the tree

(Romans 11). Unlike others who remain outside, the Jews can be assured that the spiritual road they are asked to travel is circular, always wending its inexorable way back to its source, in distinction to the vertical course laid out before the heathen. Thus, the Jew has not far to go. He need only look behind to see the fullness:

> . . . in respect of history there is a difference between Jewish and Gentile believers in Jesus Christ, though theologically there is none. The Gentile by turning to Christ renounces his heathen heritage; he turns away from idols to serve the God of Israel. The Jew by turning to Christ *returns* to the God of Israel, the God of his fathers. The Gentile therefore always remains the "proselyte," whereas the Jew is only a returner.[13]

The Jew cannot be approached as any other because he manifestly is *not* merely any "other." He does not (according to this view) have to convert at all—he must rather do *T'shuva*; that is, he must repent.[14]

But recognition of the unique relationship between Christianity and Judaism has *not* led to a clear-cut approach to the Jews. It has further confused the picture; and this confusion, I believe, is basically attributable to the ambivalence manifested in the Gospels with regard to the place of the Jew in the divine scheme in light of the rejection. On the one hand the Gospel accounts maintain that God will never abrogate the original covenant with the empirical Israel, and on the other there is reference to Christians as the "new Israel." The contention that Christ expanded the covenant to all who would believe, is opposed by the dispensationalist tenet that Christ is still king of the Jews. Against the accusation that the blood of the crucifixion is forever on the hands of the Jews stands the insistence that the Church is at root Jewish and that the Jews hold the key to the salvation of those who do not labor under a guilt so burdensome.

Admittedly all the inconsistencies just listed have been

theologically "accounted for." Answers exist that explain, and in some cases explain well, the seeming contradictions and difficulties. But few if any of these solutions have come close to gaining universal currency with the result that in the case of the Jew, there is appalling confusion and disagreement among missionaries about how to approach him. Some (Bergstrom, Newman) say he must be approached as just another human being, others (Peltz, Smith, Reich, Hoffmann) say he must be approached as something special—as a Jew. This points up the utterly problematic nature of the evangel to the Jews, in that the missionaries are not only unsure of *how* to approach him, but also as to *who* he is. Is he special or ordinary? Is he a greater sinner or an equal sinner? Is he capable of assimilating Christian truth, or is Christian dogma sufficient to assimilate him? In trying to determine the identity of the Jew, one can never escape the very question of whether the empirical Jew is the Israelite or whether the Christian is, thus confuting a clearly directed approach to an entity that resists classification. Is the Jew the deicide of old, or has the leopard really changed his spots?[15] Finally, does God want the Jews brought nigh or does He yet decree their sufferings and through their sufferings, expiation?

Unsurprisingly, such questions about the relationship between Judaism and Christianity and the difficulties engendered by the anomalous positioning of the Jew in the divine economy tend to complicate efforts to conceptualize and activate a Christian approach to the Jews. In merely noting that the relationship between Christianity and Judaism has a dimension that is lacking between Christianity and other religions, there must be recognition of at least the *possible* relevance of a "nonapproach" or an approach that has undergone radical and far-reaching revision from the ordinary undifferentiated methods that have traditionally characterized these efforts. But many missionaries believe that such recognition would undercut the universality of the Christian faith, thus posing a threat that would far outweigh any rewards that might accrue through the conversion of increased numbers of Jews. The dialectical intertwining of Judaism and Christianity thus becomes a snare in which the missionary foresees futility and failure in all missionary endeavors if the Jew (without doubt the most "likely" subject for evangelization) can successfully and with impunity wriggle out from under, claiming himself to be immune from the Christian imperative. Indeed, Smith has insisted that

> Judaism is the "acid test" of evangelization in depth. For it confronts Christianity, not only as a highly developed ethical religion *which has dispensed with Christ* [my emphasis] but as the basic form of religion upon which the whole structure of the Christian Church was built.[16]

Just *because* Judaism and Christianity bear this unique relationship to each other, the problem of how or indeed whether to approach the Jew takes on the mien and complexion of a serious threat. The Jews are seen as a testing ground for the mettle of the Church evangel. The reasoning is approximately as follows: the Church came to supplant the religion of law formulated in empirical Judaism; if the Church abdicates or fails at this first and most preliminary juncture—the supplanting of its origins—it has failed completely, and it loses both the momentum and the rationale for wider efforts. *Because* of his unique placement in the divine program, the Jew, his recalcitrance nothwithstanding, must be evangelized because he is a living denial of the need of *all* men for Christ.

> To exclude the Jew from the Church's universal missionary responsibility . . . would imply that Judaism is adequate for the Jew and that therefore he has no need of Jesus Christ, then no other people necessarily need Christ. To accept such a conclusion would be to undermine the whole mission of the Church.[17]

But even when it has been decided that the unique relationship between the two faiths "logically" demands the evangelization of the Jews, the realization of this objective is hindered at all turns by a sort of internal logic bound up in the dialectic. As Mayer has noted, the existence of the Jews (within a Christian theological framework) is both positive and negative.[18] They are the enemies of God and yet loved by Him. Freud, Samuels, Eckardt, and others have alluded to another paradoxical proposition—namely, that the Christian accepts Christ, believes in Christ, and yet wishes to reject Him, as well as the entire Christian framework. But this is an impossible desire having only one logical displacement— hatred and disgust for those who are reputed to have spawned this repressive and constrictive religion (i.e., the Jews). "Hatred of the Jews," says Eckardt, "is a result of our hatred of Christ."[19] But we deal with the Jews existentially and not on the level of abstraction. Hatred for the Jews may indeed have roots in a subconscious rejection of Christ the Jew.

THE ETHNIC AND NATIONAL CHARACTER OF THE JEWS

The character and nature of the Jewish people has never lent itself too readily to classification or explanation. To say once again that the Jews are unique sheds no new light on the problem. However, it is essential to explicate at least one core facet of this sociological "inscrutability"; namely, the inseparability of the faith of Israel from the ethnic and national character of this people.[20] From the outset, Israel has manifested a peculiar relationship between the two, making an understanding of the one dependent on an understanding of the other. In the interpretation given to their history by the Jews, Israel's historic meanderings were not capricious, not the result of mere happenstance or a directionless, blind fate, but were guided and channeled by the God of Israel, who had set this people a task in history that would persist, proceeding inexorably toward eschatological fulfillment, whereupon (and at this point alone) the union between God and Israel would disintegrate with all peoples entering the kingdom and the separateness of Israel set aside.

But until this day comes, the Jews cannot brook any artificial dichotomy between faith and peoplehood. As Baron has noted, the two (faith and peoplehood) began at that moment when before Sinai the Lord brought this people into being, sealing its national existence with the demands of the Sinaitic revelation.[21] The most imperative of substantive factors in a nation's existence, its land, was given to Israel with these words: "And I have given you a land for which ye did not labor, and cities which ye built not, and ye dwell in them. . . ." It was no concatenation of deterministic events, but the divine imperative itself which joined this people to this land, and it was by divine sanction, and divine fiat that the union was accomplished. Thus the enemies of Israel became the enemies of the Lord Himself; an attempt to unseat or disturb the political integrity of the nation was a threat and a challenge to God's revealed will, making ultimate victory the victory of God.

The festivals and observances of Israel were steeped in the national consciousness, and they assumed meanings fathomable only to those who accepted the full implication of being part of "a separate and a holy nation." The early revelation, the early formulative energies were supplemented and buttressed by the prophets of Israel, who while castigating this "stiffnecked people" for their abuses and the repeated violation of their covenant with their God, yet preached comfort and foretold restoration *as a united and national entity.*

Even under the conditions of exile and dispersal, Israel maintained this ineluctable affirmation of ethnic and national as well as religious separateness. The messianic hope, which played no small role in the survival of the Jews, revolved about the expectation of national as well as religious restoration; and those movements and forces—both from within Judaism as well as from without—which have sought to sever this linkage, to diffuse the essential particularism of Israel, have failed.

The Reform movement in its earliest stages, the enlightenment, the various assimilationist groups, have all experienced defeat insofar as they have attempted to foster a veneer of universalistic patina on what has been variously conceived as a too-stringent parochialism and narrowness inherent in the people–faith Israel. The attempt has been made to temper the injunction to "Separate thyself from the nations and eat not with them; and do not according to their works, and become not their associate; for their works are unclean, and all their ways are a pollution and an abomination and uncleanness"[22] by pointing to the universalism of the prophets, the books of Jonah and Ruth, and particularly Isaiah (LV 16, 7) wherein God promises "I will bring them [all men that acknowledge Him] to my holy mountain and make them joyful in my house of prayer; their burnt offerings and their sacrifices shall be accepted upon my altar; for mine house shall be called a house of prayer for all peoples." Oesterley assures us that

> from the exilic period onwards there were enlightened teachers among the Jews, living both in Palestine and in the Diaspora, whose conception of God demanded a wide and sympathetic outlook on humanity, realizing that their brethren were not restricted to those of their own race. There was one God and none other, and therefore all men were His children; there could be no limit put to His mercy and grace.[23]

To see universal applicability in the religioethical structure of Israel is one thing; it is quite another to infer from this a progressive divorcal of Jewish faith from the ethnic–national moorings of Israel. Yet this is the very error that has been virtually institutionalized (in its frequency of occurrence) by those attempting to bring the message of Christianity to the

Jews. In addition to the barrier of the dialectical relationship existing between Judaism and Christianity, there was also the basic and seemingly inescapable sociological complication, not merely of an ethnic encrustation, but of a total infusion of religion by "Folk" and of "Folk" by religion, serving to obfuscate and confute the evangelization of the Jews.[24] Moreover, Jewish peoplehood itself is an enigma knowing no parallel;[25] a landless people speaking with polyglot tongues, defying classification. As Gidney plaintively notes:

> There is this great difference between missions to the Jews and those to any other people, that with all others the converts remain of the same nationality as they were before their conversion, and their children after them. Not so with the Jews. There is no Jewish country, all the inhabitants of which are professed Jews. Jews are but the scattered members of a homeless race.[26]

But still there is a characteristic inability to come to grips with Israel's unique placement. The missionary sees souls, not a sanctified sociology. He may view the Jew as occupying a unique eschatological role, even as the chosen of God who remains so notwithstanding his unbelief; but this curious and illusive relationship between "citizenship" and religion" remains a stumbling block and appears to be nothing short of perverse.

> Most nations today give their citizens free choice of religion. To embrace another faith is not national disloyalty. Today if a man converts a Christian Englishman like Lord Headley to Mohamdedanism neither the missionary nor the convert is thought of as a traitor to Britain. But it is very difficult for the Jewish community to give that freedom to its members. If they become Christians they are cut off from the fellowship of their nation as well as from the synagogue. This means that the community as a nation is pained when one of its members sees in Christianity a truth greater than that in Judaism; and it visits penalties on him for acting on that belief.[27]

Jews and Judaism are thus envisaged as vindictive, even totalitarian (in the narrow sense), demanding something from its children that it has no right to demand; something that derives not from its inherent structure but rather from a desire to exercise authority and power in the sphere that is Caesar's. While there exists a nagging suspicion that the Jews do indeed represent "something different under the sun," it is difficult to acquiesce in or even to fully fathom the Jew's assertion that the relationship existing between his faith and his culture is an indivisible one, where a change in the substance of the one leads to a transformation of the other. The Christian evangelist, knowing only that Christ died for all and that all are equally in need of salvation, cannot easily shift gears, temporize, qualify, and accept a peculiar sociology as a block to the evangelization of Christ's own brethren according to the flesh. More important, this confusion of nationality, culture, and religious faith appears to be high-handed, oriental, and totally unnecessary to one who more likely than not is a product of Western society, with its compartmentalization of culture traits—its pigeonholing of religion in one niche slightly above all the other niches. Perhaps no statement is more often referred to and quoted with revulsion by those involved in the Christian approach to the Jews and by Hebrew Christians than that of the former Chief Rabbi of Great Britain, Moses Gaster:

> No one can be a Jew who does not belong to the Jewish faith, and he who belongs to the Jewish faith belongs to the Jewish nation. . . . A Jew who changes his faith is torn up by the roots. There is no longer any connection between him and other Jews. He has practically died. This is the common ground on which Jews are united. There may be degrees in the strength and quality of the faith which each one acknowledges as binding on him. But we have no inquisition. As long as a Jew has not publicly renounced his faith and embraced another, he belongs to the Jewish nation.[28]

Even when this tie of the Jew to his ethnic group and culture is accepted and recognized by the evangelist, it often leads to difficulty and an assumption of "incomplete socialization" of the Jew who does convert.[29] Once the realization hits home that the Jew *is* different, the concomittant factor of fear and suspicion of the different tends to come into play. The possibility of reversion, of backsliding to the warmth of the "racial" hearth also lurks and looms just because it is a *total* structure that the Jewish convert has left, entering as it were an incomplete and fragmentary one, where the pull of the past would exercise great attraction. Recognizing this, the Church of Constantinople required a form of culture suicide from the Jewish convert. In Schonfield's words: "as a preliminary to his acceptance as a catechumen, a Jew 'must confess and denounce verbally the whole Hebrew people, and forthwith declare that with a whole heart and sincere faith he desires to be received among the Christians.' "[30] But this of course does not readily lead to the desired end of a complete and satisfactory severance from the fold of Israel. Just *because* Judaism leaves *a total* imprint, an all-pervading coloration, the Jew who leaves this fold for another is more often than not saddled with a sense of guilt derived, I feel, from a suspicion of having gone further than he need have gone. Without assigning either value or cause to conversion (i.e., without judging whether it is an attempt to escape a specified culture or group as well as a religion), it cannot be denied that most individuals will experience pain or at least ambivalence about denying or denigrating a previous reference matrix. It is even more difficult when the group or faith to which the convert is moving has been intimately connected, historically and personally, with rejection, negation, and even persecution of his former allegiance. Even if the convert were able to accept the bifurcation of ethnicity and faith, the problem would probably persist, but in a much less pressing fashion. When, however, the new faith demands something akin to matricide, (as it must in the case of the Jew), thorns will be strewn in the path of the potential believer. Jung has said that "any religion which is rooted in the history of a people is as much an expression of their psychology as the form of political government, for instance, that the people have developed."[31] If he is correct, the Jew—the archetype of this formulation, whose government and culture *was* rooted in his religion—has been asked to submit to a self-effacement that few can endure.

But when all barriers to the conversion of the individual Jew are transcended, when the Jewish believer finds it possible to make the required leap setting aside the connective links that have bound him (whether more or less) to the *Klal Yisrael*, the people of Israel, the Christian approach to the Jew still retains a serious disability. Simply stated, the Jew who is able to make the break melts into the general population, giving the impression (to other Jews) that there are no Jewish believers, and thus no familiar base within Christianity in which the new faith can achieve roots. Not only is this a stumbling block to prospective Jewish converts, but often it is disheartening to those within evangelical Christianity who would be spurred to more intensive and rewarding efforts, were the fruitage to remain at least partly visible. In working among the Chinese, the Indians, the Africans, the missionary sees not assimilation (thus disappearance into the dominant culture) but a high degree of adaptation to Christian culture and belief, whereas

> if a Jew is converted he probably marries a Gentile, while his children for a certainty and even he himself for a probability become assimilated to Gentile surroundings and practically becomes indistinguishable from the English, French, or Germans among whom they dwell. This is no new thing. It has always been going on. The result is that every generation of Christian people has had to deal with a body of Jews whose ranks appear to front them with unbroken lines, just because no trace remains of the many who have yielded their allegiance to Christ.[32]

This very fact highlights the essential point being made here, regarding the inseparability of Jewish faith and the ethnicity of the Jew. Once the circuit is broken, as Christian faith supplants Jewish faith, the Jew inexorably moves away from Jewish consciousness and a Jewish frame of reference, with the obvious negative effect on efforts to convert Jews, as noted previously.

Christian thinkers generally and missionaries to the Jews particularly have recently begun to rethink the problem; that is, to attempt a definition of the Jew and correspondingly to tailor the Christian approach to the specific needs of the Jew. In more advanced evangelical circles there is some consciousness of the enormity and complexity of the problem generated by the unique nature of the Jewish community and its belief structure. We increasingly find statements to the effect that "Judaism is not carried by the individual, but by . . . the community of Israel. The individual is a Jew only inasmuch as he is rooted in the corporate life of his people. It is thus that nation and religion coalesce."[33] Or in a sociological vein, "the Christian must recognize the validity in the objection that conversion of the Jew usually involves not simply his acknowledgement of Christ, but inclusion in the empirical Church, that aspect of the Church whch is an institution. . . ."[34] But again, accepting the validity of this proposition goes only part of the way toward solving a problem that appears to be insoluble once it is understood in all its ramifications.

Even if the Christian approach to the Jew were to emphasize a Christological rather than a Christian strain as such, it would require a framework, a theological and intellectual scaffolding, and logically this would be drawn only from the resources of historical Christianity. Whereas on a level of theology, Eckardt may be correct in assuming that Christ can be preached to the Jew without equating "that truth with Christianity, a religion which participates in all the sinful relativities of history,"[35] its sociological implications are nil. Christ is preached in the only manner feasible—through Christianity—and Christianity confronts the Jew in his peculiar ethnic–

religious unity, challenging this unity by its demands of belief, thus posing a threat that will inevitably elicit a negative response from the Jew. Like other peoples, the Jews display a characteristic will to live, and when a doctrine is preached to them that involves not only subtle transformations of elements of their national gestalt but its outright destruction, the reaction is predictable.[36]

ANTI-SEMITISM

The dialectical relationship between Judaism and Christianity, as well as the previously described enmeshment of national–ethnic characteristics and loyalties with religion pose difficulties in carrying the message of Christianity to the Jew. Yet the strand of anti-Semitism that persists in this effort seems to be the ultimate bar to success. Wherever else the Christian message is preached, and to whatever people, be they steeped in the excesses of paganism or the sublimity of some inner enlightenment, at the outset of the relationship the slate is unmarred by a history of hostility and mutual antagonism. To be sure, tensions have arisen between the contending forces, and enduring enmities have grown up as a result of the clash between a defensive culture and the insistent bearers of a new truth. In most instances, however, the relationship between insurgent, evangelical Christianity and those who are without was at least initially unblemished by the marks of continued struggle, the memory of transcendent wrong, and a basic dislike for the people to whom the message was directed on the part of those who were its bearers.

To the missionary bent on the conversion of the Polynesians, their ignorance of the Gospel was not sin but geographical caprice—they were not so to speak within earshot of revelation. To those who sought to carry the message to black Africa, there was a feeling of exultation brought about by the opportunity to bear a burden that history, or more correctly God, had laid upon the white race (i.e., Christendom). In the efforts to convert the heathen of China and India, there was implicit the possibility of crowning already magnificent ethical structures with grace and the salvation offered only through Christ. But the Jew was neither distant from the physical arena of Christianity's development nor uninvolved in its dynamic. From the very inception of the daughter faith, Jews and Judaism have performed a role in consonance with the peculiar relationship between the two, providing on the one hand a proof of the new faith's legitimacy and on the other a threat to its truth. Once Marcionism, which had condemned the Old Testament as the work of the Demiurge, had been defeated and the Church had accepted the finality of the tie to the Old Testament, and thereby to the people and destiny of Israel, the stage was irrevocably set for the continuance of a relationship which in its very nature represented a macrocosm of ambivalence— an ambivalence that has remained and festered, showing unmistakable signs of unresolvability. The Old Testament projects a definite role for Israel, eschatological and otherwise, and in accepting the relevance of Scripture the Church had to come to grips with its meaning, resolving the positioning of Judaism and Christianity in the divine economy. The challenge, represented in the persistence of Israel, had to be met if the direction of the Church was to become clear and the promise unobstructed. But to accept the relevance of the Old Testament implied a corresponding acceptance of the dilemma that is Israel. Did God indeed cast away His people, or are they merely temporarily in eclipse? Is the Church in reality the New Israel, or has it willingly or unwillingly assumed the mantle of the usurper? Are the Jews of all succeeding generations branded as crucifiers, or are they merely the receptacle, the symbol of Everyman's guilt?

The answers to these and similar questions are significant not only as indices of the doctrinal development of Christi-

anity but also because they may have served in providing a
matrix for the formulation of attitudes, impressions, and a general "explanation" of the Jew in history. Non-Jews could be
approached with the message of Christianity merely by "stating
the case for Christ," without necessarily stigmatizing a former
belief or even assuming a defensive stance. In the matter of
the Jews, however, there were (and are) problems not alone of
a practical missionary nature to be ironed out, but difficulties
which impinge on the very destiny of the Christian church; for
if Israel is only in temporary eclipse, what does this foreshadow
for the empirical church—the wild branches grafted onto the
olive tree? If Christianity is the fulfillment, then Judaism is
false, or at best superseded, and its obstinance and obdurate-
ness become a challenge. As Grayzel has noted:

> by the time Christianity became the dominant religion of the
> Empire, the foundation for its attitude toward the Jews was
> already laid. This attitude, moreover, was the natural outcome
> of theological necessity and of defense against the danger of
> a relapse into Judaism. It was an inevitable by-product of
> Christian propaganda, which had to assume that Judaism was
> dead. . . .[37]

Whatever other factors may have been brought to bear on the
relationship between the two faiths, whether it was as Buber
suggests a sort of fear of ghosts evolving from Israel's indefin-
ability,[38] or Valentin's assertion that the hate for the Jew
stemmed from the contempt with which the winning side
always views the loser,[39] or Baron's suggestive but highly questionable view that the Jews represented a degree of moral
independence that aroused unparalleled contempt among those
dependent in this respect,[40] there can be little doubt that a
theological substratum was operative in formulating the negative picture of the Jew that appeared almost at the inception
of Christianity.[41] While it remains impossible to view anti-
Semitism in a simplistic, monistic vein, assigning final causal

imperative to economic, social, psychological, or religious factors alone, a setting for the phenomenon, a significant buttress
for its development, is to be seen in the *interpretation* placed
on early Christian experience vis-à-vis the Jews and the reflection of this experience in the Gospels and the patristic literature. Even here, however, the matter is by no means simply or
clearly defined. The same body of doctrine and sacred writ
that reports Jesus as saying of the Jews "Ye are of your father,
the Devil" (John 8:44) or "Behold an Israelite indeed in whom
is no guile" (John 1:47) is seemingly countered, or at least
tempered, in Paul. We have referred before to the assertion in
Romans 11 that God has not cast away His people who continue as the olive tree to which the gentiles are the wild
branches grafted on.

In the narrative unfolding of Christianity in the Gospels,
with its focus on an act of deicide, there was ample room for
a villain, and the Jews appeared to be historically fitted to play
this role. With the center of the stage occupied by two groups
—the Jews and the Romans, the latter capitulating to the inexorability of Christ's victory and the former remaining unre-
pentant, indeed hostile—it would have been a minor miracle
if hostility had *not* been directed at the Jews. Add to this that
the new faith was dependent on the old for the legitimation of
its claims, and one can see how emerging Christianity was constrained to interpret and reinterpret Scripture to conform to
the new scheme: In this process the Jew was not to emerge
unscathed.

> For the Gentile Church the O.T. no longer meant a way of life,
> a conception of the relation of a whole community to God, but
> a mine from which proof texts could be extracted. Instead of
> being the history of a single community, and the record of its
> successes and failures, it became the record of two communities,
> the pre-Incarnation Church symbolised by the "Hebrews" and
> the temporary and rejected people of the Jews. Out of this arti-
> ficial separation of history into two parts, on the simple prin-

ciple that what was good belonged to one group and what was
bad to the other, grew the caricature of the Jew with which
patristic literature is filled.[42]

The caricature of the Jew "as a being perpetually betraying
God and ultimately abandoned by Him,"[43] early displayed a
tenacity, a rootedness, an overriding pervasiveness that set an
immutable tone to Judeo-Christian relationships that persists
in greater or lesser degree to the present. What may or may
not have had validity or meaning on a purely religious level
alone at its origin can be made to speak in a somewhat less
lofty vein if its interpreters are so inclined or conditioned.
Thus, in many of Paul's fulminations concerning the Jews, it
becomes possible to draw conclusions about them that go
beyond the merely spiritual, and indeed border on caricature.
In the Epistle of Paul to Titus we find the following comment
on the depths of degradation possible to the Jews:

> For there are many unruly and vain talkers and deceivers, spe-
> cially they of the circumcision: whose mouths must be stopped,
> who subvert whole houses teaching things which they ought not,
> for filthy lucre's sake.[44]

When Paul then says that "Unto the pure all things are pure:
but unto them that are defiled and unbelieving is nothing
pure . . ."[45] it becomes clear that an image of the Jew as a positive or even neutral figure has become highly problematic.

Although we can trace counterbalancing factors in the portrayal of the Jew in the Gospels and the patristic literature,
the significance lies not in the striking of a balance but in the
sum of impressions that emerge and the weight that history has
bestowed on particular patterns. Thus I believe Parkes is in
the main correct in saying that although scholars may know
that the Jews do not stand alone as the villain of the piece,
"the Christian public as a whole, the great and overwhelming
majority or the hundreds of millions of nominal Christians in

the world still believe that 'the Jews' killed Jesus, that they are a people rejected by their God. . . .[46]

This image of the Jew, complicated no doubt by the inclusion of any number of other "antipathies" rooted in the specific situations of other eras, has not been laid aside nor escaped from by those committed to their conversion to Christianity. Although there have been numerous attempts to overcome this image, to approach the Jew as if he were a human being in the same need of Christ as any other, there has been little evidence of success. For a curious anomaly presents itself. Those who are able to view the Jews as "just another people" fall under the rubric of "liberals," who in any event are likely to interpret Scripture much more broadly than the fundamentalists. Not only will the various Gospel images of the Jew be tempered and interpreted in a beneficent light, but the very command to evangelize all men is called into question. I have noted elsewhere that the liberal Protestant thinker is characteristically involved in ambivalence which finds him confronted on the one hand by the unmistakable demands of his religious affirmation which knows of no distinction between "Jew and Greek" insofar as the need for salvation and the means to its achievement are concerned, and on the other by those of his nineteenth-century secular humanist ethic, based on respect for diversity, commitment to pluralism, and a pervasive equalitarianism.[47] In confrontation with evangelical commitment generally and especially with regard to the Jew, these two incompatible strains are found in upsetting imbalance and totally discomforting conflict, one with the other. In effect what these very real difficulties have done is to bring about the withdrawal of the liberals from *active* participation in evangelizing the Jews.

This withdrawal leaves the stage to the fundamentalists, or those who are most likely to be influenced by the traditional interpretations of and attitudes toward the Jews. According to fundamentalist interpretation, moreover, the Jews are not "just another people"; they are a very particular group bearing a unique and possibly threatening relationship to the fundamentalists' faith. Thus we find that the very group with the greatest commitment to the evangelization of the Jews is also the group most likely to be influenced by the negative image or images extractable from the history and literature of the Judeo-Christian relationship.

Although Eckhardt maintains that "it would be a gross misrepresentation of conservative Protestantism to contend that fundamentalism must involve anti-Semitism,"[48] the weight of evidence indicating that such a tie exists and is very strong, is incontrovertible.[49] The fundamentalist is often caught in the trap of his own literalness. Perhaps he does not intend to denigrate the Jew—possibly he desires the opposite with all his being—but only rarely is he able to extricate himself. Eckardt, contending that "the fundamentalist Christian may easily have an ambivalent attitude toward the Jew he is attempting to evangelize," comments further as follows:

> An additional contributory factor [to anti-Semitism] is that, as for example in Dispensationalism stress is often placed upon the "earthly" character of Israel. While conservative literature usually makes this claim as the result of theological conviction rather than because of prejudice, the fact is that overt anti-Semitism often carries with it the accusation that the Jews are worldly and materialistic.[50]

Even the "sacred history" of ancient Israel, when viewed through the literalists' spectacles, often loses all flexibility of interpretation, becoming the mundane record of repeated failure and mere temporal and profane striving. Israel's influence on the development of Christianity is often regarded as a tragic flaw in an otherwise pure and exemplary pattern of possibilities.

> It may be said that the Judaizing of the Church has done more to hinder her progress, pervert her mission, and destroy her spir-

ituality than all other causes combined. Instead of pursuing her appointed path of separation from the world and following the Lord in her heavenly calling, she has used Jewish scriptures to justify herself in lowering her purpose to the civilization of the world, the acquisition of wealth, the use of an imposing ritual, the erection of magnificent Churches, the invocation of God's blessing upon the conflicts of armies, and the divisions of an equal brotherhood into "Clergy" and "laity."[51]

Thus far the attempt has been made to show how a theological perspective has played a role in the structuring of a "Jewish image" that has retained its potency among those who would be most likely to act under its influence and who also happen to be those most intensely committed to the evangelization of the Jews. Left on the level of theological abstraction, this circumstance would no doubt still cause strain and tension between Jews and Christians. When, however, it is translated into a working tool for the explication of an empirical entity —the Jews—we can trace results that are far-reaching and generally negative. It is difficult to underestimate the power inherent in any structure possessing an aura of the sacred. Durkheim particularly has recognized the powerful constraining influence of the sacred and its effect on societal norms.[52] But the same quality that can act as a constraining force can provide an equally powerful release stimulus under a different set of conditions. The Jews are not viewed as sacred (except perhaps in the most esoteric sense), but they are perceived within the framework of the sacred, bearing the stigma so peculiar to the fallen—those who have profaned and who are now in turn profane. Were the Jews a secular phenomenon, they would no doubt be viewed in secular terms (i.e., according to the biases of a particular period, area, or circumstance); they would be looked at with charity and forebearance, or perhaps with scorn and disdain, but always in consonance with the "normal" situational prejudice. Even when positive in origin, however, attitudes toward the Jews almost inevitably assume a religious mien, a sacred coloration,[53] an elemental

aspect; when negative, they are seen in much the same way but
in reverse. Thus it becomes difficult for the Jew to appear as
merely an enemy of Christian faith; he becomes the enemy
incarnate, the religiously defined opponent, and the effects of
this attitude on the work of evangelization are obvious. When
a missionary assumes as a working principle the statement
that "it is a Jewish unbelief that is responsible for the post-
ponement of the Messianic kingdom . . . ,"[54] he attempts
thereby to impose an unbearable burden of guilt and assumes
in the process the stance of the aggressor, which inevitably produces countermovements among the Jews. This depiction of
the Jew as the *enemy* is in many ways ludicrous. It at times
takes on a military aspect, so that a missionary in addressing
himself to current needs in the Jewish mission field sounds
very much like a field general priming the troops when he
states:

> And, moreover, in face of the greatness and the wide ramifica-
> tions of the problem, the strength and forcefulness of the
> enemy, the waste of inefficient equipment . . . we shall surely
> add the need of a drawing together on the part of all com-
> mitted to this enterprise in order to effect their common purpose
> and to present a united front whether in action at the home
> base, or in labor in the field.[55]

It is no doubt fair to conclude that most groups faced by a
challenge so formulated will respond negatively. Furthermore,
it is not only the Jews who are proselytized so militantly but
all who are without the fold, with however, a significant difference obtaining in the nature of the threat (if any) posed by the
"enemy." The Jew is an opponent as all unbelievers are opponents, but the Jew is not merely a passive enemy, one by
default, as it were, but an active challenger whose distinctive
role in sacred history is troublesome, anomalous, and ultimately ambiguous. Much as in the case of predestination,
where the believer sought to indicate by achievement and the

good life that he was among the elect, the Christian activist often feels constrained to resolve the dilemma of the Jew's role in history and eschatology by regarding him as the apotheosis of depravity, moral as well as religious. Not only does this interpretation serve to unravel the sometimes obscure divine plan, it spurs even more strenuous attempts to rescue this benighted people and at the same time to protect Christendom from the threat of contamination. Thus in what is offered as "A Call to Prayer for Israel" we find the following:

> If not counteracted by the Gospel, Jewish irreligion and vice will mightily aid the forces of ungodliness in corrupting our national life. One of the spiritual leaders of Germany has declared that the fatherland is threatened with dechristianization by means of Jewish infidelity. The safety of society demands the instant evangelization of the Jews.[56]

The early missionaries to the Jews seemed convinced of the existence of this threat to faith and morals inherent in the Jews. Their image of the Jew often bordered on the fantastic, beginning with an interpretation of the religion of the Jews and generally ending in a bald stereotype of his capacity for evil.

> Their religion [Judaism] is legalistic formalism, more or less strict adherence to the 613 precepts of the Law as interpreted by the Talmud and the Rabbis. There is little if any sense that Scripture is a revelation of the Spirit of God; those who would follow the liberty of the spirit are regarded as destroyers of Israel. Morals and religion are separate, or otherwise morality as well as religion consists in the formal keeping of the precepts. Sin becomes merely the omission to fulfill the precepts. The summary of the way of Salvation is formal prayer, formal repentance and almsgiving. Remembering these things, remembering the tyranny of the Synagogue—the greatest tyranny the world ever knew—and that its interpretation of the precepts prescribes action in every thinkable phase in life, it is not to be wondered that a large mass of Jews, conforming to the orders of an ancient

world, are sunk in superstition as dense as will be found any-
where on earth.[57]

By and large, these appraisals of the Jew are not supplied
by men driven by blind hatred or psychotic fears. The authors
quoted would have recoiled in horror at the thought of Hitler's
"final solution"; but the similarities in sentiment to the ravings
and fantasies of the "professional" anti-Semites are clear. It
must be remembered that the purpose of these statements is to
galvanize support not for a pogrom but for the conversion of
the Jews—the inclusion of these people under the wing of the
Church. How is it possible, it may be asked, to engender love
for a people so despicable, so sunk in perversity? What Christian or group of Christians could be moved to welcome the
warped product of this religiously inspired depravity into the
communion and fellowship of believers?[58] It is my contention
that those dedicated to the conversion of the Jews have in
fact found it impossible to respond to the Jew in any way
significantly different from that propounded by those less loft-
ily inspired. And it could not be otherwise. The image of the
Jew supplied against a basic theological framework, wherein
he fulfills the role of the enemy of God, is if anything a more
powerful denigrating factor than any weapon available to the
purely "secular" anti-Semite. What perfidiousness—from poi-
soning the water supplies to undermining an economic structure—could be beyond the ability of those who would destroy
God himself? The "demonology" of the Jew becomes so binding that even the "sins" hitherto considered peculiarly the
province of the Church are shifted to the Jew with ease and
aplomb. Thus we are assured that

> The real spirit of religious intolerance springs from Talmudical
> Judaism. Those who do not conform to its tenets are persecuted
> to death; its persecuting spirit is checked by well-known circum-
> stances. Its contempt and abhorrence of the heathen and in

spite of protestation, also of others, might have taken an active
form, if there had not been restraining powers in the world.[59]

But as if the conception of the Jews as a group in a negative
light were not a sufficient block to their successful evangelization, the inclusion of individual stereotyping acts as a further
hindrance to this end. It could be expected that if the group is
viewed as a repository of evil, the individual member of the
group would not emerge unscathed. Among missionaries, the
individual Jew is generally widely viewed and pictured in
much the same manner as in the body of "secular" anti-Semitic
literature that has grown so large and so ominous in the past
75 years. One rarely comes across a tract, leaflet, or article on
the Jew in which the Jew is not pictured as a poor (but dan-
gerous) dupe of nefarious leadership, bent on something other
than the mere exercise of talmudic casuistry. From the imputation of utter depravity,[60] to the utilization of dialect and
supposed ethnic peculiarities and traits,[61] nothing in the way
of a negative typologizing seems to have been missed by those
who are—curiously enough—striving mightily to win the Jew.

The inability of mission bodies to free themselves of these
attitudes, or to sublimate them, has led to repeated failure and
ultimately to frustration. There has been considerable recognition given to the prevalence of anti-Semitism, and even to its
retarding effects on efforts to proselytize the Jews, but significantly much of the recognition has involved, at best, left-
handed condemnation of the phenomenon, and indeed, in
many instances anti-Semitism has been placed in a theological
matrix of inevitability. Anti-Semitism is accepted as tragic and
unfortunate, but somehow deserved and in an inscrutable
manner, part of the divine scheme.

> The hatred of the Jew is a tragic thing, but it should not sur-
> prise us. On the contrary there would be good reason for sur-
> prise were the Jew nowhere hated. For the Scriptures pledge

God's word that Israel should be hated in many countries, and
through the centuries, until she returns to God by accepting His
annointed Messiah. The hatred of the Jew is the fulfillment and
corroboration of the word of God.[62]

Jewish culpability for anti-Semitism is not derived from Scripture alone but also from the very temporal here-and-now behavior of the Jews. It has been difficult for missionaries to con-
demn anti-Semitism outright[63] without attempting to shift
much of the burden for its persistence to theological deter-
minance on the one hand and to certain stygian characteristics
of the Jews on the other. Especially in recent years, there has
been a growing awareness that anti-Semitism plays a not-too-
welcome role in the evangelization of the Jews; but here again,
efforts to counteract it have been stymied by the ambivalence
and indecision of those concerned. Interestingly enough, some
attempts have been made to claim that missionary activity can
ameliorate negative attitudes toward Jews; but this remains a
highly questionable thesis.[64] Among missionaries, however,
there is little effort made to show therapeutic results for their
work, and it is deemed sufficient if the Christian recognizes the
need to overlook Jewish "dereliction" to bring about his salvation. Recognition is given to the difficulty involved in overcoming the obstacles besetting the Christian in his relationship
to the Jew, but there is insistence that Christian charity and
love prevail. Nor can this approach be more successful, because
of the element of condescension and "overlooked guilt" attached to it. When an outstanding missionary to the Jews gra-
tuitously suggests that "Christians must unequivocally insist
and demonstrate that anti-Semitism is absolutely irreconcilable
with . . . the Christian faith, which means that a Christian may
never justify anti-Semitism *no matter what the provocation* (my
emphasis),"[65] equivocation is already present by the suggestion
that guilt *may* indeed exist but should be ignored or shunted
aside. This is not an isolated sentiment; it appears again and

again in missionary literature. It no doubt acts as a salve to consciences wrestling with the desire to love the Jew but somehow or other finding it difficult to do so. Thus the individual missionary who may have begun to despair of the Jews' conversion—perhaps questioning his suitability for missionary work or the salvageability of the Jew (or both)—can with comfort note that the fault is with the Jew as much or more than with himself. However, he need maintain a proper perspective, and "though it cannot be denied that in many countries severe offence and provocation have been given by the activities of certain Jews, the condemning of all Jews, good and bad, for the sins of the Jew can never be defended."[66] Once again, this approach may prove helpful to the missionary, but it will hardly result in effulgent response from the Jews. Finally, to suggest as many missionaries do that "so long as the Jew adhered to traditional custom and his age-old exclusiveness, so long would race hatred continue,"[67] acts as an irritant on Judeo-Christian relationships generally. But when the missionary adds the thought that "conversion to Christian faith is therefore the true antidote to anti-Semitism,"[68] it becomes a matter of tightening battlelines rather than opening new channels for evangelization.

NOTES

1. A. Thompson, *A Century of Jewish Missions* (Chicago: F. H. Revell Co., 1902), p. 260.

2. *Ibid.*, p. 261.

3. Carl Mayer, "Religious and Political Aspects of Anti-Judaism," in *Jews In A Gentile World,* Isacque Graeber and Steuart Henderson Brit, eds. (New York: The Macmillan Co., 1942), p. 312.

4. *Ibid.*, p. 313.

5. *Ibid.*, p. 313.

6. This "convergence" was not unidirectional. Diaspora Judaism in the West has always been influenced, sometimes very extensively, by Christian thought and theology.

7. Romans 11:1.

8. Romans, 11:16.

9. Romans, 11:15.

10. Romans, 11:21.

11. Quoted in Salo W. Baron, *Modern Nationalism and Religion* (New York: Meridian Books, 1960), p. 269.

12. Arthur Roy Eckardt, *Christianity and the Children of Israel* (New York: King's Crown Press, 1948), p. 147.

13. Jakob Jocz, *A Theology of Election—Israel and the Church* (London: Society for the Promotion of Christian Knowledge, 1958), pp. 180–181.

14. Dispensationalism—including the notion that Christ will one day rule over his people—underscores this continuous relationship between God and Israel, thus between Israel and Christianity. Dispensationalism, however, has found much more favor among Hebrew Christians than among the more traditional missionary factions (see Chapter 4).

15. After telling the tale of a Jewish shoemaker who seemed to be heading for Christianity and was beaten and sent to his grave by his brethren (for his belief or unbelief), one author states: "I felt inclined to stoop down and say to the dead: 'Forgive your poor brothers; do not be angry with them, for they know not what they do!' " Karl Emil Franzos, "The Nameless Grave," in *When Jews Face Christ*, Henry Einspruch ed. (Baltimore, Md.: The Mediator, 1932), p. 44. Note how the author indicates continuing crime—an unregenerate nature and everlasting guilt.

16. Robert Smith, "The New Dimension In Evangelism," *International Review of Missions*, Vol. 33 (July 1944), 304.

17. Conrad Hoffman, *What Now For The Jews?* (New York: Friendship Press, 1948), p. 46.
       In *Twenty-five Years of the International Missionaries' Council's Christian Approach to the Jews*, criticism of Jewish missions is disposed of as follows: "To all this criticism the International Missionaries Council could answer by referring to the basic problem for all .Christian missions both abroad and at home. If it was held that the Jews did not need Jesus Christ, or were an exception as regards Christian missions, it had to be conceded that there may also be other people who would not need Christ. This would imply that the Christian mission was deprived of the basis for its claim of the absoluteness and necessity of salvation for the individual man and for mankind . . . Judaism is as much without Christ as Mohammedanism and Hinduism, Buddhism and Confucianism. Either all people need Christ or none." *Op. cit.*, p. 5.

18. See Mayer, *op. cit.*

19. Eckardt, *op. cit.*, p. 55.

20. I am not attempting to say that a Jewish nation is the same thing qualitatively as, let us say, the French nation or the German nation. The term is admittedly imprecise; however, it does indicate that the Jews are considerably more than a religious grouping alone and that they also transcend the purely "spiritual."

21. Baron, *op. cit.*

22. "The Testament of the XII Patriarchs Levi XII, 16," quoted by William Oscar Emil Oesterly in *The Jews and Judaism during the Greek Period* (London: Society for Promoting Christian Knowledge, 1941) p. 117. According to Oesterly, Jewish particularism arose in the Babylonian period as an effort to protect the faithful from the sea of unbelief by which they were surrounded. But he also says: "It is important to note that Particularism, wholly necessary as it was if the worship of Yahweh in its purity was to survive, had the further effect of creating a nationalistic spirit which, in times to come, played an important role in Jewish history." *Ibid.*, p. 116.

23. *Ibid.*, p. 114.

24. In this context, Goldberg notes that Judaism "emanated from the Jew as truthfully as the rays of heat and light emanate from the sun, and it never existed apart from him as an abstraction, as Christianity, for example, has had existence apart from the Gentiles. Therein may be seen the fundamental distinction between Judaism and Christianity. The former, being a definite corporate spiritual equation, has never traveled away from the Jews to any other people, and other people could never embrace it in all its integrity. Christianity, on the other hand, being only a theology, could travel from one people to another, and could be embraced in all its integrity by different historical peoples. That is why, whereas Jew and Judaism are an affinity, a unified concept, Gentile and Christianity are no affinity and no unified concept." David Goldberg, "The Debacle of Religion in Russia—Judaism in the Melee—," *Central Conference of American Rabbis, Yearbook*, Vol. 12 (1931), p. 259.

25. Baron states that during the first Czechoslovak Census of 1921, eleven residents of Prague and hundreds of others in other parts of the country registered as Jewish "nationals" but of the Roman Catholic religion. Jewish leaders were shocked, and the Jewish community rejected this. Baron adds: "This would have been illogical if ethnic descent, and not religion were the exclusive criterion. But it was an inescapable reflection of the Jewish people's semiconscious realization that, however secularized it still was a 'religious nationality' glorying in its religious past and essentially held together by a common religion." *op. cit.*, p. 24.

Baron ends: "So long as the Jewish faith will largely be restricted to descendents of Jews (paradoxically of religious, and not 'racial' Jews); so long as Judaism refrains from being again an active missionary religion trying to convert vast Gentile masses; and so long as the Jews, with individual exceptions, fail to adopt other religions and formally adhere to their forefathers' creed or profess religious indifference—Judaism of every shade will appear to Jews and, still more, to their neighbors as an ethnic religion, however peculiar and unique." *Ibid.*

26. W. T. Gidney, *The Jews and Their Evangelization,* (London: Student Volunteer Missionary Union, 1899), p. 109.

27. Basil Mathews, *The Jews and the World Ferment* (New York: Friendship Press, 1935), p. 163. The confusion generated by the inability to comprehend or to accept the peculiar sociological configuration of the Jews is sometimes amusing. One often finds comment almost in the form of an appeal to good sportsmanship for the Jew to "shape up" and choose one role, one image, or another. "The point which it seems important to emphasize from the point of view of Christian missions is that Judaism cannot well combine the characters of a religious community and of a political nation. If it is a religious community, then indeed no member of it can give up the distinctive Jewish beliefs and practices without forfeiting his right to belong to the community; if on the other hand it is a political nation, a Jew might become a Christian . . . without choosing to be politically and civilly a full Jew; for it would be tyrannous according to modern conception to make one religion obligatory for all members of a nation." Edwyn Bevan, "Missions and the New Situation in Asia," *International Review of Missions,* Vol. 4, (July 1920), 339.

28. Moses Gaster, "Judaism—A National Religion," in *Zionism and the Jewish Future,* H. Sacher, ed. (New York: The Macmillan Co. 1916), p. 91.

29. Stonequist notes that Gentiles are reluctant to forget that the Jew is a Jew even after he converts. "These difficulties [escaping his Jewishness] are not necessarily reduced by the fact that a Jew may be converted to Christianity, spend a long life among Christians, marry a Christian, and yet continue not only to reveal Jewish traits of personality but also to transmit (by unconscious example and imitation) some of these traits to his children." "The Marginal Character of the Jews," in Isacque Graeber and Stewart Britt, eds., *Jews in a Gentile World,* (New York: The Macmillan Co., 1942) p. 308.

The notion that the Jew always remains a Jew is rather widespread. Baron notes that ". . . in some cases even after an indi-

vidual's conversion to Christianity, Jews were suspected of maintaining a particular brand of group solidarity and of revealing in
their behavior certain characteristics which set them aside from the
rest of the population. Loud professions to the contrary, a large
body of non-Jewish opinion simply refused to acknowledge Jewish
assimilation as an accomplished fact or to believe in its effective
realization in 'any foreseeable future.' " Baron, *op. cit.*, p. 220.

30. Hugh J. Schonfield, *The History of Jewish Christianity: From the
First to the Twentieth Century* (London: Duckworth, 1936), p. 107.
Schonfield quotes some professions of faith required of Jewish converts which show how the Church attempted to cut off the Jewish
ethnic factor. The tone of the following indicates that the fear of
Jewish backsliding or overriding ethnic attachment was quite strong.
" 'I renounce all customs, rites, legalisms, unleavened breads and
sacrifice of lambs of the Hebrews, and all the other feasts of the
Hebrews, sacrifices, prayers, aspersions, purifications, Sabbaths and
superstitutions, and hymns and chants and observances and synagogues, and the food and drink of the Hebrews; in one word I
renounce absolutely everything Jewish' . . ." p. 107 (from the
Church of Constantinople), quoted by Schonfield. Another confession
contains the following: " 'I renounce the whole worship of the
Hebrews, circumcision, all its legalisms, unleavened bread, Passover,
the sacrificing of lambs, the feasts of Weeks, Jubilees, Trumpets,
Atonement, Tabernacles, and all the other Hebrew feasts, their
sacrifices, prayers, aspersions, purifications, expiations, fasts, Sabbaths, new moons, food and drinks. And I absolutely renounce
every custom and institution of the Jewish Laws.' " Of uncertain
Eastern origin, attached to the Clementine Recognitions, quoted by
Schonfield, *ibid.*, p. 109.
   The foregoing passage ends as follows: " '. . . if I pretend to become a Christian . . . and then revert to Judaism, or be found eating
with the Jews, or observing their feasts and fasts, or speaking
secretly with them, or defaming the Christian faith, or visiting
their synagogues, or oratories, or taking them under my protection,
and do not rather confute the said Jews and their acts openly, and
revile their empty faith, then may there come upon me all the
curses which Moses wrote in Deuteronomy. . . ." *Ibid.*, p. 112.

31. Carl Gustav Jung, *Psychology and Religion* (New Haven, Conn.:
Yale University Press, 1948), p. 97.

32. Gidney, *The Jews and Their Evangelization, op. cit.*, p. 109. I elsewhere note that this need for evincing unbroken lines is an underlying cause of the emergence of Hebrew Christianity.

33. Jakob Jocz, "Judaism and the State of Israel," *Hebrew Christian
Alliance Quarterly*, Vol. 37, Nos. 2 and 3 (Fall 1951).

34. Eckardt, *op. cit.*, p. 149. To all intents and purposes Eckardt is opposed to missions to the Jews. He maintains that Christ is a gift and thus "not something we possess or require other men to possess," p. 151. But he nonetheless assumes the need for preaching Christ manifest.

35. Eckardt, *ibid.*, p. 149.

36. One such reaction, obviously facetious, was considered by the missionary leader W. T. Gidney to be a *bona fide* exposition of the Jewish insistence on retaining "Jewishness" as a condition for conversion to Christianity. The writer feels that the one thing the Church would never be able to permit is the continued existence of an autonomous Jewish people and culture." For the sake of putting an end to the strife of two thousand years, we shall be ready, if needs be, to accept the ancient right [sic] of baptism. We shall call our Synagogues Churches our Rabbis pastors, and ourselves Christians, or by any other well-chosen and suitable name. Moreover, for the sake of a compromise we should be ready to keep the Sabbath on Sunday instead of on Saturday; we would give up the dietary laws, and would entirely reject the Talmud. In a word, if our conditions were accepted, that the Church which is of the same divine origin as Judaism, should go back to Isaiah, and to Jesus, we should be ready to enter into religious fellowship, yet retaining our nationality." W. T. Gidney, *The Jews and Their Evangelization, op. cit.*, p. 115.

37. Solomon Grayzel, "Christian–Jewish Relations in the First Millennium," in *Essays on Anti-Semitism*, 2nd ed. rev. Koppel Pinson, ed., (New York: Conference on Jewish Relations, 1946), p. 87.

38. Martin Buber, *Israel and the World* (New York: Schocken Books, 1948).

39. Hugo Valentin, *Anti-Semitism Historically and Critically Examined* (New York: Viking Press, 1936).

40. Salo W. Baron, *A Social and Religious History of the Jews*, 3 vols., (New York: Columbia University Press, 1937).

41. Speaking of anti-Semitism, Leon Poliakov says, "So strange and so intense a phenomenon had necessarily to be rooted in a doctrinal system and buttressed by a strong belief, nourished on the teaching of leading thinkers. Accordingly, for centuries anti-Semitism was theological—conceived to be the expression of the divine will, whose commands the persecuters of the Jews believed themselves to be obeying by word or act— . . ." "A Look at Modern Anti-Semitism," *The UNESCO Courier*, October 1960, p. 13.

42. James William Parkes, *The Conflict of the Church and the Synagogue* (London: Soncino Press, 1934), p. 374.

43. *Ibid.*, p. 375.

44. Titus 1:10, 1:11.
45. Titus 1:15.
46. Parkes, *op. cit.*, p. 376.

Eckardt quotes the following from a study of the Institute of Social Research. "It would be difficult to exaggerate the role played by imagery of the Christ-Killer, of the Pharisee, of the money changers in the Temple, of the Jew who forfeited his salvation by denying the Lord, and not accepting Baptism." In A. Roy Eckardt, *op. cit.*, p. 8. This image of the eternal denigrator and scoffer seems to stick with the Jew even through epochs that are entirely secular in emphasis and outlook. Even when the churches recognize the dead end in which they find themselves and attempt to preach Christian love for the Jew utilizing an "even though" attitude, without effectuating a radical reinterpretation, the enterprise is doomed to failure.

Olson, for instance, has found that "The child who is told to love the Jew as part of his Christian witness cannot do so unless love for the Jew is concretely manifested, not merely in the *command* to love the Jew but *in the content which describes him* and presents him as an understandable human being." Bernhard Olson, "The Victims and the Oppressors," Ph.D. thesis, Yale University, 1959, p. 428.

47. B. Z. Sobel, "Legitimation and Anti-Semitism as Factors in the Functioning of a Hebrew Christian Mission," *Jewish Social Studies*, Vol. 23, No. 3 (July 1961), pp. 170–186.
48. Eckardt, *op. cit.*, p. 80.
49. Eckardt defines anti-Semitism as Judenhass, or hatred for the Jew, but this definition puts too narrow a collar around the neck of the problem. Anti-Semitism can involve degrees of antipathy (to say nothing of predispositions to act in a negative manner), but it does not always lend itself well to so strong a term as "Judenhass." I accept the definition of Ackerman and Jahoda: "Anti-Semitism is any expression of hostility, verbal or behavioral, mild or violent against the Jews as a group or against an individual Jew because of his belonging to that group." Nathan W. Ackerman and Marie Jahoda, *Anti-Semitism and Emotional Disorder* (New York: Harper & Row, 1950), p. 19.
50. Eckardt, *op. cit.*, p. 78.

The anti-Semite has a foothold within fundamentalism on a number of levels where it becomes possible to draw temporal conclusions from theological roots. Thus Eckardt notes "The Conservative view of the Jews as outside the 'true faith' is easily seized upon by the Anti-Semite" (p. 79). Or again, "So long as Jews cling to their exclusiveness, and hold themselves aloof from their neighbors as the possessors of certain divine privileges which belong to them solely as a chosen people, so long will they attract to themselves resentment and dislike." John Stuart Conning, "Jesus and Jewish Exclusiveness," *Hebrew Christian Alliance Quarterly*, Vol. 28, No. 2 (Summer 1943), 9.

51. C. I. Scofield, quoted in Eckardt, *op. cit.*, p. 79.

52. Emile Durkheim, *The Elementary Forms of the Religious Life* (New York: Glencoe Press, 1949), pp. 206–208.

53. Witness the reaction among so many Christians to the birth of the state of Israel, or even Niebuhr's assumption of particular qualities of grace inherent in the Jew, or the enshrinement of Jewish attributes (and faults) by the Hebrew Christian.

54. Anton Darms, "The Confirmation, Consolation, and Consummation of Israel," *Hebrew Christian Alliance Quarterly*, Vol. 29, No. 3 (Fall 1944), 13. The passage assumes a particularly ironic aspect in view of the fact that 1944 was still the time of Hitler. A Jew approached in this manner could only respond in utter confusion or anger.

55. J. T. Webster, "The Need of a New Policy in Jewish Missions," *International Review of Missions*, Vol. 7 (1918), 218.

56. Rev. T. A. Chalmers, in Thompson, *op. cit.*, p. 271.

57. Webster, *op. cit.*, pp. 206–218.

58. Indeed, as Schonfield notes the converts "frequently found that they were not wanted in the Church, and were frozen out by ill-disguised dislike. The Jewish temperament, so susceptible to atmospheric feeling, wilted with the chill of Christian austerity." Schonfield, *op. cit.*, p. 231.

59. M. Malbert, "Persecution is not the monopoly of . . . ," *Hebrew Christian Alliance Quarterly*, Vol. 5, No. 2 (April 1, 1921), 62.

60. For example: "Under their religious sanctions they will do without a qualm what would revolt the moral sense of even a low-grade type of Christian. So sunk in spiritual darkness are they that they will commit crime in fulfillment of the Law." Webster, *op. cit.*, pp. 209–210.

61. The following example of dialect was quoted in a volume intended as a tool in the evangelization of the Jews. "I used to sit there half dozing. A man got up and said, 'What shall it profit a man . . .' When I heard dot I voke up. You can't expect de Jew to sleep when he hears uf profit!" W. Price, "A Christian on the Bowery," in *When Jews Face Christ*, Henry Einspruch, ed. (Baltimore: The Mediator, 1932) pp. 45–55.

62. "The Hatred of Israel," *Hebrew Christian Alliance Quarterly*, Vol.

16, No. 1 (January–March 1931): Reprinted from *The Toronto Globe,*
Oct. 29, 1930.

63. One of the strongest statements opposing anti-Semitism was issued in
1940 by a body of Evangelical Lutherans. Statements of this genre,
however, are very much in the minority, and this statement is decidedly atypical in its across-the-board condemnation of anti-Semitism.
"We Evangelical Lutheran pastors and professors who have subscribed
our names hereto, declare that we are opposed to Anti-Semitism,
whether religious, economic, political or racial or whatever form it
may take, as inconsistent with our heritage of liberty and fair play as
citizens of America, and as unworthy of those who bear the name of
Christian. And we further declare that any attempt to use the Holy
Scriptures as an excuse for an anti-Semitic attitude is a perversion of
God's Word and irreconcilable with the spirit and teaching of the
Lord Jesus Christ. We beseech every Christian-honoring child of
God to show kindness to the Jew and to pray for his salvation."
Manifesto to the Jews by American Lutherans," *News Sheet*, Vol. 10,
No. 5 (September–October 1940), Item 1, p. 1. Quoted in *The Church
and the Jewish Question* (Geneva: World Council of Churches, 1944),
p. 14.

64. In a study made of the Lutheran parish, Floreen asserts that in congregations where there is (Jewish) missionary activity there is less
anti-Semitism. "The statistics clearly place a question mark over the
wholesomeness of mere education apart from an opportunity for overt
expression consisting of the proclamation of the Gospel to Jewish
people by word and deed or by supporting such work." The table
below shows the effect of missionary and educational activities on
attitudes in Lutheran congregations toward Jews.

Attitudes	No Activities	Educational Activity Alone	Missionary Activity Alone	Combined Activities
Friendly	37.5%	26.6%	37.7%	45.2%
Antagonistic	7.7%	7.7%	5.7%	6.4%
Indifferent	18.5%	22.5%	17.9%	14.7%
Mixed	36.3%	43.2%	38.7%	33.7%
Totals	100.0%	100.0%	100.0%	100.0%
Congregations involved	168	169	106	252

Harold Floreen, *The Lutheran Parish and the Jews: An Analytical
Study* (Chicago: The National Lutheran Council–Division of American
Missions, 1940), p. 23.

65. Hoffman, *op. cit.*, p. 1.
66. "Race Prejudice and Christian Testimony," quoted in *The Church and the Jewish Question, op. cit.*
67. Rev. Robert Allen, "Arnold Frank," *American Hebrew Christian*, Vol. 14, No. 2 (Fall 1959), 3.
68. *Ibid.*

7

Sect, Denomination, Or Mission

The question remains, What is Hebrew Christianity? The burden of the data available on the Messengers of the New Covenant and on the movement generally seems to suggest a typical sectarian developmental process. We see a membership living on a cultural periphery, having one foot in the Christian community and one in the Jewish community, but finding no solid resting place in either. In economic terms, we find a group decidedly less well off than their generational peers who remained within the Jewish community.[1] We see the prevalent sectarian reliance on self-centered religion based on personal experience taking precedence over the affirmation of an existing doctrinal structure. There is, in addition, the presence of a moral community in which strict standards of personal behavior are required and adhered to. Any individual who deviates from the ethical standards of the group is not merely frowned on as he would be in most churches, but he loses his right to participation and membership.

In terms of participation we see a voluntary group with a confessional basis, the only prerequisite for affiliation being a predisposition to believe and to act on this shared belief.[2] There is, in addition, great fervor and dedication manifest by the membership involving a full commitment to the group and to its goals. Finally, there is emphasis on conversion and on the evangelization of those who lie without the confines of the group.

But although the Messengers and the Hebrew Christian movement bear some of the signal marks of a sectarian group, other factors are less characteristic of a sect, than of a church or denomination. The members of the group have not withdrawn from the prevailing secular culture but operate within it—now more adequately, now less. The political bases of the society—representative government, the two-party system, and so on—may not elicit much concern or individual involvement but are nonetheless fully accepted by the group members. (Apropos of this, one group member answered that he probably felt more at home among Jews than among Gentiles, "because I get along with them better politically.") The broad American economic order is congenial if not overly beneficent to the individual members, and everyone readily accepts the status quo in this area. The meetings of the group and its worship service occur at regular intervals and do not interfere with other aspects of the individual's life. There is no doubt that the religious sphere pervades the believer's entire existence, and constitutes his most important concern, laying claim to the greater part of his energies, but allowing other concerns and predilections free expression.

Unlike the sectarian typology, wherein the leaders are often unspecialized and part-time workers, the leaders of the Messengers and more generally of the Hebrew Christian movement have professional qualifications for their full time task. The three professional workers of the Messengers are ordained Baptist ministers, two holding their ordination from the thoroughly fundamentalistic Moody Bible Institute.

Thus the Messengers and the Hebrew Christian phenomenon as a whole appear as a confluence of elements, some typically sectarian, others more relevant to a church structure. In both cases, that is in the Messengers and the movement, there are heated denials of being either one or the other, but

instead the repeated assertion that they are merely organizations of Jewish believers in Jesus Christ who have joined
together for purposes of Christian fellowship and in order to
provide a better witness to their unconverted brethren. Most
members of the Hebrew Christian Alliance and of the Messengers do belong to (or worship at) churches of the various
denominations. However, in the maintenance of a possibly
schismatic doctrine to the effect that Jewish Christians represent a specific order of Christians chosen not only for their
affirmation of the faith (the new Israel) but also because of
their blood line (the chosen people), there is ample room for
sectarian growth. With the recent emphasis on the founding
of specifically Hebrew Christian Churches, this tendency is
being enhanced—if not along sectarian lines, then definitely
in terms of denominational factors.[3] There are Baptist Christians and Presbyterian Christians. Why not, it is asked, Hebrew
Christians who believe essentially the same things as all "Bible-
emphasizing Christians" but are distinguished by a special
blood tie to the faith not shared with fellow believers among
the gentiles. However, although twice-chosenness is emphasized within the movement, it is "soft-pedaled" in dealing with
gentile Christian believers. The reasons for this are not difficult to comprehend, for they involve a response to (1) the basic
ambivalence of the leadership and laity concerning the motives, goals, and beliefs of the movement; and (2) the reaction
of gentile Christians both to the assertion of twice-chosenness
and to the threat of further cleavage within the church due
to an unacceptable particularism .

LEADERSHIP AND LAITY

At present there is no doubt that Hebrew Christianity, notwithstanding the existence of certain unmistakable sectarian
features, as well as the presence of a denominational "pull",

is as yet neither one nor the other but represents instead a unique missionary movement. For example, although some of the Messengers are unaffiliated, most belong to the Baptist denomination and attend a local church where they are welcome but are at the same time viewed as a bloc or subgroup. Being set apart is one of the core elements responsible for the gradual emergence of Hebrew Christianity as a sectarian structure within Protestant denominationalism. There is growing consciousness among the believers that they occupy a unique position, a sullen awareness of being "neither fish nor fowl," and a corresponding desire to express and declare themselves openly to the world. While within the confines of the movement they accept (and indeed revel in) the idea of the twice-chosenness of Israel—an idea that would stabilize their marginal group status between the gentile community and the unbelieving Jewish community—and while the continued existence of Hebrew Christian groups provides the required legitimating matrix, their continued existence as a distinct group is not an undifferentiated goal of all. Here, as in so many other aspects of the movement's genesis and development, there is considerable ambivalence. On the one hand, believers desire to assert their rightful claim to Christ and Christianity as *Jews,* and on the other they wish to become integrated (assimilated) within Christendom. But loyalty (in the case of the Messengers) to the mission and continuing need for the support and sustenance provided by and through the "community of believers" have combined to set them apart. The mission's (and the movement's) unique claim resides in its continuing to function as a repository for Jewish souls—a reborn Jerusalem Church toward which the prospective convert can look for familiarity as well as legitimation.

The leadership views the emerging Hebrew Christian Church as the wave of the future of Jewish evangelization and is understandably reluctant to let the opportunity slip by. The following exchange occurred during a leadership panel discussion at a National Convention of the Hebrew Christian Alliance which I attended as an observer.

QUESTION. Is the day of the Jewish missions approach at a dead end?

ANSWER.   I would not say that Jewish missions have reached a dead end—but certain old methods have to be changed.

QUESTION. Do you advocate a Hebrew Christian Church approach?

ANSWER.   Most decidedly.

ANSWER.   We have a Hebrew Christian Church in Philadelphia and we believe this is a natural approach to the Jews. They don't resent it like they did the missions.

ANSWER.   It is not only fellowship but a bearing of witness to the community. It is an orientation type of thing where the new Christian begins to relate to the new faith.

ANSWER.   The Hebrew Christian Church lends dignity where the mission did not. We should use all methods and all tools that prove expedient in presenting the claims of Christ to the Jews.[4]

There was no mention of any theological distinction that would mark the church, and no reason was advanced for its existence other than to provide a more reliable missionary context and to act as an "orientation" vehicle for new converts. In subsequent conversations with members of this panel and with the two or three national leaders who are most active in the formulation of a Hebrew Christian "theology," I learned that both leadership *and* laity are quite ambivalent about the implied "ideology" of the movement but have found it expedient (the laity for legitimation and personal sustenance, the leadership for wider missionary goals) to further the growth

and development of the discrete Christian phenomenon known
as Hebrew Christianity. But at the same time, there is ever
awareness of concerted opposition to this development on the
part of a sizable segment of the Protestant Church and a
resulting confusion as to what direction and form Hebrew
Christianity may assume in the future.

THE ATTITUDE OF ESTABLISHED DENOMINATIONS
TO HEBREW CHRISTIANITY

Before considering the attitudes of diverse Protestant groups
to the establishment of a Hebrew Christian Church, let us
discuss the different attitudes held with regard to the evangelization of the Jews.

All available evidence seems to indicate that the various
strata of American Protestantism—from the fundamentalist
to the liberal—still regard the proselytizing of the Jew as a
pertinent aspect of their Christian commitment. Nevertheless,
there are significant and far-reaching divergences within the
American "church" with respect to aims, methods, and the
amount of enthusiasm brought to the task. It would involve
gross oversimplification leading to distortion were we to see
in the emergence of a wide base of opposition to Niebuhr's
position (that proselytizing of the Jew should cease) a solid
phalanx of Protestant affirmation for the evangelization of the
Jew knowing of no gradation or nuance. Indeed, the plaint of
those most actively committed to a Christian approach to the
Jew refer to repeated failure to fire the imaginations of the
nominalists (i.e., liberals) to uncompromising acceptance of
Paul's charge, "to the Jew first." Although the liberal clergy
responded to Niebuhr's challenge with a "nay," it was more
a refusal to reject Paul's (and Christ's) directive than a positive acceptance of it.

As one leading Protestant clergyman put it, "I can't put

the Jew in the same boat with the Pygmies or the South Sea Islanders. Yes, I have a responsibility to tell the Jew about Christ, but I dare not assume that he is less endowed than I ethically, spiritually, or in any other way." Another minister who is directly involved in the formulation of a liberal Christian approach to the Jew was so sensitive to the problem of confronting the Jew with Christian truth and yet offering no offense or pretension to superiority that he advocated a "non-approach" to the Jew. How, after all, can one be totally committed to the equal worth of Jew and Christian and at the same time overtly or covertly demand that the Jew stop being a Jew? How is it possible to approach an individual and tell him that he is wrong, has always been in error, and will continue to err unless he accepts one's proposal for the cure, and yet assume that both parties are equal and that mutual respect exists between them? I believe that Eckardt's interpretation of the liberal position is essentially correct:

> Liberal thinking sees implicit anti-Semitism in the view that Christianity is superior to Judaism. Liberalism believes it finds effective opposition to *Judenhass* in the practice of love of God and neighbor. It would appear psychologically certain that the arrogance resulting from the conviction that we possess the truth while the Jews do not should contribute to the manifestation of anti-Semitic tendencies.[5]

Many a liberal Protestant thinker, with his sophisticated appreciation of the religious and sociological uniqueness of the Jew, accepts or certainly realizes that, in effect belief in Christ involves an immutable break with the Jewish community and a "declassing" of the Jew for which the liberal would prefer not to be responsible.

The fundamentalist Protestant confronts an entirely different set of problems. He is not concerned with whether he should approach the Jew with Christian truth; he wants to know how he can best reach the Jew for Christ. To him, either the Jew has Christ or he does not. In the first case he is a Christian, and in the other a sinner in the same need as any other. The fundamentalist is not concerned that he approach the Jew as an equal, for in view of his continued rejection of the Savior he is patently not an equal. The fundamentalist is decidedly not an ambivalent product of secular humanism: he believes in the Gospel and holds that one is either for men or for God; and if one is for God, one must preach His message to all.

Thus, for the liberal, attitudes maintained towards a phenomenon such as Hebrew Christianity will prove largely academic in nature, and especially so in view of the present enrapturement with the idea of ecumenism. But the fundamentalist churchman takes the movement seriously enough, although generally speaking he is thoroughly confused as to how to treat it. Even though support for the idea of Hebrew Christianity has come almost exclusively from fundamentalist circles, there always seems to have been a certain fear about having created a Frankenstein monster that would one day devour its fabricator. Even as early as the nineteenth century, before the birth of a Hebrew Christian movement, the churches expressed concern over the possibility of further fragmentation within Christendom. Eichhorn, in talking about Church opposition to a mission house hospice for Jews, states that the churches (in 1846) "thought that the American Society for the Melioration of the Condition of the Jews (ASMCJ) was trying to establish a new Protestant denomination, a distinct Hebrew Christian Church . . . and refused to support the ASMCJ because they believed that it was adding to Protestant confusion and disharmony."[6] The leadership of the movement, since its very inception, has felt obliged to steer a careful course in an attempt to avoid the opposition that has arisen in spite of all efforts to head it off. The question, What is so special about Jewish believers? has been raised again and again by churchmen who see in a separate Hebrew Christian Church either a threat to the purity of the believer's faith

or a challenge to some fancied unity within world Protestantism. Robert Smith, for example, states:

> If we ask why . . . no Hebrew Christian Church has ever grown
> up, is not the answer this: that when the light of Christ comes
> to a Jew the logical development of his faith leads not to a new
> national Church, but direct to the World Church which is the
> fulfillment of Israel.[7]

Others, who recognize that no "world church" exists expect
or demand that Hebrew Christians seek to establish one.
Kraemer feels that the Hebrew Christian ideal of a community
is a dying concept and essentially wrong in terms of the Christian idea. He has observed:

> The Christianization of Europe meant the building up of the
> *Corpus Christianum* in which state, Church and community
> became identified. The dissolution of this *Corpus Christianum*
> and the chastening lessons which the Christians of the modern
> age have learnt thereby have made this a deflated ideal.[8]

Still others have insisted that separation will prove to be
"bad" for the Jewish believer because if his claim to distinctiveness is recognized, he will be "pampered" and possibly
lost.[9] If the Jewish believer is not lost by attrition, he may
absorb and swallow up Christianity in his own powerful particularism, for

> unless the Jew makes a complete break with his tradition, par-
> ticularist tendencies are apt to reassert themselves. He remains a
> Jew, and Jewish associations obscure his interpretation of the
> new faith. That was why St. Paul had to warn the Galatians
> against Judaizing tendencies. Jewish consciousness is so strong
> that it can only be transcended in the communion of the uni-
> versal Church.[10]

Widespread doubts such as those just voiced have led to
despair among some concerned Hebrew Christians,[11] and

others have become willing to soft-pedal the idea of a separate church.

Some opponents of the church idea are motivated by fears less tangible than those already adduced. They are not overly concerned with the deterioration of faith if left in unintegrated Jewish hands, nor do they fear being swept up in a new Jewish-based and Jewish-oriented Jerusalem Church. What appears to disturb these opponents is the apparent usurpation of a special Christian role by Jews, who envision for themselves a mission already appropriated by that shadowy entity, the universal Church. And indeed, in the assertion that the Jews will in the end prove to be the instrument of God for the conversion of the world, we can see a striving going beyond legitimation.

> Three thousand converted Jews formed the first Christian Church. Sons of Israel were the first Christian martyrs. Sons of Israel were the first missionaries, who filled with the Holy Ghost went forth into the world with the glorious message, and Sons of Israel first brought the Gospel to Europe and were founders of the first Christian Churches. What God has done in the days of the New Testament to Israel and through Israel, He can and will do again in our day. If we place our lives at the disposal of Jesus with deep humility, childlike belief and complete surrender, He will give us the power of the Holy Spirit to enable us to be His servants and standard-bearers for the conversion of the Jews and the salvation of the World.[12]

Although missionary theorists like Geoffrey Allen maintain that "the function of the mission is to found and build the Church,"[13] this seems to be intended only for those not involved in the Jewish–Christian dialectic. The purpose and destiny of the "Church" is seen as the absorption of the Jews, not the sponsorship of their autonomous development as special Christians.

Some church groups, such as the Episcopal Church, have recorded their opposition to the establishment of a Hebrew

Christian Church.[14] Usually, however, it is the individual clergyman who is opposed. In a questionnaire I sent to 100 Protestant clergymen in the general area covered by the outreach of the Messengers, only one of 59 respondents thought that the idea of a Hebrew Christian Church was a good one, while two thought they might give it qualified approval. The answer that was repeatedly given to the question "Do you think the establishment of a Hebrew Christian Church (that is, a church composed of Jewish converts to Christianity) is the best means of caring for the spiritual growth of Jewish converts?" was "We are all one in Christ Jesus," or a variation of this phrase. (This "negative" response was given by 39 out of the 43 who responded to this question.) In interviews with the Reverend Alexander Shaw, secretary of the New Jersey Council of Churches, and with various officials of the National Council of Churches, there was no approval at all expressed for a Hebrew Christian Church or, for that matter, for Hebrew Christianity. The ministers responding to the questionnaire, as well as those interviewed, overwhelmingly approved of integration, and if a mission approach was advocated, the parish approach seemed to be most favored and the Hebrew Christian approach least favored.

In sum, I think the evidence supports the contention that the idea of a Hebrew Christian Church, if not of Hebrew Christianity itself, has found little support within American Protestantism, either in the liberal camp (which could be expected) or in the fundamentalist branches of the Church.

THE REACTION OF JEWISH COMMUNITY LEADERSHIP

The reaction to the phenomenon of Hebrew Christianity of Jewish community leadership, lay as well as religious, holds no surprises for the interested observer and can be summarized very briefly. Few of the Jewish leaders spoken to in the area of Newark, N.J., where the Messengers are located, had ever heard of the group or of Hebrew Christianity. They expressed interest in this group and wanted to be told more about it; but invariably, the responses contained the same two elements: (1) "They are mad—how can they be Jews and Christians at the same time?" and (2) "It's all the same old missionaries." No one expressed any concern or voiced fears that Hebrew Christianity would increase the rate of "apostasy" or conversion from Judaism.

With the recent appearance of the Jews for Jesus phenomenon, this attitude has changed, and concern tinged with not a little hysteria has replaced indifference.

NOTES

1. Liston Pope, *Millhands and Preachers* (New Haven, Conn.: Yale University Press, 1942), pp. 122–124. This is not the case with the young Jews for Jesus studied in Jerusalem, who are representative in class term of American Jewry on a broader spectrum.

2. See H. H. Gerth and C. Wright Mills, *From Max Weber: Essays in Sociology,* (New York: Oxford University Press, 1946) pp. 304–306.

3. There are now six Hebrew Christian Churches on the North American continent. They are in Chicago, Philadelphia, Los Angeles, Miami, New York, and Toronto. In addition, there are Alliance branches in Newark, Detroit, St. Louis, and Tampa, and nuclear groups in most of the larger cities in the country.

4. Hebrew Christian Alliance National Convention, Cincinnati, Ohio, June 1961. Panel participants: Rev. Daniel Finestone (moderator), Rev. Arthur Glass, Dr. Victor Bukbazen, and Dr. Robinson.

5. Arthur Roy Eckardt, *Christianity and the Children of Israel* (New York: King's Crown Press, 1948), p. 117.

6. David M. Eichhorn, "A History of Christian Attempts to Convert the Jews of the United States and Canada," Ph.D. dissertation, Hebrew Union College, 1938, p. 20.

7. Robert Smith, "The New Dimension in Evangelism," *International Review of Missions*, Vol. 33 (July 1944), 310.

8. Hendrik Kraemer, *The Christian Message in a Non-Christian World* (New York: Harper & Row, 1938), p. 58.

9. Julius Richter, "The Gospel for the Modern Jew from the Standpoint of the German Churches and Missions," *The Church and the Jewish Question* (Geneva: World Council of Churches, 1944), p. 70.

A quite opposite viewpoint is maintained by Hebrew Christian Fred Kendal: "Our greatest problem is in bringing up our Jewish babes in Christ. They are often on the door-step of a Church that is not adapted for their development as the incubator is for the chicks. Some Churches freeze them and others roast them. Some greet them with suspicion and others smother them with attention. There is a natural Jewish pride which will flourish if too much is made of the new convert." "Hebrew Christian Temptation," *Hebrew Christian Alliance Quarterly*, Vol. 38, No. 1 (Spring 1952), 9.

10. Hans Kosmala and Robert Smith, *The Jew in the Christian World* (London: Student Christian Movement Press, 1942), p. 169.

11. "Yet we know that even now with all the liberality of faith that has come with more enlightened days, the Jewish Christian who wishes to retain his national and ancestral practices, while utterly loyal to his Saviour, is looked upon askance and the genuineness of his Christian convictions is doubted." Hugh J. Schonfield, *The History of Jewish Christianity: From the First to the Twentieth Century* (London: Duckworth, 1936), p. 83.

12. No author or title given, *American Hebrew Christian*, Vol. 36, No. 4 (Winter 1951), 20.

13. Geoffrey Allen, *The Theology of Missions,* (London: Student Christian Movement Press Ltd., 1943), p. 14.

14. Eichhorn, *op. cit.*, p. 375.

8

Conclusion

HEBREW CHRISTIANITY AND THE
SECOND GENERATION

No one can accurately predict the future course of Hebrew Christianity. Nevertheless, it now appears that there is scant likelihood of its long-term survival in any form other than as a fringe phenomenon. It has not sparked significant response within the varied Jewish communities to which it appeals, while failing even to elicit "real" support from its only logical base in Protestant fundamentalism.

But the roots of its ultimate failure go even deeper, lying less in external failure or lack of unstinting Protestant support than in a notable and inevitably fatal inability to achieve generational continuity. Hebrew Christianity is confronted by the very difficulty it claims to have offset and obviated within the missionary enterprise—namely, it has not been able to create a self-perpetuating witness to the Jews based on the ready and continuous visibility of a body of converted Jews. Hebrew Christianity, in mistakenly enshrining the assertion that the threat of sociological suicide is the primary obstacle to large-scale conversion among the Jews, has failed to take note of the evidence available in their very midst to the contrary—the children of Hebrew Christians inevitably opt for the Christian rather than the Hebrew element of their parents' faith. Even when the Hebrew or "Jewish" element is presented to the children as an important gift that they not only need not give up in affirming their Christian belief, but that lends an added aura to their faith, it has failed (at least thus far) to strike any roots. And it could not be otherwise, in view of the essentially missionary nature of the movement and the negative attitudes toward Jews and Judaism maintained by almost all Hebrew Christians. One cannot expect that a child will be willing or able to affirm as an item of his personal identity what is blatantly a missionary ploy—interpreting himself as a Hebrew Christian when it is obvious that he is a Protestant. No matter how far Hebrew Christianity might want to go in legitimating the act of conversion to Christianity through the inclusion of Jewish feasts, festivals, or even liturgy, it cannot provide a meaningful link to a past never experienced by the individual born into this anomalous position. The Hebrew Christian child has no need to legitimate his Christian faith—it is his heritage and as much a part of the reality that surrounds any other Baptist or Methodist or other Christian in similar socioeconomic circumstances. This is not to say that the "Hebrew" of Hebrew Christian passes him by having no effect and leaving no residue. The very fact that he is told he is a Hebrew Christian, even if no other reinforcing factors or patterns existed, would be sufficient to establish a distinctive element in his makeup. But it is a far cry from *consciousness* of difference to integration of its diffuse elements into a meaningful whole. The efforts that have been made to do just this (i.e., to meaningfully integrate the Jewish past of the parents into the lives of the children) reflect the same transparency and lack of commitment that marked most of the Judaizing trends that have occurred in the movement. A certain sadness pervades the efforts of Hebrew Christian leadership to foster a tradition that logically and pragmatically has no basis—a sadness that is moving because of its futility and because a need has been created that cannot be satisfactorily answered. What is to be the tradition, the past and the future of the Hebrew Christian child? In what direction will he be permitted to seek fully and without artificial constraint? If any laws of "sociological gravity' were in force, the direction sought surely would be that of the church. But given the ideological motives with which Hebrew Christianity has charged itself, the attempt is made to impose a sometimes strange syncretism and a marginal status on children who will probably reject this role when the decision is theirs to make. The plaint that the Hebrew Christian child is ambivalent about his tradition is specious. His tradition is what his parents had chosen it to be—Protestant Christianity.[1] There is little doubt that the attempts at turning the Jewish holy days to Christian meanings will ultimately appear as what they are —curiosities with no basis other than that available to any believing Christian, whether of Jewish origin or not.[2] Since pains are taken to assure the believer of the religious meaninglessness of these traditions, they are sure to be short-lived. For when it can be asserted that "In our attitude to all these things—the holydays, the music, there is the blessed freedom with which Christ has made us free,"[3] there is an implied rejection of commitment and an assumption of sterile voluntarism having no intrinsic relationship to faith and practice. The Hebrew Christian child who fails to develop a "missionary burden" for the Jewish people will also fail in remaining a Hebrew Christian. A missionary enterprise is not a faith, and when the community of experience that bound their parents together is absent (as it must be), the loyalties of the young tend to move toward inclusion in one of the Protestant denominations. This tendency has been duly noted and recognized by leadership, who have tried to formulate a Hebrew Christian youth movement, which, however, was stillborn.[4]

Thus in the most basic desideratum for survival—the ability to hold its youth and to instill in them a sense that the aims of the movement are meaningful—Hebrew Christianity has fallen far short of the mark.

But another difficulty alluded to earlier assumes almost equal weight as an ultimate cause for failure. This is the inability of Hebrew Christianity to clarify for itself its reason for being and to lay out a course of action expressing a commonly affirmed ethos. Is Hebrew Christianity to be a movement seeking a return to the Jewish roots of Christianity, which would of necessity involve its proponents in a split with normative Protestant Christianity, giving rise to increased cleavage within the Church? Or is Hebrew Christianity to be a missionary endeavor? Ideally the movement has opted for both, indicating that the former will ensure the success of the latter; but it has found that the proposed marriage of goals is too often noncomplementary and difficult of achievement. For example, a return to the pregentile roots of Christianity would mean a certain break with gentile Christendom—and this step would have been possible only for a Rabinowitz or a Lucky, not for the vast majority of Hebrew Christians who must experience for themselves a sense of belonging within the empirical church. It would, furthermore, involve the Hebrew Christian in the *Klal Yisroel*, the people of Israel, believer and non-believer alike, and he would become a defender of Israel and of its autonomy, thus precluding a missionary role in the accepted sense. This too, Hebrew Christianity has not been able to do, and this failure to fully identify with the *Klal Yisroel* is best exemplified in the revulsion with which the movement viewed the seemingly beneficial goodwill movement of the 1930s and 1940s in the United States and Great Britain.

THE GOODWILL MOVEMENT AND HEBREW CHRISTIANITY

In the history of Hebrew Christianity no single issue has aroused the almost pathologically negative response that was elicited by the goodwill movements arising in the decade of the 1930s and culminating in the creation of the National Conference of Christians and Jews. One might have suspected that a movement whose very genesis and existence was largely due to the recognition that evangelistic failures of the past were partly attributable to anti-Semitism would have welcomed displays of goodwill from the Christian community. This, however, was not the case.

> Under the guise of an attempt to establish religious liberty, the whole Good Will movement is nothing less than a conspiracy of Reform Judaism and Modernistic [sic] Christianity to destroy the liberty which is at present our cherished heritage.[5]

The writer next accused the goodwill movement of being under a cloud of "injustice, bigotry, hate and fraud."[6] Another Hebrew Christian author went a step further, seeing in goodwill the very hand of Satan:

> Satan, seeing that the old hatred game could no longer be used in Protestantism because of its tolerance and good will to the Jew, bethought to himself and decided to get on the bandwagon of Tolerance and Goodwill. And Satan now is using this argument in Protestant Churches ad infinitum.[7]

Zeidman envisioned only four ways in which Satan could keep the Jews from receiving the Gospels, with the depredations of Rome in first place and "Tolerance and Goodwill" right behind in second. After listing such "untoward" acts as the exchange of pulpits between rabbis and ministers, the sale of a church building for use as a synagogue, union meetings of Jewish and Christian youth, the carrying out of Reform Jewish services in a church loaned for this purpose, the editor of the *Quarterly* crisply notes: "To some, these departures may mean progress, but to us they are signs of compromise, retrogression, denial and retreat."[8]

Why did the Hebrew Christian Alliance react so negatively to a seemingly harmless attempt to improve the lot of their Jewish brethren? The answer is of course that the Alliance (no doubt correctly) recognized that "normalizing" the position of the Jew in American life could do them no good. The very next line after that just quoted plaintively suggests that "In the midst of all this there are abundant signs in America and in other parts of the world that Judaism is crumbling to pieces."[9] The implication is that too many so-called Christians are rocking the evangelistic boat in making it easy for the Jews. In making it "easy" for the Jews, it becomes tougher for the missionary bearers of the Gospel. If the Jews could see the possibility of living a "Christian life" (an ethically oriented, God-fearing life) among gentile Christians and in fellowship with them, but without having to accept the Cross, they would indeed prove impossible to win.[10]

I think that there were two elements in this opposition to the good will movement, with the one adduced previously taking precedence over the other. The second element was, I think, the believers' healthy refusal to allow their Christian faith to be watered down and impinged on for any reason whatever, including the prospect of eliminating anti-Semitism. Reacting to an article by Horace Kallen,[11] suggesting certain revisions in the New Testament, the *Quarterly* editor states:

Having succeeded thus far in persuading modernist Christian leaders to compromise Christianity as the price of good-will Jewish leaders are now making a further demand. They now insist that the New Testament itself must be revised and portions of it deleted and discarded in order to eradicate anti-Semitism.[12]

The editor concludes that this is the price of good will demanded by Jewish leaders and their liberal Christian bedfellows, appealing to Christians not to allow themselves to be hoodwinked by "these enemies of the Cross."[13]

But whether for one reason or the other, this reaction to the good will movement is important because the Alliance and Hebrew Christianity were forced to make a choice (or did so without being forced) on *the* issue confronting Jews as a group —anti-Semitism—and the choice made irrevocably placed the movement *without*, while shouting into the wind that they are *within* the Jewish fold. I believe that the die was cast on this very issue of the good will movement, although Hebrew Christians still do not recognize its significance. When it can be said that "Whenever and wherever Good Willers and Kosher food tasters meet, and they meet quite often, there the subject of the crucifixion pops up,"[14] an attitude is suggested and a loyalty underscored which leaves little room for misinterpretation or confusion.[15]

THE IDIOSYNCRATICALLY DISINHERITED

Thus Hebrew Christian efforts at stabilization, growth, and survival are hamstrung not only by the movement's inability to reproduce itself, but by its lack of a viable and consistent self-image as well.

In addition, there seems to be a fatal flaw in the very membership composition of the movement. Its membership, as I have noted previously, is comprised largely of the disinherited, but of a peculiar variety. In almost any social movement, and certainly in religious ones, there is the presence of those who are denied acceptable status within the dominant order but who otherwise range the entire scale with regard to personality structure, qualities of mind, and general ability to function adequately. The factor that binds them together can by and large be isolated in the sociological rather than the primarily psychological sphere. With the phenomenon of Hebrew Christianity however, one is able to discern the ethos of the disinherited, but of a personally idiosyncratic rather than of a social nature. That is to say, the movement attracts what one might call a "type" characterized by personal upset, serious psychological disorder, and failures of all kinds. More than being bound together by their common Jewish origins, they are bound by a common need for comfort and reassurance directed at *them* as individuals, rather than as bearers of a peculiar weltanschauung. One of the most perceptive, sensitive but significantly fringe ideologues of the movement, Ludwig R. Dewitz says:

> A further difficulty that may, however not be peculiar to Jewish missions, but which is creating a definite problem, lies in the fact that to some extent people with a somewhat unbalanced mental condition often find the atmosphere of a Mission, the very place where they find the care and affection which they would find nowhere else. It is of course a privilege to serve those who are in special need, but at the same time, newcomers to the meetings may easily get the impression that the Christian message is only for people who differ from what is generally regarded as normal.[16]

Dewitz is referring to missions rather than to specifically Hebrew Christian bodies, but his comments are entirely applicable. As Dewitz notes, such a constellation of factors can do the overall effort no good. The base of Hebrew Christianity is, at least at the present time, limited in the extreme to individuals who can best be characterized as the victims of extreme emotional buffeting, thus little suited to the task of strengthening this or any other movement.

In what would appear to be a direct assault on this notable stumbling block, the movement has, at least since the 1970s, begun a series of campaigns aimed at overcoming this negative image. From time to time over the last four years Hebrew Christian groups have sought through advertisements in the general press, television programs, and a revamped tract program to change their image from that of a fringe phenomenon appealing to fringe types to that of a dynamic, progressive, and youthful movement with wholly legitimate claims to being Jewish.

In 1971 a television film entitled "The Passover" was produced and an attempt was made to give it widespread coverage in the United States. The program was not shown extensively, however, because of opposition from the organized Jewish community which maintained that it was misleading in its portrayal of a Hebrew Christian family celebrating the Passover Seder. The message of the film was that Hebrew Christianity is Jewish and emphasizes a faithful adherence to biblical precepts.

In 1971 a full-page advertisement appeared in some of the leading newspapers in the United States captioned "So many Jews are wearing that smile nowadays."[17] The ad featured an overhead shot of a group of smiling, happy looking people who looked no different than any other group of prosperous middle-class American Jews. The text was well done (even snappy) and managed to adhere to the traditional Hebrew Christian approach wherein Christian faith was underscored as an addition to Jewishness and not a rejection, for in "acknowledging the Great Jew (Jesus Christ) as the Messiah . . . we are not giving up being Jews, we are in fact adding a beautiful dimension to being Jewish." The thrust of the advertisement and the television program was an attempt to emphasize normalcy both in the religious stance held by Hebrew Christians as well as in those who held to this particular doctrine. Both of these forays into the mass media reflect an evolving recognition on the part of leadership that the movement could not enjoy greater success as long as it remained identified with the deviant and the marginal. The new campaign reflects a sophistication and skill previously absent in the movement, and this together with the verve and enthusiasm of groups of young, vibrant Jews for Jesus could presage a new period of growth. Even with respect to the most traditional of all missionary devices—the tract—the 1970s have witnessed the development of a stronger and more attractive tool. Whereas in the past tracts tended to be heavy-handed and overly insistent, the new publications of the movement emphasize scholarship and quiet persuasion and are written by biblical experts and trained divines. The major emphasis has not changed but the subtlety with which it is posited has developed to a remarkable extent. The Hebrew Christian movement has always asserted Jewish legitimacy for its point of view but, as previously demonstrated here, in a rather heavy-handed manner. In the 1970s the assertion seems to be not so much that Hebrew Christianity is the *only* Jewish way, but that it is rather *another* Jewish way entirely consistent with the "denominationalism" of the contemporary Jewish scene. This is highlighted in the booklet *The Confession of the Hebrew Christian* where the advertising blurb asks: "What is the Jew of today to believe? Orthodoxy demands one thing: Reform Judaism another; Liberal Judaism still another. Does a Jew cease to be a Jew when he believes in Jesus Christ"?[18]

Thus, the 1970s should be viewed as a time of growing sophistication, a farther "outreach," and a new emphasis on youth. But the evidence currently available in both Israel and the United States does not yet warrant an assertion of revolutionary change in either direction or fortunes. The fruits remain slight and the converts as noted throughout this work were and remain marginal people with respect to a wide spectrum of sociological variables.

What then is the prognosis for Hebrew Christianity? As I indicated at the outset, I cannot play the prophet, saying with finality that this or that trend or item will inevitably bring about either the demise or the success of the movement. I think that the evidence adduced here and elsewhere strongly suggests that the movement will not be notably successful, but time alone will tell. It is conceivable (as many Hebrew Christians hope) that a resurgent Hebrew Christianity with more viable and stronger Hebraic roots will grow from the soil of the Jewish state in Israel; such growth will be more realistically indigenous, thus suffering less from the stultifying and enervating ambivalence that marks the phenomenon in the West. It is further conceivable that a more intelligent and farseeing leadership will continue to emerge to give Hebrew Christianity the vision and determination that it sorely lacks, replacing present and past flaccidity with solid muscle fiber. It is possible that the movement will break loose from the straitjacket placed on it by the overwhelming bleakness that makes its people a festival-less and dour community whose satisfactions cannot be communicated. Only the comfort they draw from one another can be shared:

> To be in possession of an absolute truth is to have a net of familiarity spread over the whole of eternity. There are no surprises and no unknowns. All questions have already been answered, all decisions made, all eventualities foreseen. The true believer is without wonder and hesitation.[19]

NOTES

1. The following quotation contains an example of the raising of this specious question. In my experience with Hebrew Christians, covering a two-year period, I never met or heard of a Hebrew Christian child who thought of himself as anything but a Christian. "Woven into the background of our lives, runs the strong thread of tradition —how strong we are often slow to realize. Because we are Christian Hebrews, are our children then to have only broken threads? Pitiful indeed is the child without some bright gleam out of the past in his life fabric; and just as pitiful is the child who being denied traditions of his own, stretches out his little hands to the traditions of others!" Annie A. Zeidman, "How Can Hebrew Christian Children Remain Hebrew and Christian?" *Hebrew Christian Alliance Quarterly*, Vol. 23, No. 2 (Summer 1938), 20.

2. "Our Seder service is really beautiful, with its blending of the fore-shadowing and the fulfillment. The table is set in the traditional

manner except for the shankbone, for Christ our Passover is slain for us. I make the Charoises [a paste symbolizing the clay from which the bricks in Egypt were made] and the Knodelich [Passover dumplings] myself, and my little girl helps me. The Scripture passages read are from the Haggadah [the Passover order of service] and the New Testament. From 40 to 50 Hebrew Christians and their children— even babies—sit down together at the table, and commemorate our deliverance from the bondage of Egypt and our greater deliverance, through the dying of the Lord Jesus, from the bondage of sin and death." A. Zeidman, *op. cit.*, 22.

3. *Ibid.*, p. 23.

4. The youth movement was formed in July 1955. "To the original objectives of reaching Jewish young people for Christ and encouraging fellowship of Hebrew Christian Youth, were added, (1) advancing the spiritual development and general welfare of Hebrew Christian young people, and (2) bringing about better understanding of the Jews by Christians, and of the Christian message by Jews." Richard G. Katz, *Hebrew Christian Alliance Quarterly*, Vol. 44, No. 1 (Summer 1958), 16.

5. Elias Newman, "The Hebrew Christian Alliance Program and the Crises of Today," *Hebrew Christian Alliance Quarterly*, Vol. 17, No. 4 (October and December 1932), 33.

6. *Ibid.*, p. 34.

7. Morris Zeidman, "Satan's Great Fear," *Hebrew Christian Alliance Quarterly*, Vol. 27, No. 2 (Summer 1942), p. 13.

8. Elias Newman, "Missionary Events," *Hebrew Christian Alliance Quarterly*, Vol. 16, No. 3 (July and September 1931), 24.

9. *Ibid.*, 24.

10. And indeed one must sympathize with this point of view (that ethics do not the Christian make) given the lengths to which it has been taken. I find the following response of the Alliance leadership refreshing: "Since when, or where in the Word of God can we find proof that a man can be Christian without actually believing in Christ? It is such silly claptrap that keeps Jews away from Christ." "Notes by the Honorable General Secretary," *Hebrew Christian Alliance Quarterly*, Vol. 22, No. 4 (Winter 1938), 15.

11. *Opinion*, May 16, 1932.

12. "Notes and Comments," *Hebrew Christian Alliance Quarterly*, Vol. 17, No. 3 (July and September 1932), 7.

13. *Ibid.*, 8.

14. Editor, "Across the Desk," *Hebrew Christian Alliance Quarterly*, Vol. 30, No. 3 (Fall 1947), 19.

15. Alliance reaction against goodwill was not solely their own but was

part of a larger "reaction." Kosmala and Smith, for example, put forth an interesting theory against the good will movement. They claim that it represented an attempt at a universal faith of Noachism, for which liberal Judaism is pushing. The good will movement is, they claim, Israel's missionary approach to the world. (Hans Kosmala and Robert Smith, *The Jew in the Christian World*, (London: Student Christian Movement Press, 1942), pp. 101–104.)

Dewick notes a reaction against good will that is consistent with the Hebrew Christian attitude. "Of late, a reaction against interreligious cooperation is evident in many quarters. If we compare the resolutions of the Jerusalem Conference of 1928 with those of the Tambaram Conference of 1938 we shall observe that . . . Tambaram considered that the greatest danger comes from the revival of the non-Christian religions, and insisted that it is the duty of the Christian missionary to 'call men out from these'—a policy which can hardly be reconciled with real cooperation." E. D. Dewick, *The Christian Attitude to Other Religions*, (Cambridge: Cambridge University Press, 1953), p. 56.

16. "Problems of Jewish Evangelization," *Hebrew Christian Alliance Quarterly*, Vol. 37, Nos. 2 and 3 (Fall 1951), 28.

17. Published in the *New York Times*, December 10, 1971.

18. *The Confession of the Hebrew Christian* (J19), n.d., American Board of Missions to the Jews.

19. Eric Hoffer, *The True Believer* (New York: Harper & Row, 1951), p. 80.

Bibliography

BOOKS

Ackerman, Nathan W. and Marie Jahoda. *Anti-Semitism and Emotional Disorder: A Psychoanalytic Interpretation.* New York: Harper & Row, 1950.

Adams, Richard N. and Jack J. Preiss. *Human Organization Research: Field Relations and Techniques.* ·Homewood, Ill.: The Dorsey Press, Inc., 1960.

Allen, Geoffrey. *The Theology of Missions.* London: Student Christian Movement Press Ltd., 1943.

Baeck, Leo. *Judaism and Christianity.* New York: Harper & Row, 1956.

Baker, Archibald G. *Christian Missions and a New World Culture.* Chicago: Willet, Clark and Co., 1934.

Baron, Salo Wittmayer. *Modern Nationalism and Religion.* New York: Meridian Books, 1960.

———. *A Social and Religious History of the Jews.* 3 vols. New York: Meridian Books, 1960.

Barton, James L. *The Missionary and His Critics.* London: Fleming H. Revell Co., 1906.

Benedict, George. *Christ Finds a Rabbi: An Autobiography.* Philadelphia: privately printed, 1932.

Bernstein, Peretz. *Jew-Hate as a Sociological Problem.* New York: Philosophical Library, 1951.

Blalock, Hubert M., Jr. *An Introduction to Social Research.* Englewood Cliffs, N.J.: Prentice-Hall, Inc., 1970.

Bless, H. Arthur with Walter Wagner. *Turned on to Jesus.* New York: Hawthorn Books, Inc., 1971.

Bonar, Andrew Alexander. *Narrative of a Mission of Inquiry to the Jews from the Church of Scotland in 1839.* Edinburgh: W. Whyte & Co., 1848.

Braden, William. *The Age of Aquarius.* New York: Pocket Books, 1971.

Bronstein, David, Jr. *Peniel Portrait.* Chicago: D. Cameron Peck, 1943.

Bruyn, Severyn T. *The Human Perspective in Sociology: The Methodology of Participant Observation.* Englewood Cliffs, N.J.: Prentice-Hall, Inc., 1966.

Buber, Martin. *Israel and the World.* New York: Schocken Books, 1948.

Clarke, William Newton. *A Study of Christian Missions.* New York: Charles Scribner's Sons, 1910.

Cohen, Arthur. *The Myth of the Judeo-Christian Tradition.* New York: Harper & Row, 1970.

Cohn, Joseph Hoffman. *Beginning at Jerusalem.* New York: American Board of Missions to the Jews, 1948.

Clarke, William Newton. *A Study of Christian Missions.* New York: Charles Scribner's Sons, 1910.

Dewick, E. D. *The Christian Attitude to Other Religions.* Cambridge: Cambridge University Press, 1953.

Dubnow, Simon. *Nationalism and History,* S. Pinson, ed. New York: Meridian Books, 1961.

Dunlop, John. *Memories of Gospel Triumphs Among the Jews During the Victorian Era.* London: Partridge, 1894.

Durkheim, Emile. *The Elementary Forms of the Religious Life.* New York: Glencoe Press, 1949.

Eckardt, Arthur Roy. *Christianity and the Children of Israel.* New York: King's Crown Press, 1948.

Eckstein, Stephen D. *From Sinai to Calvary: An Autobiography.* Kansas City, Mo.: Stephen D. Eckstein, 1959.

Einspruch, Henry, ed. *When Jews Face Christ.* Baltimore, Md.: The Mediator, 1932.

Enslin, Morton Scott. *Christian Beginnings.* New York: Harper & Row, 1956.

Erikson, Erik. *Childhood and Society.* London: Penguin Books, 1970.

———. *Identity, Youth and Crisis.* London: Faber & Faber, 1971.

Festinger, Leon, Henry W. Reicken, and Stanley Schachter. *When Prophecy Fails.* New York: Harper & Row, 1956.

Floreen, Harold. *The Lutheran Parish and the Jews: An Analytical Study.* Chicago: The National Lutheran Council, Division of American Missions, 1948.

———. *The Lutheran Parish and the Jews—A Survey.* The National Lutheran Council, Division of American Missions, 1949.

———, Jakob Jocz, and Otto Piper. *The Church Meets Judaism.* Minneapolis, Minn.: Augsburg Publishing House, 1960.

Frank, Arnold. *What About the Jews?* Belfast: Graham and Heslip Ltd., 1944.

Friedenberg, Edgar. *Coming of Age in America*. New York: Vintage Books, 1967.

Fuchs, Daniel. *How to Reach the Jew for Christ*. Jewish Mission Correspondence Course: A Manual of Study for Christians Who Love the Jews. Grand Rapids, Mich.: Zondervan Publishing House, 1943.

Gartenhaus, Jacob. *The Influence of the Jews upon Civilization*. Grand Rapids, Mich.: Zondervan Publishing House, 1943.

————, *What of the Jews?* Atlanta, Ga.: Home Mission Board, Southern Baptist Convention, 1948.

Gerth, H. H. and C. Wright Mills. *From Max Weber: Essays in Sociology*. New York: Oxford University Press, 1946.

Gidney, W. T. *History of the London Society for Promoting Christianity Amongst the Jews, from 1809 to 1908*. London: Society for Promoting Christianity Amongst the Jews, 1908.

————. *Jews and Their Evangelization*. London: Student Volunteer Missionary Union, 1899.

————. *Missions to Jews: A Handbook*. London: London Society for Promoting Christianity Amongst the Jews, 1899.

Gordon, Albert. *The Nature of Conversion*. Boston: Beacon Press, 1967.

Harrison, Paul M. *Authority and Power in the Free Church Tradition: A Social Case Study of the American Baptist Convention*. Princeton, N.J.: Princeton University Press, 1959.

Hebrew Christian, A. *Go Tell My People*. New York: Vantage Press, 1958.

Hedenquist, Gote, ed. *The Church and the Jewish People*. London: Edinburgh House Press, 1954.

————, ed. *The International Jew—and the Ecumenical Church: Addresses Delivered at the Pre-Evanston Conference on the Christian Approach to the Jews at Lake Geneva Wisconsin, August 8–11, 1954*. New York: National Council of the Churches of Christ in the U.S.A., 1954.

————, ed. *Twenty-five Years of the International Missionary Council's Committee on the Christian Approach to the Jews: 1932–1957*. Uppsala: Almqvist & Wiksells, 1957.

Heller, Bernard. *Epistle to an Apostate*. New York: The Bookman's Press, Inc., 1951.

Hoffer, Eric. *The True Believer*. New York: Harper & Row, 1951.

Hoffman, Conrad. *The Jews Today: A Call To Christian Action*. New York: Friendship Press, 1941.

————. *What Now for the Jews? A Challenge to the Christian Conscience*. New York: Friendship Press, 1948.

Holmio, Armas Kustaa Ensio. *The Lutheran Reformation and the Jews: The Birth of the Protestant Jewish Missions*. Hancock, Mich.: Finnish Lutheran Book Concern, 1949.

Hort, Fenton John Anthony. *Judaistic Christianity*. London: Macmillan and Co., 1898.

Jacobs, Glenn, ed. *The Participant Observer*. New York: George Braziller, 1970.

James, William. *The Varieties of Religious Experience*. New York: The Modern Library, 1929.

Jocz, Jakob. *Is it Nothing to You?* 2nd ed. London: Church Mission to the Jews, 1941.

————. *A Theology of Election: Israel and the Church*. London: Society for Promoting Christian Knowledge, 1958.

Jung, Carl Gustav. *Psychology and Religion*. New Haven, Conn.: Yale University Press, 1948.

Junker, Buford. *Fieldwork*. Chicago: University of Chicago Press, 1960.

King, C. Wendell. *Social Movements in the United States*. New York: Random House, 1956.

Klapp, Orin. *Collective Search for Identity*. New York: Holt, Rinehart & Winston, 1969.

Klausner, Joseph. *From Jesus to Paul*. New York: The Macmillan Co., 1943.

Kosmala, Hans and Robert Smith. *The Jew in the Christian World*. London: Student Christian Movement Press, 1942.

Kraemer, Hendrik. *The Christian Message in a Non-Christian World*. New York: Harper & Row, 1938.

Kreider, Roy. *Judaism Meets Christ: Guiding Principles for the Christian Jewish Encounter*. Scottdale, Pa.: Herald Press, 1960.

Lamott, Willis Church. *Revolution in Missions*. New York: The Macmillan Co., 1954.

Latourette, Kenneth Scott. *The Christian World Mission in our Day*. New York: Harper & Row, 1954.

Levinger, Lee Joseph. *Anti-Semitism in the United States*. New York: Bloch, 1925.

Levy, Rosalie, ed. *Why Jews Become Catholics: Authentic Narratives*. New York: the author, 1924.

Levertoff, Paul. *The Order of the Service of the Meal of the Holy King*. Milwaukee, Wis.: Morehouse, 1928.

Liebow, Elliot. *Tally's Corner: A Study of Negro Streetcorner Men*. Boston: Little, Brown and Co., 1967.

Lindberg, Milton B. *Witnessing to Jews: A Handbook of Practical Aids*. Chicago: American Messianic Fellowship, 1954.

Liptzin, Solomon. *Germany's Stepchildren*. New York: Meridian Books, 1961.

Lowenstein, Rudolph M. *Christians and Jews: A Psychoanalytic Study*. New York: International Universities Press, 1952.

Mathews, Basil. *The Jew and the World Ferment*. New York: Friendship Press, 1935.

Mintz, Alan L. and James A. Sleeper. *The New Jews*. New York: Random House, 1971.

Neusner, Jacob. *American Judaism*. Englewood Cliffs, N.J.: Prentice-Hall, Inc., 1972.

Oesterley, William Oscar Emil. *The Jews and Judaism During the Greek Period: The Background of Christianity*. London: Society for Promoting Christian Knowledge, 1941.

Parkes, James William. *The Conflict of the Church and the Synagogue*. London: Soncino Press, 1934.

Parsons, Talcott. *The Social System*. New York: Glencoe Press, 1951.

Pinson, Koppel, ed. *Essays on Anti-Semitism*. 2nd ed. rev. New York: Conference on Jewish Relations, 1946.

Pope, Liston. *Millhands and Preachers*. New Haven, Conn.: Yale University Press, 1942.

Rubenstein, Richard. *My Brother Paul*. New York:. Vintage Books, 1971.

Sabatier, Auguste. *Outlines of a Philosophy of Religion Based on Psychology and History*. New York: Harper Torchbooks, 1957.

Schonfield, Hugh J. *The History of Jewish Christianity: From the First to the Twentieth Century*. London: Duckworth, 1936.

————. *Judaism and World Order*. London: Secker and Wärburg, 1943.

Selltiz, Claire, Marie Jahoda, Morton Deutsch, and Stuart W. Cook. *Research Methods in Social Relations*. Rev. one-volume ed. New York: Holt, Rinehart & Winston, 1961.

Soper, Edmund Davison. *The Philosophy of the Christian World Mission*. New York: Abingdon Press, 1943.

Specter, Ruth R. *The Bud and the Flower of Judaism*. Springfield, Mo.: Gospel Publishing House, 1955.

Speer, Robert E. *Missionary Principles and Practice*. London: Fleming H. Revell Co., 1902.

Stanley, Arthur Penrhyn. *Lectures on the History of the Jewish Church*. New York: Charles Scribner's Sons, 1871.

Streiker, Lowell D. *The Jesus Trip: Advent of the Jesus Freaks*. New York: Abingdon Press, 1971.

Tawney, R. H. *Religion and the Rise of Capitalism*. New York: Mentor Books, 1947.

Thompson, A. *A Century of Jewish Missions*. Chicago: F. H. Revell Co., 1902.

Troeltsch, Ernst. *The Social Teaching of the Christian Churches.* 2 vols. New York: Harper & Row, 1960.

Underwood, Alfred Clair. *Conversion: Christian and Non-Christian.* New York: The Macmillan Co., 1925.

Valentin, Hugo. *Anti-Semitism Historically and Critically Examined.* New York: Viking Press, 1936.

Weber, Max. *Theory of Social and Economic Organization.* ed. and transl. A. M. Henderson and Talcott Parsons. New York: Oxford University Press, 1947.

Weiss, Johannes. *Earliest Christianity: A History of the Period* A.D. *30–150.* 2 vols. New York: Harper & Row, 1959.

Weiss-Rosemarin Trude. *Judaism and Christianity.* New York: Harper & Row, 1965.

West, Ray B., Jr. *Kingdom of the Saints.* New York: Viking Press, 1957.

Williams, A. L. *Missions to the Jews: An Historical Retrospect.* London: Society for Promoting Christian Knowledge, 1897.

Williams, Robin M., Jr. *American Society: A Sociological Interpretation.* 2nd ed. New York: Alfred A. Knopf, 1960.

Williams, T. R. *Field Methods in the Study of Culture.* New York: Holt, Rinehart & Winston, 1967.

World Council of Churches. *The Church and the Jewish Question.* Geneva: The Council, 1944.

Wright, Louis B. *Religion and Empire.* Chapel Hill: The University of North Carolina Press, 1943.

ARTICLES, MONOGRAPHS, AND REPORTS

American Hebrew Christian. See: *Hebrew Christian Alliance Quarterly.*

Baeck, Leo. "Romantic Religion," in *Judaism and Christianity,* transl. Walter Kaufman. Philadelphia: Jewish Publication Society of America, 1958.

Barnes, J. A. "Some Ethical Problems of Modern Fieldwork," *British Journal of Sociology.* Vol. 14 (1963), 118–134.

Baron, Salo W. "Who is a Jew: Some Historical Reflections," *Midstream,* Vol. 6, No. 2 (Spring 1960), 5–16.

Bernard, Jessie. "Biculturality: A Study in Social Schizophrenia," in *Jews in a Gentile World.* Isacque Graeber and Steuart Henderson Britt, New York: The Macmillan Co., 1942.

Bernard, Solomon S. "The 'Jesus Movement,'" *ADL Bulletin,* November 1972.

———. "Key 73—A Jewish View." *The Christian Century,* Vol. 90 (January 3, 1973), pp. 12–14.

Bernards, S. S., Henry Siegman, and Marc H. Tanenbaum. "Christian Evangelism and Jewish Responses: An Exchange," *Congress Bi-Weekly,* Vol. 40, No. 3 (Feb. 9, 1973), 21–27.

Bonsirven, Joseph. "The Missionary Work of the Roman Catholic Church Among the Jews," *International Review of Missions,* Vol. 25 (July 1936), 354–363.

Cohon, Samuel. "The Jew and Christian Evangelization," *International Review of Missions,* Vol. 22 (October 1933), 470–480.

Ehrenber, Hans P. "The Rediscovery of the Jew in Christianity," *Inter-National Review of Missions,* Vol. 33 (October 1944), 400–406.

First Hebrew Christian Conference of the United States, Printed Minutes, Maryland, 1903.

Gaster, Moses. "Judaism—A National Religion," in *Zionism and the Jewish Future,* Howard Sacher, ed. New York: The Macmillan Co., 1916.

Gelwick, Richard. "Will the Jesus Revolution Revive Anti-Semitism?" *The Christian Century,* May 10, 1972.

Gill, C. "The Vienna Conference of the International Committee on the Christian Approach to the Jews, June 28–July 2, 1937," *International Review of Missions,* Vol. 26 (October 1937), 531–536.

Gold, Raymond L. "Roles in Sociological Field Observations," *Social Forces* Vol. 36 (1958), 217–223.

Goldman, Felix. "Converts," *Universal Jewish Encyclopedia,* Vol. 3 (1941), 341.

Grace to Israel. Irregularly published by the Messengers of the New Covenant, Newark, N.J.

Grayzel, Solomon. "Christian-Jewish Relations in the First Millennium," in *Essays on Anti-Semitism,* Koppel S. Pinson, ed. New York: Conference on Jewish Relations, 1946.

Handlin, Oscar. "Historical Perspectives on the American Ethnic Group," *Daedalus* (Spring 1961), 220–233.

Harling, Otto von. "The Present Situation in Missions to Jews and its Challenge," International Review of Missions, Vol. 22 (July 1933), 345–352.

Hebrew Christian Alliance Quarterly. 1917–1951. Name changed to *American Hebrew Christian,* 1952–1960. Chicago.

Hoffman, Conrad. "Jewry and the Future," *East and West Review,* Vol. 16 (July 1940), 233–237.

———. "Modern Jewry and the Christian Church," *International Review of Missions,* Vol. 23 (April 1934), 189–204.

Holmberg, Allan R. "Participant Observation in the Field," *Human Organization,* Vol. 14 (1955), 23–26.

International Missionary Council's International Committee on the Christian Approach to the Jews. *Christians and Jews: A Report of the Conference on the Christian Approach to the Jews, Atlantic City, May 12–15, 1931.* New York: International Missionary Council, 1931.

Jarvie, I. C. "The Problem of Ethical Integrity in Participant Observation," *Current Anthropology,* Vol. 10, No. 5 (December 1969), 505–508.

"Jews, The," *Integrity,* special number, August 1947.

"Jews and Jesus," *Newsweek,* March 19, 1973, p. 54.

"Jews for Jesus," *Time,* June 12, 1972, p. 24.

Kloos, Peter. "Role Conflicts in Social Fieldwork," *Current Anthropology,* Vol. 10, No. 5 (December 1969), 509–512.

Kluckhohn, Florence R. "The Participant Observer Technique in Small Communities," *American Journal of Sociology,* Vol. 46 (1940), 331–343.

Kohler, Kaufmann. "Conversion to Christianity," *The Jewish Encyclopedia,* Vol. 4, New York: Funk & Wagnalls, 1903, p. 249.

Kosmala, Hans. "The Jews in Their New Environment: Intellectual and Spiritual Trends," *International Review of Missions,* Vol. 29 (October 1940), 497–505.

———. "The Two Judaisms," *International Review of Missions,* Vol. 32 (October 1943), 420–426.

———. "What is Judaism?" *International Review of Missions,* Vol. 35 (October 1946), 416–421.

Langford, D. B. "The Why of Christian Missions to Jews." *The Mission World,* Vol. 15, April 1917.

Lohman, Joseph D. "The Participant Observer in Community Studies," *American Sociological Review,* Vol. 2 (1937), 890–897.

Mayer, Carl. "Religious and Political Aspects of Anti-Judaism," in *Jews in a Gentile World.* Isacque Graeber and Steuart Henderson Britt., eds. New York: The Macmillan Co., 1942, 311–328.

Miller, S. M. "The Participant Observer and 'Over-Rapport,'" *American Sociological Review.* Vol. 17 (1952), 97–99.

"New Rebel Cry: Jesus is Coming! *Time,* June 21, 1971, pp. 32–43.

Palms, Roger. "Jews for Jesus," *Home Missions Magazine,* January 1973. pp. 7–9.

Parsons, Talcott. "Some Sociological Aspects of the Fascist Movements," in *Essays in Sociological Theory,* New York: Glencoe Press, 1954, 124–141.

Polner, Murray. "The Convert Business," *Congress Bi-Weekly,* Vol. 39 (May 1972), 24–26.

Report of the First General Conference, Hebrew Christian Alliance of America, April 6–9, 1915.

Schwartz, M. S. and C. G. Schwartz. "Problems in Participant Observation," *American Journal of Sociology,* Vol. 60 (1955), 343–353.

"Searching Again for the Sacred," *Time,* April 9, 1973, pp. 90–93.

Shils, Edward A. "Social Inquiry and the Autonomy of the Individual," in *The Human Meaning of the Social Sciences*, Daniel Lerner, ed. New York: Harcourt Brace Jovanovich, 1959, pp. 114–157.

Smith, Robert. "The New Dimension in Evangelism," *International Review of Missions*, Vol. 33 (July 1944), 304–311.

Sobel, B. Z. "Legitimation and Anti-Semitism as Factors in the Functioning of a Hebrew-Christian Mission," *Jewish Social Studies*, Vol. 23, No. 3 (July 1961), 170–186.

———. "Jews and Christian Evangelization: The Anglo-American Approach," *American Jewish Historical Quarterly*, Vol. 48, No. 2 (Dec. 1968), 241–259.

———. "Protestant Evangelists and the Formulation of a Jewish Racial Mystique," *Journal for the Scientific Study of Religion*, Vol. 5, No. 3 (Fall, 1966), 343–356.

———. "The Tools of Legitimation: Zionism and the Hebrew Christian Movement," *Jewish Journal of Sociology*, Vol. 10, No. 2 (December 1968), 241–250.

Stonequist, Everett V. "The Marginal Character of the Jews," in *Jews in a Gentile World*, Isacque Graeber and Steuart Henderson Britt, eds. New York: The Macmillan Co., 1942.

Vidich, Arthur J. "Participant Observation and the Collection and Interpretation of Data," *American Journal of Sociology*, Vol. 60 (1955), 354–360.

Wax, Rosalie Hankey. "Observation: Participant Observation," *International Encyclopedia of the Social Sciences*, David Sills, ed. New York: Crowell, Collier and Macmillan. 1968. Vol. 11, pp. 239–240.

Weiss-Rosmarin, Trude. "The Jesus People Movement," *Jewish Spectator* (September 1972), 2–7.

———. "Key, 1973," *Jewish Spectator*, Vol. 38 No. 2 (February 1973), 2–4.

Webster, J. T. "The Changing Policy in Jewish Missions," *International Review of Missions*, Vol. 6 (1917) 206–218.

World Missionary Conference. Report of Commission 1: *Carrying the Gospel to All the Non-Christian World*. New York: Fleming H. Revell Co., 1910.

TRACTS AND PAMPHLETS

Abramovitch, L. "The Meaning of the Jewish Holy Days." New York: Sar Shalom Publications, n.d.

Aids to Jewish Evangelism. Dallas: Dallas Theological Seminary, 1959.

Cohn, Joseph Hoffman. *The Afikoman or: The Broken Matzo*. New York: Sar Shalom Publications, n.d.

Cohn, Leopold. *Story of a Modern Missionary to an Ancient People: Being the Autobiography of Leopold Cohn, Missionary to 250,000 Jews of Brooklyn.* n.p.: n.d.

Denman, F. L. *Hebrew Christians as Missionaries to Gentiles.* London: Society for Promoting Christianity Amongst the Jews, 1914.

Eisenberg, Charles. *" 'For With Jehovah is the Fountain of Living Waters.' "* New York: Sar Shalom Publications, n.d.

Finestone, Isaac Levy. *The Abrahamic Hope.* Newark, N.J.: The Messengers of the New Covenant, n.d.

———. *Reaching the Jewish Nation for Christ,* Newark, N.J.: The Messengers of the New Covenant, n.d.

Freshman, Jacob. *Manual of First Hebrew Christian Church in America.* n.p.: n.d.

Goldney, Edward. *A Friendly Epistle to the Jews and a Rational Prayer Recommended to Them in Order for Their Conversion to the Christian Religion.* London: 1760.

Here is the Story Behind All Those Smiling Faces. New York: Beth Sar Shalom Fellowship, n.d.

Ideal Book for the Ideal Home. London: Scripture Gift Mission, n.d.

Jewish Views on Jewish Missions. London: London Jewish Religious Union for the Advancement of Liberal Judaism, 1933.

Kimball, Earl. *Of Whom Does Isaiah 53 Speak?* New York: Sar Shalom Publications, n.d.

Kligerman, Aaron Judah. *Sharing Christ with our Jewish Neighbors.* Cleveland: Bible House, 1946.

Kosmala, Hans. *Anti-Semitism in the Present.* n.p.: 1944.

———. *The Racial Bar: Anti-Semitism in the Present.* n.p.: n.d.

Levy, Mark John. *Hebrew Christianity and Jewish Nationalism.* Charleston, S.C.: 1931.

Love and Obedience. London: Scripture Gift Mission, n.d.

"Ministry of Beth Sar Shalom Hebrew Christian Fellowship." New York: Sar Shalom Publications, n.d.

Newton, W. *For His Great Love.* London: British Society for the Propagation of the Gospel Among the Jews, 1959.

Newman, Chaim, ed. *Gentile and Jew: A Symposium on the Future of the Jewish People.* London: Alliance Press Ltd., 1945.

Prince, Derek. "Repent and Believe." Fort Lauderdale, Fla.: Derek Prince Publications, n.d.

———. "3 Messages for Israel." Fort Lauderdale, Fla.: Derek Prince Publications, 1969.

Schlink, M. Basilea. "*Godspell*: Advertised as 'Killingly Funny' but at Whose Expense?" Radlett, Herts.: Evangelical Sisterhood of Mary, n.d.

Singer, Charles. *The Christian Approach to Jews*. n.p.: 1937.

The Rabbi Told Me So. New York: The American Board of Missions to the Jews, n.d.

UNPUBLISHED MATERIALS

Bernards, Solomon S. "Fact Sheet: Key 73 and the Jewish Community." (mimeographed) New York: Anti-Defamation League, January 15, 1973.

"Christian Missions to the Jews: A Brief Reading List." (mimeographed) New York: Union Theological Seminary, Missionary Research Library. January 1, 1953.

Eichhorn, David M. "A History of Christian Attempts to Convert the Jews of the United States and Canada." Ph.D. dissertation, Hebrew Union College, 1938.

Fishman, Samuel Z. "Jewish Students and the Jesus Movement: A Follow-up Report." Washington, D.C.: B'nai B'rith Hillel Foundations, n.d.

Glick, Ira O. "The Study of a Marginal Religious Group." Master's thesis, University of Chicago, 1951.

Nichols, Eunice. "A Study of the Christian Approach to Jewish People in the City of Chicago." Master's thesis, Presbyterian College of Christian Education, Chicago, 1941.

Olson, Bernard Emanuel. "The Victims and the Oppressors; A Depth Analysis of the Protestant Images of Their Own and Other Groups in Situations of Conflict, Deprivation, and Persecution, as They Appear in Religious Educational Materials." Ph.D. dissertation, Yale University, 1959.

Press, Dolores. "The Contemporary American Jew and the Christian Faith." Master of Religious Education thesis, Princeton Theological Seminary, 1961.

PUBLICATIONS IN HEBREW

Ostrovsky, Y. S. *Who Is a Jew?* Tel-Aviv.

Prince, Derek. "Repent and Believe." The Center for Religious Publications, 1971.

Sroli, Moshe. "The Coming of Peace." Jesusalem, n.d.

Periodical Bibliography

Irving I. Zaretsky

The following is a representative sample of news reports about the "Jesus Revolution" in Israel, the United States, and other countries as reported primarily by the Jewish press. The news events reported and the attitudes expressed in the cited items have not been available in the general American press. From November 1972 to November 1973 a variety of periodicals and newspapers in several languages published in Israel, the United States, and elsewhere were surveyed for hard news stories and feature articles dealing with the Jews-for-Jesus Movement, conversion of Jews, intermarriage between Jews and non-Jews, and evangelistic efforts such as Key '73 and their impact on Jews. Most of the media surveyed are organs of diverse Jewish institutions representing a cross section of indigenous political, religious, professional, and institutional viewpoints which together profile the issues posed to the Jewish community by the Movement. Since the major effort of the Jews-for-Jesus Movement is to have its members be accepted as complete Jews or whole Jews by the Jewish community, it has been the Jewish press that has followed the Movement's growth most carefully. There are few additional sources of information on the current activities of the Movement in communities within and outside Israel.

Names of foreign language periodicals are transliterated into English and the place of publication is given. For economy and brevity news items are not individually indexed but grouped together under the date when they appeared in the periodical. Each date may refer to several news items within the periodical. Names of months in the calendar are transliterated and placed in parenthesis after the name of the equivalent month in the American calendar.

ENGLISH LANGUAGE PRESS

Australia

Australian Jewish News (Melbourne)	1/5/73; 5/11/73
Australian Jewish Times (Darlinghurst, N.S.W.)	4/19/73

England

The Jewish Chronicle (London)	3/9/73; 3/16/73; 3/23/73; 4/6/73; 4/13/73; 4/5/73; 6/15/73; 6/29/73; 7/6/73; 7/20/73; 9/14/73
Jewish Observer and Middle East Review (London)	3/16/73
Jewish Review (London)	3/28/73
Jewish Tribune (London)	2/8/73; 2/9/73; 2/23/73; 3/9/73; 3/23/73; 6/5/73
Jewish Voice (Southend-on-Sea)	12/15/72; 3/16/73; 6/1/73
PAI Views (London)	July 1973
The Times (London)	4/3/73

Canada

Canadian Jewish News (Toronto)	1/19/73; 2/16/73; 2/23/73; 3/2/73; 3/16/73; 4/6/73; 4/20/73; 6/4/73; 7/6/73
Canadian Jewish Outlook	April-May 1973
Jewish Post (Winnipeg)	2/1/73; 3/15/73
Jewish Standard (Toronto)	1/15/73; 3/15/73; 3/1/73; 6/1/73; 7/15/73
The Chronicle Review (Toronto)	May 1973
The Western Jewish News (Winnipeg)	2/22/73; 4/5/73; 4/12/73; 6/14/73

Israel

Israel Digest (Jerusalem)	3/30/73
Jerusalem Post (Jerusalem)	3/8/73; 3/11/73; 3/12/73; 3/15/73; 3/18/73; 3/22/73; 3/27/73; 3/28/73; 4/2/73; 4/10/73; 4/13/73; 4/15/73; 4/16/73; 4/18/73; 4/24/73; 5/31/73; 6/5/73; 6/17/73; 7/8/73; 7/10/73; 7/11/73; 7/12/73; 7/13/73; 7/15/73.

	7/18/73; 7/25/73; 8/19/73; 9/2/73;
	9/12/73; 9/18/73; 9/19/73
Judah '73 (Jerusalem)	April 1973
Newsletter (Jerusalem)	6/19/73; 8/26/73
The Mount Zion Reporter	
(Jerusalem)	May 1973
Women's World	February 1973

New Zealand

New Zealand Jewish Chronicle	
(Wellington)	3/26/73

Scotland

Jewish Echo (Glasgow)	12/8/72; 2/23/73; 3/9/73; 3/30/73;
	4/6/73; 4/13/73

Union of South Africa

Jewish Herald (Johannesburg)	2/27/73; 3/6/73; 3/13/73; 4/10/73
South African Jewish Times	
(Johannesburg)	2/23/73; 3/9/73
Zionist Record (Johannesburg)	3/9/73; 3/16/73; 4/6/73

United States

American Jewish World	
(Minneapolis, Minn.)	4/13/73; 5/4/73
Ayin L'tzion (New York, N.Y.)	March 1973
B'nai B'rith Messenger	1/5/73; 1/26/73; 2/2/73; 3/9/73;
(Los Angeles, Calif.)	3/16/73; 3/23/73
Brotherhood (New York, N.Y.)	March-April 1973; May-June 1973
Buffalo Jewish Review	12/8/72; 2/23/73; 3/23/73;
(Buffalo, N.Y.)	5/25/73; 6/22/73
Burlington Times	
(Willingboro, N.J.)	2/15/73
California Jewish Voice	
(Los Angeles, Calif.)	12/8/73; 1/26/73
Cleveland Jewish News	
(Cleveland, Ohio)	1/12/73; 3/9/73
Heritage (Los Angeles, Calif.)	12/29/72; 1/26/73; 2/2/73; 2/16/73;
	3/2/73; 3/16/73; 3/23/73
Intermountain Jewish News	12/8/72; 4/6/73;
(Denver, Colo.)	6/8/73; 6/18/73
Israel Horizons (New York, N.Y.)	April 1973

Jewish Advocate (Boston, Mass.)   11/16/72; 1/4/73; 3/22/73; 3/29/73
Jewish Civic Leader
  (Worcester, Mass.)   3/8/73
Jewish Digest (New York, N.Y.)   April 1973
Jewish Exponent
  (Philadelphia, Pa.)   3/30/73
Jewish Heritage (New York, N.Y.) Winter 1972
Jewish Journal
  (Brooklyn, N.Y.)   3/2/73; 3/16/73; 3/23/73
Jewish Ledger (Hartford, Conn.)   12/21/72; 2/8/73; 6/28/73
Jewish Life (New York, N.Y.)   January 1973
Jewish News (Detroit, Mich.)   12/22/72; 1/5/73; 1/11/73;
                                     2/16/73; 3/2/73; 3/16/73;
                                     3/23/73; 3/30/73; 5/11/73
Jewish Press (Omaha, Nebr.)   11/24/72; 12/1/72; 1/12/73; 2/23/73
Jewish Press (New York, N.Y.)   1/11/73; 1/25/73; 2/8/73;
                                     2/16/73; 2/23/73; 3/29/73;
                                     3/30/73; 4/6/73; 4/20/73;
                                     4/5/73; 5/18/73; 5/25/73; 6/14/73
Jewish Spectator (New York, N.Y.) December 1972
Jewish Standard   12/1/72; 1/12/73; 3/9/73; 3/30/73;
  (Jersey City, N.J.)   5/25/73; 6/22/73
Jewish Times (Baltimore, Md.)   2/9/73; 3/23/73; 4/6/73;
                                     4/13/73; 4/20/73
Jewish Week (Washington, D.C.)   11/9/72; 12/21/72; 1/4/73;
                                     1/11/73; 2/15/73; 3/1/73; 3/15/73;
                                     4/11/73; 4/19/73; 4/26/73
Jewish Week (New York, N.Y.)   2/8/73; 2/15/73; 2/26/73;
                                     3/8/73; 3/29/73; 6/28/73
Kansas City Jewish Chronicle   2/9/73; 2/16/73; 2/23/73; 3/9/73;
  (Kansas City, Mo.)   3/30/73; 4/13/73; 5/18/73; 6/8/73
National Jewish Monthly
  (Washington, D.C.)   November 1972
National Jewish Post and Opinion 12/1/72; 12/15/72; 12/29/72; 1/5/73;
  (Indianapolis, Ind.)   1/12/73; 2/2/73; 3/2/73;
                                     3/9/73; 3/30/73; 4/6/73;
                                     4/27/73; 5/11/73; 6/15/73
New York Times   3/13/73; 6/25/73; 7/26/73; 11/20/73;
  (New York, N.Y.)   11/21/73; 11/27/73
Ohio Jewish Chronicle
  (Columbus, Ohio)   2/15/73; 3/1/73
Philadelphia Jewish Times   12/1/72; 1/4/73; 1/18/73;
  (Philadelphia, Pa.)   1/25/73; 3/1/73; 5/31/73; 6/21/73
Phoenix Jewish News
  (Phoenix, Ariz.)   12/15/72

San Francisco Jewish Bulletin (San Francisco, Calif.)	1/12/72; 1/5/73; 1/26/73; 2/2/73; 2/23/73; 3/16/73; 3/23/73
Southern Jewish Weekly (Jacksonville, Fla.)	1/19/73; 3/2/73; 3/30/73
St. Louis Jewish Light (St. Louis, Mo.)	1/24/73; 2/7/73; 2/21/73; 3/21/73; 4/25/73
Texas Jewish Post (Fort Worth, Tex.)	1/25/73; 4/12/73
The Hebrew Watchman (Memphis, Tenn.)	5/24/73
The Jewish Chronicle (Pittsburgh, Pa.)	12/14/72
The Jewish Observer	March 1973
The Jewish Monitor (Birmingham, Ala.)	November 1972; December 1972; March 1973
The Sentinel (Chicago, Ill.)	1/18/73; 2/8/73; 3/1/73; 3/8/73; 3/15/73; 4/5/73; 5/3/73
Toledo Jewish News (Toledo, Ohio)	May 1973
United Synagogue Review (New York, N.Y.)	Winter 1973; Spring 1973
Waterbury American (Waterbury, Conn.)	2/19/73
Wisconsin Jewish Chronicle (Milwaukee, Wis.)	2/16/73
Young Israel Viewpoint (New York, N.Y.)	November 1972; December 1972

FRENCH LANGUAGE PRESS

Belgium

La Libre Belgique (Brussels)	3/20/73

Israel

L'Information D'Israel (Tel Aviv)	3/7/73; 3/30/73; 5/30/73; 7/11/73

France

Information Juive (Paris)	May 1973
Journal des Communautés (Paris)	January 1973
Le Monde (Paris)	2/19/73; 3/9/73
Tribune Juive (Strasburg)	3/8/73

GERMAN LANGUAGE PRESS

Germany

Allgemeine Wochenzeitung Der
   Juden in *Deutschland*
   (Düsseldorf, West Germany)   7/6/73
Donau-Kurier (Ingolstadt)   2/21/73

Israel

Jedioth Chadashoth (Tel Aviv)   3/9/73; 3/12/73; 3/16/73; 3/19/73;
                                   3/23/73; 4/2/73; 4/6/73; 4/12/73;
                                   4/27/73; 7/9/73; 7/19/73
MB Mitteilungsblatt (Tel Aviv)   3/16/73; 3/30/73
Volksblat (Tel Aviv)   February 1973

Switzerland

Israelitische Wochenblatt
   (Zurich)   3/9/73; 3/23/73; 6/8/73

HEBREW LANGUAGE PRESS

Israel

Amudim (Tel Aviv)
*(Bulletin of the Religious
   Kibbutz Movement)*   May (Eyar) 1973
Al Ha'Mishmar   3/3/73; 3/8/73; 3/14/73; 3/18/73;
                                   3/19/73; 3/28/73; 5/14/73; 5/29/73;
                                   6/1/73; 6/11/73; 3/25/73; 7/8/73;
                                   7/16/73; 7/18/73; 7/23/73;
                                   8/19/73; 8/23/73; 9/30/73
Ba'Mo'atsah (Jerusalem)
*(Bulletin of Labor Council of
   Jerusalem)*   May 1973
Ba'Maleh (Tel Aviv)
   (Bulletin of Hano'ar Ha'oved) May 1973
Ba'Ma'aracha (Jerusalem)   April 1973
Bat Kol (Ramat Gan)
   (Bar Ilan University Bulletin) 1/28/73
Chotam (Tel Aviv)   5/11/73
Davar (Tel Aviv)   3/8/73; 3/11/73; 3/15/73; 3/16/73;
                                   3/18/73; 3/19/73; 4/30/73; 5/3/73;

338   PERIODICAL BIBLIOGRAPHY

	5/10/73; 5/29/73; 5/31/73; 6/1/73; 7/3/73; 7/11/73; 7/12/73; 7/16/73; 7/29/73; 8/14/73; 8/17/73; 8/19/73; 8/23/73
Daf Ha'Tnuah (Tel Aviv) (*Bulletin of Ha'Noar Atzioni*)	3/14/73
Gesher (Tel Aviv)	April 1973
Ha'Tsofeh	3/7/73; 3/8/73; 3/9/73; 3/11/73; 3/13/73; 3/14/73; 3/18/73; 3/20/73; 3/26/73; 4/5/73; 4/6/73; 4/10/73; 4/13/73; 4/25/73; 5/4/73; 6/4/73; 6/5/73; 6/7/73; 6/22/73; 6/27/73; 6/28/73; 7/6/73; 7/8/73; 7/10/73; 7/11/73; 7/12/73; 7/13/73; 7/17/73; 7/19/73; 7/20/73; 7/24/73; 7/25/73; 7/30/73; 8/6/73; 8/14/73; 8/16/73; 8/17/73; 8/19/73; 8/23/73; 8/27/73; 8/31/73; 9/20/73; 9/23/73; 9/24/73
Ha'Modiah	3/6/73; 3/8/73; 3/11/73; 3/14/73; 3/23/73; 4/6/73; 4/10/73; 6/1/73; 6/4/73; 6/7/73; 6/26/73; 7/8/73; 7/9/73; 7/11/73; 7/16/73; 7/17/73; 7/24/73; 7/25/73; 8/10/73; 8/17/73; 8/23/73; 9/24/73; 9/28/73; 9/30/73 April 1973
Ha'Derech (Tel Aviv)	3/7/73; 3/8/73; 3/11/73; 3/16/73;
Ha'Arets (Tel Aviv)	3/19/73; 5/14/73; 5/29/73; 6/4/73; 6/5/73; 6/7/73; 6/20/73; 6/24/73; 6/27/73; 7/18/73; 8/24/73; 7/29/73; 8/9/73; 8/17/73; 8/19/73; 8/23/73; 8/26/73; 8/31/73; 9/10/73; 9/23/73; 10/2/73
Ha'Olam Ha'Zeh (Tel Aviv)	3/28/73; 4/25/73
Halichot (Tel Aviv) (*Bulletin of Ha'Moatsah Ha'Datit*)	April (Nissan) 1973
Hed Hachinuch (Tel Aviv)	6/14/73
Israelski Par (Tel Aviv)	3/12/73; 7/10/73
Kol Ha'Shabat (Jerusalem)	March (Purim) 1973; May-June-July 1973
La'Isha (Tel Aviv)	4/22/73
Ma'ariv (Tel Aviv)	3/8/73; 3/11/73; 3/14/73; 3/16/73; 4/10/73; 4/12/73; 4/15/73; 4/24/73; 4/30/73; 5/4/73; 5/29/73; 6/1/73;

	6/4/73; 7/5/73; 7/10/73; 7/11/73; 7/12/73; 7/15/73; 8/14/73; 8/19/73; 8/23/73; 9/30/73
Mabat (Tel Aviv)	3/14/73
Negohot (Jerusalem)	3/28/73
Panim el Panim (Tel Aviv)	3/23/73
"Ot" Shavu'on Mifleget Ha'Avoda (Tel Aviv)	3/29/73
Omer	5/29/73
Shavu'ah Magazine Hadshot le'Israel (Tel Aviv)	8/23/73
She'arim	3/12/73; 3/13/73; 3/14/73; 3/16/73; 3/19/73; 3/23/73; 3/25/73; 3/28/73; 4/9/73; 4/11/73; 4/12/73; 4/22/73; 4/25/73; 4/26/73; 5/10/73; 6/1/73; 6/5/73; 6/19/73; 6/22/73; 7/5/73; 7/6/73; 7/12/73; 7/15/73; 7/16/73; 7/18/73; 7/24/73; 7/26/73; 7/29/73; 9/20/73; 9/24/73
Tmurot (Tel Aviv)	3/24/73
Tfutsot Israel (Tel Aviv)	February 1973
Zo Ha'Derech	3/14/73
Yesh Bre'rah (Tel Aviv)	March 1973; June 1973
Ydi'ot Acharonot (Tel Aviv)	3/5/73; 3/8/73; 3/11/73; 3/12/73; 3/15/73; 3/16/73; 3/19/73; 3/25/73; 4/1/73; 4/4/73; 4/7/73; 4/19/73; 4/30/73; 5/15/73; 5/29/73; 7/3/73; 7/4/73; 7/8/73; 7/9/73; 7/11/73; 7/17/73; 7/15/73; 7/24/73; 8/23/73; 9/23/73

United States

Hado'ar (New York)	2/2/73; 2/23/73; 3/16/73

ITALIAN LANGUAGE PRESS

Israel

La Terra Santa (Jerusalem)	April 1973

POLISH LANGUAGE PRESS

Israel

Noweini i Kurier (Tel Aviv)	3/7/73

RUMANIAN LANGUAGE PRESS

Israel

Viata Noastra (Tel Aviv)   3/22/73

HUNGARIAN LANGUAGE PRESS

Israel

Uj Kelet (Tel Aviv)   3/7/23; 3/12/73

SPANISH LANGUAGE PRESS

Israel

Aurora (Tel Aviv)   7/12/73

YIDDISH LANGUAGE PRESS

Canada

Das Nayeh Yiddisheh Vort
  (Winnipeg)   2/16/73; 4/19/73

Israel

Israel Shtimeh (Tel Aviv)   3/7/73; 3/21/73
Illustrirteh Velt Voch (Tel Aviv)   4/11/73
Letsteh Na'ies (Tel Aviv)   2/16/73; 3/9/73; 3/13/73; 3/14/73;
                                     3/30/73; 6/1/73; 7/11/73; 7/16/73;
                                     7/24/73; 9/3/73; 9/26/73

United States

Der Yid (New York)   2/23/73; 3/16/73
Der Algema'iner Journal
  (New York)   2/2/73
Forwards (New York)   3/5/73; 3/8/73; 3/25/73; 3/26/73;
                               3/31/73

Appendix

Jesus in Jerusalem 1973: Mission Impossible?

IRVING I. ZARETSKY

"Shmad." "Jüden gegen Christen." "Christians Hunting Jewish Souls." "Israël contre les missionaires." "Church Heads Fear Threats and Violence." Even though one may raise an eyebrow, historically there is nothing surprising about these headlines, which, in 1973, were often found in both the secular and religious press in the Americas, in Europe, and in Israel. Such statements have been within the periodic norms of various localities and have accompanied outbursts of religious persecution at various times during our Common Era. Today, however, they deserve reappraisal.

What are the current conditions that have given rise to such statements? By the end of 1973, we had seen rapprochement of religious institutions followed by several years of efforts at interdenominational ecumenism, both Catholic and Protestant. There had been attempts at the unification of Christian churches, and this potential unification was celebrated by a calendar week. Dialogue between the Vatican and Israel had burgeoned, culminating in an understanding of Israel's jurisdiction over Jerusalem. A grass roots religious renaissance across all religious persuasions had occurred. Youth had promoted and popularized the belief that the Age of Aquarius was upon us, ushering in an era of spirituality and love. And a new Middle East war had taken place, followed by diplomatic negotiations to secure a regional peace and the existence of Israel as a homeland for Jews. These activities on our religious and sociopolitical horizon are contemporaneous with religious suspicions phrased in terms of pogroms and persecutions, which cast a shadow on church-synagogue relations. One reason for this is detailed and explained in this book. That reason is missionary activity.

This book is a comparative study of the Hebrew Christianity movement in the United States and Israel.[1] The raison d'être of this movement is to proselytize Jews into a new and personal religious consciousness and affiliation. The movement suggests that in accepting Christ as a personal Messiah, an integral part of Divinity, an agent for Salvation and an instrument for self-help in conquering existential problems, a Jew may transform himself into a Complete Jew, a Whole Jew, a Messianic Jew, a True Jew—a Hebrew Christian. He may thus help advance the Second Coming and bring about social change through personal religious transformation. He need not abandon his Judaism; he enhances it through his acceptance of Christ. He thereby becomes part of the vanguard that will lead Judaism in what is regarded as a natural evolutionary development toward "completion."

The approach to Hebrew Christianity in this book is consistent with the empirical evidence we have at hand. The approach is historical, contemporary, and comparative.[2] It outlines historically the roots of the movement as a whole and the institutionalization process of its component groups in their respective localities. Based on field work and library research, it is a comparative study of the Messengers of the New Covenant, headquartered in the House of the Lord Our Righteousness in New Jersey; of The First Hebrew Christian Church of Chicago, and of the individuals currently attracted to form similar groups in Israel, particularly in Jerusalem. It is contemporary in its discussion of the ideological and theological framework within which the movement is bounded and of the generating social conditions that host its growth and spread.

Although the dialogue between Christians and Jews over the Jews' acceptance of Christ as a Messiah and an integral part of Divinity is not an historically new phenomenon, some of the institutional forms and recruitment patterns used to proselytize and convert Jews are of rather recent origin. In particular this volume treats the Anglo-American model for the Missions to the Jews. Such missions are basically a Western innovation, rooted in early nineteenth-century England and simultaneously developed in the United States during the last half of the nineteenth and during the early part of the twentieth centuries. The term Hebrew Christianity is therefore used in the postnineteenth century sense of Mission to the Jews and not as a reference to the Apostolic church or to early Christianity.

As we approach the last quarter of the twentieth century, Hebrew Christianity is perhaps strongest in the United States, where it is not geographically localized, but has a national spread with particular intensity on both coasts. Spurred on by the current enthusiasm for varieties of religious experience, self-appointed missionaries and delegates of Hebrew Christian and fundamentalist Protestant religious bodies are looking East to the Holy Land, the place where Jesus walked, to hand-deliver the "New Covenant" to the residents of Israel.

The export of the missionary model from West to East has been a hegira accompanied by conflict. Repeated opposition has been rallied, especially in Israel by church, synagogue, and some secular authorities. The formulation and resolution of conflicts between missionaries and indigenous religious and secular opposition to them pose the most interesting issues for analysis, understanding, and further research. The diffusion of the Anglo-American model to overseas communities allows us to speak of Missions to the Jews and Hebrew Christianity, one of its institutional and recruitment forms, as articulating a movement of social change through personal religious transformation.

The following comments only briefly summarize and allude to the significant issues which Hebrew Christianity may raise: the multiple senses and component meanings of the linguistic concepts in English and Hebrew of missionary work such as proselytization by the word and not by the sword; Hebrew Christianity and conversion; Hebrew Christianity in the context of contemporary religious movements; the description and analysis of Missions to the Jews as movements of social change through personal religious transformation; church-state issues resulting from proselytizing activities in the United States and Israel; and a prognosis for the impact of the movements on proselytized populations.

MISSIONARY ACTIVITY: THE MEDIUM AS MESSAGE

Much of social science research on missionary activity has been devoted to the impact of Western traditions on developing societies in Africa, Latin America, or Asia since the onset of Colonialism. But proselytization, within Western, urban, industrialized societies, organized on a variety of different legal and political models, and the problems it poses in the religious and secular life of those societies has remained, on the whole, a neglected topic of research within contemporary scholarship. In particular, the ecology and demography of inter- and intradenominational population shifts has not been examined in relationship to the present religious revival. This is partly because explicitly proselytizing campaigns such as Explo '72 and Key '73 are of very recent origin, and partly because such groups as Hebrew Christianity have been numerically marginal and were thought to be catering to a population outside the mainstream of American life. Until recently, these groups have been relatively inconspicuous.

Studies of missionary activity have focused rather on the recruitment methods of various religious bodies. Thorough studies such as those by Lofland (1966) and Gerlach and Hine (1970), examine the recruitment and proselytization patterns of groups or movements, largely to understand the group's internal organization and its own potential for growth and expansion. Efforts have also been made to understand the social conditions that generate the emergence of religious groups, processes of institution building, and functional solutions to the personal and collective problems brought by their membership.

The two foci for analysis have been, therefore, the social institution and the individual parishioner. In terms of the individual we have focused on church affiliation models that emphasize social deprivation or disorganization and personal pathology or deviancy (Hine, 1974). Where attention has been given to the impact of the individual's affiliation on the religious institution, it has been essentially in terms of multiple affiliations in several religious bodies, a pattern frequently followed by religious "seekers" (Lofland, 1966; Festinger, 1957; Zaretsky, 1974; Zaretsky and Leone, 1974).

Although we need not abandon our interest in the individual and his religious affiliation, it would be useful to place such personal affiliation in terms of its institutional impact on religious bodies competing for a potentially limited population pool. All currently active religious groups must recruit members to compensate for the natural attrition of membership through deactivation, disaffiliation, or death. Extant churches are therefore in constant competition for new members with other extant churches or with emerging groups, whether they be schismatic or newly created movements.

Missionary activity, as one process of recruitment, promotes population shifts and redistribution among religious bodies

that may result in interdenominational political confrontations. Grounded in the institutional fear of losing members
and in the suspicion of other institutions gaining members,
such confrontations may be phrased in terms of church-and-
state issues, such as the free exercise of religious beliefs. The
right to proselytize freely may be claimed as an integral part of
one's religious beliefs and worship. Viewed ecologically and
demographically, shifting populations and the realignment of
certain religious niches may be among the reasons for church-
state confrontations over proselytization activities as is the
more traditional argument that problems arise when a particular group's religious beliefs and practices threaten or offend
the secular interests or values orientation of the social order
(Pfeffer, 1974). We shall return to this point after examining
the concept of missionary activity.

Missionary Activity

"Missionary activity" or "proselytization" are lexical terms
used in several senses that subsume different communication
processes and institutional forms. The terms denote an activity
that may be promoted by and/or may result in the creation of
religious institutions. As a process, missionary activity is a
neutral information exchange that turns parochial through
particular persuasion techniques and messages being transmitted. It may be undertaken by ordained clergy; by profes-
sionally trained missionaries, both clerical and lay; or by laymen self-appointed and/or institutionally approved for the job.

Proselytizing is not necessarily synonymous with witnessing
and testifying for a faith. Witnessing and testifying may occur
within a religious service as a profession of faith of the gathered
participants. They may also take place in religious conventions, such as those sponsored by the Full Gospel Business
Men's Fellowship International. These conventions, which are

held from time to time in various cities in the United States, bring together members of participating religious groups for a religious experience. When newcomers are present, witnessing or testifying may be motivated by a missionary effort. This is particularly true when they are not expressed in the form of speaking in tongues (glossolalia) or other personal ecstatic manifestations, but in the form of ordinary conversation with others that informs them of the virtues of the faith and the advisability of joining it. In this latter sense, witnessing and testifying become two senses of the term "proselytizing."

Missionary activity may occur interdenominationally or intradenominationally between competing persuasions advocating different degrees of religiosity or variant belief systems. Although intradenominational recruitment is not commonly thought of as missionary work, analytically, as a communication and persuasion process, it may be useful to consider it as such.

Missionary activity is endemic to all Christian religious traditions, but by and large it is not part of contemporary Judaism. During some historical periods, Judaism did allow missionary work (Isaac, 1965:284–289; *Ha'Arets,* August 3, 1973), and some have interpreted the current phenomenon of the *Chabad* movement of the Lubavitscher Rabbi, which works within Judaism, as a variant of an intradenominational missionary effort. The Christians for Moses group organized in Israel by the Jewish Defense League in 1972–1973 is regarded by some as a Jewish missionary effort toward Christians, but this movement is more accurately described as a symbolic political reaction, rather than one motivated and actively pursued for genuine religious purposes.

Missionary activity may be undertaken by religious institutions; it may also lead to the building of religious institutions. Three basic institutional types can be considered—although they may not be mutually exclusive because in reality analytical distinctions blur. First, there is the group that sees itself as a terminal point for religious affiliation. It supplies the individual with a belief system, with ritual functions, and with a complete set of life cycle rites of passage. Examples are major denominations such as Pentecostalists, Baptists, Episcopals, Methodists, and some Hebrew Christian groups. Second there are churches that are transitional both in intention and function. These churches socialize the proselytized individual from one religion or no religion to another or new religion on his way to full participation in one of the major denominations. Examples are sidewalk churches, living-room temples, and transient groups organized around street Christianity of the type common in the 1960s at the peak of the "Jesus Revolution." The third type of group combines features of the first two types. These groups may serve the total needs of the individual and render the proselytized into a missionary whose religious life revolves around continued witnessing to potential converts. The raison d'être for joining such a group and sustaining it is the process of proselytizing. Examples are B'Nai Yehoshua, and Board of Mission to the Jews' Beth Sar Shalom.

Most Hebrew Christian groups are of the second and third types, with a unique distinguishing attribute. The Hebrew Christianity movement is basically a missionary effort that has targeted only one group for its proselytizing efforts, namely Jews. It has chosen its theological framework to be particularly adaptive in missionary work by explicitly synthesizing two major traditions, Judaism and fundamental Protestantism. Although recruitment efforts of most movements are aimed at potential converts from diverse religious backgrounds, and even though some churches, such as the Mormons, may be particularly active with a group such as the American Indians, they do not solely recruit from any one group. Hebrew Christianity primarily focuses on Jews, of all ages and all degrees of religiousness, Orthodox, Conservative, Reform, or Reconstructionist.

Also unique to Hebrew Christianity, in its own stated terms, is the fact that it benefits from the missionary effort of many Christian churches. Campaigns such as Explo '72 and Key '73, although not primarily focused on Jews, did make contact with many Jewish people. They do not specify institutional alternatives for the proselytized and are generally compatible with Hebrew Christian beliefs in a fundamental Christianity, rooted in a literal interpretation of Scriptures.

As a generic term within the context of missionary activity, "Hebrew Christianity" is conventionally viewed as synonymous with terms such as "Missions to the Jews," "Messianic Judaism," "Invisible Church," "Jews for Jesus," "Judeo-Christians Who Bleed for Christ." From Jews' viewpoint, these terms are all incorporated in the term "Jesus Revolution." As generic terms, each of these synonyms refers to the process of proselytizing Jews by Christians and Jewish-born affiliates within the movement, and to institutional religious bodies with their unique history of institution building based on the Anglo-American missionary model. These are decentralized, independent, localized groups sharing basic ideologies, recruitment patterns, and goals. They may be churches such as the Messengers of the New Covenant or The First Hebrew Christian Church of Chicago, or they may be missionary societies such as the Board of Missions to the Jews with their own worship locale, or assembly of believers, Beth Sar Shalom (House of Peace). (The worship locale is usually given a biblical or Hebrew name transliterated into English characters.) These synonyms also refer to the identity of a member as a whole Jew who has not abandoned his Judaism but enhanced it. Specifically, there is little attention paid in the movement to the identity of the Christian proselytizing the Jew. While he too, through affiliation, may be called a Hebrew Christian, he does not become one as a result of converting to Judaism. Usually, the missionary retains his identity as a Christian.[3]

Hebrew Christianity therefore is not a midway station between traditions, resembling both but transcending either, nor

a composite of two equal and mutually interacting components achieved through reciprocal conversion of its members
into each other's former religions. Rather, in terms of institutional identity, it is unidirectional for Jews, who accept an
identity hitherto thought of as intrinsically non-Jewish. It
might appear to some as exotic, although institutionally difficult, to found a movement whose members, coming from different traditions, would convert to each others' religion and form
a new synthesis. Orthodox denominations, particularly in
Judaism, hesitate to convert individuals who convert with the
ulterior motive of forming a new religious group. This is precisely what some converts have succeeded in doing prior to their
arrival in Israel. Non-Jews have converted to Judaism in the
United States and used their new status to immigrate to Israel
under the Law of Return. Once there they began to proselytize
for Hebrew Christianity or for other fundamental Protestant
denominations. The case of Shira Lindsay is said to be an
example, to which we will return below. Independent religious
movements in America are exceptions to orthodox denominations, in that they allow individuals to use ordination certificates and church charters received from one church, such as the
Universal Life Church, to form churches other than and often
radically different from those issuing the certificates and charters (Judah, 1965; Zaretsky, 1974; Zaretsky and Leone, 1974).

Conversion

A key issue in missionary activity is that it urges the individual
being proselytized to confirm his new religious identity
through formal affiliation with the proselytizing group. The
affiliation may involve formal conversion by a rite of passage
such as baptism. Conversion is an explicit act of personal religious definition and redefinition. It is also an act of affiliation
into a group and frequently involves a formal disaffiliation

from a natal or previously adopted religious group. To translate an ideational act of self redefinition to an empirically grounded social fact, conversion and affiliation must be validated and acquiesced to by the group receiving the convert. In some cases, it may also involve a formal disaffiliation from the group already having a claim on the convert.

Conversion and affiliation are of import to the individual, to his past and new religious groups, and to both of their social milieus. Therefore, conversion is not a neutral, isolated act of only personal import to the convert. It is quintessentially a social act involving at least a dyad, the individual and his new religious institution, and frequently a triad, the convert, his past institutional affiliation, and his new institutional affiliation. In a triad, the convert becomes the bridge between two religious institutions and a potential battleground for their individual claims to his loyalty. When the act of affiliation and conversion stems from personal seeking, it is not as likely to produce conflict. But when it is stimulated by the missionary efforts of a group, it harbors a confrontation between the institution losing a member and the institution gaining him. The reason is simple. Every religious group has a vested interest in retaining its membership, and institutions growing at its expense arouse suspicion. Further, major orthodox traditions consider their own theological views in relationship to other traditions to be at least *primus inter pares* and are committed to the efficacy and primacy of their own beliefs. Adhering to institutionally expressed theological formulations is important not only to the success of the church, but also to the state of the member's soul and indeed to the fate of humanity, as with those who believe their actions can advance the Second Coming.

A conflict between institutions over members' conversions, and over population shifts caused by missionary activity, is not solely rooted in theology, however. It also has practical implications in terms of the secular status of the convert after conversion, the potential political status of a growing religion, and the status of missionary activity as an integral right in the free exercise of religion. These implications would seem to be more important in nation-states like Israel than in the United States in terms of mechanisms and concepts for dealing with these issues.

In Israel, laws of personal status involving marriage and divorce are recognized by the state as being within the sole jurisdiction of religious communities. And even in the United States, in the private sector, religious status may prejudice an individual in terms of opportunities to get health or life insurance, and jeopardize his employment possibilities. While these issues have been taken to the United States courts, they still demonstrate the importance that religious status has in many secular matters.

Similarly, growing religious groups by virtue of population size become political forces whose rights are more likely to be vindicated, especially in political systems with coalition governments such as Israel, where religious parties, although proportionally small in representation, participate in the coalition and have political significance in maintaining a balance of power within the government. In Israel, moreover, politically institutionalized religious groups, which include certain trade unions and housing developments, exercise political influence of import not only to their religious adherents but also to the secular society at large.

MISSIONARY ACTIVITY AND CONVERSION:
THE PARADOX OF COMMUNICATION

Since much of the data on the Hebrew Christianity movement, especially in Israel, and the data that expresses Jews' viewpoint is in Hebrew, we need to understand the Hebrew language labels used and their meaning for the user.

In English such terms as "missionary activity," "proselytizing," and "conversion" carry several layers of meaning. Their
Hebrew counterparts are in some cases more general and in
others more specific. On the whole, they are not neutral or
value free. In standard Hebrew as it is spoken in Israel, the
terms *"Mis'ion"* (mission) and *"Mis'ioner"* (missionary) exist.
They are collective nouns subsuming many more senses of
meaning than their nearest English counterparts. Some of their
senses are mutually exclusive with the English terms.

In standard Hebrew, *Mis'ion* has the following definitions.
First, it refers to Christian churches and their supportive institutions, such as schools, established and recognized under the
Ottoman colonial administration, inherited by English Mandate, and adopted by the Israeli legal-political system (see
England, 1966; Rubinstein, 1967). Examples are the Anglican,
Catholic, and Greek Orthodox churches. In comparison with
noninstitutionally affiliated missionaries, these churches do not
engage in conspicuous local proselytizing of Jews. Second, a
Mis'ion may be a Christian church not recognized in the Israeli
legal-political system. The third definition encompasses missionary institutions, clerical or lay, that have no denominational tie and proselytize for a belief rather than for an
institutional affiliation. The term thus links all Christian
institutions, whether houses of worship, schools, or missionary
societies, along the dimensions of being non--Jewish and inherently proselytizing in orientation. It usually is not used to refer
to Moslem institutions.

The term *"Mis'ioner"* (missionary) is used to label the clergy
and staff of non-Jewish religious groups, Christian rather than
Moslem, and the staff of Christian institutions who are neither
ordained or denominationally affiliated, who might not explicitly partake in active proselytizing. The same term also
refers to active missionaries. Again the relevant dimension of
meaning is the religious status, Christian, rather than the functional occupation of the individual related to missionary activ-

ity. These definitions also hold true for the same terms in Yiddish.[4] This linguistic ambiguity should be kept in mind when surveying the Hebrew and Yiddish press in Israel and elsewhere.

The lexical ambiguities have been instrumental in both reflecting and effecting a crystallization of Jewish public opinion—Jews and non-Jews are seen as separate entities, without allowing for distinctions in self-definition, denominational affiliation, and religious occupations. In this light, the lexical terms may function as performative utterances (Austin, 1962).

If the terms labeling the religious status of institutions and the religious status and occupation of individuals are inclusive and overly general, the terms for the process of conversion are most specific and detailed. This is consistent with social realities in Israel. The status of non-Jewish institutions and individuals is of less interest to Israeli Jews than that of their Jewish counterparts. But the conversion process, especially of Jews, is a sensitive and a highly political act, and is taken with great seriousness for reasons too vast for this discussion. It involves laws of personal status and consequences to interpersonal relationships within the social organization of the Jewish society.

In English the verb "to convert" is a neutral term, in the sense that it denotes a process of change without specifying from what to what. In Hebrew, three verbs, for example, signify the act of conversion, and each focuses unidirectionally on the group to which the individual is converting. Transliterating the infinitive form, they are: *Le'Hitgayer*, to convert to Judaism; *Le'Hitnatser*, to convert to Christianity with no distinction as to denomination; *Le'Hitaslem*, to convert to Islam. The only term that approximates the English neutral verb "to convert" is *"Le'Hamir dat,"* to change one's religious affiliation. Its adjectival form (*Mumar*) denotes a convert from Judaism to another religion. These terms are used but not nearly as frequently as the verb *Le'Hishtamed* (or the noun form *Shmad*), which signify, both in Hebrew and in its Yiddish variations, conversion in violent circumstances. This verb for both a forced and a voluntary conversion also denotes spiritual death and social suicide for the convert—tearing oneself away from kin and community—followed among very observant Jews by a ritual of mourning (*Shivah*) by the convert's family as if for a relative's physical death.

While the choice of terms depends on the lexical repertoire of the speaker and the context for the communication event, the frequent use of the word *Shmad* (as I encountered it among some of my informants and in the Yiddish and religious press) connotes Israel's mood with regard to missionary activity. It is regarded as an aggressive act against members of the Jewish community and a threat to interfaith harmony between resident religious communities in Israel. The lexical items that we have been dealing with have been used historically in the context of Jewish experiences in the Diaspora whenever Jews professed a faith other than Judaism under duress. They have also developed within Judaism as a result of the social stigma attached to voluntary and sought conversions of Jews.

It might appear paradoxical that *Shmad*, connoting profession of faith under duress, should be used in Israel today with regard to conversions stimulated by the missionary effort. While in the Diaspora *Shmad* bespoke a reality of Jews converting to the religion of the powerful nation-state, in Israel the nation-state is primarily in the hands of Jews. Conversion out of Judaism is tantamount to affiliation with a politically less powerful group, a minority. The reason for the use of *Shmad*, especially by speakers of standard Hebrew who are immigrants to Israel, underlies the fact that cognitively they perceive current realities in terms of their personal historical experiences in communities within the Diaspora. It takes perhaps longer than 25 years (the period of Israel's existence) for individuals to align their cognitive and linguistic categories with a changed political reality. A corollary to this is that there is a differential use of this term among speakers of standard Hebrew. The term is less frequently used by Israeli born, non-Yiddish speaking, secularists. It is more frequently used by immigrants whose primary language is other than Hebrew (that is, Yiddish or languages spoken in Europe or Afro-Asia) or who are religiously oriented or who perceive the political security of Israel and world Jewry as fragile and vulnerable.

HEBREW CHRISTIANITY: THE CONTEMPORARY
RELIGIOUS CONTEXT

Hebrew Christianity should not be viewed in a social vacuum. It exists in the context of current religious life. The movement has sociostructural organization features resembling the evangelical Christianity of fundamentalist Protestant churches, such as the Baptist and Pentecostal.[5] Since the nineteenth century, Catholic and Greek Orthodox churches have been involved to a much lesser extent with proselytizing Jews, and have generally concentrated their efforts on developing societies.

The contemporary "Jesus Revolution" has been largely a Protestant phenomenon (notwithstanding the Charismatic Renewal Movement in the Catholic church) spearheaded and coalesced during the past two years by Explo '72 and Key '73 campaigns, and by such efforts as the Campus Crusade for Christ, which are "calling our Continent to Christ" and "winning souls for Jesus." It is estimated that Key '73 was endorsed by some 150 churches and religious organizations, both liberal and conservative, including 43 Roman Catholic dioceses. Over half of the 40,000 Methodist congregations participated in Key '73 in some way. These efforts were financed by some $10 million on the local level and by nearly $1 million for national media communications and advertising (*New York Times,* January 20, 1974: E–7).[6]

Although both are missionary in nature, the fundamentalist

Protestant effort differs from the Hebrew Christian approach. Explo '72 and Key '73 were evangelistic campaigns directed at the North American population at large, urging people to follow in the religious arena the political slogan "Come Home, America." Listeners were exhorted to abandon their erroneous ways and to return to a surer and more wholesome Christianity; to shun religious forms imported from other countries and other traditions and return to their natal churches; to seek their social alternatives under the overarching canopy of an original Christianity that is literally rooted in Scriptures and exemplified by the life of Christ and the Apostles. The evangelical effort is not directed at any one group but at all people within reach of the communication media—television, radio, press, mail, and face-to-face messages from missionaries. Among those reached in this way were Jews and other non-Christians.

The current evangelical revival is both general and specific. It is general in that the evangelizing call does not direct converts to specific Christian institutions. This is significant today because it allows organized and established churches to give structural and financial support to a grass roots initiative that began in the 1960s, and thus allows the movement greater potential success than other grass roots religious initiatives have enjoyed. It is unique in that all Christian groups, seeing their shared interests threatened by some of the current entrepreneurial grass roots religious efforts, have combined their resources to redirect a population back into their own sphere of influence. The growth and impact of the "Jesus Revolution" is great not necessarily because there are more people attracted to it or that it offers a more successful program, but in part because it is sponsored by established groups with successful financial means of reaching nearly 100 million Americans in their homes.

The revival is specific in that "Jesus people" communes and various crusades inform the individual that there are alternatives to reactivating oneself in one's natal or adopted church. One can join a new group, be it a commune or a church, that offers a fundamental approach, often not different from the doctrinal message of Key '73.

Within these two approaches, which are by no means mutually exclusive but can be symbiotic and reinforce each other, Hebrew Christianity, although it benefits from the general media approach, is closer to the specific, institutional one. Clearly, if Jews returned to their natal synagogues, the Hebrew Christian movement would not be completely successful. Therefore, new institutional forms must be provided as transition stations. A middleman church is needed to socialize people and allow them to formulate their new religious identity in the company of others who are similarly motivated. They may eventually join other Protestant groups or may even have an acknowledged or concealed dual membership with a standard Jewish synagogue or a Jewish cultural group like B'nai B'rith.

There are a great deal of statistical data on Hebrew Christianity both in the United States and in Israel. Sobel presents a statistical profile in this book. His warning about some statistics in this area deserves to be underscored. Most of the statistics are speculative, postured, and biased by ideological motivation, and are often published for tactical political considerations. Censuses may be misleading, since respondents do not wish to identify themselves officially as Hebrew Christians. Essentially Hebrew Christianity both in the United States and in Israel is a numerically marginal movement. Its significance, however, lies not in its numerical strength, but in its impact on church, synagogue, and state relationships in Israel, and in triggering legislation as a countermeasure that might be detrimental to the free excercise of religion by all religious persuasions. In the United States its impact is mainly on interfaith harmony. It should be noted in passing that the missionary issue and what is regarded as the appeal of Hebrew Christianity have not presented new problems, but have only crystalized and brought to the fore issues that have been in existence for some time. Some sectors of the Jewish population have used the current missionary thrust as an occasion to focus on what have been defined as problems in Israel and elsewhere: intermarriage, lack of competent Jewish education (including competent education especially in Israel about non-Jewish religious persuasions), secularization, and the perennial encounter between Jewish Orthodox and non-Orthodox sectors over the liberalization of laws of personal status in Israel. We shall return to this point below.

HEBREW CHRISTIANITY: A MOVEMENT OF SOCIAL CHANGE THROUGH PERSONAL TRANSFORMATION

Hebrew Christianity shares some structural features with fundamental Protestantism, particularly the Pentecostal movement. Although Hebrew Christianity need not be defined as a Pentecostal occurrence—and Sobel does not present it as such in his book—the analytical models built through the support of data from Pentecostalism may be useful in viewing Hebrew Christianity within a broader context of contemporary religious movements.

The model for the creation of a religious group specified by Goodman (1972, 1974a, 1974b) and the model describing the institutionalization of a local group into a national and international movement of social change through personal religious transformation detailed by Gerlach and Hine (1970) and Gerlach (1974) may be suggestive of one kind of analysis of some of the Hebrew Christianity data. These models are not, however, presented to suggest an inevitable developmental pattern for Hebrew Christianity, nor to predict the efficacy of the movement's social organization to achieve its stated goals. Rather, by focusing on the shared features of social organization of several different kinds of movements, including religious movements, these models help us to place the structure and activities of Hebrew Christianity in a larger analytical and scholarly context (the Gerlach and Hine model, in particular, is derived not only from the analysis of Pentecostalism, but also from the data available on the Black Power and ecology movements).

Goodman's (1974a) model states that some religious groups may emerge as a local Upheaval in a society, a kind of crisis cult during periods of stress, social dislocation, and personal deprivation. Goodman outlines four stages in the development of such an Upheaval: onset, gathering momentum, peak, and platform phase. Within the generating conditions for such an Upheaval, several factors deserve particular attention. The supernatural premises on which the emerging group's message rests should be resident in the culture and available to participants prior to the onset of the Upheaval. The mechanisms (e.g., altered states of consciousness) for validating or confirming the premises should be in part present in the culture and in part innovated by the emerging group. The charismatic leader, the message bearer, the symbol, the catalyst, should be situationally appropriate and structurally and functionally indicated for the particular locality in a given historical period. Goodman concludes by pointing out that on the basis of her data from an Apostolic church in Yucatán during the period 1969 to 1973, culture change was unaffected by the Upheaval.

Within the context of Hebrew Christianity, the supernatural premises of particular import deal with the participant's belief in Jesus Christ as a personal Messiah, an integral part of Divinity, an agent for Salvation, and an instrument for self-help in conquering existential problems. Whether these premises will become confirmed for individuals in the United States and Israel through participation in the movement remains to be seen. Sobel suggests several alternatives for the prognosis for Hebrew Christianity in the locales where it currently exists.[7]

FROM UPHEAVAL TO SOCIAL MOVEMENT

Let us now see if these small Hebrew Christian groups can be regarded as a large-scale movement of social change through personal religious transformation, and if they have a unified impact on the larger society.

Hebrew Christianity can be classified as a movement using the model of Gerlach and Hine (1970: xvi),[8] who define a movement as

> A group of people who are organized for, ideologically motivated by, and committed to a purpose which implements some form of personal or social change; who are actively engaged in the recruitment of others; and whose influence is spreading in opposition to the established order within which it originated.

Gerlach and Hine identify five key factors that must interact before a collectivity becomes a true movement, and for the movement to become an autonomous social entity that can grow independently of the original generating conditions (1970:199). They are organization, recruitment, commitment, ideology, and opposition (1970: xvii).

1. *A segmented, usually polycephalous, cellular organization* composed of units reticulated by various personal, structural, and ideological ties.
2. *Face to face recruitment* by committed individuals using their own preexisting, significant social relationships.
3. *Personal commitment* generated by an act or an experience that separates a convert in some significant way from the established order (or his previous place in it), identifies him with a new set of values, and commits him to changed patterns of behavior.
4. *An ideology* that codifies values and goals, provides a conceptual framework by which all experiences or events relative to these goals may be interpreted, motivates and provides rationale for envisioned changes, defines the opposition.

and forms the basis for conceptual unification of a segmented
network of groups.

5. *Real or perceived opposition* from the society at large or
from that segment of the established order within which
the movement has risen.

Of particular import to the discussion at hand is the fifth
factor—opposition. Once the premises of the Hebrew Christian message are confirmed for a participant in the movement,
he will willingly face any opposition to his own participation
in the group and to the movement as a whole. Gerlach and
Hine (1970:217) point out:

> Conscious participation in the processes of social evolution
> involves . . . expectation of and willingness to face opposition
> from those dedicated to the maintenance of the status quo in
> spite of its present deficiencies, weaknesses and flaws. Opposition
> may come in the form of physical force, or various types of
> pressure exerted through institutional channels. Or it may come
> in the form of ridicule from those who are still secure in the
> notion that power is based only on position within and ability
> to manipulate the existing power structure.

Whatever the result of the opposition, it is usually difficult
to return to a *status quo ante*. Opposition is significant in
testing the commitment and risk undertaken by the participants in the movement. It is also the most significant factor
in the current situation in Israel in its potential for church,
synagogue, and state confrontation and in the United States
in terms of interfaith harmony.

THE WORTHY OPPOSITION:
ISSUES OF CHURCH AND STATE

Opposition to fundamentalist Protestant proselytization and in
particular to Hebrew Christianity has come from a variety

of sources. We are here primarily concerned with the Jewish response. Opposition both in the United States and in Israel has been expressed in ad hoc physical force, as in the deprogramming (in the United States) of young people living in religious communes; through an antimissionary movement with structural features similar to those of the missionary movement (outlined above); through interdenominational institutional channels; and through the courts. The forces of opposition have had a greater societal impact in the area of the individual's rights to the free exercise of his religious beliefs than the missionary effort has had in bringing about substantive religious change. Although the impact of the missionary movement in realizing its stated goals has been numerically marginal, its significance thus transcends its numerical strength or geographical spread. It has pressed on social and religious nerve centers, especially in Israel. Reaction to the movement may produce social changes of far greater magnitude on the present society and its fundamental democratic foundation of civil rights and religious liberties. We shall first examine the American situation and then proceed to the Israeli context.

Opposition in the United States

In the United States, opposition to Hebrew-Christian proselytization has assumed two forms—interdenominational dialogue and an ad hoc antimissionary movement.

The most consistent response of the Jewish community has been to express its opposition publicly and privately to religious leaders of the evangelistic campaigns and their component groups, and to request that missionary activities toward Jews be curbed. The exchange of letters between Rabbi Marc H. Tanenbaum and Dr. Theodore Raedeke is an example (*The Jewish Week*, Washington, D.C., January 11, 1973:4). In a letter to Rabbi Tanenbaum, director of the interreli-

gious affairs department of the American Jewish Committee,
Dr. Raedeke, executive director of Key '73, assured Rabbi
Tanenbaum:

> There is no anti-Semitism in either the ideology or the thrust
> of Key '73. I trust that you understand this, just as we under-
> stand your position to be not anti-Christian. We do not wish
> to persecute, pressure or force Jews to believe or do anything
> against their will. On the other hand we are confident that the
> Jews do not wish to undermine our holy faith or deprive us of
> our rights to propagate our faith—the privilege which we
> enjoy in America. Rest assured that we will attempt in no way
> to deny our deepest Christian convictions in this regard so that
> we wrong the Jewish community in any way. At the same time,
> I hope that we may be confident that you who are not Christians
> will not in any way intimidate or pressure the many Christian
> participants in Key '73 against confessing before men the saving
> Gospel.[9]

Tanenbaum noted:

> While these views do not respond adequately to all the questions
> that the Jewish community would want clarified, the statement
> repudiating anti-Semitism and any evangelical resort to coercion
> are welcome clarifications indeed. One can only hope and expect
> that this message will reach many of the Key '73 evangelists,
> especially on college and high school campuses, some of whom
> in their zeal need such reminders that the right of religious
> liberty involves the duty of respecting the conscience of others
> who do not feel the need to be witnessed to. (*The Jewish Week*,
> Washington, D.C., January 11, 1973:4)

The United Church of Canada, which took part in the
Key '73 campaign, responded to the claim by some rabbis and
clergymen that an anti-Semitic bias was contained in the North
American Key '73 document used as a handbook for organ-
izers. In dissenting from the statements in campaign literature
aimed at converting Jews, the executive of the Church's general council approved the statement:

We view with deep concern the fact that some literature produced in the USA and some movements associated with Key '73
in that country have suggested that this is an opportunity to
"present the Messiah to your Jewish friends" and "to win Jews
for Jesus." We take exception to the implications of those
statements [in the Key '73 document] . . . Theologically this is
not the only place United Church people would find parts of
this document less than compatible with present United Church
belief . . . We are also aware of the fact that some Jewish leaders
have found these implications offensive . . ." The Church affirmed
that it would "oppose any tendency within the Key '73 pro-
gramme to single out groups as a particular target" for its evangelistic thrust. (*The Jewish Chronicle*, London, April 6, 1973)

The second form of opposition has come from ad hoc anti-
missionary campaigns organized by Jewish individuals and
groups. Examples are the Hebrew Truth Crusade organized
in Philadelphia (*Philadelphia Jewish Times,* January 25, 1973),
the *Hineni* and Jews for Judaism organized by Zionist and
religious youth groups, and groups such as the Jewish Defense
League. In addition to organizing a countermissionary movement called Christians for Moses that attempts to deactivate
through face-to-face contact Jews involved in the missionary
effort and to proselytize Christians, the Jewish Defense League
recruited individuals who would go to Israel to help in their
antimissionary campaign. Formal opposition to missionary
advertising in the media has been expressed (*National Jewish
Post and Opinion,* Indianapolis, January 5, 1973, February 2,
1973; *The Jerusalem Post,* April 2, 1973). These efforts have
been paralleled by an increase of attention to Jewish education
and by the calibration of Jewish institutions to become more
responsive to the needs of their membership.

The reason the opposition is expressed in these forms is to be
understood in the context of the constitutional foundation for
the free exercise of religion and the separation of church and
state. It may also be suggested that the current evangelization
efforts do not infringe on the shared secular interests of our

society. The theology, doctrines, and religious experiences of the proselytizing groups, whether Hebrew Christian or fundamentalist Protestant, do not threaten the norms and value orientation of the society at large. An exception may be found in cases of deprogramming, where the proselytizing groups are alleged to threaten the family unit, a point we shall return to below.

Proselytization is permitted and accepted as a form of religious worship protected by the First Amendment. The battle over proselytization was fought in the courts during the 1930s and 1940s, when concern was with missionary activities of the Jehovah's Witnesses, whose assertion of their right to engage in such efforts is clearly summarized by Burkholder (1974) and Pfeffer (1974).[10] In the 1930s the apocalyptic theology of the Jehovah's Witnesses, revised under Judge Rutherford, triggered extensive proselytization in this country. In the face of strong opposition, the Witnesses sensed a divine mission to save the world from satanic influences. Their door-to-door canvassing, augmented by sound trucks, street meetings, and parades, provoked public hostility and led to arrests. Communities passed ordinances prohibiting such activities, or established restrictive licensing policies, but the Witnesses ignored them. Proselytization and ad hoc opposition to it resulted in 1149 arrests in 1936. This confrontation with the social order was eventually brought to the courts for resolution.[11] Early appeals to the Supreme Court on freedom of religion claims did not receive support. In 1938, when the tactics were changed to arguments grounded on freedom of the press, the Court struck down an ordinance against literature distribution [*Lovell* v. *Griffin* 303 U.S. 444 (1938)]. A series of cases dealing with new rights to use public places, distribution of literature, and door-to-door solicitation soon followed (see Stokes and Pfeffer, 1964:118).

A further development on freedom to propagate was dealt with in the case of *Cantwell* v. *Connecticut* [310 U.S. 296

(1940)]. In overturning a conviction for breach of the peace by a Witness evangelist, Justice Roberts noted:

> Thus the Amendment embraces two concepts,—freedom to believe and freedom to act. The first is absolute but, in the nature of things, the second cannot be. Conduct remains subject to regulations for the protection of society.

The Court decision held that:

> In the absence of a statute narrowly drawn to define and punish specific conduct as constituting a clear and present danger to a substantial interest of the State the petitioner's communication, considered in the light of the constitutional guarantees, raised no such clear and present menace to public peace and order as to render him liable to conviction of the common law offense in question.

Whether proselytizing is equivalent to the worship practices of more conventional churches was a question raised in the case of *Murdock* v. *Pennsylvania* [319 U.S. 105 (1943)]. Justice Douglas stated:

> The hand distribution of religious tracts . . . occupies the same high estate under the first amendment as do worship in the churches and preaching from the pulpits. It has the same claim to protection as the more orthodox and conventional exercises of religion.

Finally, *Prince* v. *Commonwealth of Massachusetts* [321 U.S. 158 (1944)], the case of a Witness prosecuted for allowing her nine-year-old niece to accompany her in selling religious literature on the street, crystallized the issue of "balancing" freedom of religion against secular interests in the welfare of children. The Court opinion took note of the contention that "the street, for the Jehovah's Witnesses and their children, is their church, since their conviction makes it so; and to deny them access to it for religious purposes as was done here has the same effect as excluding altar boys, youthful choristers and other children from the edifices in which they practice their religious beliefs and worship." According to Justice Rutledge, however, "The public highways have not become their religious property merely by their assertion. And there is no denial of equal protection in excluding their children from doing there what no other children may do." The Court ruled in favor of the state to protect the "welfare of children." Justice Murphy dissented. In observing that "from ancient times to the present day, the ingenuity of man has known no limits in its ability to forge weapons of oppression for use against those who dare to express or practice unorthodox religious beliefs," he argued that "The state . . . has completely failed to sustain its burden of proving the existence of any grave or immediate danger to any interest which it may lawfully protect."

Notwithstanding their attack on organized religion and particularly on the Catholic Church, the activities of the Jehovah's Witnesses may have been regarded more as a primary concern to the community than as an affront to interfaith harmony (Pfeffer, 1974). For example, one of the several church and state confrontations of the Witnesses was occasioned by the refusal of Jehovah's Witnesses children to salute and pledge allegiance to the national flag in public schools, a ceremony the Witnesses deemed a violation of the commandment against having other gods and making graven images (Pfeffer, 1974). In the *Gobitis* case [*Minersville School District v. Gobitis,* 310 U.S. 586 (1940)], the Court upheld the constitutionality of the expulsion of the children of Witness Walter Gobitis from the public school of Minersville. The Court's opinion, written by Justice Felix Frankfurter, shows how strongly it felt that the refusal of the Gobitis children to salute the flag even though religiously motivated represented a threat to the secular interests of nationalism and security.

> National unity [the Court said] is the basis of national security
> . . . The ultimate foundation of a free society is the binding tie
> of cohesive sentiment. Such a sentiment is fostered by all those
> agencies of the mind and spirit which may serve to gather up
> the traditions of a people, transmit them from generation to
> generation, and thereby create that continuity of a treasured
> common life which constitute a civilization. "We live by symbols."
> The flag is the symbol of our national unity, transcending all
> internal differences, however large, within the framework of the
> Constitution. (cited in Pfeffer, 1974)

The period following the Court's decision saw much violence and persecution visited upon the Witnesses. Three years
after the *Gobitis* decision the Court, by a vote of 6 to 3,
reversed itself and ruled that children could not constitution-
ally be barred from public schools for refusing to salute the
flag [*West Virginia State Board of Education* v. *Barnette*
319 U.S. 624 (1943)].

The current proselytization activities of Hebrew Christian
and Protestant churches in America do not pose a secular
threat to the shared secular concerns of the social order. The
religious beliefs and practices of the proselytizing churches
are not a direct affront to the deeply held values of the society.[12]
The fact that particular religious groups are unhappy that
their members are being proselytized is unlikely to result in
a church-state confrontation. Therefore, interdenominational
opposition and conflict over missionary activities frequently
have to be resolved informally or institutionally through
political negotiations involving a range of reciprocal interests.
But when the constitutional rights of either participant are
perceived to be curtailed, and/or with an escalation of such
occurrences, intervention of the judicial system becomes inevitable, as demonstrated below.

Some of the church-state issues that are emerging from the
current "Jesus Revolution" deal with deprogramming cases,[13]
which involve the kidnapping of individuals, both minors and

adults, from religious groups (usually communes), by their parents or their parents' representative. The kidnapped person is then deprogrammed so as to believe that he or she has erred in joining the commune and in subscribing to its belief system. Thereby, it is hoped that the individual will renounce his affiliation with the group and return to his natal church and affiliation, and/or assume a life style other than communal.

Deprogramming is best known through the efforts of Ted Patrick, a deprogrammer of individuals involved in a variety of religious groups including Jesus communes. Along with some parents of commune members and individuals who have no such personal involvement with the "Jesus Revolution," Patrick seems to believe, according to some press accounts, that those who belong to a variety of fundamentalist groups and those who live in religious communes have lost their religious freedom. They have been brainwashed, hypnotized, spiritually captured, and should be liberated from this captivity and deprogrammed to erase their unorthodox and unreasonable religious beliefs and practices. Patrick further argues that parents have a human and constitutional right to rescue their children who are in danger (Kaufmann, 1973). To accomplish the goal of deprogramming, some parents concerned over their children's involvement with religious groups have joined forces with Patrick to form a group called The Committee to Free Our Sons and Daughters From the Children of God, or FREE COG. It is alleged that Patrick, assisted by others, at the request of parents and acting as their agent or representative, will abduct or "kidnap" their son or daughter from a group or commune and undertake to deprogram them at a specified location for a number of days.

The individuals who have undergone deprogramming, with varying degrees of success according to Patrick's goals, have included men and women, minors and adults, Jews and non-Jews. The groups and communes from which they have been abducted are located in a number of states, including Cali-

fornia, Florida, Massachusetts, and New York, and include
the Children of God; New Testament Missionary Fellowship;
Tony and Susan Alamo Christian Foundation; and The Way,
The Truth, and The Life.[14]

Recently, participants in Eastern religious groups and individuals who are not institutionally involved with a group but
whose actions are regarded as rooted in a religious outlook
not sympathetic with that of their parents have also been a
target for deprogramming.

Individually and generally, these cases raise many issues of
import to church-state relations and civil liberties. Among
them are: kidnapping; deprogramming; freedom of association; freedom of movement; parental authority over minor
children; parental authority over emancipated children whose
activities are viewed as endangering their mental, psychological, or emotional health, general welfare, and morals;
freedom to worship; physical coercion to obtain religious conformity; religious observances that harm society by destroying
family relationships; the rights of children to religious freedom
and to the protection of First Amendment rights.[15]

None of the cases concerning these issues has yet reached
the Supreme Court. Local enforcement agencies such as the
police have been reluctant to get involved and have, it has
been said, sometimes not interceded in the abductions even
when they were witnesses to them. Similarly, lower courts
tended to be sympathetic to the parents' interests and unresponsive to the claims of the abducted and/or deprogrammed
individual. It has been suggested that the deprogramming
cases that have arisen during the past two years and the issues
they pose are reminiscent of the questions posed in *Prince* v.
Commonwealth of Massachusetts in which Justice Rutledge
focused on the competing claims of "the obviously earnest
claim for freedom of conscience and religious practice" allied
with "the parent's claim to authority in her own household,"
and "the interest of society to protect the welfare of children."

The Prince case did not oppose the interests of the parents and those of the child; rather, kinfolk united in facing the state, which was concerned with the welfare of children who were thought to be insufficiently protected by their kinfolk.

Similarly, the *Yoder* case [*Wisconsin* v. *Yoder* 406 U.S. 205 (1972)] may be viewed as posing issues related to those involved in the deprogramming cases. In the Yoder case, members of the Old Order Amish and Conservative Amish Mennonite Church who had refused to send their children to public or private schools following graduation from the eighth grade were convicted for violating the state's compulsory school attendance law, which requires children to attend school until age 16. The Amish claimed that high school attendance was contrary to the Amish religion and way of life and that they would endanger their own salvation and that of their children by complying with the law. The Supreme Court upheld the parents' claim that Wisconsin's attempt to force the Amish children to attend school through age 16 was an unconstitutional infringement on freedom of religion. Justice Douglas dissented. He urges that children are "persons" within the context and meaning of the Bill of Rights and that the Bill of Rights is not for adults alone. He goes on to say:

> The Court's analysis assumes that the only interests at stake in the case are those of the Amish parents on the one hand, and those of the state of the other. The difficulty with this approach is that, despite the Court's claim, the parents are seeking to vindicate not only their own free exercise claims, but also those of their high-school-age children. . . . Although the lower courts and a majority of this Court assume an identity of interest between parent and child, it is clear that they have treated the religious interest of the child as a factor in the analysis. . . . Crucial, however, are the views of the child whose parent is the subject of the suit. . . . On this important and vital matter of education, I think the children should be entitled to be heard. . . . It is the student's judgment, not his parents', that is essential if we are to give full meaning to what we have said about the

Bill of Rights and of the right of students to be masters of their own destiny.

In the *Yoder* case, some of the Amish children were questioned about their religious beliefs and they supported their parents' opposition to secular education after the eighth grade. The questions raised in this case are different from but nonetheless related to those raised by deprogramming cases involving minors—how to balance the freedom of religion of both parents and their children with the secular interests of the state in protecting the welfare of children.

How deprogramming cases will be handled by the Supreme Court, should they reach it and be accepted for a hearing, remains an open question. The answers will depend to some extent on the composition of the Court and on the mood of the country with regard to those religious groups who are forging alternative life styles for themselves. Such religious groups presently claim that they are misunderstood and misinterpreted by a society hostile and fearful of social innovations and alternative life styles. Also relevant might be the political pressures exerted by denominations who feel that the current revival has made inroads into their church or synagogue membership. Although not of legal importance for the free exercise of religion, this ecological and demographic factor of population shifts provides strong political motivation for lobbying by orthodox denominations against legal support that might encourage the further growth of new religious groups. The legal encounter will provide one index of the degree of acceptance that new religious groups have achieved within the larger society.[16]

A comparison of the United States and Israel in terms of the mechanisms and concepts available to those who oppose proselytizing by certain groups or individuals should be placed in a wider context. There have been religious movements developing in Europe and there are European missionaries in

Israel. Like the American missionaries, they challenge the values of some sectors of the Israeli population. Opposition to missionary activity can also be found in Moslem countries, which discourage it, and in some European countries that regulate proselytization by either Protestants or Catholics in terms of the civil status of the missionary in the country in which he proselytizes—whether he is a citizen or foreign national visiting or permanently residing in that country.

The Israeli situation is unique in that Israel is the Holy Land to many religious persuasions. Many individuals feel that either as pilgrims or missionaries the act of witnessing for the Gospel in the land where Jesus was born, died, and was resurrected, where the Word was made Flesh, is endowed with an even greater import than witnessing for the Gospel in communities outside the Holy Land. The claim on Israel as the Holy Land coupled with the fact that Israel is an independent state with its own legal-political system and historical framework for dealing with the plurality of religious communities residing there gives rise to unique problems.

Many Israelis feel that a portion of the missionary activity is not a grass roots, indigenous religious movement generated by Israelis. Rather it is imported by foreign nationals. As such, some argue that Israel as a State may deal with missionaries as foreign nationals and regulate their activities the way some European countries do. Others argue that notwithstanding the civil status of the missionaries, in the interest of freedom of religion indigenously and in the context of Israel as the Holy Land, the free exercise of religion must not be impeded. These two viewpoints, which are advocated with equal passion, are superimposed on the reality that Israel is still in the process of creating a viable legal-political framework to deal with its own problems arising out of social diversity and pluralism and is now faced with challenges by foreign nationals who demand fair treatment. This is not to say that the missionary challenge to Israel would not have been experienced in other historical periods, but rather that the frequency and intensity with which missionaries have been arriving there have caused some sectors of the population to feel that Israel is receiving the results of a religious revival generated outside its borders. They now feel forced through circumstances to deal with such challenges at a rate not conducive to maintaining a balance within their own political process and not amenable to dispassionate and carefully reflected inquiry.

Opposition in Israel

In Israel, popular opposition to the missionary activity of Hebrew Christians, Protestant evangelists, and Christian churches that are recognized in the Israeli legal-political system (Englard, 1966; Rubenstein, 1967) gives rise to different issues.

Israeli consulates inform individuals inquiring about church-state relationships in Israel and those who apply for a tourist or immigrant's visa to do missionary work of their government's position by supplying a public information sheet entitled "The Christian Mission in Israel." The sheet reads:

> According to Israeli government estimates there are about 200–300 Christian missionaries in Israel.
>
> Being able to offer social benefits and services to the poor, Christian missions originally attracted such people to send their children to church schools, but with the growth of State education and welfare programs, the number of those Jews interested in Church support has declined sharply, and some Mission schools have had to close down because of lack of pupils.
>
> Only two Israeli laws have any bearing on the mission and these are liberal in character.
>
> Under the Legal Guardianship Act of 1965 (Amendment), the conversion of religion of a legal minor may only take place with the consent of both of his parents, or of one of them with the consent of a Court of Law. If the minor is over 10 years old he or

she must also express consent. Anyone converting a child or trying to convert a child illegally faces a penalty of 6 months imprisonment.

The other law is the Law of the Return (Amendment) which says that a Jew may immigrate to Israel not only if he is a Jew according to Jewish law (Halacha) (a son of a Jewish mother) but also if he is the son of a Jewish father or even grandson of a Jewish grandfather, on condition that the immigrant has not been converted from Judaism prior to immigration. Should an immigrant, having become an Israeli citizen, convert from Judaism, he does not lose his citizenship.

Beyond these two laws there is no legal restraint on Mission Activity in Israel. Many Christian missions are in regular contact with the Ministry for Religious Affairs of the Government of Israel which provides them with some of their material needs and permits them to function with minimal interference.

Applicants for a tourist visa at Israeli missions abroad who state their intention to engage in missionary work are politely advised to reconsider that intention, but they are nonetheless granted visas. Should a missionary-tourist wish to extend his visa beyond the normal 3 month tourist limit in order to carry out mission work, the authorities are entitled to refuse this, and in fact do generally exercise this prerogative.

Israeli society, being democratic and tolerant, has only marginally been affected by these Christian efforts. There have been occasional and individual acts of violence against missions, and these acts are punished by law whenever the culprits are caught. The problem is a complex one with deep emotions generated on both sides. The government protects the freedom of the Christian missionary within the context of law and democracy. Although complex, the issue is much smaller than the exaggerated claims of pro- or anti-mission elements alike, and is essentially marginal and peripheral to the mainstream of Israeli culture and society.

It remains peripheral because of the generally offended sensibilities of the vast majority of Israeli Jews at what they consider to be an unwarranted and unwanted encroachment on their Jewish way of life.

Although there has always been a missionary effort in Israel and a normative stand of the Israeli legal-political system with regard to it, current popular opposition to missionary activities has reached an intensity unparalleled since the foundation of the state in 1948. The current opposition to missionaries differs from what the normative stand provides for. But this opposition must be understood in the context of several factors in the relationship between the state and religion.[17] These factors are the infrastructure of the national legal-political norms, the sociopolitical reality, and the religious norms of Orthodox Judaism.

NATIONAL LEGAL-POLITICAL NORMS

1. Israel does not yet have a written constitution; it does, however, have a Declaration of Independence.

That Declaration, while specifically stating that Israel is a Jewish State, goes on to say: "The State of Israel . . . will be based on freedom, justice and peace as envisaged by the Prophets of Israel; it will ensure complete equality of social and political rights to all its inhabitants irrespective of religion, race or sex; it will guarantee freedom of religion, conscience, education and culture." This part of the Declaration is not regarded as binding and certainly carries no constitutional authority [*Ziv v. Gubernik* 1 P.E. 33 (1948)]. It does, however, embody the "Credo and vision" of the people. Moreover, it has been said that, although the Declaration cannot serve as a foundation for any actionable legal right, "it laid down the way of life of the citizens of the State, and its principles must guide every public authority in the State." (Rubinstein, 1967:381)

2. Parliament is sovereign in the enactment of legislation and may counter or overrule any Supreme Court decision through contrary legislation. This results in a tension between the Supreme Court as an agency for social change, in reality, when vindicating minority rights, and the coalition government in Parliament which is necessarily more conservative.[18]

3. Within the framework of the State, Jews and non-Jews live side by side. The status of religious communities and

religion in Israel issues from Israeli statutes superimposed on
some of the Mandatory Regulations, which in general preserved the preceding Ottoman system. The application of
ecclesiastical law in certain jurisdictions is not an Israeli
invention; it was instituted by earlier regimes (Ottoman-
Mandatory) and existed in Palestine long before Israel was
created (see also Rubinstein, 1967:384).

4. Religious communities retain jurisdiction over their members in a variety of areas, as in the laws of personal status.
Israel enacted legislation applicable to Jews, such as the Law
of Return, which specifies among other things who is a Jew
for the purposes of that Law.

5. There are no laws against missionary work *per se*. It is
asserted by the Declaration of Independence and it is also
accepted informally that the freedom of conscience of the
individual is to be respected by all religious communities.[19]

SOCIOPOLITICAL REALITY

6. Unique to Jews, however, are religious political parties
who represent the religious sectors of the population and who
may take part in the coalition government in the Knesset
(Parliament). There are also secular parties, some of which are
nationalistic. The religious parties champion the pervasiveness
of religious law (*Halakha*, interpreted by orthodox Rabbinic
authorities) in the life of the Israeli. They are frequently challenged by the secular sectors and some political parties who
do not accept the principle of unity between the state and the
Jewish religion. The secularists consider the state to be guided
by the principles of tolerance and equality between religions,
and consider it above religion (see also England, 1966:254).[20]

7. A view of Israel, held by some sectors, as the beginning
of fulfillment of the Messianic idea of Israel's redemption.
As England (1966:254) summarizes it:

The idea of nationhood is deeply rooted in the outlook of
Judaism. There is, in its view, a unity between religion and

nation. The ingathering of exiles, the return of the Jewish people to the land of Israel and the establishment of an independent government there—these are among the features of Messianic redemption.

RELIGIOUS NORMS OF ORTHODOX JUDAISM

8. *Halakha,* the norms accepted as binding by Rabbinical Orthodox Judaism, is extremely important in the legal and social framework within which the state exists.

As England (1970:109) points out:

> The Halakha is predominantly legalistic. It is a normative order which lays down a particular pattern of behavior. In principle, it recognizes no distinction between temporal matters, which are subject to the State's authority, and spiritual interests concerning the soul's salvation, which are the exclusive affair of religion. The Halakha, wishing to be the sole arbiter of all aspects of the individual's existence, regulates both man's relations with God and his conduct towards his fellow-man.

Halakhic law and its interpretation by appropriate rabbinic authorities is significant in both secular and religious matters. Of particular relevance here is that it controls certain laws of personal status and that it bears on the question of defining who is a Jew.

9. "The Halakha is also a coercive order," as England points out, "which demands obedience to its precepts . . . Halakha is not opposed to coercion in order to achieve the desired behavior, even in the case of a person who denies the principle of faith" (1966:257).

10. The idea of coercion is given support by the principle that "all Israel is surety for one another," implying collective responsibility to some degree for one another and to a greater degree, to one another; this notion of collective responsibility is held especially with regard to what is considered to be the privilege of living in the Holy Land. This may further be summarized:

The clear knowledge handed down to us in the written and oral Tora that the Jewish people cannot long endure in the Land of Israel except by observing the Tora, and that a Jewish state that obliterates the name of Heaven from upon itself has no right to exist; this knowledge itself enjoins us toward joint action so as to impress the stamp of the Tora, as far as possible, on the way of life of the people in the State. (S. Israeli, cited in England, 1966:257)

11. The *Halakha* is universalistic in its norms. As England (1966:258) summarizes it:

The Halakha sees itself as applying to everybody, gentile as well as Jew, everywhere, at every time . . . Indeed, for gentiles the Halakha prescribes a minimum set of norms, allowing them wide autonomy.

Non-Jewish communities are free to organize themselves, and some of them are officially recognized by the government. There are few religion and state problems that arise with regard to religion other than Jewish.

These eleven factors provide a kind of infrastructure for analyzing the opposition to current missionary activity in Israel. Although both the United States and Israel may be labeled secular democracies, their legal, political, and social organizations are clearly different. It is not surprising, therefore, that the forms of opposition to missionary activities and their resolution vary between the two countries.

In Israel, the primary opposition comes from the religious sectors of the population, represented by religious parties such as the National Religious Party, and often supported by the nationalistic parties such as Cherut and The Movement for a Greater Israel, currently united in the *Likud* party. The National Religious Party's viewpoint is that Israel must be governed by Jewish law, *Halakha,* interpreted by Orthodox Rabbinic authorities; that *Halakha* demands that Jews abide by its laws, and that the state in aiding the implementation of

Halakhic law may demand that the individual obey the law or at least not allow for circumstances that would tempt him to abandon living by religious precepts—that is, the state should discourage missionary activity, for example. This is further premised on the principle that "all of Israel is surety for one another," which implies a collective responsibility to protect individuals from erring, in matters of religion, and *ipso facto* to protect their unborn Jewish progeny; and the fact that Judaism does not proselytize and does not want to lose adherents to other religious persuasions through a process in which it does not engage.

The secular sectors of the population, the freethinkers and those who do not adhere to Orthodox Judaism, do not share many of these views, and have opposed the religious sectors on a variety of issues quite apart from the missionary question. They have attempted to loosen the hold of religious authorities on a number of areas—they have tried, for instance, to institute civil marriage and divorce. They have been active in the problematic area of defining who is a Jew, an aspect of which is the acceptance by Israeli Orthodox Rabbinic authorities the conversions to Judaism supervised by Conservative and Reform rabbis in Jewish communities outside Israel. They have further tried to resist the strength and efforts of the religious parties in the coalition government to balance party cooperation on legislation of secular and political import in return for support on withholding legislation on significant religious issues, such as retaining sole religious jurisdiction on laws of personal status.[21]

These comments help us understand the background for opposition to missionary activity, but they do not explain the current intensity of the opposition in a country where non-Jewish religious communities have always existed and have always proselytized. The loss of millions of Jews in the Holocaust is of course of primary significance. Another key lies in the attitude of the religious sectors to the worldwide social

movements of the 1960s, and to the style and content of the
activities of the young missionaries presently arriving in
Israel.

The religious sectors recognize that most of the young missionaries working in Israel now are from Western countries.
Many are American university students or exstudents. The
resident religious population in Israel has, at least publicly
through its press, identified and categorized the American
youth as religiously freethinking and secular, and thus destruc-
tive of Orthodox religious institutions; and politically committed to the New Left, a political orientation not known for
its sympathy either with Israel's foreign policies in the Middle
East or with its domestic politics. He is therefore regarded as
posing a threat to the national security of the state and its
value orientation. Socially, he is seen as partaking of the drug
culture, which is regarded as a threat to Israeli youth.

That these opinions are not completely consistent with the
facts, that it is hardly possible to generalize about all youth
in this vein, and that the Jesus people—whether Jews or
non-Jews, missionaries or not—are frequently politically conservative, religiously committed, live by a strict moral code,
and disapprove of using drugs to achieve altered states of
consciousness, does not seem to prevent their opponents from
stereotyping them. Labeling all young people causes them to be
perceived according to the faulty labels, and thus causes general alarm about the social and religious threats posed by
some Westerners. These stereotypes are also fueled by the
history and experiences of Jewish communities in the Diaspora,
the basic attitude of Judaism toward rights and duties of Jews
qua Jews, and the perceived threat of missionary activity to
the integrity of the Jewish people collectively.

The style and content of current missionary work raises
more complicated issues. The recruitment style of the young
Hebrew Christian missionaries closely approximates the Gerlach and Hine model. Many of the missionaries have no

denominational ties with recognized non-Jewish religious communities in Israel.[22] They are therefore not represented by institutions that can be negotiated with, formally by government authorities or informally by the Jewish religious leadership.

Lacking formal denominational ties with existing religious institutions, the missionaries have not created supportive institutions to absorb the converted. Following the Gerlach-Hine model, these new institutions have a mirage quality and are therefore suspect. They are flexible, temporary, easily assembled and reassembled and are not always plainly visible. They take such forms as living-room churches, prayer meetings, and privately operated clubs.

As some Jews see it, recruitment and proselytization attempt to commit Jews to the Hebrew Christian message without giving them permanently established institutional support structures that can become part of the formal non-Jewish religious community. The missionaries claim that they are afraid to and unable to establish visible formal institutions because of the continual harassment and opposition to their work. Furthermore, they claim that converts do not need formal non-Jewish institutions, since they have not abandoned their Judaism—they are *Hebrew* Christians.

The religious sectors do not accept the argument that Hebrew Christianity is a form of Judaism, and say that whatever else it is, it has no place within the institutional life of the Jewish community. Therefore, for missionaries to proselytize Jews and not to give them a permanent, officially recognized institutional support means that the converts are forced to affiliate with non-Jewish churches that are already recognized in Israel. These churches are however hesitant to accept the proselytized Jews. They fear being accused of aggressive and widespread missionary activity and of facing conflict with the state, even though the converted might not have been proselytized by their own denominational missionaries. They

fear that the state will decree that they have not been respectful of freedom of conscience of Jews to pursue Judaism unen-
cumbered by missionary efforts. If the established churches
were to accept and service the proselytized Jews, they fear that
the Jewish population will accuse them of aiding entrepreneurial missionaries for the purpose of increasing their own
membership. This too could lead to possible church-state confrontation between the organized and established churches and
the state.

To further complicate things, proselytized Jews who are
Israeli citizens and who wish to disaffiliate from the Jewish
community and are not accepted by one of the recognized
and established non-Jewish communities are left in a difficult
position with regard to laws of personal status dealing with
marriage and divorce. In extreme, such individuals may be
characterized, metaphorically, as stateless persons.[23] Although
such cases have been provided for, the provisions concerning
them are ineffective.[24] The primary alternative for these individuals—to marry or divorce outside Israel, in Cyprus, for
example—depends on the availability of financial and personal resources. As a result, the proselytized population with
no affiliation with one of the established religious communities
is polarized into a layered collectivity of haves and have nots.
As many of the proselytized are poor and disadvantaged, this
is a real concern.

To add to the complications, the second area of conflict with
missionaries stems from the location of their activities. Some of
the missionaries have proselytized in Ulpanim (educational
centers for the study of the Hebrew language by newcomers to
Israel); in absorption centers for new immigrants, such as
Russian immigrants, where they have encouraged emigration
from Israel; among mixed-marriage couples; on university campuses primarily among foreign Jewish students for whom authorities feel a responsibility approximating *in loco parentis*;

and among the poor and disadvantaged. These activities have been widely reported in the press, particularly the missionary work in Carmiel,[25] a new town between Haifa and Safad that is currently absorbing many of the Russian immigrants to Israel (*Ma'ariv,* July 5, 1973, July 7, 1973, July 10, 1973; *The Jerusalem Post,* July 11, 1973, July 13, 1973, July 18, 1973; *Ha'Tsofeh,* July 13, 1973; *Ydi'ot Acharonot,* July 9, 1973, July 24, 1973; *Ha'Arets,* July 18, 1973; *Al Ha'Mishmar,* July 18, 1973).

But these activities have not been initiated only by missionaries. In some cases, Jewish Israelis who feel helpless and defeated by daily problems and in their efforts to secure better housing or employment have threatened the government that unless they receive assistance in such matters, they will turn to the missionaries and convert or have their children baptized. This form of blackmail has angered the government authorities, causing them to oppose even more vigorously missionaries who offer financial assistance to the disadvantaged as an incentive for conversion. In the past, few Jews who were economically disadvantaged threatened to convert to one of the established churches, thus manipulating both church and state to call attention to their economic plight. This however has not been the case with those independent missionaries proselytizing for a belief rather than for a church affiliation, and who have no financial resources to adequately stimulate conversions. The state has strenuously opposed any missionary offering financial rewards and/or help in emigration from Israel to potential converts.

Finally, the formal conversion to Judaism of individuals in communities outside Israel by non-Orthodox rabbinates has received wide publicity since some of these individuals became missionaries. Such conversions have been used by individuals as a springboard to enter Israel as Jewish immigrants under the Law of Return. With specified qualifications, the Law of Return guarantees all Jews the automatic right to be absorbed as immigrants to Israel should they chose to immigrate. The Law of Return, which was signed in 1950 and amended in 1954 and 1970, can be translated as follows:

1. Every Jew has the right to come to this country as an *oleh* [a Jew immigrating to Israel permanently].
2. (a) *Aliyah* [immigration] shall be by *Oleh's* Visa.
   (b) An *Oleh's* Visa shall be granted to every Jew who expresses his desire to settle in Israel, unless the Minister of the Interior is satisfied that the applicant:
      (1) is acting against the Jewish people; or
      (2) is likely to endanger public health or the security of the State; or
      (3) is a person with a criminal past, likely to endanger public welfare.
3. (a) A Jew who comes to Israel and subsequent to his arrival expresses his desire to settle in Israel is entitled, while in Israel, to receive an *Oleh's* Certificate.
   (b) The restrictions specified in Section 2(b) shall also apply to the grant of an *Oleh's* Certificate, but a person shall not be considered to be endangering public health on account of an illness contracted after his arrival in Israel.
4. Every Jew who came to this country as an *Oleh* before the coming into force of this Law and every Jew born in this country, whether before or after the coming into force of this Law, shall have the same status as a person who comes to this country as an *Oleh* under this Law.
   A. (a) The rights of a Jew under this Law, the rights of an immigrant under the nationality Law, 1952 and the rights of an immigrant under any other legislation are also granted to the child and grandchild of a Jew, to the spouse of a Jew and to the spouse of the child and grandchild of a Jew—with the exception of a person who was a Jew and willingly changed his religion.
      (b) It makes no difference whether the Jew through whom a right is claimed under sub-section (a) is still alive or whether or not he has immigrated to this country.

(c)   The exceptions and conditions appertaining to a
Jew or an immigrant under or by virtue of this
Law or the legislation referred to in subsection (a)
shall also apply to a person claiming any right
under sub-section (a).

B.   For the purpose of this Law, a "Jew" means a person
born to a Jewish mother or converted to Judaism and
who is not a member of another religion.

5.   The Minister of the Interior is charged with the implementation of this Law and may make regulations as to all matters
relating to its implementation and also as to the grant of
Oleh's Visas and *Oleh*'s Certificates to minors up to the age
of 18 years.

Relevant to the present discussion is section 4B and its definition of a Jew. Defining who is a Jew and determining if there
is an Israeli or Jewish nationality distinct from Jewish religion
have been two of the most difficult, intensely debated and
litigated issues since the founding of Israel in 1948.[26] The first
question is essentially answered by two criteria: religious law,
Halakha (as interpreted by orthodox Rabbinical authorities),
and civil law. The civil criterion (section 4B) states that a
Jew, whether born to a Jewish mother or converted to Judaism, is not considered a Jew if he is a member of another religion. But what is the meaning of the phrase, "a member of
another religion"? And what are the significant issues in the
process of conversion that bear on this question?

The case of *Rufeisen* v. *Minister of Interior* dealt with an
individual born to a Jewish mother who was an active Car-
melite and who wanted to immigrate to Israel under the Law
of Return. In its opinion, the Israeli Supreme Court noted that
Israel is not a theocratic state, but a state where civil law gov-
erns its people in civil matters. While granting Rufeisen immigrant status, it stated that as an active member in the Car-
melite Order, he is not considered a Jew within section 3A of
the Law of Return and is to describe himself in the population

registry forms as "without nationality." But what happens
when "membership in another religion" is not so clearly defined? The case of Shira Lindsay provides an illustration.

Converted to Judaism by a Boston Rabbinate, Shira Lindsay
then came to Israel under the Law of Return and began to
engage in what were interpreted as missionary activities. She
claimed that although converted to Judaism, she never lost her
faith in Christ. Israeli religious groups raised major opposition
to her immigrant status under the Law of Return and informally requested that the Boston Rabbinate rescind the conversion on the premise that it was fraudulent. The conversion was
rescinded. Lindsay left Israel, and what her status will be upon
any eventual return remains an open question. Interesting
questions arise from this case. For example, does the proselytizing of Jews to a belief in Christ by a converted Jew who is
not otherwise denominationally affiliated constitute "membership in another religion"? The Lindsay case did not answer
the question because the Boston Rabbinate rescinded Lindsay's
conversion thus reinstating her non-Jewish identity and therefore her ineligibility to use the Law of Return for immigration
purposes.[27]

Conversion is a rite of passage that creates for the convert an
external social identity and personal status. It reflects the
personal commitment, acknowledgment, and intention of the
convert to accept and live by the basic beliefs of the religion
to the exclusion of beliefs previously maintained that are contrary to those of his new religion. But what if conversion was
undertaken honestly and in good conscience, but with the
passage of time, through the natural process of aging, the
individual readopts his preconversion religious beliefs? Does
he lose his status as a convert and become reinstated in his
preconversion religion?

In Israel, there is a legal dichotomy between belief and action.
In terms of the civil status of the convert, personal beliefs that
are not manifested in socially visible behavior and that are not

clearly identifiable as motivating inappropriate behavior are not penalized and the religious status of the convert is not challenged. But behavior such as missionary activity, which is socially identifiable and both self-consciously and consensually validated, may stigmatize the convert and result in defining him as a member of another religion by civil law criteria. While the distinction between proselytizing for a belief as opposed to proselyting for an institutional affiliation is analytically possible, in the Israeli context it is not deemed significant.

All of this suggests that converts to a religion who want to innovate religious alternatives within their newly acquired religion—for example, presenting Hebrew Christianity as a genre of Judaism—may find it a nearly impossible task. Their conversions may be rescinded and they may be ousted. This does not mean that individuals born to a religion will find it any easier to introduce similar innovations, but that the penalties against them are not as easily available and the consequences of penalizing an individual born to a religion might have a far greater impact on the collectivity of which he is a part. The convert remains always marginal, even though he is centrally placed within rigid boundaries.

The opposition to these activities and occurrences occasioned by currently arriving missionaries, working either independently, or with denominational ties to existing non-Jewish religious communities, has taken several forms. First, there have been antimissionary ad hoc physical attacks on missionaries and their residential and missionary headquarters (*Ma'ariv,* May 4, 1973; *Ha'Modi'ah; Ydi'ot Acharonot,* July 17, 1973; *Al'Ha'Mishmar,* July 8, 1973; *Ha'Arets,* June 5, 1973; *Ha'-Tsofeh,* June 7, 1973, August 23, 1973). Attacks on missionaries have been investigated by the police and wherever found culprits have been prosecuted (*Ma'ariv,* August 14, 1973). Second, antimissionary groups such as The Association for the Prevention of Missionary Activity, EZRA, *Yad Le'Achim,* and Christians for Moses (organized by the Jewish Defense League)

have been organized with help from similarly organized
groups in the United States such as *Hineni* and Jews for
Judaism (organized by Zionist and religious youth groups)
(*The Mount Zion Reporter,* Jerusalem, May 1973; *Jewish Press,*
New York, April 20, 1973; *Philadelphia Jewish Times,* January
21, 1973; *Ha'Arets,* July 29, 1973). Third, there has been opposition to media advertising by missionaries (*Ha'Tsofeh,* August
16, 1973). Finally, legislation has been requested to curb missionary activities, including insistence that the Law of Return
be amended to regard as valid only those conversions supervised
by orthodox rabbis, and to exclude individuals who immigrate
to Israel for missionary purposes; and requests that strict licensing regulations be imposed on the creation of clubs and public
facilities for missionary purposes, as well as other administrative measures[27] (*She'arim,* July 12, 1973; Jewish Press, New
York, May 4, 1973; *The Jerusalem Post,* July 10, 1973, August
19, 1973; *Ha'Modi'ah,* June 29, 1973).

The consequences of this opposition has been to strain
church, synagogue, and state relationship in Israel and to
strain interdenominational relationships, as the following material illustrates.

Resident non-Jewish churches fear that antimissionary legislation by the state will work a hardship on their religious work
and interfere with their free exercise of their religious beliefs.
The Baptist Convention in Israel outlined this fear in a letter
to the editor of *The Jerusalem Post* (April 10, 1973):

Sir,—We, the members of the Baptist Convention in Israel, have
today sent the following letter to Her Excellency the Prime
Minister:
We respectfully submit to you the following reasons why we
believe that the enactment of anti-missionary legislation would
work neither to the best interests of the State of Israel, nor to
the Christian minorities: 1. Such legislation, however mild,
would provide those unsympathetic to the State with grist for

their mills to grind out anti-Semitic propaganda, by their distorted use of such legislation. 2. Any anti-missionary legislation could be construed as a negation of Art. 18 of the United Nations Universal Declaration of Human Rights signed by Israel, which guarantees religious freedom to all faiths. This freedom was also affirmed in the Declaration of the State of Israel.

While going on record as opposing any anti-missionary legislation, we wish to express our agreement with the Joint Declaration of Christian Communities of Israel, signed by heads of the Christian Communiites in July 1963, which opposes the use of unethical proselytizing practices, such as exploiting "the economic situation of an Israeli citizen—his poverty, unemployment, inadequate housing or desire to emigrate—in order to induce conversion. . . ."

We also do not endorse the practice of some who come for short periods of time and in an offending manner—oftentimes both degrading and insulting to the Jewish faith—attempt to press their religion in an argumentative manner on Jewish individuals.

This does not mean in any sense that we oppose the presence of Christians in this land, living among the Jewish people, sharing their faith in a deep-rooted, day-by-day ministry and dialogue, conducted in a manner guided by proper ethical standards and recognized by this government as a basic right. We deeply appreciate the democratic spirit existing in this country that permits these rights to be exercised freely, allowing Christians of many different communities to enjoy full freedom of worship, the privilege of maintaining churches, schools, hospitals, bookshops, theological training centres and other Christian institutions and ministries without interference.

As you lead this State towards its manifest destiny under God, we assure you of our esteem and our loyalty, and offer you the assurance of our prayers to this end.

Interdenominational tension between Christian churches is illustrated by the following letter of Brother Joseph Cremona, OFM, a Franciscan Friar, who wrote on his own behalf to the editor of *The Jerusalem Post* (March 12, 1973):

Sir,—I think that the Catholic Church is also concerned about the activity of Protestant missionaries of various sects. In my thirty years as a parish priest in the Middle East, I have had ample experience of them and I feel that they are not true missionaries, but rather mercenaries who want to make proselytes at any price.

For example, I know some Catholic families here in Jerusalem who are regularly "visited" by three different missionaries of three different sects. These families are Catholic, baptized, and believe in Jesus Christ. One can scarcely understand why these three missionaries should insist by their continued "visits" to compel those good families to betray their Catholic faith and to adhere to their sects. Is it not the same Jesus we adore?

In Nazareth, there are no less than eight Protestant sects. They have no flock or very few adherents. The Catholic Church in Nazareth has plenty of churches, schools, hospitals, orphanages and other social welfare agencies for her members. What are these missionaries intending to do in Nazareth? To convert the Moslems? Not at all. They are trying to ... sow confusion and doubt among other Christians . . . To take advantage of the poverty of other Christians and compel them to abandon their faith by promising them "seas and mountains" (and sometimes heaven) is a crime. Undoubtedly they say that the Catholic Church does the same. But the Catholic Church does not proselytize by going from house to house and sowing confusion and doubt in the minds of other Christians. She humbly waits the movement of Divine Grace.

I am not here to suggest that the Israel Government curb missionary activity, but I want to suggest to these Protestant sects that they should not be so fanatical and aggressive, but should respect the "freedom of conscience" of everyone.

How these issues will be resolved remains in doubt. The National Religious Party remained strong in the December 1973 elections, and may continue to participate in the new coalition government. To what degree it will press for anti-missionary legislation and to what degree secular sectors of the population will be able to resist such pressure remains to be seen.[28]

The significant point is that missionary activity is neither the first nor the only issue over which Jewish religious and secular forces have clashed. It is only one recent and highly charged issue that crystalizes the different attitudes of the Israeli population toward the role of Orthodox Judaism and its legal norms, *Halakha,* in the legal and political life of the state. How the missionary issue will be handled will in large measure depend on how each side defines its relative strength and formulates political strategy to be effective not only in this issue but in the light of other controversial issues that will involve legislation and litigation. While not denying the issues inherent in the missionary controversy, antimissionary legislation will be a testing ground for a fight over yet larger issues dealing with laws of personal status; acceptance of genres of Judaism other than Orthodox, such as Conservative and Reformed; and the definition of who is a Jew.

These issues should also be viewed in the context of international relations. Insofar as proselytizing churches have branches in Israel and there are Jews living outside Israel, the churches might choose to ease missionary efforts to Jews if Israel were to refrain from legislating in areas that might handicap Christian communities. It remains to be seen whether this will happen. Any such reciprocal consideration would certainly clarify the question of whether Israel is a political factor in ensuring the integrity of Jewish communities overseas.

CONCLUSION

Hebrew Christianity is a numerically marginal movement in both the United States and in Israel. Its significance rests not in its numerical strength or efforts at religious change, but in the impact of its opposition on the social order and its political and legal framework.

We have viewed Hebrew Christianity in terms of missionary work, the alternative institutional affiliations available to the proselytized, and the act of conversion as a social act with political implications in systems where religious affiliation determines in some areas the laws under which the individual is to live.

In the context of contemporary religious movements, for an incipient religious group or movement to take root requires that the supernatural premises of its ideology be resident in the culture and available to participants before the creation of the original group or movement. Through the process of recruitment and commitment to the movement these supernatural premises become confirmed, and the organized group may continue to exist. Committed individuals will willingly face any opposition from any quarter to their own involvement in their religious group and to the movement as a whole.

Two points deserve emphasis. A religious group is not solely or automatically the product of ongoing forces of social change such as secularization or technological innovation. It is also the product of a particular set of conditions, supernatural premises, and mechanisms such as altered states of consciousness for implementing them, available in the culture. A religious group may initiate social change whose realization may depend on similar preconditions operative for the realization of a group into a social movement.

Religious movements that are exported to a locality that lacks the generating conditions and prerequisites for maintaining the ongoing movement may be expected to have a short life span in the face of strong opposition. The case in point is the Hebrew Christian movement exported from the United States to Israel.

While opposition phrased in terms of church-state issues may serve to define, realize, and broaden commitment to the free exercise of religious beliefs, it may also result in greater restrictions and the obliteration of religious freedom. The one hope one can entertain is that both missionary and antimissionary groups will join forces and decide to recruit for their mutual interest—tolerance.

NOTES

1 Field observations on missionary activity in Israel were conducted from February through April 1972 and during February 1973. I am indebted to Professor Heda Jason of the Department of Poetics and Comparative Literature, Tel Aviv University, for her invaluable help. I have discussed many of the issues dealt with in this appendix with my colleagues who have generously contributed of their knowledge, insights, and time: Professor Leon Lipson, Dr. Pnina Lahav, Dr. June Starr, and Dean Carol Weisbrod of Yale Law School; and Dr. Seth L. Wolitz of the Department of Romance Languages and Literature, Hunter College, City University of New York. Final responsibility for the conceptualization of the material herein rests with me. I am grateful for editorial assistance from Valda Aldzeris and Christine Valentine. I have been supported during the research period by the Russell Sage Foundation, and am indebted to the Russell Sage Program in Law and Social Science at Yale Law School.

2 Most of the material on the contemporary Hebrew Christian movement comes from journalistic accounts and is incomplete. One has to piece together very truncated reports in order to create a composite picture of the movement's development. Many of the reports appear in the foreign language press and linguistic caution should be exercised in interpreting the terms used in it to describe the movement.

3 Hebrew Christianity is regarded as a movement useful particularly for Jews, whose religious identity is seen as incomplete. Christians do not feel the need to convert to Judaism, in the context of Hebrew Christianity, since their identity as Christians is complete.

4 There are a great many more terms in Yiddish, and some in Hebrew, than have been mentioned here. They follow similar patterns of meaning however.

5 Frequently one encounters Hebrew Christians who have ministerial certificates issued by Pentecostal or Baptist churchs. These certificates allow individuals to perform as clergy for a variety of purposes.

6 These statistics are not exact, but serve only to give a sense of the scope of the campaigns.

7 The question that comes to mind is how one compares the current missionary effort toward Jews in Israel with the inception of Christianity during the life of Christ and the Crucifixion. In passing, we might observe that the Jewish community's initial acceptance of the Christian message was based on an event claimed to be witnessed and consensually validated by a living collectivity who transmitted the message to descending generations. With the passage of time, the personal testimony of witnesses to the event was transmitted by others on the basis of faith; proselytization became different and perhaps necessitated the conditions specified in this model in order to be effective.

Confirmation of the Christian message is a result of a personal, deeply felt religious experience that may remain isolated and lacking in consensual validation until it is institutionalized in a setting where multiple personal, intense religious experiences are shared. Personal experiences become shared experiences under a rubric of communication modes, semantic labels, ritualized activities, and an ethos encouraging communion. In terms of the proposed model, it is the collective experience of the witnesses to Christ's life and message that is functionally equivalent to the supernatural premises available in the general culture of today's society. Just as the personally described experiences of Jesus' first disciples had to be resident in the culture to make affiliation with early Christianity possible, the supernatural premises must be rooted in today's culture for individuals to have these confirmed through intense personal religious experience. Such premises may be so well established that they are considered indigenous to the culture—as in the issue of whether the United States is a Christian nation, a question that has been dealt with by legal and legislative bodies from time to time. Or they may have been introduced by a large-scale and pervasive movement active in the society prior to the onset of a religious enthusiasm.

8 The Gerlach and Hine (1970) model and its component parts—organization, recruitment, commitment, ideology, and opposition—are herein cited directly from the text with permission of Bobbs-Merrill Company, Inc.

9 All letters are quoted by permission.

10 In the summary of the Jehovah's Witnesses I am citing directly from the texts of Burkholder (1974) and Pfeffer (1974) with permission of Princeton University Press.

11 For additional information on Jehovah's Witnesses see Manwaring, 1962; Pfeffer, 1967; 1974; Rotnem and Folsom, 1942; Stokes and Pfeffer, 1964; Stroup, 1945; and Waite, 1944.

12 In Israel on the other hand, current missionary activity is regarded, by the religious sectors of the population, as a threat to national security and to the value orientation of the social order. Therefore, one way of viewing the current opposition to missionary work in Israel is as a functional equivalent to the perceived threat of the Jehovah's Witnesses by some Americans during the 1930s and 1940s.

13 I am indebted to Daniel Voll of Yale College for his bibliography on the deprogramming cases and for the information he shared on the events that transpired in such cases.

14 For additional information on deprogramming, see Fiske, 1973a, 1973b, 1973c; Kaufmann, 1973; Kramer, 1973; Miller, 1973; Perlez, 1973; Sullivan, 1972; and Willoughby, 1973.

15 Recently a District Court jury in Denver, Colorado, found Ted Patrick guilty of falsely imprisoning two young Denver women. The offense is a misdemeanor. The jury found Ted Patrick not guilty of felony, kidnapp-

ing, and conspiracy charges. The two young women left their homes and the Greek Orthodox faith against the wishes of their parents (*New York Times*, May 3, 1974:40). "The parents contended they abducted their daughters in an effort to free them from alleged mind control resulting from religious influences" (*The Denver Post*, April 30, 1974:4).

[16] On the issue of legitimation of marginal religious groups, see Burkholder, 1974, and Pfeffer, 1974.

[17] For information on the general area of church-state relation in Israel, and in particular on topics such as the organization of Jewish, Christian, Moslem and other religious communities; laws of personal status; religious freedom; religious law and secular law; missionary activity; definitional questions of who is a Jew, etc., see England, 1965, 1966, 1972; and Rubinstein, 1967.

[18] For additional information see Rubinstein, 1967:384–388. On the discussion of the Supreme Court as an agent for social change, see England, 1972:113; 1965.

[19] For discussion of missionary work, see England, 1972:115–116.

[20] For additional information, see Rubinstein, 1967:391–399.

[21] See the discussion of laws of personal status in England, 1966:265–271; and Rubinstein, 1967:384–387)

[22] Most missionaries are recruiting for a belief in Christ rather than for any denominational or institutional affiliation. This poses a threat to the Jewish religious sector because recruitment for a belief that is not accompanied by concrete institutional alternatives causes uncertainty as to what the proselytized will do when they try to find institutional support for their beliefs. The possibility exists that proselytized Jews could seek to form a Hebrew Christian alternative and insist that it be accepted as a genre of Judaism. This is a fight that is not eagerly awaited by anyone in a country that has not yet even fully accepted Conservative or Reform Judaism.

[23] Jewish foreign nationals in Israel are subject to the jurisdiction of religious laws, *Halakha*, in personal status matters involving marriage and divorce [Rabbinical Courts (Jurisdiction) Act 1953 Section I.] For foreign nationals of other faiths, see Rubinstein, 1967;385–386.

[24] Jurisdiction over the religiously nonaffiliated is discussed in Rubinstein, 1967:386.

[25] Missionaries and missionary activity have been used as scapegoats in many of the difficulties that the state faces, such as, the absorbing and socializing of immigrants. The cry of "missionary activity" whenever a problem arises is often meant to mask bureaucratic difficulties totally unrelated to missionary work.

[26] Israeli Supreme Court cases dealing with the definition of a Jew, Jewish or Israeli nationality as distinct from religious affiliation, conversion, and

the Law of Return include *Clark v. Minister of Interior et al., Hadad v. Zezil et al., Lansky v. Minister of Interior, Schick v. Ha'Yoets Ha'Mishpati La'Memshala, Shalit v. Minister of Interior et al., Rufeisen v. Minister of Interior, and Tamarin v. The State of Israel.* Citations are found in the bibliography. See also the following in regard to the definition of a Jew and laws of personal status in the Langer case: *New York Times,* November 20, 1973:5, November 21, 1973:8, November 27, 1973:15.

27 The Emma Berger case (*Ma'ariv,* March 16, 1973; *She'arim,* September 20, 1973; *Yedi'ot Acharonot,* September 23, 1973; *Ha'Arets,* September 20, 1973; September 23, 1973; *Ha'Modi'ah,* September 20, 1973) illustrates both the kinds of opposition that has been administratively expressed against those suspected of missionary activity and the role of the Israeli Supreme Court in vindicating minority rights. Emma Berger, a German national, resides in Israel and heads a non-Jewish religious group called Beth El. She had purchased real estate in Zichron Ya'akov where she resides, some of which was expropriated by the District Committee for Planning and Construction under the rights of eminent domain. She protested the expropriation claiming that the Town Council wanted to displace her from Zichron Ya'akov because she is a German national and a Christian heading a religious group. Her protests to administrative authorities were not responded to affirmatively. She petitioned the Israeli Supreme Court which ruled that the expropriation was null and void. The Court noted that there are no laws in Israel that say that West German civilians or Christians cannot buy land in Israel, nor is there a law that forbids missionary activity. The religious sector attacked the Court decision as harsh and promoting of missionary activity. However, the Court decision simply affirms that expropriation of land under eminent domain will not be conducted if it is a tactic motivated by a desire to harass, penalize, and single out individuals with whom a community disagrees religiously or otherwise.

28 Some claim that the conversion of individuals to Judaism prior to their application to enter Israel under the Law of Return is motivated by a desire to do missionary work there on a permanent basis. Tourist-missionaries usually do not have their three month visas renewed. The religious sectors claim that the conversion to Judaism by such individuals is a premeditated act to engage in missionary activities as well as a politically conscious effort to sow seeds of conflict in Israel over the issue of the definition of who is a Jew within the context of the Law of Return. For this, and other reasons, they have pressed for legislation to amend the Law of Return.

REFERENCES

Akzin, Benjamin. "Who Is a Jew? A Hard Case." 5 *Israel Law Review*, 259 (1970).

Austin, J. L. *How to Do Things with Words*. New York: Oxford University Press. 1962.

Bamberger, Bernard J. *Proselytism in the Talmudic Period*. Cincinnati: Hebrew Union College Press, 1939.

Burkholder, John Richard. "'The Law Knows no Heresy: Marginal Religious Movements and the Courts." In Zaretsky, Irving I. and Mark P. Leone (eds.). *Religious Movements in Contemporary America*. Princeton: Princeton University Press, 1974.

Eichhorn, David Max (ed.). *Conversion to Judaism: A History and Analysis*. Ktav Publishing House, Inc., 1966.

England, Izhak. "The Chief Rabbinate and the High Court of Justice's Right of Review." *HaPraklit*, Vol. 22 (1965), 68–79 (in Hebrew).

England, Izhak. "The Relationship between Religion and State in Israel." In Tedeschi, G. and U. Yadin (eds.). Studies in Israel Legislative Problems. *Scripta Hierosolymitana*, Vol. 16 (1966), 254–275. Jerusalem: The Hebrew University.

England, Izhak. "The Relationship between Religion and State in Israel." *Christian News from Israel*, Vol. 22, No. 3–4 (1972), 109–116.

Festinger, Leon, Riecken, Henry W., and Stanley Schachter. *When Prophecy Fails*. New York: Harper and Row (Harper Torchbooks), 1956.

Fiske, Edward B. "Area Youth, After Week's Ordeal, Now Happy Over 'Rescue' From Sect." *The New York Times*, May 7, (1973a), p. 41.

Fiske, Edward B. "Parents vs. Religious Communes." *The New York Times*, March 15, 1973b.

Fiske, Edward B. "Fundamentalist Sect Changes Style of Life to Avert Abductions." *The New York Times*, May 31, 1973c.

Gerlach, Luther P. and Virginia H. Hine. *People, Power, Change: Movements of Social Transformation*. Indianapolis: The Bobbs-Merrill Company, Inc., 1970.

Gerlach, Luther P. "Pentecostalism: Revolution or Counter-Revolution?"

In Zaretsky, Irving I. and Mark P. Leone (eds.). *Religious Movements in Contemporary America*. Princeton: Princeton University Press, 1974.

Ginossar, Shalev. "Who is a Jew: A Better Law?" 5 *Israel Law Review*, 264 (1970).

Goodman, Felicitas D. *Speaking in Tongues: A Cross-Cultural Study of Glossolalia*. Chicago: University of Chicago Press, 1972.

Goodman, Felicitas D. "Prognosis: A New Religion?" In Zaretsky, Irving I. and Mark P. Leone (eds.). *Religious Movements in Contemporary America*. Princeton: Princeton University Press, 1974.

Goodman, Felicitas D. "Disturbances in the Apostolic Church: A Trance-Based Upheaval in Yucatan." In Goodman, Felicitas D., Henney, Jeannette H., and Pressel, Esther J. *Trance, Healing, and Hallucination: Three Field Studies*. New York: John Wiley and Sons, Inc., 1974b.

Greeley, Andrew M. "A Christmas Biography." *The New York Times Magazine*, December 23, 1973.

Hine, Virginia H. "The Deprivation and Disorganization Theories of Social Movements." In Zaretsky, Irving I. and Mark P. Leone (eds.). *Religious Movements in Contemporary America*. Princeton: Princeton University Press, 1974.

Isaac, Erich. "Judaism for the Nations." *Judaism*, Vol. 14, No. 3 (Summer 1965), 277–289.

Kaufmann, Marc. "Saving Your Children from Salvation." *New York Magazine*, April 16, 1973, p. 58.

Klein, Claude. "The Lansky Case." 8 *Israel Law Review*, 286 (1973).

Kramer, Carol. "Kidnapping of Young 'Jesus Freaks' Faces Test in Court." *The Chicago Tribune*, June 17, 1973, p. 8.

Lofland, John. *Doomsday Cult: A Study of Conversion, Proselytization and Maintenance of Faith*. Englewood Cliffs, N.J.: Prentice-Hall, Inc., 1966.

Manwaring, David R. *Render Unto Caesar: The Flag-Salute Controversy*. Chicago: University of Chicago Press, 1962.

Miller, Gene. "She Was Going to Give 180,000 to 'The Way.'" *The Miami Herald*, March 19, 1973, p. 1.

Perlez, Hane. "Is It a Kidnapping or Is It a Rescue?" *New York Post*, March 5, 1973.

Pfeffer, Leo. *Church, State and Freedom*, rev. ed. Boston: Beacon Press, 1967.

Pfeffer, Leo. "The Legitimation of Marginal Religions in the United States." In Zaretsky, Irving I. and Mark P. Leone (eds.). *Religious Movements in Contemporary America*. Princeton: Princeton University Press, 1974.

Rotnem, Victor W. and F. G. Folsom, Jr. "Recent Restrictions Upon

Religious Liberty." *American Political Science Review,* Vol. 36, December (1942), 1053–1068.

Rubinstein, Amnon. "Law and Religion in Israel." 2 *Israel Law Review,* 380 (1967).

Stokes, Anson Phelps and Leo Pfeffer. *Church and State in the United States.* New York: Harper and Row, 1964.

Stroup, Herbert. *The Jehovah's Witnesses.* New York: Columbia University Press, 1945.

Sullivan, Marguerite. "Parents Seek to Counter Jesus Groups." *The San Diego Union,* December 18, 1972.

Waite, Edward F. "The Debt of Constitutional Law to Jehovah's Witnesses." *Minnesota Law Review,* 208 (1944).

Willoughby, William. "Parents Kidnapping Their 'Jesus Freaks." *The Evening Star and the Washington Daily News,* February 22, 1973, p. A-10.

Zaretsky, Irving I. "The Language of Spiritualist Churches." In Spradley, James P. *Culture and Cognition: Rules, Maps, and Plans.* San Francisco: Chandler Publishing Company, 1972.

Zaretsky, Irving I. "In the Begining Was the Word: The Relationship of Language to Social Organization in Spiritualist Churches." In Zaretsky, Irving I. and Mark P. Leone (eds.). *Religious Movements in Contemporary America.* Princeton: Princeton University Press, 1974.

Zaretsky, Irving I. and Mark P. Leone (eds.). *Religious Movements in Contemporary America.* Princeton: Princeton University Press, 1974.

AMERICAN COURT CASES CITED

Cantwell v. Connecticut 310 U.S. 296 (1940)

Lovell v. Griffin 303 U.S. 444 (1938)

Minersville School District v. Gobitis 310 U.S. 586 (1940)

Murdock v. Pennsylvania 319 U.S. 105 (1943)

Prince v. Commonwealth of Massachusetts 321 U.S. 158 (1944)

West Virginia State Board of Education v. Barnette 319 U.S. 624 (1943)

Wisconsin v. Yoder 406 U.S. 205 (1972).

ISRAEL SUPREME COURT CASES CITED
(TEXTS IN HEBREW)

Clark v. Minister of Interior 27 (I) Piskei-Din 113 (1973)

Hadad v. Zezil and Ha'Yoets Ha'Mishpati La'Memshala 23 (I) Piskei-Din 729 (1969)

Lansky v. Minister of Interior 26 (II) Piskei-Din 337 (1972)

Schick v. Ha'Yoets Ha'Mishpati La'Memshala 27 (II) Piskei-Din 3 (1973)

Shalit v. Minister of Interior 26 (I) Piskei-Din 334 (1972)

Rufeisen v. Minister of Interior 17 Piskei-Din 2428 (1962); 17 Piskei-Din 2453 (1962)

Tamarin v. The State of Israel 26 (I) Piskei-Din 197 (1972); 26 (I) Piskei-Din 225 (1972)

Index

Ackerman, Nathan W.,
102, 105, 291
Affectuality, linked to
rationality, 220
Alfonsi, Pedro, 136
Allen, Geoffrey, 198,
304
American Hebrew Chris-
tian Alliance, 181-
182
American Jewish Year
Book, 182
American Society for
Ameliorating the
Conditions of the
Jews, 139, 171, 302
American Society for
Promoting Christi-
anity among the Jews,
139
"Anglo-American" evan-
gelization of Jews,
140-166, 172-173,
343
Anti-Semitism, 11, 12,
43, 98-105, 132, 135,
136, 147, 148, 232,
236-241, 264, 272-
285, 301, 313, 364
Assimilation, cultural,
132-133, 139-140,
146, 149, 162, 200,
270, 298
Assurance, as lacking

in Judaism, 77-78,
82, 108
Aston, F.A., 235

Baeck, Leo, 41, 131
Baptism, 21, 39-40, 71-
72, 128, 133, 136,
154
Baptist Society for the
Evangelization of
the Jews, 139
Barnes, J.A., 5, 12
Baron, David, 180, 181
Baron, Salo W., 211,
221, 265, 274, 287-
288
Barth, Karl, 146, 170,
260
Barton, James L., 142-
143
Becker, Howard S., 13
Benedict, George, 100
Beni Abraham, 177, 180
Berger, Peter L., 212
Bergstrom, Nels E., 160,
161, 164-165, 262
Bernard, Jessie, 113-114
Bevan, Edwyn, 288
Biblical exegesis, as
instrument of con-
version, 66-70, 81-
82, 84, 88, 90, 92,
140, 179, 218, 237
Birnbaum, Nathan, 103

412   INDEX